Peru and Bolivia

THE BRADT TREKKING GUIDE

THE BRADT STORY

It is nearly 30 years since my (former) husband, George, and I spent three days on a river barge in Bolivia writing our first guidebook for like-minded travellers: *Backpacking Along Ancient Ways in Peru and Bolivia*. Known then as 'The Little Yellow Book', it has sold around 50,000 copies in its various manifestations, and was the book that launched Bradt Travel Guides. Now, with over 60 titles on our list, we continue to fill the demand for detailed, well-written guides to unusual destinations, while maintaining the country's original ethos for low-impact travel.

I hope that you will get the most out of your trip, and perhaps have the opportunity to give something back in return. Do write and tell me about your travels, sharing new experiences, places and treks. I love receiving your letters and our readers play a vital role in each new edition, ensuring that favourite places are shared, new businesses get a mention, and deletions are made when necessary.

Buen viaje!

Hilary Bradt

19 High Street, Chalfont St Peter, Bucks SL9 9QE, England
Tel: 01753 893444; fax: 01753 892333
Email: info@bradt-travelguides.com
Web: www.bradt-travelguides.com

Peru and Bolivia

THE BRADT TREKKING GUIDE

Eighth Edition

Hilary Bradt
Kathy Jarvis

Bradt Travel Guides Ltd, UK
The Globe Pequot Press Inc, USA

Eighth edition published in 2002 by Bradt Travel Guides Ltd,
19 High Street, Chalfont St Peter, Bucks SL9 9QE, England
web: www.bradt-travelguides.com
Published in the USA by The Globe Pequot Press Inc, 246 Goose Lane,
PO Box 480, Guilford, Connecticut 06437-0480

First published in 1974 by Bradt Enterprises

Text copyright © 2002 Hilary Bradt/Kathy Jarvis
Maps copyright © 2002 Bradt Travel Guides Ltd

The author and publishers have made every effort to ensure the accuracy of the
information in this book at the time of going to press. However, they cannot accept any
responsibility for any loss, injury or inconvenience resulting from the use of information
contained in this guide.

British Library Cataloguing in Publication Data
A catalogue record for this book is available from the British Library

ISBN 1 84162 033 5

Library of Congress Cataloging-in-Publication Data applied for

Cover photograph Children of the Cordillera Vilcabamba, Peru (Hilary Bradt)
Illustrations Botanical drawings (Carole Vincer),
ethnographic designs from Inca and pre-Inca ceramics and weavings
Maps Alan Whitaker

Typeset from the author's disc by Wakewing
Printed and bound in Italy by Legoprint SpA, Trento

Authors and Updaters

Hilary Bradt has been writing about South America since her first trip there in 1969 when she fulfilled her dream of seeing the land of the Incas. For 13 years she led treks to Peru and Bolivia for Wilderness Travel of California and High Places in Britain, culminating in a 'Wrinklies Special' in 2000, revisiting her favourite places and experiencing a few new ones. She writes, lectures and broadcasts on aspects of travel and low-impact tourism. She is the founder and publisher of Bradt Travel Guides.

UPDATERS
Kathy Jarvis, who updated Part 1 and Part 2 of this book, has been a regular visitor to Peru and Bolivia since 1994, when she led her first adventure tour. She contributed to the seventh edition of this guide, and went on to write *Ecuador, Peru and Bolivia: The Backpacker's Manual*. Kathy also writes and photographs for other publications and presents slide shows and lectures on various aspects of the Andes. She is a partner in the Edinburgh-based adventure travel company, Andean Trails, which specialises in trekking, mountaineering, mountain-biking and cultural tours to the Andes.

Peter Hutchison updated the Bolivia section. He lived and worked in Bolivia as a journalist in the mid-1990s and has since developed an obsession for the country and Latin America. He was co-author of *The Amazon: The Bradt Travel Guide* and has contributed to other Bradt guides. In 2002 Peter received a Winston Churchill Memorial Trust Travelling Fellowship to lead an expedition that attempted the first descent of the River Parapeti, in southeast Bolivia – an expedition approved by the Royal Geographic Society.

CONTRIBUTORS AND RESEARCHERS
The following contributors provided material for earlier editions which have been retained here.

Jonathan Derksen lived and worked in Bolivia during the early 1990s during which time he explored the country from top to bottom, and is about to return to his favourite country. **Jonathon Exley** is a New Zealander who spent 18 months wandering through the Andes before heading for Britain. **Jane Letham** lived in Peru for several years, running the Lima branch of the South American Explorers Club and hiking many of the trails in this book. **Ann and**

Frank Spowart-Taylor have trekked in Peru many times. The warmth and kindness of the Peruvians is the biggest draw. **Jürgen Stock**, a German geographer, has visited Bolivia eight times to hike in the Cordillera Real. He now runs his own business encouraging sustainable tourism.

Thanks also to contributors **John Forrest** of the Tambopata Reserve Society (web: www.geocities.com/treesweb), and **Tania McCrea Steele** and **Anne Kendall** of the Cusichaca project for their contributions.

Contributors to this eighth edition

Roberto Arévalo works for the Mountain Institute in Huaraz (web: www.mountain.org).

John Biggar has trekked and climbed in the Andes since 1989. He is author of a trekking and climbing book on these mountains, and also owns Andes (web: www.info.andes.com), which takes expeditions there.

Paul Cripps is an expert on rafting in the big rivers of Peru and Bolivia. He runs Amazonas Explorer (web: www.amazonas-explorer.com), a Cusco-based rafting and mountain-biking adventure tour operator.

Dr Chris Fenn is a nutrition consultant and motivational speaker. For more details, check her website at www.chrisfenn.com.

Tom Gierasimczuk lived in Northern Peru for several years and is co-owner of Vilaya Tours (web: www.vilayatours.com) in Chachapoyas, Peru. He is also a journalist and often writes about Latin America for North American media.

Chris Hooker is co-owner of Andean Trails (web: www.andeantrails.co.uk), a specialist tour operator organising trips to the Andes. He has an in-depth knowledge of the Andes, where he was born and brought up, and has spent many years of his adult life there.

John Pilkington is the author of three travel books and a popular lecturer and broadcaster on BBC Radio 4. He recently spent eight months walking the Inca Royal Road from Quito to Cusco. His website can be found at www.pilk.net.

Dr Jane Wilson Howarth led a two-month-long scientific expedition to the caves of Palcamayo in central Peru, where the team researched the effects of altitude on decision-making. She has gone on to make about 20 trips to altitudes over 3,000m and has worked for 11 years on health projects in the developing world. She now works as a GP in England and has written *Bugs Bites and Bowels* (Cadogan) and *Your Child's Health Abroad* (Bradt).

LIST OF MAPS

Contents

Introduction

This guide has been in print since 1974, going through seven editions and numerous reprints. Looking back at the first foreword, I can see that although the cities and tourist areas of Peru and Bolivia have changed substantially in the intervening 28 years, the remote mountain areas are just the same. Then we wrote: 'Hiking in Peru and Bolivia provides a truly unique perspective on a wonderful continent which is full of natural beauty, adventure and hospitality. You will enjoy all three aspects by taking some of the walks described here...' In the 1970s all my walking in South America was done carrying a 40lb pack, along mainly unmapped trails, and with an unknown destination.

Over 30 years after my first visit I organised a 'Wrinklies' Trek' for family and friends where the emphasis was on comfort, though to be true to myself I specified a route away from the popular trekking areas. The actual organisation was done impeccably by the specialist Peruvian tour operator, Aracari. We had a fabulous time, and the only real difference from the olden days was the level of comfort. There were the same shy, but courteous, campesinos farming the land in traditional ways and the same wonderful snow peaks overlooking deep valleys.

So, whether you're a hardy backpacker or a wrinkly trekker – or something in between – you will find much to delight you in the Andes. Enjoy it!

Hilary Bradt

Though a relative newcomer, with only ten years travelling throughout Peru and Bolivia, I never tire of the Andes and all they have to offer. I often had a copy of this book in hand in my early days of exploration, faithfully following the excellent trek descriptions. Helping to update this edition has given me a great opportunity to repeat some of those now classic, well-worn trails and to add some of my favourite new routes that have more recently been opened up. Peru is a country of innumerable hidden treasures, more and more of which are gradually coming to light. Each year we hear of discoveries of previously unknown Inca sites, burial grounds replete with Inca Mummies, old Inca roads uncovered from beneath dense vegetation, proving the immensity of the wealth of Peruvian history and culture. Taking some time to explore the stunning landscapes and experiencing the ancient as well as the vibrant modern Andean culture is, to my mind, one of the best ways of learning something of the fascination of the Andes. I can't recommend it too highly.

Kathy Jarvis

Part One

General Information

A Quechuan Prayer

Pachi Pachamama,
Imaraycuchus ricusayku caipicainiykita,
P'achallisga p'isqomanta,
sut'iyaimanta Urq'manta.
Pachi asirihuasqaykurayku
chay ashka chaupi t'ika ukhumanta.
Pachi, imaraycuchus ch'inkayniykiwan
sapa chisiyaspa yachachiwaiku:
'Wajchakayqa, nan winay Janajpachaman'
Pachi kay k'acha kutimanta.

Thank you, *Pachamama,*
because we feel
your presence, dressed as a bird,
a mountain or a dawn;
thank you for smiling at us
through flowers of many colours;
thank you because, in silence,
you show us each nightfall.
'Humility is the way to eternity'.
Thank you for this wonderful opportunity.
(Free translation)

Reproduced from *The Gate of Paradise* by Luis Espinoza Chamulú,
published by Gateway Books

Background Information

1

GEOGRAPHY

The Central Andes are the dominant feature of Peru and Bolivia, their glaciated peaks rising to over 6,000m (Huascarán, in Peru, is 6,768m and Illimani, Bolivia's highest, is 6,480m). The two countries share the world's highest navigable lake, Titicaca, and the *altiplano*, a high, chilly, windswept plain which begins in southern Peru and extends southwards through much of Bolivia. This land provides grazing for llamas and alpacas. Frost-resistant potatoes are grown here, but few other foodstuffs can withstand the drying sunshine of the days coupled with the freezing nights.

Only Peru has a coastal desert strip and rainless western mountains; Bolivia, being landlocked, is not influenced by the Humboldt Current. In both countries the well-watered eastern *cordillera* supports cloudforest at high altitudes and true rainforest as the foothills meet the Amazon basin. Tributaries of the Amazon run through both countries, the Ucayali and Marañón in Peru, and the Beni in Bolivia. These rivers flow west and north into Brazil, which forms a common boundary to both countries.

GEOLOGY

The Andes are young mountains formed during the late Secondary and early Tertiary periods, at about the same time as the Alps. On the geological time-scale 'young' is a relative term; before the Andes were born some 50 to 60 million years ago, the South American continent was a going concern with the Amazon flowing into the Pacific!

Continental drift, resisted by the earth's crust beneath the Pacific, created intense compression and crumpled the land's surface, releasing igneous rocks which form most of the high peaks and folding the original strata into grotesque shapes. You will see evidence of this in many of the high valleys.

The effects of glaciation, volcanic action and water erosion have completed this process and helped form the deep gorges and sheer mountainsides that we see today.

Glaciers are still shaping the Andes. As the ice moves down a mountain, its snout forms a cutting edge and glacial debris piles up on each side, forming lateral moraines. The maximum extent of the ice is marked by a terminal moraine. This glacial footprint remains long after the glacier retreats, and can be seen far below the treeline on the eastern slopes of the Andes of Peru. Those flat, rock-strewn, grassy areas so commonly found at the base of

ECOLOGY AND EVOLUTION ON TROPICAL MOUNTAINS

Jonathan Hughes

In travelling from the base of a tropical mountain to its peak, you undertake a journey similar, in ecological terms, to a much longer trip from the equator to the poles. At the foot of the mountain, if rainfall is sufficient, there is tropical forest. As you climb, the temperature drops, and the palms and evergreens give way to deciduous and then coniferous trees – a displacement that occurs gradually over entire continents as the distance from the equator increases. Above about 3,000m, regular night frosts occur and trees cannot survive, hence the upper limit of forest or tree line. The severity of night frosts continues to increase with altitude until, at about 5,000m, the temperature drops below freezing every night and a permanent snow line exists, bordering the arctic environment of the highest peaks.

Between the tree and snow lines there is a cool, treeless habitat, similar to the tundra found in Siberia, Canada and Patagonia, and often referred to as alpine, after the European mountain range. To survive at these altitudes a species must be frost resistant, a characteristic not normally demanded within the tropics. Hence alpine communities are composed of atypical species, and in the tropics are subject to peculiar evolutionary rules.

Darwin was famously inspired to contemplate evolution after witnessing the unusual species found on the Galapagos Islands. He surmised that these species had immigrated from the South American mainland and then adapted to the various environments by natural selection – survival of the fittest. This created a wealth of new and unusual species in a process known as adaptive radiation.

Any isolated habitat is subject to this 'island effect'. Tropical mountain tops can be viewed as islands in the sky, isolated by a low-altitude 'sea'. The animals and plants inhabiting these originally arrived, by long-distance dispersal, from more typical tundra environments in higher latitudes. Once isolated, they adapted to the individual patterns of season, landform and precipitation that they encountered, eventually becoming new species, significantly different from their ancestors.

Where a mountain range exists there is an archipelago of sky islands. The alpine species island-hop along the chain, adapting each time to the local environments. Species that are less mobile, such as plants, or reproduce more quickly, such as insects, tend to undergo a more dynamic adaptive radiation as they migrate. The end result is a string of new species along the range, in some cases each mountain having its own unique flora and fauna. This evolutionary history, although fascinating, makes tropical alpine communities particularly vulnerable to extinction.

mountains were once lakes, dammed by boulders or ice, into which the rocks and silt carried down from the mountains were deposited. Gradually the lakes dried up and meadows were created.

NATURAL HISTORY
With contributions by Tino Auca of ECCO, Peru, and Dr James Luytens of New York Botanical Gardens, updated by Brian Hamilton, trustee for the charity Eye on the Wild

The Quechua word *puna* is still used in the Andean countries to describe the windswept grasslands between the trees and snowline on the high plateau. The *puna* area can best be defined as above the limits of agriculture, generally between 3,800m and 4,800m. *Puna* is characterised by expanses of coarse grassland with low vegetation and a large variety of cushion plants adapted to survive the strong daytime sun and freezing nights. The fauna is unique, and equally well adapted to the environment.

This is the landscape most familiar to hikers and the only biological zone which can feasibly be described here. The lower regions are so rich in flora and fauna that specialist books or information are needed. Local conservation groups may be able to help you here, or biologists working in local universities.

Flora
Although descriptions in English of the flora of the Andes are hard to find, much research has been done in this field, mostly by local biologists and university students. The descriptions below are not intended to be a complete list but will help you identify and appreciate the more common flora you come across. The local name is given in parentheses.

Family Compositae (Asteraceae)
This is the well-known daisy family, most of which are short-stemmed.

Werneria dactylophylla (*Margarita andina*). Also known as the *Boton Boton*, it has crinkly leaves and a small white daisy flower growing in felty clumps.

Werneria nubigena (*Margarita andina*). A common and attractive Andean daisy with large white flowers, often tinged with pink, and blue-green strap-like leaves. This daisy seems to grow directly out of the ground, which it hugs closely from its long tap roots.

Bidens andicola. Grows at altitudes up to 4,000m and has a tendency to use other plants as a support. They grow to the size of a small, twiggy bush.

Espeletia. This genus has a giant species which is more often seen in the northern Andes, where it is known as *frailejon*, or 'tall friar'. In Peru's *puna* a smaller variety is seen at high altitudes where the downy hairs on the grey-green leaves and stems prevent it from freezing at night. The flowers are yellow.

Espeletia

Family Berberidaceae

Berberis, some of which grace our gardens, exhibit spiny bluish-green evergreen leaves like miniature holly, orange and blue flowers, and blue waxy-looking fruit.

Berberis lutea (*Checche*). A shrub which fruits from April to June. They make very effective hedges to enclose farmland. The locals have a further use for the saffron-yellow wood, which is used for dyeing wool.

Family Cactaceae

Opuntia floccosa (*Chapu chapu*). A spiny, hairy cactus with white flowers, typical of the cushion-forming plants of the *puna*. The hairs act as insulation in the freezing nights.

Opuntia subulata (*Cholla* or *P'atakiska*). This columnar cactus is also known as a harpoon cactus since its thorns are shaped like harpoons, so difficult – and painful – to remove from the skin.

Trichocereus cuzcoensis (*J'ahuaccollay*). A large branched cactus growing to a height of 8m. It has creamy white flowers.

Opuntia subulata

Opuntia ficus indica (*Tuna*). This is the familiar prickly pear cactus, introduced from Mexico. The fruits are eaten by many of the Indians (hence their popular name 'Indian fig'), and the large pads provide fodder for cattle. Sometimes a white powder-like substance is found on the leaves. This is excreted by the bright red cochineal beetle, which – crushed – is used as a red dye or paint base.

Family Caprifoliaceae

Sambucus peruviana (*Sauco*). This shrub is a relative of the familiar European or North American elder, *Sambucus nigra*; it fruits from March to May and the berries are used to make jams and drinks.

Sambucus peruviana

Family Fabaceae (Leguminosae sp. Palilionaceae)

The lupin family is familiar to most people. The seeds have traditionally been used as food, but the long preparation needed to get rid of the bitter chemicals has caused them largely to be replaced by broad beans (known to the Americans as Lima beans).

Lupinus weberbaueri (*Q'uera* or *Tarwis*). A giant species of the lupin family, which grows to nearly two metres.

Lupinus mutabilis (*Q'uera* or *Tarwis*). This is the species most often used for its seeds, which must be leached in running water to remove the poison. The water is then used as a fish poison.

Family Gentianaceae

The majority of this family cultivated in British gardens is from Europe or Asia; the gentians of South America are rarely seen in cultivation yet are the most spectacular, ranging from the common blue to vivid red or yellow. The flowers vary in shape, too, being crocus or cup shaped, rather than the more familiar trumpet shape. The plants range from tiny plants to upright stems of one to two metres, clothed in gorgeous pendulous bells.

Gentiana sedifolia (*Phallcha*). These are the tiny, star-shaped flowers seen on open *puna* especially near moist areas.

Family Loasaceae

All members of this family have hairy leaves with a powerful sting. Beware!

Cajophora horrida (*Helechos* or *Otis colorada*). Most commonly seen in Bolivia, it has large orange-red scrotum-like flowers and – as its name implies – is unpleasant to touch. It stings.

Cajophora horrida

Family Malvaceae

This family includes the Mallow genus, commonly grown in British gardens. They are compact rosettes of tiny grey-green leaves, often covered in hairs or fine wool, with proportionately large flowers which may be bright yellow, white, rose or magenta, all exhibiting stamens with a prominent globose head protruding from the centre of the flower.

PUYA RAIMONDII

The monster of the Andes, this *puya* is the tallest flower spike in the world, sometimes topping 10 metres. It is said to live 100 years and flower once before it dies. And how it flowers! An estimated 8,000 greenish-white blossoms grow on one stalk between October and December, and attract the hummingbirds and moths which pollinate it. Other birds nest among the spiky leaves and some stab themselves to death on their doorstep. The sharp spikes are also a danger to livestock. *Puya raimondii* are found only in Peru and Bolivia where they are protected in Andean national parks. In the north the local name is *Llacuash* and in the south, *Titanca*. There is an easily accessible group in Parque Nacional Huascarán, in the Cordillera Blanca (see page 147).

Family Melastomataceae

Brachyotum rostratum (*Macha macha*). It occurs more on the eastern side of the Andes, in the *queñoa* forests between the *puna* and the cloud forest. The shrub has pairs of oval, deeply parallel-veined, dark green leaves and purple or greenish flowers with pendulous furled petals. Their fruits look like little red apples.

Family Onagraceae

This is the fuchsia family. Most of the hundred or so species come from South America. They vary from scarlet tubular flowers, almost bush-like, to peach-coloured downy flowers struggling to gain a foothold between ancient stone walling. The name comes from a 16th-century German herbalist, Leonhart Fuchs.

Fuchsia simplicicaulis

Epidendrum ciliare

Family Orchidaceae

Of the several species of terrestrial orchid found in the Andes, the purple and orange *Epidendrum* genus is the most familiar. In Peru the purple species is known as *wiñay wayna*, which means 'forever young'; the ruins near Machu Picchu bear the same name.

Family Polemoniaceae

Cantua buxifolia (*Kantu/Q'antu*). The national flower of Peru. The red, bell-like flowers hang from bushes near rivers. The *kantu* is a popular motif in ancient weaving designs, and is still used in some religious ceremonies and fiestas. This is also the one species of the genus cultivated in British gardens, usually against south-facing walls.

Cantua buxifolia

Family Ranunculaceae

Ranunculus is the botanical name for buttercup, a very primitive family with many species in the Andes, some of which look more like anemones than buttercups.

Ranunculus guzmanii (*Rima rima*). This beautiful flower is quite common in the Cordillera Blanca. It has large, red flowers and the whole plant is covered in dense golden hairs. *Rima* means 'speak' in Quechua (as in the river Apurímac – 'The Great Speaker') and the popular name for the flower indicates its use in folk medicine: it is given to children who are slow to learn to speak. It is also known as 'the rose of the Andes'.

Ranunculus guzmanii

Ranunculus weberbaurii (*Chapu chapu*). It resembles a Turk's head or turban with its fist-sized, bulging yellow-orange flower.

Family Rosaceae

There are about 15 different *Polylepis* species; these Andean endemics grow at altitudes between 3,000m and 4,800m, just below the treeless *puna*. They have a characteristic peeling, papery, red bark, with small dark-green leaves. The most common species are *Polylepis incana* (*Queñoa*), and *Polylepis besseri* (also known as *Queñoa*).

Family Crassulanaceae

Escallonia are common garden shrubs in Britain with a profusion of pink blossom in the summer months.

Escallonia resinosa (*Chachacomo*). As the name implies, the resin content makes this tree suitable for kindling.

Family Scrophulariacea

Calceolaria engleriana (*Ayac Zapatilla*). This butter-yellow ladies' slipper (or slipperwort) is one of the most attractive and recognisable trailside flowers.

Calceolaria engleriana

Family Agavaceae

Agave americana (*Pacpa*). These fleshy, thorn-tipped agaves, introduced from Mexico, are characteristic of high farming land where they are used as (very effective) hedges.

Agave americana

Family Brassicaceae (Cruciferae)

The cabbage family has several representatives in the Andes.

Eudema nubigena

Eudema nubigena is a striking-looking 'cushion' plant' with a rosette of shiny dark green leaves, and yellow or cream-coloured slowers. It grows on the puna or above.

Family Alstroemeriaceae

Bomarea sp. These beautiful flowers are found in many mountain valleys. Some are cane-forming from 30cm to 2m. Others are twining climbers, straggling over bushes and displaying different vivid colours of tubular flowers in a terminal cluster. All flowers grow from little white tubers.

Bomarea caldasii

Family Amaryllidaceae

Stenomesson miniatum (*Michi michi*). Also *Zephyranthes parvula* (again known as *Michi michi*). The dark green leaves stay on the ground, while the flower grows on a long stem. It is a small crocus-like yellow flower, its reverse streaked with violet. In Britain it is grown as a pot plant and commonly called Rainlily or Windflower.

Family Bromeliaceae

This family includes the pineapple and Spanish moss among its 2,000 or more species, but its most spectacular member in Peru is the *Puya raimondii* (see page 7). Other species that are more often encountered include the smaller and more common *Puya herrerae* (*Achupalla*) and *Guzmania morreniana*, which grows in trees as an epiphyte at 1,500–2,500m (so is not a *puna* species).

Family Labiateae

This family includes the Salvia genus, of which the familiar sage (used in cooking) is one species. Salvias are popular with British gardeners, and include many flowering shrubs.

Minthostachys glabrescens (*Muña*). This species smells like mint but the leaves are smaller, growing on little bushes in the higher altitudes. When made into a tea this is a popular natural remedy for high altitude sickness. The Incas used this herb to cover their potato harvest, preventing it from sprouting and repelling insects. Potatoes stored this way were said to keep for up to a year.

Family Liliaceae

Nothoscordum andicola (*Chullcus*). This lily is often found in the ruins of Sacsayhuaman. It resembles an onion flower, but is delicately scented and coloured a white-tinted mauve.

Family Poaceae (Gramineae)

Stipa sp. (*Ichu*). This is the spiky, tough grass commonly found in the *puna*, and the cause of many a resting trekker rising hastily. It is used for thatching houses.

Fauna
Birds

Given the scarcity of large mammals in the high Andes, birds are, for most hikers, the most interesting fauna. They are also easy to see and quite easy to identify.

The polylepis forest holds 57% of Peru's endemic birds, and 65% of those are classified as endangered. Deforestation is a major problem in the Andes, and this habitat destruction is threatening the survival of many species. Trekkers have a particular responsibility not to disturb the fauna, particularly nesting birds.

The list below covers all the species you are most likely to see while hiking in the mountains, classified by size (largest first). The local name is in parentheses.

Caracaras, hawks, eagles, vultures and falcons

Being the largest, these are at least easy to see, although telling them all apart takes some practice.

The **Andean condor**, *Vultur gryphus* (Quechua *Kuntur*). The largest and heaviest flying bird in the world. A male can weigh 12kg and has a wingspan of 3m. He differs from the female by his crinkly comb. You may be fortunate enough to see an Andean condor circling below you as you rest at the top of a high pass. From this vantage point they are unmistakable, with broad white bands on the top of their wings, and you'll probably pick out the neck ring of fluffy white feathers. Seen high above you, against a bright sky, they are harder to identify, but the 'fingering' on the end of the wings is a distinctive feature. Despite their name, Andean condors are more often seen on the coast of Peru scavenging the sea lion colonies; carrion is harder to find in the high places. A condor's feet are not designed for grasping prey, so the occasional stories you hear about them carrying off babies are untrue. Their legs often hang down as these birds glide on air thermals, rarely flapping their wings.

Mountain caracara, *Phalcoboenus megalopterus* (Quechua *Alkamari, Acchi,* Spanish *China linda*). These scavengers have a wingspan of 1m. They are very common throughout the Andes, and there's no mistaking them with their black-and-white plumage, bare red faces and orange legs. Caracaras find roadkills a particularly good source of food and often follow vehicles. You will see them solo or in groups of two or three.

Black-chested buzzard eagle, *Geranoaetus melanoleucus* (Quechua *Ank'a,* Spanish *Aguila*). In the air they look like flying triangles, with tail and wings as one. They are always seen alone. The plumage is grey and white, with a conspicuous dark-grey breast, white belly and black tail.

Puna (or variable) hawk, *Buteo poecilochrous* (Quechua *Hat'um hua-mancha,* Spanish *Aguilucho*). A white, grey and brown hawk seen at high altitudes: 3,000–5,000m. The altitude and the white tail with a black bar aid identification.

Red-backed hawk, *Buteo polyosoma* (Quechua *H'uchuy hua-mancha,* Spanish *Aguilucho común*). Very similar to the *puna* hawk but smaller, and with a larger tail relative to its size. Found below 3,500m.

Aplomado falcon, *Falco femoralis* (Spanish *Halcón perdiguero*). An elegant falcon with long wings and tail, easily seen and recognised by its light eyebrow, thin but distinct moustache, and dark 'vest'.

American kestrel, *Falco sparverius* (Quechua *Quillichu,* Spanish *Cernícalo*). A small ruddy-coloured raptor often seen hovering. It has a characteristic pattern on its head of two vertical black stripes, and a rufous-coloured tail tipped with black. Widespread in all kinds of open country at all altitudes.

Waterfowl (grebes, ducks, geese and others)

Puna lakes are excellent places for bird-watching, especially the shallow reedy ones which support a large number of waterfowl. The ones you are most likely to see are given below.

Silvery grebe, *Podiceps occipitalis* (Spanish *Zambullidor blanquillo*). Recognisable by its grey back and grey plumes behind the eyes. Back of neck black.

Crested duck, *Lophonetta specularoides* (Spanish *Pato cordillerano*). A large, handsome duck with a blue bill and brown crest and back: the largest of the ducks likely to be found on a mountain lake.

Andean duck or **ruddy duck**, *Oxyura jamaicensis*. Recognised by the blue bill and black head and tail of the male, it may be mistaken for the much smaller *puna* teal.

Puna teal, *Anas versicolor* (Spanish *Pato de puna*). This small duck has a conspicuous blue bill, which is yellow at the base, creamy-white sides of head and throat and a black cap.

Speckled (yellow-billed) teal, *Anas flavirostris* (Spanish *pato sutro*). Recognised by its yellow bill and speckled black-and-brown head and neck.

Torrent duck, *Merganetta armata*. These fascinating little ducks are found not in lakes but on boulders in the middle of fast-flowing rivers. They dive into the torrent in search of larvae and insects and can swim against almost any current using their very large, powerful feet for propulsion and long, stiff tail as a rudder. They are found in pairs up to an altitude of about 4,000m. The male is very conspicuous with a black-and-white patterned head and bright red bill. The female is a more subdued reddish brown.

Andean goose, *Chloephaga melanoptera* (Spanish *Ganso de los Andes*, Quechua *Huallata*). These handsome and very common birds feed in pairs or in large groups on marshy ground near lakes or on the open *puna* in boggy areas. Their white head and body and black wings are instantly recognisable.

Andean lapwing, *Vanellus resplendens* (Quechua *Lek'echo*). Another very common bird, which is found on the *puna* even in quite dry areas, as well as around lakes. Its black-and-white V-shaped markings, visible as it flies off with a noisy alarm call, make it unmistakable.

Andean gull, *Larus serranus* (*Spanish Gaviota de los Andes*). This is a species of the familiar black-headed gull of the Old World but it spends the summer (and some of the winter) in the high *puna*. In the winter its black head turns white.

Puna ibis, *Plegadis ridgwayi*. This handsome bird has a greeny-blue sheen to its black feathers.

Buff-necked ibis, *Theristicus caudatus* (Spanish *Bandurria*). Another ibis found in flocks on marshy ground, with grey wings and a fawn-coloured neck.

Giant coot, *Fulica gigantea*. Identification is easy: a goose-sized coot with a dark-red bill tipped with white, white frontal shield, and enormous feet. It builds a huge floating nest of weeds, nearly 2m in diameter.

Slate-coloured coot, *Fulica ardesiaca*, and Common gallinule, *Gallinula chloropas*. These familiar water birds are similar to their North American counterparts, with a black body and white (coot) or red (gallinule) 'shield' above the bill.

Tinamous

These chunky birds look a bit like a small chicken and hide in the long grass, to fly off with a great commotion when nearly stepped on. It scares the hell out of most hikers! The locals call them *los perdizes de los Andes*, or Andean partridges, a misnomer although superficially they do look and behave like partridges. Their speckled colouring offers perfect camouflage. There are many species; all are ground-nesting, laying olive-green or purple eggs which have a beautiful porcelain-like sheen.

Ornate tinamou, *Nothoprocta ornata* (Quechua *Llut'u*, Spanish *Falsa perdiz*). They are a speckled greyish ochre, with a grey breast and a whitish head spotted with black.

Swifts and swallows

Andean swift, *Aeronautes andecolus* (Spanish *Bencejo Andino*). White collar, rump and underparts, including vent.

Brown-bellied swallow, *Notiochelidon murina* (Spanish *Golondrina plomiza*). Dark smoky-grey below. Found between 2,100m and 4,300m, mostly in humid and semi-humid regions.

Andean swallow, *Petrochelidon andecola* (Spanish *Golondrina andina*). A chunky bird with triangular wings and only slightly forked tail. The throat is grey-brown, and the belly whitish. It is found between 2,500m and 4,600m in open arid country.

Woodpeckers

Those found in the *puna* have hardly seen a tree in their lives. They live in holes in rocky areas and are extremely well camouflaged.

Andean flicker, *Colaptes rupicola* (Quechua *Jac'acho*, Spanish *Carpintero de las piedras*). An attractive bird with a speckled brownish back, yellowbuff breast, and a tell-tale yellow rump which shows when it flies away whistling its loud alarm call.

Sparrows, finches and siskins

Rufous-collared sparrow, *Zonotrichia capensis* (Spanish *Gorrion americano*, Quechua *Pichingo*). It has a distinct rufous half-collar and blackish spot on the sides of its breast. A very common bird.

Ash-breasted sierra finch, *Phrygilus plebejus* (Quechua *Pichitankas*). These very common little birds live in large groups, feeding in the open fields or on farmland. They are greyish with a white belly and a large bill.

Siskin, *Spinus sp.* (Spanish *Jilguero*). Another common Andean bird with several similar species. Like the finches, they feed in large groups in open fields. They are identified by their black and yellow colouring.

Thrushes
Chiguanco thrush, *Turdus chiguanco* (Spanish *Tordo*, Quechua *Chihuaco*). They are woodland birds but are common in open areas, feeding on a large variety of seeds and fruits. Recognised by their brown colour with a yellow bill and legs and a great variety of calls: this bird is said to produce 14 different sounds.

Hummingbirds
General information on the Trochilidae family is given in the box opposite; the following species are most likely to be seen by hikers.

Giant hummingbird, *Patagona gigas* (Quechua *Huascar q'ente*, Spanish *Picaflor gigante*). A very large hummingbird, the size of a small dove, with a whitish rump and cinnamon below. It flies with erratic wingbeats interspersed with gliding, and does not hover over the flower like other hummingbirds.

Great sapphirewing, *Pterophanes cyanopterus* (Quechua *Sihuar q'ente*). A very large hummingbird, dark green with blue wings, with a thinner and straighter bill than the giant hummingbird, and with a more typical hummingbird flight pattern, though it still has some erratic wingbeats and glides.

Greentailed trainbearer, *Lesbia nuna*. The tail is deeply forked, about the length of the bird's body, and the tips of feathers are a glittering emerald green. The bill is generally small and straight. Common.

Sparkling violet-ear, *Colibri coruscans* (Spanish *Picaflor vientre azul*). Quite a large shining-green hummingbird with a dark, subterminal bar on its tail. The blue of its ear-plumes continues as a chinstrap.

Field guides to birds
An expensive but extremely beautiful book, *Birds of the High Andes* by Jon Fjeldså and Niels Krabbe, has been published in Denmark (Apollo Books, Lundbyvej 36, DK-5700 Svendborg, Denmark) priced at DKK 700. There is no other similarly comprehensive guide to the birds of the Andes but *South American Birds* by John Dunning is very useful and has some good colour photos (Harrowood Books, USA).

Among the specialist books listed in the extensive catalogue of the Natural History Book Service (Britain, tel: 01803 865913) are *A Birder's Guide to Travel in Peru*, *Birds of South America* in four volumes, and *The Birds of the Department of Lima*.

HUMMINGBIRDS

These little birds, widespread throughout the Americas, elicit many superlatives: the smallest, the most brightly coloured... and the most interesting of the birds found in the Andes. The local name for these tiny nectar-feeders is *picaflor* and the Quecha name is *Q'entes*. Surprisingly, many species of hummingbird live on the chilly slopes of the Andes, and they show a remarkable adaptation to their habitat and food source. About half of the flowering plants of the *puna* are pollinated by hummingbirds, and these have evolved trumpet-shaped flowers, so the nectar can only be reached by the hummingbird's long bill and even longer tongue, and long stamens which dust the bird's forehead with pollen. An example of this mutual dependency is the white, trumpet-shaped *datura* flower, which is pollinated by the swordbill hummingbird whose bill is actually longer than its body. Such flowers generally have little scent because hummingbirds have no keen sense of smell. Cross pollination is ensured by providing the birds with just enough nectar to to reach the next plant. Hummingbirds need to feed every 12 minutes or so; they use energy faster than any other animal. Their wings beat 70 times a second (one third of their body weight is wing muscle), and in flight their heartbeat may reach 1,200 per minute!

The Andean hillstar, a hummingbird that lives just below the snowline, shows a special adaptation which allows it to survive the freezing nights. It saves energy by perching on, rather than hovering over, the flowers (usually the *chuquiagua*), and at night goes into a state of torpor. Its body temperature may drop to 15°C (from its normal daytime 39.5°C) and its heart slows down to 36 beats per minute. Thus the bird is able to conserve energy. The large, well-insulated nests of the Andean hillstar are usually built on the eastern face of rocky cliffs to catch the morning sun.

Mammals

In post-conquest Peru and Bolivia the wildlife suffered the same depredations as gold and silver artefacts: it was squandered for immediate gain. Whereas during Inca times hunting was controlled and restricted, now it was available to anyone and the Spaniards' superior weapons must have decimated the edible mammals. As always, however, destruction of habitat played, and still plays, a more serious role in the extinction of species. The widespread cutting down of forests, particularly the slow-growing native woodlands of the *sierra*, has resulted in wildlife being scarce and timid.

That said, however, an alert hiker will see quite a few animals in the *puna*, especially in remote areas where they inhabit small groves of trees or seek protection among rocks.

Carnivores

Puma, *Felis concolor*. The name is Quechuan (one of the few Quechua words to join the English language); the animal was the symbol of power in Inca and pre-Inca cultures in Peru. This elegant tawny cat is now an endangered species, having been hunted as an enemy of farmers.

Colpeo fox, *Dusicyon culpaeus* (Quechua *At'oc*). A grey fox seen throughout the Andes and regarded as a predator of livestock, so killed whenever possible. It is also a useful scavenger.

Andes skunk, *Conepatus rex* (Spanish *Zorillo*). Rarely seen, but often smelled! An attractive black-and-white animal.

Weasel, *Mustela frenata* (Spanish *Comadreja*). A common animal in the *puna* but seldom seen, living in rocky crevasses. They are about 50cm long.

Herbivores

Spectacled bear, *Tremarctos ornatus* (Spanish *Oso*). The only bear in South America is an endangered species most commonly found in cloud forest. Lucky hikers have occasionally seen them in Parque Huascaran and along the Inca Trail in Peru.

White-tailed deer, *Odocoileus virginianus* (Spanish *Venado de cola blanca*, Quechua *Luychu*). Despite being heavily hunted, this animal is still common in the more remote areas. Very adaptable, it occurs from the coastal plain to 4,000m, and on the humid eastern slopes of the Andes.

Andean guemal, *Hippocamelus antisensis* (Spanish *Taruca*). This is an endangered species, less adaptable than the white-tailed deer so more affected by loss of its favourite habitat, small isolated patches of woodland at high altitudes. It is recognised by its location (just under the snowline), its greyish brown colour and having no white tail.

Mountain viscacha, *Lagidium peruvianum inca*. The wild mammal you are most likely to see is this member of the chinchilla family. It looks like a cross between a squirrel and a rabbit, and whistles when alarmed. Groups of viscachas live at the foot of scree slopes where they can take refuge among the rocks. If you see one you'll see 20, bounding from rock to rock, or standing upright to see you better. At rest they are hard to spot, their yellow-grey colouring providing perfect camouflage.

Domesticated animals
Guinea pig

The South American guinea pig, *Cavia cobayo*, has been domesticated in Peru for thousands of years. Archaeologists investigating Culebras, in the north of the country, found the remains of hundreds of the animals. Those ruins date from 2500BC, and *cuy* housing was already part of the architecture. The Paracas culture, too, evidently raised guinea pigs, and by Inca times they were well established: excavations in Pisac have revealed *cuy* 'cages' beneath the classical

CUY ROULETTE
One of the charms of travelling to out-of-the-way places in South America is the home-made entertainments devised by the locals. At a small fiesta I once watched a most effective form of roulette.

A circle was made of up-ended cardboard boxes with holes cut in the sides and numbers chalked on the tops. Onlookers bought numbered tickets and a guinea pig was released into the centre of the circle. It scurried into one of the boxes, and the holder of the corresponding ticket won a prize. Simple and fun!

niches of Inca buildings. Indians in the *sierra* still raise guinea pigs in much the same way, and they are one of the main sources of meat in the central Andes.

One explanation for their continuing popularity is that they are so easy to raise. Even city dwellers keep them, and every rural house has a horde of squeaking *cuyes* – the name is onomatopoeic, since the animals seem to chirrup 'cuy cuy cuy' – scuttling around in the kitchen. Sometimes they are confined in cages or boxes, but they usually run free, making full use of the thoughtfully provided holes in adobe 'furniture'. I once visited a house in a remote part of the Cordillera Blanca and questioned the householder about a row of tortoise shells ranged neatly by the wall. She lifted one up and out popped a *cuy*! A fiesta was starting the next day...

Guinea pigs eat household scraps, with an occasional supplement of alfalfa or green barley, and are remarkably clean, producing small dry droppings that are easily swept up. Like all rodents, the animals are prolific breeders: litters of three or four are born every three months. Adults usually weigh about 1kg (2lb) – not much meat considering the time taken to prepare them. Various research projects in Peru have produced super-*cuyes* weighing in at about 2kg (about 4.5lb), but the benefit of higher meat production is counterbalanced by the extra work involved in selected rather than haphazard breeding, and in keeping the animals separated in cages.

Guinea pigs are usually raised for home consumption or sold within the village. You may sometimes come across a *cuy* transaction taking place in the market: a squeaking sack on the ground and the potential buyer expertly testing the animals for plumpness.

The cameloid family: llamas, alpacas, guanacos and vicuñas
Llamas and their relatives were the only animals domesticated by the Incas, and have been associated with man for at least 7,000 years. They were described appreciatively by Augustín de Zarate, a Spaniard, in 1544: 'These sheep of Peru are large enough to serve as beasts of burden ... their wool is very good and fine ... and they can go for four or five days without water. Their flesh is as good as that of the fat sheep of Castile.' De Zarate also noted that the Spanish used to ride the llamas – something unknown to the Indians past and present. Not surprisingly a tired llama 'turns his head

CUY CURE

Guinea pigs, *cuyes*, have always played an important part in Indian rituals to ensure health and good fortune. Recent findings suggest that the animals were sacrificed in Inca times, and no doubt the *jubeo* ceremony, practised nowadays by *curanderas* (native healers), goes back thousands of years. If a person falls seriously ill in Peru or Bolivia, his or her family is as likely to call in a *curandera* or, more specifically, a *jubeadora* as a doctor, even though the former may be more expensive.

To diagnose and cure the patient, a black guinea pig is required, and these animals cost three times as much as those of other less potent colours. The *jubeadora* must also be paid and, since her powers are increased by good food, she is feasted as well. Her job is considered a risky one – she may catch the patient's disease or, more obliquely, her 'destiny may change', so she can command a high price.

The relatives of the patient ensure that this money is well spent by scrupulous attention to the details of *jubeo*. The ceremony should take place on a Tuesday or Friday (although in an emergency any day of the week will do). A black guinea pig of the same sex and equivalent age to the patient is selected, and a candle burns by the sick person, along with aromatic herbs.

around and discharges his saliva, which has an unpleasant odour, into the rider's face'. Llamas and their relatives do spit (the contents of their stomach, not saliva!) but rarely at humans. They prefer to get the message across to other llamas.

These are the New World camels, as perfectly suited to the harsh environment of the *altiplano* as the humped camel is adapted to the deserts of the Old World. These cameloids show a special adaptation to the altitude. They have more red cells in their blood than lowland mammals, thus increasing the amount of oxygen-carrying haemoglobin available, and a higher respiratory rate. Special water cells in the stomach rumen enable them to survive long periods without drinking.

There are two wild cameloids, the guanaco (which is common in the southern part of South America but seldom seen in Peru or Bolivia) and the vicuña. Their two domesticated descendants (almost certainly the result of a vicuña/guanaco cross) are llamas and alpacas.

Llamas Bred as beasts of burden and for meat, llamas are willing to carry only about 25kg of cargo, so large herds are necessary for efficiency. Llamas can be distinguished from alpacas by their long ears (curved like parentheses), long legs and necks, and the cocky angle of their tails.

Alpacas These are bred for their wool, and consequently have a much heavier fleece than llamas, with a characteristic 'apron' of wool bushing out from their chests. Their noses, legs and ears are shorter and more sheep-like than those of llamas. Ideally, alpacas should be sheared every three years, but if their

The *jubeo* begins at midnight, but preparations involving coca chewing and the consumption of *aguadiente* (a regional alcoholic beverage) begin well before that hour. At midnight the *jubeadora* picks up the guinea pig and, filling her mouth with *aguadiente*, blows the alcohol over the animal's belly, face, nose and ears. After a prayer and the sign of the cross, the guinea pig is held firmly by its fore and back legs, belly well exposed, and systematically passed over all parts of the patient's body, beginning with the chest. As the animal takes on the symptoms of the sick person, it struggles violently and – so they say – dies. (If it doesn't die the patient's illness is not considered to be serious.) Relieved of his symptoms the patient is well on the road to recovery, but diagnosis is still necessary before herbal remedies can complete the cure. The dead *cuy* is carried into the next room wrapped in a black cloth; and after further coca chewing, helped along with shots of *aguadiente*, it is opened up and its organs examined. An enlarged heart shows that the patient was suffering from a cardiac problem, an inflamed liver points to hepatitis, and so on. The animal may even be skinned so that the muscles and joints can be examined. Mission accomplished, the *jubeadora* is further fortified with food and drink, collects her fees, and goes on her way.

owner needs money this may be done more often. Just as frequently, however, the animals are not sheared at all but slaughtered with a full coat of wool, which is sold with the hide.

Owners of llamas and alpacas will put colourful ear tassels in the animals' ears around June 23 at the celebration of the festival of San Juan Pastor, the *fiesta de campesinos*. Large herds of llamas and alpacas are easily driven over the mountains since each group has a leader, so the herdsmen only need to control one animal.

Vicuña Reputed to have the finest wool of any animal, the vicuña was reserved for the Inca emperor himself. The animals were captured, shorn and then released. But after the conquest vicuñas were killed for their wool, and the numbers declined to near-extinction. After careful protection the species has recovered and vicuñas are not uncommon in southern Peru and in Bolivia. It is a singularly beautiful little animal, slim and graceful with a golden coat and white underparts.

Guanaco Not often seen but unmistakable since it looks like a llama but with an orangey-brown coat shading to white on the underbelly.

THE PEOPLE: PAST AND PRESENT
Incas and Aymaras
Most sources believe that the South American 'Indian' crossed the Bering Strait from Asia to North America and gradually migrated south over thousands of years. Myths, however, are more interesting than facts, and the

beliefs of the origin of Man are central to the spiritual life of both the Quechua and the Aymara people. The former are by far the largest linguistic group in the Andes, being descendants of the Incas. Aymaras are a small group of tenaciously independent people living around the shores of Lake Titicaca, mainly in Bolivia. Patriotic Bolivians believe that the Aymara civilisation is very old, and the Quechua much more recent, but there is little evidence to support this.

The myths and way of life of the two groups are similar, but they remain two races with different physical and psychological characteristics, different dress and agriculture and, most important, a different language. A Quechua tribesman cannot even understand an Aymara: the grammar and vocabulary of the two languages are different, although they share fundamental words. This inability to communicate doubtless helps to keep the two tribes separate, even today. Some villages are half Aymara and half Quechua, and each half is recognisably different. The two groups rarely intermarry.

Quechua-speaking Indians are found throughout the old Inca Empire, from the Colombian border with Ecuador to southern Bolivia and beyond. This wide dispersal of the language is due to the Inca custom of subduing newly conquered tribes by establishing Quechua-speaking settlements within their territory. They are the linguistic majority in Peru, and the minority in Bolivia where they are found in the southern part of the Altiplano, in the Department of Oruro, and around Cochabamba, Potosi and Sucre.

The Incas sought to rule by consent, not compulsion, but met fierce resistance from the Aymara, who did not submit to Inca rule until the end of the 15th century. They adopted the Inca religion, with embellishments, but kept their own language and customs.

Inca mythology has Lake Titicaca as the birthplace of Man, with the son of the sun and the daughter of the moon arising from two islands on the lake. The Aymara belief is similar: the creator, Viracocha (the name means 'creator' in Quechua and Aymara), rose out of the lake and created a world without sun, light or warmth, and peopled by giants. These creatures angered Viracocha, so were destroyed by a flood, after which Viracocha appeared from an island in the lake and created the sun, moon and stars along with men made in his own image.

Whatever the truth about the origin of the Incas, their visible monuments arguably surpass all others in the Americas. Yet it is the unseen achievements that are so awe-inspiring: their empire still stands as one of the most perfect examples of organisation and administration in the history of Man.

Further reading

Further accounts of the Inca culture and conquest are found throughout this book, so check the index. However, with such a complex and fascinating subject, it is worth doing some reading before or during your trip. Coffee-table-style books are increasingly available in Peru and Bolivia making lasting souvenirs and normally written or compiled by nationals. A selection of recommended books can be found at the end of this book in *Further Reading*.

Inca roads and communications

One of the most exciting aspects of hiking in Peru is that the ancient trails linking village to village and mountain to valley were once the means whereby an empire was conquered and controlled. The Inca empire was criss-crossed with roads forming a complex administrative, transport and communications system. Roads radiated out from the centre ('navel') of the empire, Cusco, to the farthest point of its four quarters. Since horses and the wheel were unknown, relays of runners provided the speed and efficiency required. Roads were engineered to give the shortest and easiest route between two points. Steps were quicker to negotiate than a short steep slope, so steps were cut into the rock or laid as paving. Less precipitous slopes were made manageable by zigzag paths, and tunnels were cut through the outcrops of rock obstructing the direct route.

From sea-level to 5,000m, and down again to the Amazon, the roads looped and curved over a distance of 5,200km. In particularly mountainous areas the footways were steep flights of steps no more than half a metre wide, but across flat open spaces the surface was often 6m wide with a fan arrangement of shallow steps going round corners.

The Inca runners, *chasqui*, relayed verbal and numeric messages to all parts of the empire from the Sun King in Cusco. The Incas had no written language, only one of several reasons we know so little about their culture, so the numeric messages consisted of knotted llama wool strings, *quipus*. With strings of different colours and thicknesses the Incas were able to keep detailed records. A *quipucamaya*, a record- or account-keeper, could look at a *quipu* and learn a great deal. Gold, for example, was represented by a golden string, while the amount of gold was recorded by a series of knots along the cord. Silver was represented by white threads, while a series of red cords detailed the fighting strength of an army unit. Once the size, length and colour of a cord had been standardised throughout the empire, it was relatively easy to keep records.

The *chasqui*, sons of civil servants, were youths of great pride and physical strength. In order to fulfill their labour tax they had to run messages for two weeks in every month for about a year. Each runner was equipped with a conch-shell to blow as he approached the next *tambo* or *tampu* (resthouse), where he would pass his message to the next man. In this manner the runners could do about 9km an hour, even at altitudes close to 5,000m. No point in the empire was more than five days' run from Cusco. From Cusco to Lima, 672km, took 72 hours. The Inca was known to send down to Acari, on the coast, for seafood. In less than two days he was eating fresh fish.

Tampus or *tambos* were built at intervals of about 20km along the roads. These also functioned as storehouses, stocked with provisions from the surrounding countryside. Some also had corrals for llamas, because not only *chasquis* made use of these roads; they were crowded with traders, tax collectors, farmers, priests, soldiers, gangs of labourers and perhaps a royal delegation off to foreign parts.

Each community was responsible for the maintenance of the road in its

MOTHER EARTH

Robert Randall

For the Andean Indian the earth is his entire world – he exists as another plant in it and life apart from the land is inconceivable. The earth is called *Pachamama* (Mother Earth). She is alive, and during most of the year is passive and receptive, feeling nothing and leaving man free to cultivate her. There are days, however, when she is actively happy or sad, giving rewards or punishment, and it is prohibited to touch her. There is also a period of time (Holy Week) when she dies.

She is mother of all things, including men and women. This is meant literally, biologically. Thus offerings are made to her. At certain times there are large offerings (usually involving alcohol), and these you are more likely to witness or participate in. They are fairly simple but extremely important:

T'inka Before drinking alcohol, one allows several drops to fall from the glass on to the soil. Thus Pachamama is served first. This is done whether outside or inside the house.

Ch'ura Similar to the *t'inka* except the alcohol is scattered with the fingers. Often it is sprinkled this way on a house, animal or other object to be blessed.

Ch'alla From a small glass the alcohol is thrown to the major *apus* (spirits or gods – usually the snowpeaks) of the area. The *ch'alla* is done standing up, and the person doing it completes a full circle.

These rituals may vary from place to place, but they are omnipresent in the Andes. They only begin to indicate a value system of extreme complexity

area, and for the construction of bridges over major rivers. These were made from twisted *manguey* fibre, and had to be remade every other year. The most famous bridge of this type, over the Apurimac river, was immortalised by Thornton Wilder in *The Bridge of San Luís Rey*. Nowadays only the supports can be seen, but the festival of San Luís Rey is still celebrated annually.

Modern travellers rather glibly refer to any stone-paved trail as 'Inca' but we know that many of the civilisations conquered by the Incas had achieved a high standard of stone masonry and it is likely that these pre-Inca people also had an interest in well-built roads to help the transport of tropical produce from the low valleys to the highlands and vice versa.

Little is left of the Inca and pre-Inca roads. They have been asphalted for the motor car or lie hidden in dense jungle, but some wonderful stretches do remain, giving us glimpses of the past as impressive and tantalising as the ruins of temples. For this reason, if no other, the Inca Trail to Machu Picchu and the Takesi Trail in Bolivia should not be missed.

and richness. From these basics, however, we should be able to glimpse the Indians' humility before, and respect for, the environment.

The Andean Indian, before first digging his *chaquitaclla* (footplough) into the soil, asks pardon and permission of Pachamama. This is an attitude which we should attempt to adopt and be constantly aware of as we walk through the Andes. The earth is alive, and we are a very small organic part of her. We should therefore approach her and the people who live with her with a profound sense of respect and humility.

We have much to learn from the Indians. Although it is impossible to generalise about so many different tribes, the people are usually honest, warm, and friendly. They have not lost the sacred connection with their environment and are aware of the spirits of the mountains, springs and rivers. If one reason we are walking through these mountains is not to re-establish some such connection, then we probably have no business there in the first place.

Robert Randall died of rabies (following a bite from a puppy) in November 1990. During his 15 years in Ollantaytambo, near Cusco, he had done more to support the local community and their culture than any other foreigner. A friend, Max Milligan, wrote in The South American Explorer: *'He held up life for us to look at while he marvelled at it... No one knew the walking routes in the locality better than he..., an intimate knowledge, gained after the language and trust of the Quechua people that gave him a clearer picture of the Andean concepts of space and time, and the beliefs and myths handed down still in the highland villages.' At Randall's funeral in Ollanta a village elder spoke: 'Most who have come to our valley have come to take. This good man... came and gave back to us. He reminded us of who we are, of the value of our heritage and tradition.'*

Village life today

Since the Spanish conquest the Indians of Peru and Bolivia have developed various protective mechanisms which help them cope with present-day exploitation and discrimination. They are remote not only geographically but culturally, and often seem indifferent to the modern world. This provided a fertile breeding ground for the ideology of El Sendero Luminoso (The Shining Path) terrorists. Communication is not only difficult between Indians and whites (be they Peruvian, Bolivian or European) but between Lima and the highlands, and neither side seems anxious to change the status quo. The difference between the two worlds will be very obvious to the backpacker who spends a few days in Lima before journeying up to the Andes.

In highland villages the way of life is based on structure and rituals and visiting backpackers will have much more empathy with the locals if they understand some of these. They are a hybrid of Spanish and Inca, but the Spanish influence is – at least outwardly – dominant.

Village land is generally owned collectively, although private ownership still prevails in some places. Each village has its headman, who may be the governor (*gobernador*), mayor (*alcalde* or *warayo*), or council chief (*agente municipal*). He carries a ceremonial stick (*personero*) as a symbol of his position. The headman holds office for one year, and during this time is expected to sponsor traditional fiestas, paying for the musicians and supplying food and drink for these occasions. So most headmen are wealthy when they first take office, and as poor as the other villagers when they leave it.

Rural Indians live virtually outside the cash economy, and day-to-day life is organised on the basis of reciprocity or mutual help. Any big job, such as harvesting, threshing, and house building, is done with the help of neighbours who receive aid in return when they need work done. Finishing a house is an occasion for great celebration. *Safacasa*, putting the roof on, is done by a godmother or godfather who goes up on to the unfinished roof, lays the last tiles or thatch, and puts a ceramic figure or pot, or a cross, on the ridge for good luck. Ceramic bulls, to ensure fertility, are popular, as are little vessels of *aguadiente* ('firewater' brewed from sugarcane). The godparent then throws gifts of sweets, cigarettes, and so on down to the family and neighbours below who have helped build the house.

You and them: village etiquette

The villages you pass through on the hikes described in this book are mostly well accustomed to backpackers and no special behaviour is needed apart from greeting people in a friendly manner, and avoiding potentially offensive behaviour or dress (men should not go shirtless, for instance).

If you explore on your own you should always remember that because you are there in the village and on their land, you will be treated as either guest or intruder. The former is much more common. Indians have a strong tradition of extending hospitality to strangers. It is not rude politely to refuse such hospitality if you want to move on; however it is considered rude to reject offers of accommodation and then put your tent up just outside the village and cook your own meal. Be sensitive to this: either accept the hospitality and stay with the family or move on and camp some way beyond the village.

If you are well off the beaten track, in a very remote area, the people – the women and children, at least – may flee in terror from this alien. Don't further intimidate them by approaching their house. Move on quietly, unless you want to make contact, in which case let them come to you.

On popular trails (most of the trails in this guide) you can be more relaxed. Even so, you should always ask permission to camp, both as a courtesy and for security. Don't feel you have to overdo the friendliness, and especially do not hand out sweets or other *regalos*. Your entertaining presence will be reward enough. You'll probably be surrounded by curious kids – and adults – who are fascinated by your state-of-the-art camping gear. Chat to them as you set up, explain what everything is, where you came from and where you are going to. Try to use a few words of Quechua or Aymara. But be formal and polite. If the

BECOMING A GODMOTHER
Kathy Jarvis

After two years of visiting the Island of Taquile on a regular basis, and having spent many happy hours playing with the local children, I was asked to become a godmother. This meant being the person responsible for performing the elaborate pagan/Catholic ritual of the first haircut, known as *rutuchiy*. Practised all over Peru when a child reaches the age of two and is beginning to learn to talk, this rite signifies the child becoming a part of the community. Its unbrushed hair has been left to grow untended until then, in the belief that the greater the number of knots and tangles, the luckier the child will be in the future.

My godchild-to-be was called Cristian, the two-year-old son of Dolores and Benigno in whose house I often had the good fortune to stay on my visits to the island. Cristian was beautifully dressed for the occasion in his best white *almilla* (shirt), a clean white *phantila* (a kind of wrap-round skirt), an *incaj chullu* (knitted woollen cap with fringe) and *wawa chumpi* (a narrow woven belt). Although these clothes are worn every day on Taquile, many months are spent weaving or knitting new items for important occasions such as this.

A large woven cloth was laid on the ground and the family members, parents and grandparents, gathered round. From a small heap of coca leaves each family member took three leaves and, holding them over the child, made a blessing: three wishes for his future. These leaves were then placed in a separate bowl. Next I made my wishes, that he grow up to be healthy, happy and prosperous, and placed my coca leaves in the bowl too. Dolores then explained how I should sprinkle grains of *quinoa* on Cristian's head in the form of a cross. Then came the hair cutting, each chunk being added to the bowl of used coca leaves. I say chunk because of the extremely large pair of blunt scissors I was given to cut the hair with. Several people who were with me also rather nervously had a go. They thus became hair-mothers or hair-fathers too, and are always welcome back to stay with the family. After the hair had been cut and put together with the coca leaves and *quinoa* in the bowl, the contents were buried as an offering to *Pachamama*, Mother Earth. Throughout all of this rather strange ritual Cristian looked on somewhat bewildered, but returned to his usual, admittedly now short-haired, joyful self as we celebrated with large platefuls of fresh-lake fish, rice and eggs, washed down with beer and soft drinks. As we enjoyed this gift from the family we presented a photo album, some toys and money for Cristian's future to his mother. I sincerely hope that I can return many times to Taquile to watch this child grow up to fulfil the wishes made for him.

attention becomes tiresome withdraw into your tent for a while, having bid a firm goodbye.

If you accept a meal and accommodation, make sure you share some of your food with your hosts; that is what is generally expected, not money or presents. On popular routes, however, an offer of accommodation is most likely made on a commercial basis, so offer to pay.

Indians are usually both friendly and shy, polite and curious. However, there are always exceptions. If you realise that you are not welcome, or if the locals ask you to leave, then do so without fuss. It is their land and there will be a good reason for them feeling hostile, whether through fear or – more likely – because they have had a bad experience with other gringos.

Keep your distance from drunkards. As in all societies they may be aggressive or lecherous. Excessive drinking is common; indeed it is part of the culture, especially during fiestas.

Respecting a culture, warts and all, is one of the great challenges confronting travellers. It does not just mean enjoying their music, their weavings and their *chicha*, it means accepting inefficiency and poor hygiene, and turning a blind eye to cruelty to animals (unless it seems the latter is done to impress or please you, in which case explain calmly how you feel). It means trying to answer yourself the question that keeps springing to mind: 'Why don't they...?'

Many travellers feel awkward answering the constant questions about how much they earn and how much their gear or clothing cost. Assuming you speak reasonable Spanish, try to put your enormous wealth into perspective. Tell them how much a house costs in your country, or a kilo of oranges, or a horse. Something they can relate to. Explain also about unemployment in the West. Sharing stories about your respective ways of life is an excellent way of getting to know each other providing it does not lead to envy on their side. I vividly remember my first visit to Chinchero near Cusco in 1973, when South America was part of the Hippie Trail. An American, who had chosen to live in that community as part of the process of dropping out, was deeply upset by the materialism of the villagers, who in turn were puzzled by his praise of the quality of their lives. Few of the world's unavoidably poor people view their position as enviable. Most envy our affluence. Few, come to that, share our admiration (especially if we are taking photographs) for their heavy, earthenware pots and banana-leaf wrappers. They would much prefer plastic pots and plastic bags, and would see no reason to dispose of them in an environmentally responsible manner.

If you are hiking into really remote areas, try to find out about the people and their customs before you go. A local guide will do much to prevent misunderstandings as well as showing you the way.

The traditional role of coca

For the Andean people the chewing of coca leaves heightens the significance of almost all social or ritual activities. Both Quechua and Aymara Indians view the leaves as a sacred gift from *Pachamama* (Mother Earth). The name *coca* comes from the Aymara language and means 'food for travellers and workers' because the narcotic effect of chewing the leaves dulls the pangs of hunger and relieves fatigue. The practice has been going on for at least 2,000 years: pre-Inca Mochican ceramics show the tell-tale ball of coca leaves in one cheek. Under the Inca empire, coca was probably a privilege reserved for the royal family and priests (although historians disagree about this) and specific communities were given the job of growing it. The leaves were carried in a finely woven shoulder bag, the *chuspa* or *k'intu*.

Contrary to popular belief, the highland Indians do not use cocaine (which is extracted from the leaves through a complicated process) but the leaves themselves are used for many purposes:

Chacchar/chaccheo Quechua words for chewing coca leaves. To extract the narcotic juice the leaves are chewed until they are soft, then formed into a ball with some *llipta* (known in Bolivia as *lejía*), a mixture of lime (the mineral not the fruit) and potash. The ball of coca and *llipta* is held in the cheek and chewed from time to time.

Social Sharing coca leaves with a stranger is the equivalent of our shaking hands.

Offerings Before entering a valley or climbing a mountain, *campesinos* will offer coca leaves to *Pachamama* asking the *Apus* of this region permission to tread on their slopes and for protection during the journey. Three nice coca leaves are put under a rock or in a ditch.

Medical Traditional healers put great value on the use of coca leaves for many curative processes (and not just as a medicine – see page 90).

Reading of the leaves The leaves are 'read' for advice on a variety of problems and for predictions. Some Quechua elders interpret the leaves by examining the form, shape and colour.

Protection The leaves are believed to protect the person carrying them.

Death When a person dies, coca leaves are given to the mourners as a sign of affection and sympathy. After three days these coca leaves and the clothes of the deceased are burned. The belief is that his/her soul goes to heaven with the smoke.

Fiestas (festivals)

The rich traditions of history and religion come together in local festivals. In the larger towns and cities these are often little more than an opportunity to close banks and businesses and take off for a long weekend, but in the mountain regions the people grab this chance to escape the rhythm of their daily lives and explode into an orgy of colour, music and dance. And drinking.

Most fiestas are similar in atmosphere, but are different in detail. They are common all year round throughout the Andes, but particularly in Bolivia, so you can hardly avoid being caught up in the action.

If you are a lone woman be cautious about participating in fiestas: the combination of alcohol and dancing liberates the male spirit. Your apparent availability could lead to rape. Attend in the company of a man, either local or gringo. If you feel you can handle it on your own you should expect some sexual harassment and be prepared to laugh it off or leave. Do not get angry or upset.

Never participate in a local festival unless you are invited. If you are invited, be prepared to enjoy yourself. Western inhibitions have no place here. For the locals, gringos are part of the fun.

To give a flavour of the fiesta experience, I am retaining the descriptions of three fiestas that George and I attended in the 1970s. These three towns now see plenty of tourists so the attitude to gringo participants may have changed, but not the fiestas themselves.

Chacas, Peru This village in the Cordillera Blanca is proud of its Spanish heritage, and the principal events in its week-long fiesta have a Spanish flavour. We arrived for the *carrera de caballos* (horse race). The morning was occupied by a religious procession, with the plaza full of expectant villagers as the Virgin of Chacas was carried from the church, elaborately attired for the occasion. The procession was led by the village elite with a banner-carrying horseman representing the *caballeros*. Then came the dancers, gloriously dressed and masked, some with large head-dresses of peacock feathers, and dancing to music from pipes, a fiddle and an enormous harp. After the procession had wound its way round the square and the Virgin was returned to the church, the plaza started filling up with horsemen riding magnificent Peruvian 'walking horses' (*caballos de paso*). The riders' wealth was represented by the beautiful animals they rode. We'd been expecting horse races, but in fact the afternoon contest measured the skills of the riders rather than the speed of their animals. Between two posts hung a row of sashes with a ring sewn on to the lower end. The riders had to spear this ring with a short wooden pick as they galloped between the posts. The prize for the most successful was the leadership of next year's contest. There were, perhaps, more desirable prizes; the village maidens had written their names on the sashes.

Paucartambo, Peru This is one of the finest of all Peruvian fiestas, and deservedly popular. The dancing is continuous for three days, and performed with a tribal intensity by the Indians involved. The costumes are varied and incredible: one group reminded us of agitated birds' nests, others of animated sacks. The dancers were fantastically masked and dressed. There were monsters, gringos and negroes: symbolic figures that had played a part in the Indians' history or mythology.

The procession of the Virgin of Carmen was the climax of the last day. She swayed towards us, resembling a stiff white cone of lace and jewels, smothered in flowers and with her doll's face almost hidden under an elaborate crown. Preceding her came a pure white llama, beautifully decorated. On the rooftops of the houses lining her route were dancing devils, demons and winged creatures, but before the Virgin could come under their evil influence, a flight of angels conquered them, beating them out of view. Later, at night, we heard music. Peeping in through a doorway we saw a large room with tables laden with food, and the victors and vanquished dancing together in the middle. A friendly shout went up; we were pulled into the room, filled with food and drink, and danced with until we had to beg for mercy.

Achacachi, Bolivia Our favourite participatory fiesta was Achacachi, near Lake Titicaca, one of our 'accidental' celebrations. We were actually heading for the festival in the neighbouring town of Sorata when our bus was forced to stop by a large and noisy brass band blocking the road. We hastily gathered up our things, got out and found ourselves immediately swept into the parade. The costumes here were quite incredible. The principal dancers looked like the White Queen in *Alice through the Looking Glass*. It was hard to believe they could walk, let alone dance, in such outlandish apparel.

At the fiesta, stove alcohol was the preferred drink. Fortunately the custom of returning some of each cupful to Pachamama saved us from embarrassment. I slipped away at one point, and returned to see George dancing down the street, arm in arm with a large white bear, and hitting bystanders on the head with a banana. Later he swore that it was part of the dance; certainly the bear and the bystanders enjoyed it enormously.

Fiestas in Peru and Bolivia
Below are the main festivals in Peru. Check dates with the tourist office in the nearest large town before you go.

January 1	Año Nuevo: all Peru
January 1–6	Fiesta del Año Nuevo: Apurimac, Huancayo (Peru)
January 6	Día de los Reyes Magos: Cusco, Puno (Peru)
January 6	Niño Occe: Huancavelica (Peru)
Juanary 12	Fiesta de Negritos: Huancavelica (Peru)
January 20	San Sebastián and San Fabián: Huancayo, Cusco (Peru)
January (last week)	Alacitas: La Paz (Bolivia)
February (one week)	Carnival: throughout South America
February 2	Virgen de Candelaria: Huancayo, Ayacucho, Cusco, Puno (Peru); Virgen de Copacabana, Lake Titicaca (Bolivia)
March 8	San Juan de Dios: Puno (Peru)
March or April	Semana Santa: throughout Peru and Bolivia
April 25	San Marcos: throughout the Andes
May (first week)	Feria de Alacitas: Puno (Peru)
May 1	Labour Day: all Peru and Bolivia
May 3	La Invención de la Santa Cruz: throughout the Andes
May 15	Fiesta de San Isidro: Moche (La Libertad), Huaraz (Peru)
End of May	Semana del Andinismo: Cordillera Blanca (Peru)
End May/early June	El Gran Poder, Calvario, La Paz (Bolivia)
Early June	Qoyllor Rit'i: Cordillera Vilcanota, Cusco (Peru)
Mid June, Thursday after Trinity Sunday	Corpus Christi: throughout Peru and Bolivia

June 15	Virgen de las Mercedes: Huancayo (Peru)
June 24	Inti Raymi: Cusco and San Juan Bautista. Día del Indio: Lima (Peru)
June 28	San Pedro and San Pablo: all Peru and Bolivia
June	Fiesta de Torre-Torre: Huancavelica (Peru)
July 6–8	Santa Elizabeth: Callejón de Huaylas (Peru)
July 16	Virgen del Carmen: throughout the Andes
July 24–28	Fiesta de Santiago: throughout the Andes
July 26	Santa Ana: Puno (Peru)
July 28	Independence Day, Peru: all Peru
August 4	Santo Domingo: throughout the Andes
August 5–8	Virgen de Copacabana, Lake Titicaca (Bolivia)
August 6	Independence Day (Bolivia)
August 15	Fiesta de Asunción: throughout the Andes
August 16	San Roque (patron saint of dogs): several places in Peru and Bolivia
August 30	Santa Rosa de Lima: Lima (Peru)
September 8	Virgen de la Natividad: Cajamarca, Huancayo, Cusco (Peru)
September 14	Fiesta de la Exultación: Huaraz and some other mountain villages (Peru)
September 23–24	Virgen de las Mercedes: throughout the Andes
September 30	San Gerónimo: throughout the Andes September Fiesta de Huarachicoy: Sacsayhuaman (Cusco) (Peru)
October 4	San Francisco de Asís: throughout the Andes
October 7	Fiesta de Señora Rosario and Uma Raymi (Festival of the Water): most Andean villages
October 18	El Señor de los Milagros: Lima and San Lucas, Huancayo and some other mountain villages (Peru)
October 20	Dia de La Paz (La Paz, Bolivia)
November 1–2	Todos Santos and Día de los Muertos: cemeteries all over Peru and Bolivia
November 4–5	Festival of Manco Capac: Lake Titicaca, Puno (Peru)
December 3–13	Virgen de Guadalupe: Huancayo (Peru)
December 8	Fiesta de la Purísima Concepción: throughout the Andes
December 24	Santo Rantikuy (the buying of saints): Cusco (Peru)
December 25	Los Galos: Huancavelica (Peru)
December 28	Fiesta de los Santos Inocentes (similar to April Fools' Day): all of Peru and Bolivia

Language
Spanish

'What kind of language is it when:
sopa means soup not soap
ropa means clothes not rope,
and *como no* means yes?'

In fact, Spanish is not a difficult language and backpackers should make every effort to learn the essentials. Your ignorance of the language shouldn't discourage you from making the trip, but I do advise you to learn a few greetings and a basic backpacker's vocabulary, even if you don't aspire to discussing politics and philosophy.

Both a dictionary and a phrasebook are essential. The dictionary should have a Latin-American bias; avoid buying one based on the language of Spain – too many words are different.

An excellent way to become fluent in Spanish and at the same time learn about Andean cultures is to sign up for a language course in Latin America. The following companies are among those who organise such courses in the UK and the USA:

Caledonia Languages Abroad The Clockhouse, Bonnington Mill, 72 Newhaven Road, Edinburgh EH6 5QG, Scotland; tel: 0131 621 7721/2; fax: 0131 621 7723; email: info@caledonialanguages.co.uk; web: www.caledonialanguages.co.uk. Spanish language courses in Cusco, including homestay accommodation with meals, classes, transfers, salsa and cooking classes. Also volunteer work in Peru.

VentureCo Tel: 01926 411 122; fax: 01926 411 133; email: mail@ventureco-worldwide.com; web: www.ventureco-worldwide.com. Four-month Gap Year opportunity comprising a Spanish course followed by volunteer work, followed by an expedition.

AmeriSpan Unlimited PO Box 40007, Philadelphia, PA 19106-0007, USA; tel: 800 879 6640; worldwide: 215 751 19861100; email: info@amerispan.com; web: www.amerispan.com. Spanish language programs in Cusco and Sucre as well as throughout the rest of Latin America.

Perhaps the best option is to sign up directly with one of the schools in Cusco, Huaraz or Huancayo.

Cusco

Cusco Spanish School Calle Garcilaso 265–Of 6, 2nd floor, Cusco; tel/fax: 084 226928; email: cuscospan@cuscospanishschool.com or sbuenoch@terra.com.pe; web: www.cuscospanishschool.com. Spanish lessons, all levels, one-to-one or small groups. Flexible schedules, salsa classes, hiking, homestay, volunteer programmes.

Amauta/don Quijote Calle Suecia 480, Cusco; tel: 084 262345; email: infocentral@donquijote.org

Excel Language Centre Cruz Verde 336, Cusco, tel: 084 232272; fax: 084 232272; email: info@excel-spanishlanguageprograms-peru.org

Huaraz

Sierra Verde Lucar y Torre 538; tel: (044) 721203; email: svlc@qnet.com.pe

Huancayo

Incas del Peru Av Giraldez 652, Huancayo; tel: 064 223303; web: www.incasdelperu.com

Many of the language schools offer courses in Spanish and Quechua, as well as in various arts and crafts. I love the idea of using both sides of my brain and emerging from a beautiful and fascinating part of Peru not only speaking Quechua but able to weave, cook, or play the *charango*!

The Spanish words given below are used in this book because their English translation is too long or doesn't convey quite the same meaning.

campesino	peasant, small farmer
cerro	hill
cordillera	mountain range
hacienda; *estancia*	farm; estate
mestizo	a person of mixed Indian/European ancestry
pasaje, portachuelo	pass
nevado	snow-covered mountains
quebrada	ravine; narrow valley with stream
selva	jungle
sierra	highlands

'Gringo' is so common it's not even italicised. It means any white-skinned foreigner and is a term of convenience, not abuse.

Quechua and Aymara

Spanish is still the second language for many people in Peru and Bolivia. Quechua and Aymara are still widely spoken. Place-names in the *sierra* are usually Quechua, which explains the variety of spellings: the Spanish transcribed the names as best they could.

The following list of Quechua and Aymara names is designed to help you to understand the Inca culture, interpret place-names, and ease your travels through non-Spanish-speaking communities. Some basic vocabulary is given in *Appendix 1*, pages 397–8. In addition you will find the Quechua phrasebook published by Lonely Planet a great help.

Inca words

Amanta	royal Inca's advisers
Ayllu	the basic community, or clan, of the empire
Capac	lord or chief (literally, magnificent)
Capac Raimi	December fiesta in honour of the sun
Condorachi	the annual killing of a condor to ensure good crops or banish evil spirits from a town
Coya	star; wife of the ruling Inca, often his sister
Cuntisuyu	the Inca empire
Huatana	to tie, eg: Inti Huatana, the hitching post of the sun
Inti	sun
Inti Raimi	summer solstice fiesta
Tahuantinsuyu	the land of the four quarters; the Inca empire
Tambo	warehouses or resting places along the roads
Wasi	house or home

Origins of place-names

Bamba	place of	Paca	valley fork
Caja	pass	Pampa	meadow
Cota	lagoon	Pata	summit, hillside
Cucho	corner	Paucar	flowery
Jirca	mountain	Raju	glacier, snowpeak
Huanca	rock	Rucu	old
Huaru	ford	Rumi	stone
Huaylla	meadow	Tambo	roadside resthouse
Lacta	land	Tingo	junction of two
Llacta	village		rivers
Machay	crevice	Urcu	mountain
Marca	city	Yurac	white

Practical Information

PREPARATIONS
Getting to Lima and La Paz

There is a fair number of airlines flying in to Lima from all parts of the world, and there are always some special prices available, though usually in the low season. Air tickets are more expensive in the high season: from April until September and around Christmas time.

There is far less choice to La Paz and fares are much more expensive. There is a good reason for this: because the airport, appropriately named El Alto, is so high (nearly two miles!), planes have to be specially adapted to land safely in the thin air. Few airlines are willing to take on this expense, and with less competition prices are inevitably higher.

Your best bet is to use one of the specialist agencies for South America who offer low prices and informed advice. Check the travel sections of newspapers and magazines; many flight operators advertise special deals here.

It's always cheaper to buy a round-trip ticket, and, anyway, all countries require a return ticket for their tourist visa (though this is not always strictly checked).

From Europe

At the time of writing there is no direct flight to Lima from the UK.

Several airlines fly from mainland Europe to Lima: KLM, United and American Airlines (via the USA) offer the best fares. American Airlines offers the advantage of flying direct to Cusco, with a change of planes in Lima. It is best to go through one of the companies specialising in discounted flights to South America, such as Journey Latin America (tel: 020 8747 3108; fax: 020 8742 1312; email: flights@journeylatinamerica.co.uk; web: www.journeylatinamerica.co.uk) or South American Experience (tel: 020 7976 5511; fax: 020 7976 6908; email: info@southamericanexperience. co.uk; web: www.southamericanexperience.co.uk). A sample low-season fare at the time of writing is with Iberia: £560 with tax direct from Madrid to Lima. High season would be about £130 more.

As noted, getting from Europe to La Paz is expensive. Flights often go through Miami connecting with American Airlines and Lloyd Aéreo Boliviano (LAB) flights to La Paz, or through a South American country using a national carrier such as Sao Paulo in Brazil with Varig. The cheapest current low-season price is £500, but a more realistic price is around £700. High season

(Christmas, Easter, July and August) has the highest prices, up to £890. It maybe cheaper to fly to Lima and take LAB to La Paz or a domestic flight to Cusco or Juliaca in Peru and make the short overland trip to La Paz.

From the USA

Several airlines serve the route Miami–Lima: United, Continental and American Airlines. The latter operates flights from the USA to Lima and directly on to Cusco (with a change of planes). All have direct connections with New York. Direct flights from Los Angeles to Lima are served by Aerolíneas Argentinas and Varig, but these direct flights tend to be more expensive than flying via Miami.

Flights to La Paz are more limited. In addition to American Airlines, Lloyd Aéreo Boliviano (LAB) flies from Miami and so, since it can be combined with an Airpass (see below), may be worth investigating.

The North American specialists for cheap flights to Latin America are eXito (see *Tour operators*, page 39).

From Australia

The worldwide operator STA Travel has branches throughout the major towns of Australia. Links are through a South American operator such as LAN Chile or Aerolíneas Argentinas, or through the United States.

Airpasses

If you have only a limited amount of time and want to cover a lot of ground, an airpass is a good option. In Peru, Lan Peru do a 90-day pass, which offers unlimited domestic flights. In Bolivia, Aero Sur have an airpass but it is not available for purchase outside the country – in general airpasses can only be purchased outside the country.

Tour operators

Many companies run organised treks to Peru and Bolivia, as well as flight-only arrangements. Below are some specialists (see also *USA tour operators*, page 39).

Andean Trails The Clockhouse, Bonnington Mill Business Centre, 72 Newhaven Road, Edinburgh EH6 5QG; tel/fax: 0131 467 7086; email: info@andeantrails.co.uk; web: www.andeantrails.co.uk. Specialists in group departures and tailor-made tours: trekking, trekking peaks, mountain-biking and jungle trips in the Andes.
Andes 93 Queen St, Castle Douglas, Dumfries and Galloway DG7 1EN, Scotland; tel: 01556 503929; fax: 01556 504633; email: john@andes.com; web: www.info.andes.com. Trekking, climbing, skiing and biking holidays in the Andes.
Austral Tours 20 Upper Tachbrook St, London SW1V 1SH; tel: 020 7233 5384; fax: 020 7233 5385; email: tours@latinamerica.co.uk; web: www.latinamerica.co.uk. Peru treks include a llama trek Olleros-Chavin/Huaraz, plus five treks or climbs in Bolivia.
Exodus Travels Ltd 9 Weir Rd, London SW12 0LT; tel: 08675 5550; email: sales@exodus.co.uk; web: www.exodus.co.uk. Inca Trail, Cordilleras Blanca and Huayhuash; llama trek in Bolivia.

Explore Worldwide 1 Frederick St, Aldershot GU11 1LQ; tel: 01252 760000; fax: 01252 760001; email: info@exploreworldwide.com; web: www.exploreworldwide.com. Treks in Peru, including Mollepata to Cruzpata.

Gane and Marshall 98 Crescent Rd, New Barnet, Herts EN4 9RJ; tel: 020 8441 9592; fax: 020 8441 7376; email: holidays@GaneandMarshall.co.uk; web: www.GaneandMarshall.co.uk. Inca Trail, Salkantay, Cordilleras Blanca and Vilcanota.

Journey Latin America 12 & 13 Heathfield Terrace, Chiswick, London W4 4JE; tel: 020 8747 3108 (flights) or 020 8747 8315 (tours); fax: 020 8742 1312; email: adventure@journeylatinamerica.co.uk; web: www.journeylatinamerica.co.uk. *Also at* 12 St Ann's Square, 2nd Floor, Barton Arcade, 51-63 Deansgate, Manchester M2 7HW; tel: 0161 832 1441; fax: 0161 832 1551; email: man@journeylatinamerica.co.uk. Inca Trails, Vilcabamba treks, and treks in the Cordillera Blanca and Huayhuash. Also multi-activity treks including rafting the Tambopata, Tuichi and Apurimac rivers.

Magic of Bolivia Group 182 Westbourne Grove, London W11 2RH; tel: 020 7221 7310; fax: 020 7727 8746; email: zoe@bolivia.co.uk; web: www.bolivia.co.uk

South American Experience 47 Causton St, Pimlico, London SW1P 4AT; tel: 020 7976 5511; fax: 020 7976 6908; email: info@southamericanexperience.co.uk; web: www.southamericanexperience.co.uk. Flights and tailor-made tours to Latin America.

Steppes Latin America The Travel House, 51 Castle St, Cirencester, Glos GL7 1QD; tel: 01285 885333; fax: 01285 885888; email: james@steppeslatinamerica.co.uk; web:www.steppeslatinamerica.co.uk. Treks in Peru and Bolivia include the Cordillera Blanca, the Ausangate and Huayhuash circuits, Cusco area, and Bolivia treks in the Cordillera Real.

Walks Worldwide Kings Arms Building, 15 Main St, High Bentham, Lancaster LA2 7LG; tel: 01524 262255; fax 01524 262229; web: www.walksworldwide.com. Peru treks include Choquequirao and Alpamayo.

World Expeditions 3 Northfields Prospect, Putney Bridge Rd, London SW18 1PE; tel: 020 8870 2600; fax: 020 8870 2615; email: enquiries@worldexpeditions.co.uk; web: www.worldexpeditions.co.uk. Inca Trail, Cordillera Vilcanota, Cordillera Vilcabamba and Huayhuash. Climbing in the Cordillera Real (Bolivia). Trekking for the over 50s. Cycling trips.

Worldwide Journeys & Expeditions 27 Vanston Place, London SW7 1AZ; tel: 020 7386 4646; fax: 020 7386 4655; email: chris@worldwidejourneys.co.uk. Trekking in Cordilleras Blanca and Huayhuash, Inca Trail and alternative Inca Trail.

Other UK companies that run trekking tours in Peru and Bolivia include:

Abercrombie & Kent Tel: 0845 0700610; email: info@abercrombiekent.co.uk; web: www.abercrombiekent.co.uk

Bukima Adventure Tours Tel: 0870 7572230; fax: 0870 7572231; email: bukimauk@cs.com; web: www.bukima.com. 3-week overland expeditions from Lima to La Paz or vice versa.

Chile Tours Tel: 020 7730 5959; email: London.Chiletours@btinternet.com; web: www.Chiletours.uk.com

Discover Adventure Ltd. Tel: 01722 741123; email: info@discoveradventure.com; web: www.discoveradventure.com

Dragoman & Encounter Adventure & Overland Journeys Tel: 01728 861133; email: bradt@dragoman.co.uk; web: www.dragoman.com and www.encounter.co.uk

Explore Worldwide Tel: 01252 760000; email: info@exploreworldwide.com; web: www.exploreworldwide.com

Far Frontiers Ltd Tel: 01285 850926; email: info@farfrontiers.com; web: www.farfrontiers.com

Footloose Adventure Travel Tel: 01943 604030; fax: 01943 604070; email: info@footlooseadventure.co.uk; web: www.footlooseadventure.co.uk

Footprint Adventures Ltd Tel: 01522 804929; email: sales@footprint-adventures.co.uk; web: www.footprint-adventures.co.uk

Golden Hill Travel Tel: 015395 52281; email: sales@goldenhilltravel.co.uk; web: www.goldenhilltravel.co.uk

High Places Ltd Tel: 0114 275 7500; fax: 0114 275 3870: email: treks@highplaces.co.uk; web: www.highplaces.co.uk

KE Adventure Travel Tel: 017687 73966; email: info@keadventure.co.uk; web: www.keadventure.com

Kumuku Tel: 020 7937 8855; fax: 020 7937 6664; web: www.kumuka.com

Last Frontiers Limited Tel: 01296 653000; email: info@lastfrontiers.com; web: www.lastfrontiers.com

Naturetrek Tel: 01962 733051; email: info@naturetrek.co.uk; web: www.naturetrek.co.uk

Oasis Overland Tel: 01258 471155; fax: 01258 471166; email: travel@oasisoverland.com; web: www.oasisoverland.com

Reef and Rainforest Tours Ltd. Tel: 01803 866 965; email: mail@reefandrainforest.co.uk; web: www.reefandrainforest.co.uk

Roxton Bailey Robinson Worldwide 25 High St, Hungerford, Berks RG17 0NF; tel: 0488 689700; fax:01488 689730; email: richard.laker@rbrww.com. Occasional treks plus horse riding in Peru and Bolivia.

Sherpa Expeditions Tel: 020 8577 2717; fax: 020 8572 9788; email: sales@sherpaexpeditions.com; web: www.sherpaexpeditions.com

South American Safaris Tel: 020 8767 9136; fax: 020 8682 1323; email: info@southamericansafaris.com; web: www.southamericansafaris.com

Sunvil Latin America Tel: 020 8758 4774; email: latinamerica@sunvil.co.uk

Terra Firma Travel Tel/fax: 01691 870321; email: info@terrafirmatravel.com; web: www.terrafirmatravel.com

Tim Best Travel 68 Old Brompton Rd, London SW7 3LQ; tel: 020 7591 0300; fax: 020 7591 0301; web: www.timbesttravel.com

Travelbag Adventures Tel: 01420 541007; email: info@travelbag-adventures.com; web: www.travelbag-adventures.com

Tribes Tel: 01728 685971; fax: 01728 685973; email: info@tribes.co.uk; web: www.tribes.co.uk

VentureCo Tel: 01926 411 122; fax 01926 411 133; email: mail@ventureco-worldwide.com; web: www.ventureco-worldwide.com. Gap Year programme (see page 31) plus horse-riding trips.

Walks Worldwide Tel: 01524 262255; email: info@walksworldwide.com; web: www.walksworldwide.com

World Expeditions Tel: 020 8870 2600; email: enquiries@worldexpeditions.co.uk; web: www.worldexpeditions.co.uk
World Wide Adventures Abroad Tel: 0114 247 3400; fax: 0114 251 3210; email: info@adventures-abroad.com; web: www.adventures-abroad.com

USA

eXito 1212 Broadway, Suite 910, 5699 Miles Ave, Oakland, CA 9461894611; tel: 1 800 655 4053 or 510 655 2154; fax: 510 655 4566; email: exito@wonderlink.com; web: www.exito-travel.com. Discounted tickets and tours.
Wildland Adventures 3516 NE 155 St, Seattle, WA 98155, USA; tel: 206 365 0686; email: info@wildland.com; web: www.wildland.com
Wilderness Travel 1102 Ninth St, Berkeley, CA 94710; tel: 510 558 2488; fax: 510 558 2489; email: info@wildernesstravel.com; web: www.wildernesstravel.com

When to go

Most people, if given the choice, will prefer to go in the dry season: May to October. The best months for hiking are April, May, September and October (when the rainy season is not delayed or early!). The few travellers who decide to do some coastal hiking in Peru will choose the months when it is raining in the mountains but sunny along the coast: December to March or April. Visits to the jungle are best early in the dry season when there is still plenty of water in the rivers.

There are two main advantages to going in the rainy season: cheaper air fares and fewer other trekkers; and a lush greenness to the countryside that you miss in the long, dry winter months. It is also slightly less cold. Generally speaking the mornings will start fine but clouds will build up during the day and rain is likely in the afternoon. There are, however, days of unbroken sun as well as days of continual rain – or snow, which brings discomfort and the somewhat unpleasant experience of white-outs or of being surrounded by clouds with very poor visibility.

What to take

Try to keep your backpack as light as possible; you will enjoy your trip much more and it is easier to look after your stuff during bus and train rides. However, you do need to bring all the essential equipment for your trip as it is difficult and expensive to buy it in Peru and Bolivia and the quality is variable. Renting is increasingly an option, especially in Huaraz (Peru) and La Paz, but not ideal if you are planning several treks. Select your camping equipment with care: it can make or break your trip. Although, in general, lasting quality costs money, keep in mind that the expensive things aren't always necessarily the best for your purposes and you don't need to buy every gimmick on the market. Consider buying second-hand equipment – you will be worrying less about things being stolen and will look less like a rich gringo.

There are some good products available from catalogues. In Britain, Field and Trek (tel: 01268 494444; email: catalogue@fieldandtrek.com) have a comprehensive selection of outdoor gear at discounted prices. They provide a

24-hour telephone service. Other mail-order companies include Hawkshead (tel: 0870 599 3344 for a free catalogue; web: www.hawkshead.com), Rohan (tel: 0870 601 2244; web: www.rohan.co.uk), SafariQuip (tel: 0870 330 0113; email: mail@safariquip.co.uk) and Cotswold Camping (tel: 01285 643434, web: www.cotswoldoutdoor.com). For internet shopping, in addition to the above try the following websites which offer a secure shopping facility: www.snowandrock.com, www.yhaadventure.co.uk and www.ellis-brigham.com. Nomad (tel: 020 8889 7014; web: www.nomadtravel.co.uk) specialise in pharmaceuticals but have a good range of tropical camping equipment.

Americans also have plenty of choice, with REI (web: www.rei.com) and EMS (web: www.ems.com) leading the field on the west and east coasts respectively.

Clothing

Remember the old travellers' maxim: 'Bring twice as much money and half as many clothes as you think you'll need.' All of your clothes should be chosen for comfort, but select one outfit which will render you respectable for that blow-out in a good restaurant, or an invitation to visit an upper-class home.

A popular saying describes a day in the Andes as including all the seasons of the year: nights are as cold as winter, mornings are spring-like, the afternoon heat can be as fierce as summer, and evenings have an autumn crispness. This means extreme temperature changes, and backpackers should be prepared accordingly. In the mountains, cold is the biggest enemy (temperatures drop to well below freezing at night). Obviously you must keep yourself warm without adding too much weight to your pack. There is plenty of high-tech outdoor clothing around nowadays to suit all activities and tastes. It is expensive though, so think carefully about what you need and how much on-going use you will get out of it before splashing out huge sums of money. If you choose one expensive item of clothing, make it a good fleece jacket.

The best way of keeping warm and comfortable is by wearing layers of clothes. Since you'll warm up rapidly in the sun and through exercise, you can peel off successive layers of clothing during the day. New designs by the big names (Paramo, Berghaus, Sprayway, Karrimor, Low Alpine, Mountain Equipment and Mountain Hardwear etc) over the last few years combine light weight with warmth, windproofing and breathability to give versatile layers that cope with all but wet weather. Cotton holds moisture next to the skin, which means you will get cold as soon as you stop moving, so is not recommended. Better by far to go for synthetic fibres that wick the moisture away. Thermal underwear is very useful for these freezing nights, being light but very warm. A down parka (duvet jacket) is warm, lightweight and perfect for high altitudes, but not really necessary unless you are going near or above the snow line. Down is useless when wet. At lower altitudes a fleece or wool sweater and windproof top are adequate. The local alpaca woollens are warm, cheap and a good way to support local labour. Don't forget a good warm hat as much heat is lost through the head.

It is likely to rain, even in the dry season and a waterproof jacket or coat and waterproof trousers of some kind are essential. A big rain poncho which covers your backpack is also very useful and doubles as a groundsheet. Waterproof jackets to wear over the warm, windproof layers come in an astonishing range of materials, designs and prices. You will definitely want a breathable fabric for trekking and, in addition, look for useful features such as sealed seams and zips that stop water getting in, ventilation zips, pockets in the right places, and a hood that moves with your head.

Quick-dry walking trousers (pants) over long underwear, or fleece (Polartec Powerstretch is particularly good) trousers are the best options. Lightweight polyester trousers that unzip above the knee are increasingly popular, providing a two-in-one, trousers-and-shorts option, but they are not that good for warmth once the sun goes down. Jeans are not suitable for hiking because denim is heavy and takes ages to dry. Shorts are fine for hiking though they may give offence in some towns. Fleece trousers are lightweight, quick to dry, can be used as pyjamas at night or leisure wear in hotels, and worn under other clothing give an extra warm layer. Give some thought to pockets; all trousers should have deep pockets, secured with a button or zip, and they are handy in shirts as well. Rohan are renowned for putting voluminous and secure pockets in their garments.

Sunburn is a danger at these altitudes. Bring a quick-dry long-sleeved shirt for protection against sun (and insects) and remember that T-shirts leave the base of your neck vulnerable. A broad-rimmed hat is essential, creating a better shadow than a simple baseball cap.

Note It is inadvisable to wear military-style clothing in Peru or Bolivia. The army is not viewed with much affection by rural people.

Backpacking equipment and provisions

Experienced backpackers probably already own all the equipment necessary for a South American trip but newcomers should get expert advice. Good backpacking shops should be able to advise you and climbing/hiking magazines always have good, independent information. It is worth looking in the classified adverts of outdoor magazines or on noticeboards in bigger equipment shops for second-hand equipment.

The requirements of backpackers differ from those of trekkers who need not be quite so careful about weight or bulk (the long-suffering mules or porters will be carrying their stuff) so comfort becomes the primary objective.

Backpack Be willing to spend some money on this – it will be your most important 'companion'. Spend time trying on different makes and models; only settle for the best one for you: size, weight and capacity. Some manufacturers make packs especially for women. Choose one that can be adjusted to your back. The leading manufacturers in Europe are Karrimor and Berghaus and in the USA, Lowe and Kelty. Trekkers need large-capacity daypacks, with strong hip belts, to carry all their daily needs, from cameras to waterproof clothing, as they will not have access to their main luggage during the day.

Boots Together with your backpack, these are the most important items for an enjoyable trip. Seek professional advice, and remember that a boot either fits or it doesn't; you should not need to break them in. The combination of leather and GoreTex is preferred by many people because they are waterproof, but in the dry seasons of Peru and Bolivia lightweight hiking boots made from synthetic materials are perfectly adequate. They are always comfortable, rarely cause blisters, and with less weight to carry on your feet you will become less tired. Boots should have ankle support and good thick soles. Trainers (running shoes) may be all right for some trekking routes but are not suitable for backpacking, where you are at risk of turning an ankle because of the extra weight on your back. Remember that the more weight you carry the more support you will need from your boots. Avoid boots that bend too easily at the sole – they will not last.

Blisters can be avoided by wearing correctly fitting boots and good-quality walking socks, and by not walking too far for the first few days. The most common cause of blisters is prolonged walking downhill – an unavoidable part of hiking in the Andes. When buying boots, lace them firmly and stand on tiptoe, like a ballerina. Your boot should be snug and your toes should still be comfortable.

Tent Although my first year of backpacking in the Andes was spent under a shower-curtain, I concede that a good tent is necessary. It not only protects you from the elements but protects your gear from the acquisitive eyes of the locals when you are camping close to villages. Good tents are expensive so, again, explore the option of buying second-hand. If you buy a cheap or used tent, be sure to bring some sealant to block those dripping seams. It is also useful to bring a tent-repair kit for broken poles or rips in the fabric.

Sleeping bag Although some very effective synthetic fillers are now on the market, you still can't beat goose-down, which is the lightest and warmest insulation available. It is virtually essential for backpackers – synthetic bags take up too much space. Backpacking or trekking in the Andes poses a problem, however, in that in the valleys the nights can be quite warm and you may be too hot in the bag which is just right for 4,000m. Your best bet is to have a sleeping-bag cover or liner which gives you the versatility for moderate and freezing temperatures. A sheet sleeping bag not only keeps your down bag clean, but is perfect for jungle hiking and for use in cheap hotels where sheets may not be provided. Silk is warmer and lighter than cotton. A pillow is made from a T-shirt stuffed with a sweater or duvet (down) jacket.

Mattress/sleeping pad It is essential to have some sort of insulation from the cold ground, as well as padding. Closed-cell foam is cheap and adequate, but the best mat of all is the Thermarest, a combination of air mattress and foam pad. It's lightweight and compact, but expensive. However, if you can't afford a full-length Thermarest, there's a cheaper (and lighter) three-quarter length one.

Mosquito net This is not necessary if you are trekking or backpacking in the highlands, but overland travellers taking in the low-lying areas and staying with local people should bring a lightweight net to protect themselves from insect-borne diseases (see *Health* section). Great advances are being made in improving the design of mosquito nets, and the most effective are now treated with permethrin, which kills insects on contact.

Torch A small but powerful torch (flashlight) such as a Maglite, or a headtorch, should be on your list and kept handy for hotels, which are subject to power cuts, and for exploring ruins, as well as for camping. Candles are not recommended; quite a number of backpackers manage to burn their tent down.

Stove A good stove is one of the most important items on your equipment list and worth spending some money on. The most practical are the multi-fuel stoves (widely available from good outlets) which run on any fuel – but note that spare parts are not available in Peru or Bolivia. You can buy white gas/stove alcohol/benzene (*benceina*) at pharmacies (*farmacias*, *boticas*) or hardware shops (*fereterias*). Kerosene/paraffin (*kerosina*) is available at most petrol stations or in small stores. *Alcohol potable* (drinking alcohol) is readily available and works as a fuel with some stoves.

Bleuet Camping Gaz stoves, which use butane gas canisters, are clean and handy, particularly for lone hikers, but can fail at altitudes above 5,000m. You can buy the cartridges in the bigger cities of Peru and Bolivia. It is forbidden to carry them on planes. For emergencies, it's sensible to bring a tiny 'hot pot' – an aluminium cup and stand that burns tablets of solid fuel (you can buy these in Peru). Bring waterproof matches.

Making fires is strictly forbidden in national parks and reserves because of the damage caused by careless use of campfires. In former days, the National Reserve of Machu Picchu lost many hectares of endemic forest through hikers' carelessness, and much of the ancient Inca stonework has been permanently damaged through campers lighting fires against the walls. Even the most careful siting of fires still requires dead wood which can not then play its part in regenerating the soil. So, cheery and warming though a campfire may be, please resist the temptation and do not allow your local guide to make a fire unless you are outside a protected area and well away from mountain villages who need the scarce fuel more than you do.

Pots and pans If you don't already own a lightweight aluminium saucepan, buy it in Peru or Bolivia. Make sure it has a good fitting lid as this makes cooking more efficient – a process already hindered in the highlands by the reduced oxygen in the rarified atmosphere. Pots are cheap and available in even the smallest towns. Plastic or tin plates and mugs are both suitable, and great for warming hands as well.

Food There is a good choice of suitable pack food available in Peru and Bolivia, so you don't need to bring food from home. You can shop in the local markets or at supermarkets in the bigger towns.

Packet soups, noodles, purée potato, sugar, oatmeal, dried sausage and dried milk all provide a good basis for your hot meals. Ginger, chillies, onions, garlic, salt and pepper and stock cubes add flavour. For lunches, cheese, fresh bread and dried fruits are excellent. Powdered fruit drinks make treated water more palatable.

Dried fruit and vegetables (sliced carrots, cabbage, onions and apples) make excellent backpacking food, and are easy to do yourself in the strong sun of the mountains.

What to bring from home? Maybe your favourite special treat, and a packet or two of dehydrated food for emergencies. See also box on pages 54–5.

Miscellaneous useful items

Below is a checklist of items we have found to be indispensable: toilet paper, trowel for digging 15cm toilet hole, rubbish bags, a travel alarm clock, good quality penknife, sewing kit, safety pins, large needles and strong thread (or dental floss) for tent or other repairs, scissors, heavy-duty sticky tape, felt-tipped pens, pencils and ballpoint pens, a small notebook, a large notebook for diary and letters home, plastic zip-lock bags, large plastic bags for keeping your clothes dry, universal plug for baths and sinks, elastic clothes-line or cord and clothes pegs, small scrubbing brush, concentrated detergent, liquid soap (non-polluting!), shampoo, small towel, toothpaste, earplugs, insect repellent, sunscreen, handcream, lipsalve and sunglasses.

If you wear glasses or contact lenses, bring a spare pair. Bring a medicine kit (see *Health* section, page 86), compact binoculars and camera, film, a couple of paperback books, a phrasebook and Spanish dictionary, a pack of cards or other small pocket games, spare batteries, water bottle and one 2-litre container, water-purifying tablets, waterproof matches, slow-burning candles, compass, waterproofing for boots, large plastic dustbin liners (garbage bags) for covering packs and other equipment at night and a survival blanket.

Presents

You will be the recipient of great kindness and generosity from local people and will want to show your appreciation with gifts. But be cautious with the giving of presents. Thoughtless backpackers and trekkers have created the beggars you meet in rural areas: children who demand *caramelos* or *dulces* (sweets) or *plata* (money) or simply want a present ('*Regalame*'). Gifts – even worthless things such as pens and sweets – should never be handed out indiscriminately. Instead, exchange stories, songs, games and drawings. Rural poverty is not synonymous with unhappiness, and if you examine your motives for wanting to give presents it may be that *you* feel good bringing smiles to children's faces, whereas with a bit more effort you could bring the same smile by playing a game. If you still feel guilty remember that your very presence is vastly entertaining and simply tolerating the stares as you go about your daily business is reward enough. See also pages 71 and 74.

Handicrafts

Textiles and woollen goods from Peru and Bolivia are widely available throughout the world, but the variety, selection, quality and prices in the Andes means that few can resist picking up a few special items. For details on handicrafts in Peru see page 106–7, for Bolivia see page 318–19.

Making do

If you arrived in South America planning to relax but are seduced by the mountains and inspired by the tales of other backpackers, don't feel that your lack of equipment is a barrier. Back in 1973 George and I were in the same position when much of our equipment was stolen: we used a shower curtain as a tent (rigged between trees with a cord) and a poncho as a sleeping bag (until we found a fellow-traveller in need of funds). Renting equipment is no problem in the major cities of the hiking areas, like Huaraz, Arequipa and Cusco in Peru, or in La Paz in Bolivia. At the South American Explorers in Lima you can find some used equipment for sale, and at the popular backpackers' hostels you can put up a notice requesting equipment. When it is your turn to go home, consider selling your gear to help out other backpackers and make more space for all those alpaca sweaters.

Money

The currencies of Peru and Bolivia are dealt with in the country sections. Here we cover general considerations.

Simply put there are three options. Cash, travellers' cheques and credit cards.

The most easily exchanged currency is US dollars – trying to change other currencies can be time consuming and frustrating. Make sure that dollar bills are not damaged (little tears or pieces missing) or they may not be accepted. Forged dollar bills are common so be wary about buying dollars in South America.

You can also bring your money in travellers' cheques. The most used and accepted travellers' cheques are American Express and Thomas Cook. It is easy to change travellers' cheques in cities at the major banks and *casas de cambio* (the best time to change is in the mornings; open weekdays only). You cannot change travellers' cheques in the smaller towns or villages. Always keep a list of the cheque numbers and note the date they are used; failure to do this will make it difficult to replace lost or stolen cheques. Never sign your cheque until the bank clerk has given the go-ahead. Bring the receipt you were given when you purchased them as this may be requested also.

Finally, cashpoints or Automated Teller Machines (ATMs) are increasingly common in major cities and are a convenient source of local currency for holders of Cirrus, MasterCard and Visa cards. You can also get cash from major banks with an American Express card and other credit cards (but a commission is charged) and most upper-range hotels, restaurants and shops accept credit cards.

If you are on an organised trek and only in Peru or Bolivia for a couple of weeks you can manage with a combination of cash and debit/credit cards since your expenditure will be minimal. Backpackers and long-term travellers will probably need to bring travellers' cheques and US$100–200 in cash for emergencies and changing in small towns. Do not take all your money with you on the hikes, only the amount you'll need and some extra. Leave the rest at a hotel that has a safe (make sure that you get a receipt).

Keep all your valuables in a money-belt, under your clothing, while travelling, and if possible leave them in a hotel safe against a receipt when in town. It is a good idea to make photocopies of all your documents, travellers' cheque numbers and flight tickets; keep them separate from your money; and email copies of all important numbers, contact addresses and so on to yourself.

Budgeting
Peru and Bolivia are inexpensive by the standards of the developed world, but you will still need to assume an expenditure of around US$20–25 per day although probably you will spend less. Whilst you will spend virtually nothing when hiking the trails, it's a rare backpacker who can resist the lure of a bit of luxury on hitting the cities. Keep costs down by buying food in the markets and staying in the cheap gringo hotels recommended in the popular guidebooks.

Bargaining is standard practice in Peru and Bolivia, especially with handicrafts, although personally I prefer to pay a fair price for the often painstaking work than pride myself on how little I paid for it.

Photography
Camera and lenses
You have to make a considered decision here: do you expect to take professional-quality photos on your trip or do you just want to have some memories afterwards? Serious photographers need to take more care over the safety of their equipment, give themselves time during the hikes for photography, organise a pack-animal to carry the camera equipment and have good insurance. Others will be happy with a small, automatic camera, preferably with a built-in zoom. The comfort of carrying less weight and the security of looking less like a rich tourist are ample compensation for the poorer-quality photos at the end.

Film
Fuji is the most suitable slide film – ASA 100 or 200 is fine for daytime outdoor shots but bring a few rolls of fast film for poor light or interiors. For prints, 100 ASA will cope with bright and cloudy days. Although film is often available in Peru and Bolivia, you cannot rely on it so it is best to bring all you need from home.

Keeping the film in good condition can be a problem on longer trips where it is exposed to heat and humidity. It is worth bringing a few special bags to keep the film in. And it's probably best to wait until you get home before developing your pictures, as the quality is poor and the cost high in Peru and Bolivia.

Note Unexposed film should be carried in your hand luggage. Newly introduced and more powerful x-ray scanners used on luggage being stored in the hold is believed to fog some films.

Camera courtesy

Both countries are wonderfully photogenic, and few visitors can resist capturing as much as possible on film. However, you must bear in mind that, for people living in the remote mountain areas, this can be a highly intrusive practice. The rural people are reserved but very courteous and their initial contact with strangers has a ritualised pattern. By photographing them without establishing some sort of human contact you are being rude and insensitive. Once you have established contact you should ask permission to take a photo. If you are refused, or the person is uneasy, put your camera away.

It is a different matter for people living in the popular tourist areas. Here they can make a nice living posing for photos. This is a business and should be respected as such: if you don't want to pay, don't take a photo. Try to find out the proper price beforehand – there is something obscene in paying a child posing with a llama the same fee that her father may earn working all day in the fields. If money is not demanded, don't offer it. Many people love to have their photos taken, particularly those who do not look 'ethnic'. You can get some delightful portraits of these grinning kids. Do get their address and send them a print – and honour your promise. The result will be far more treasured by the recipient than by you.

Never take photos of any military objects. If in doubt, ask someone in authority.

Further information

The best place for hiking information – and *all* information – is the South American Explorers (SAE) in Lima (see page 53). And of course from the other travellers whom you'll meet at the towns closest to the trails. Unfortunately many guides are unreliable sources of information, being preoccupied by the commercial side of it all. 'No' or 'I don't know' are not part of their vocabulary.

Maps

The maps in this book will give you an adequate idea of the hikes described, and the SAE has some good detailed maps on the popular hikes in Peru. If you want to go off the beaten track and do some serious hiking and exploring by yourself (and we strongly urge you to do this), we recommend you carry a topographical map of that area. In both countries the government-run Geographic Institute (Instituto Geografico Militar – IGM) publishes maps which are available in the capital. Details are given in the relevant sections.

TRAVEL IN PERU AND BOLIVIA
Transport

In terms of availability, public transport is excellent in Peru and Bolivia. Specifics of travel are dealt with in each country section, but in general any village served by some sort of road will have some sort of vehicle running there on some sort of irregular schedule. On major routes the quality improves dramatically so it's up to you whether you go for comfort or for cheapness.

Buses

These come in various shapes and sizes, from luxury vehicles speeding along the intercity routes to ramshackle affairs serving the rural villages. In Peru, and to a lesser extent in Bolivia, you can get luxurious buses on the well-travelled routes (mostly along the coast and on paved roads into the mountains) with video, toilet and reclining seats. They charge about 30% more than the normal price. Make sure you buy a ticket with a well-known company where the buses mostly leave on time, stick with the route and don't stop at every corner. The smaller bus companies never leave on time or cancel the scheduled departure altogether if there are not enough passengers.

Try to travel during the day for more comfort, safety and scenery. Also avoid long bus rides; break your journey. You'll enjoy the trip much more, avoid problems with theft (most of which happens when you are tired), and arrive in better shape. The cheaper buses have more character, and more sights and smells. The amount of fruit peel, paper, babies' pee and vomit that the average Peruvian family can dispose of during a lengthy trip in the mountain region has to be seen to be believed.

Most buses stop for meals (except the luxury buses, which feed you on board), but not necessarily at mealtimes. Make sure you understand how long you will be stopping for, or the bus will leave without you. Better still, have your meal within sight of the driver. Plenty of snacks are available from local vendors who will pour on to the bus and crowd round the windows at every village. Remember to fill your water bottle before you leave although soft drinks are usually available from vendors.

Your luggage will be lashed to the roof or stowed away in the luggage compartment. Checked luggage is usually safe: most bus companies have an effective security system to prevent someone else claiming your luggage. Either way, it will be inaccessible, so bring warm clothes and something to use as a pillow during night trips (those crescent-shaped inflatable neck pillows are ideal). You'll also need games or a book for entertainment during unexpected delays or breakdowns. Keep your passport on you for police checks. Watch your luggage like a hawk, especially when boarding and alighting the bus. Padlock small items to the luggage rack or seat. Robbery is common on buses, but by professional criminals, not your fellow bus passengers. Some bus companies impose a luggage weight limit of 20kg per person. Expedition members may therefore find themselves paying excess baggage charges.

Colectivos

These are vans or cars which use the same routes as buses, but the long-distance ones are about double the price. This is because they are more comfortable and faster once they get moving, but since they only leave when they are full there might be a long waiting time. The short-distance *colectivos*, mostly between towns, are the same price as (or a little more than) the buses. They are a comfortable option (if not filled up to the roof!) and very popular in Peru and Bolivia.

Trucks

Lorries/trucks used to form the backbone of public transport in Peru and Bolivia. This is no longer the case, with buses now serving all but the most remote villages. However, if you are heading way off the beaten track you may find your only transport option is the back of a truck.

Although buses are more comfortable – and warmer – the views from an open truck are so fantastic that these should be your choice for short journeys through spectacular scenery. Although some trucks run to a schedule, most wait until they have collected enough passengers to make the trip worthwhile. Don't be misled by the driver telling you he is leaving *ahorita*. His and your concept of 'now' will be different; you may wait for hours before he makes a move.

Remember, it is bitterly cold riding in an open truck in the Andes. Keep all your warm clothes (including gloves, cap and even your sleeping bag) handy, and carry your foam pad to cushion those bare boards. Not all trucks have a tarpaulin, so bring protection from rain and snow. It's a good idea to strap your pack on to the side of the truck (inside) so that it's neither trampled by other passengers nor resting in a nice pool of oil or urine during the trip. Protect it from the effluent of furred or feathered passengers by putting it in a strong bag such as a flour or rice sack (which can be purchased at any market). Bring something to eat and drink during long trips, although long-distance trucks, like buses, stop for meals.

Don't take a truck at night unless you're absolutely desperate and well prepared for freezing weather. Assume an afternoon departure will become an evening/night departure.

Taxis

There is no shortage of taxis in either Peru or Bolivia. If you can join up with other travellers to share the cost, and strike a good bargain with the driver, a taxi need cost little more than conventional transport and will save you a lot of time and effort – for example when you need to get to the trailhead and are carrying a heavy backpack. Save your energy for the hike.

Always settle the price beforehand and make sure the taxi is reasonably likely to make the journey without breaking down. Make sure, too, that the driver knows where you want to go (in the hiking areas most know the popular trailheads) but don't expect him to know how to read a map.

Trains

Although slower than buses, trains are a pleasant alternative – and the views are better. On the negative side, however, is the increased risk of theft. Professional teams work the most popular tourist trains and even experienced travellers can fall prey to their tricks. Thieves commonly slash bags left under the seat or take them from the rack and throw them through the open window to an accomplice. Padlock your stuff to the luggage rack and try to team up with other travellers to watch each other's luggage. You should be extra vigilant on trains and in and around all stations. An unsuccessful attempt was made on my pocket recently on a train in Peru, but later several locals on the same train realised their wallets had been stolen.

In Peru recent changes in regulations mean that tourists generally have to travel on designated tourist train services; travelling on the colourful local train is no longer an option. The one advantage of this is that the risk of theft is reduced.

It is well worth buying a ticket the day before, and reserving a seat (but this still doesn't guarantee that your seat will not be occupied!). It is advisable to go first class if you are carrying much baggage. Second class throws you into the hub of local life and conversation but it is difficult to enjoy this if you are trying to watch your luggage, and a moment's inattention may be fatal. You may also have to fight for a seat since they cannot be reserved. In first class you are still exposed to plenty of local colour when vendors stream on to the train at stations, and some of the more well-to-do locals (those that are likely to speak English) travel first class. Note, however, that first is not actually the best class. The authorities have taken notice of the gringo fear of robbers and on some lines have provided them with a carriage protected from the incursion of any but the most respectable locals. Buffet- or tourist-class carriages have locked doors and only ticket holders are allowed on. There will be no vendors so no local colour, but you *will* be safer.

Peru

The famous train from Lima to Huancayo via La Oroya is not currently operating, but there is a daily train between Huancayo and Huancavelica. In the south of Peru a line runs from Arequipa to Juliaca, from where one branch continues on to Puno and the other to Cusco. From Cusco there is a line via Ollantaytambo and Aguas Calientes (nearest station to Machu Picchu) to the Hidro Electric station just below Machu Picchu. Train schedules can be reduced or cancelled in the rainy season.

Peru Rail

Peru Rail run the tourist train services in southern Peru. For details of timetables and prices contact them by email: reservas@perurail.com; web: www.perurail.com; or at one of their local offices: Lima Avenida Armendariz 397, Miraflores; tel: 01 4445020 or 4445025, Mon to Fri 08.30–18.00; Arequipa Av Tacna y Arica 200; tel: 054 205640, Mon to Sat 07.00–17.00; Cusco Estacion Wanchac; tel: 084 238722 or 221992 Mon to Sat 07.00–13.00, 14.00–16.00; Juliaca Plaza Bolognesi; tel: 054 321112, Mon to Fri 06.00–10.00 and 14.00–18.00, Sat/Sun 06.00–10.00; Puno Av La Torre 224; tel: 054 351041 or 369179, Mon to Fri 07.00–17.00, Sat/Sun 07.00–12.00.

Bolivia

Bolivia has a more extensive railway network than Peru. It is said that every time Bolivia lost a war (which has happened with regularity throughout its history) the victors built a railway in compensation. If you want to travel by train in Bolivia it is a memorable experience but none of the lines pass through the main trekking areas.

As well as ordinary trains, Bolivia has the *ferrobus*, which looks just as it sounds – a bus designed to run on rails. There are two classes. On the *ferrobus* these are called *Pullman* and *Especial*, and on trains simply first and second class, although a few lines have Pullman carriages. There are no sleeping cars.

Hitchhiking

This is possible but hardly worth it if you're looking for a cheap way of travelling as most drivers charge for the ride. There are exceptions, of course, but it is courteous to offer payment unless you are quite sure this would be offensive. However, hitchhiking can come in to its own when you've finished a trek and the twice-weekly bus service left a couple of hours previously.

Aeroplanes

Andean roads are often in very poor condition, especially in the rainy season, so sometimes it's wise to consider taking a domestic flight. If you have an airpass (see page 36) you will be taking them frequently. Otherwise domestic airfares are fairly expensive, especially in the high season, and international flights within South America are outrageously expensive. It is far cheaper to fly from border to border, and cross the frontier by bus. In the low season domestic flights are often sold at very cheap prices.

Always confirm and reconfirm your flight, and this must be from the town of departure. The tourist peak season is from June until September, with July as the busiest month, and from December until February, when Peru and Bolivia enjoy their main holiday season. Be prepared for overbooked and delayed flights, and cancellations. Flights are often cancelled in the rainy season, so allow extra time in your schedule. For security always make sure that your checked luggage is locked and put backpacks in another strong, protective bag. Most domestic airlines are pretty generous with extra luggage and don't charge for excess.

Accommodation

There is always a wide variety of hotels to choose from in Peru and Bolivia, from a little dark cell with a too-small bed that feels more like a hammock, to a luxury room with a king-size bed and en suite bathroom and limitless hot water. Then there are the middle-range hotels. The star-rating of hotels may mislead you – few are up to European or American standards – but then they're half the price. In Peru expect to pay US$4–5 per person for a cheap *hostal*, around US$10–30 for a mid-range hotel, and US$50–100 for most of the top-class hotels. Prices vary according to the size and tourist interest of the town, high or low season, and for groups. Prices in Bolivia are similar, maybe just a little cheaper overall, US$3–5 for the cheapest, US$10–30 for mid-range and anything above should start to be a bit special.

The hotel feature of abiding interest to gringos, most of whom have diarrhoea or are expecting to have diarrhoea, is the toilet. In the cheapest hotels this will be out in the yard and very smelly; in cheapish hotels it will be inside, but communal and probably occupied when you most need it. You may prefer to go for the upper end of the middle range to ensure that your room has its own bathroom. Plumbing systems in Peru and Bolivia are rather half-hearted, so except in the posh hotels don't try to flush your toilet paper (yes, you must supply your own) down the lavatory, but put it in the basket or box in the corner. No, it's not nice, but a clogged toilet is nastier. South American electricians enjoy having lots of exposed wires in the shower. Be very careful when using the on/off switch for hot water. Dry hands and rubber flip-flops are a sensible precaution if the wiring looks really suspect.

Cheap hotels are often lit by 40-watt bulbs. If you are really keen, get your own 100-watt bulb to allow you to read at night.

All towns of interest have their backpacker hangouts. The travellers' grapevine or guidebooks will tell you where these are. It is worth deciding beforehand where you will stay and taking a taxi there to avoid being hassled by hotel touts in the larger cities. On the other hand, finding your own, unlisted, hotel ensures lower prices and fellow guests who are not all foreigners. The cheapest hotels are almost always clustered around bus and train stations. In villages that have no obvious hotel, there is always a *señora* with a room to rent for the night, so just ask around.

Your possessions can be at risk in any hotel. The better places have safe-boxes in which you can leave your valuables (take the precaution of putting them in a sealed envelope, and make sure you get a receipt). Don't leave enticing valuables on show in your room – even an honest chambermaid can succumb to temptation. Leave them at the bottom of your backpack, in a bag that you can recognise by touch. If something goes missing, do report it to the hotel owner and if this has no effect go to the police.

Make sure you know the hotel rules: checkout times, discounts, electricity or water cuts, hot water availability and whether there is an extra charge for this, and if the price includes taxes (especially in middle- and upper-range hotels), special services, and so on.

Camping

It is generally perfectly safe to camp well off the beaten track and usually all right in or near the smaller villages, although in remote areas you may infringe the rules of rural etiquette if you refuse offers of accommodation and then pitch a tent. In some places there may be a nominal charge for camping. Avoid leaving your campsite unattended and always keep all your valuables inside the tent, which should be lockable. Never camp in, or close to, towns or cities; a hotel is much safer. It goes without saying that you should take *all* your rubbish with you.

For more about camping see *Chapter 1.*

South American Explorers

This is a non-profit organisation that functions mainly as an information network for South America. Since 1977, researchers, explorers, students, and long-term travellers from all over the world have used the SAE as a base to network and plan their activities. Over the past 20 years, the club has gathered the knowledge and experience to become one of the leading sources of information on Peru, Ecuador, Bolivia, and Latin America as a whole. Information, however, is only a part of the club's activities: as a foundation, it helps plan and promote academic research, exploration, and conservation projects in Latin America.

Services to members include: use of Trip Reports (reports written by members about all their experiences in Peru, including the grading of tour companies, hotels etc); sending/receiving faxes; use of mailing address; free storage of luggage, equipment and valuables; reconfirmation of flights from Lima; discounts on the wide range of books and maps for sale; use of library and map room; book exchange; notice-board; and a relaxing place to have a cup of tea and meet other travellers. They also have an extensive database on volunteer positions in Peru. *Membership* is US$50 for an individual for a year and US$80 for a couple and includes a 1-year subscription to South American Explorer magazine. Remember, to get all these benefits you need to be a member. The hard-pressed volunteers who work there do not have time to answer enquiries from non-members (except briefly by phone) so even if you are only planning a short trip it is worth joining. You can sign up at the clubhouses, or through Bradt Travel Guides in England (tel: 01753 893444; fax: 01753 892333; email: info@bradt-travelguides.com – an administrative fee is charged on top of the membership fee – or at the Ithaca office.

General website: www.samexplo.org. Clubhouse contact information:

Lima Calle Piura 135, Miraflores; tel/fax: 511 445-3306; email: limaclub@saexplorers.org; postal address: Casilla 3714, Lima 100, Peru. Open Mon–Fri 09.30–17.00 (Wed until 20.00); Sat 09.30–13.00.
Cusco Choquechaca 188 no 4; tel: 51 84 245484; email: cuscoclub@saexplorers.org; postal address: Apartardo 500, Cusco.
USA 126 Indian Creek Rd, Ithaca, NY 14850; tel: 607 277 0488; fax: 607 277 6122; email: ithacaclub@sae.explorers.org

Food

Eating in Peru and Bolivia is enjoyable. There are all sorts of tasty snacks sold on street corners and in cafés, and even the cheapest restaurant food is usually good, although starchy. These are meat and fish countries and vegetables are rarely served. If you don't fancy what is on the menu, most restaurants will serve eggs, potatoes and rice on request. But of course it is more fun to experiment with the local food. Bring your dictionary to the restaurant and don't be embarrassed to wander round looking at other people's choices. Sometimes that's the easiest way to select a meal – simply point to someone else's.

HIGH ALTITUDE NUTRITION
Dr Chris Fenn

Fluid is easily lost at high altitude via your lungs and as a result of sweating. Breathing cold, dry mountain air can result in a loss of two litres of water each day at moderate altitudes. You need to make a conscious effort to replace this fluid loss. Thirst is not a good indication of your need to drink – it's too late by then, dehydration has already set in. Aim to drink at least three litres of water a day, more if you sweat a lot. Hot drinks made from boiled water are the safest way of drinking fluid. If you prefer plain water, make sure that you filter and sterilise it thoroughly.

The need for salt
It is logical to think that you need to take extra salt to replace that lost in sweat. However, taking salt without adequate water can be dangerous. Sweat is a very dilute solution of salts and proportionally more water is lost from the body, causing the concentration of salts in the body to rise. Taking extra salt without adequate water will disrupt the salt and water balance in the body even more. Salt tablets are then not useful, but if you find you develop an increased taste for salt, you could be a little depleted. Remedy it by adding extra salt to your food.

Trek food
During strenuous exercise the body uses carbohydrates as the main fuel to provide energy. Several research studies have shown that a diet based on carbohydrates can also help reduce the symptoms of acute mountain sickness. At high altitudes the body is more able to metabolise carbohydrate foods than fatty foods, and generally speaking you will find that carbohydrates are more appealing at altitude than fatty food. All carbohydrate foods will help keep your energy levels high, but for energy and health it is best to eat more of the starchy carbohydrate foods. This is because the starchy ones also provide valuable nutrients such as vitamins,

All the cheaper restaurants serve set meals at lunch time, listed as *menú*, or *almuerzo* (the menu, in the English sense, is *la carta*). In a set menu you'll get soup of the day, *sopa del día*, a main dish, *la segunda*, and a dessert, *postre* or/and a cup of herb tea, *mate*. The helpings will be substantial and the price low at around US$2–5.

Anything chosen from the à la carte menu will be more expensive and take longer to prepare, so save this for the evening meal.

In the mid- and upper-range hotels and restaurants a meal will cost between US$5 and US$40, with an added tax (in Peru) from 18 to 31%.

Always check your bill carefully, and count your change. Tipping is not customary in the cheaper restaurants, nor in the mid-range restaurants where it will be added to your bill. Waiters in international restaurants expect a tip on top of the service charge and tax.

minerals, fibre and proteins. So aim to eat at least half of your daily calories in the form of carbohydrates. Sugary foods should not form a regular part of your eating pattern as too much sugar leads to a rapid rise and subsequent rapid fall in blood sugar. Foods with natural sugars are a much more healthy option than chocolate, biscuits and cakes.

Food containing starchy carbohydrates Bread, pasta, rice, noodles, potatoes, sweetcorn, peas, beans, lentils, cereals, oats.
Sugary food containing simple carbohydrates Sugar, jams, biscuits, cakes, tinned fruit.
Food with natural sugar Fresh fruit, dried fruit, honey.

Snack food for the trek
Whether you enjoy the trekking food or not, it is a good idea to take an extra supply of your favourite snacks. These should be foods that supply a lot of carbohydrates for energy. Regular nibbling on carbohydrate snacks will help to prevent mental and physical fatigue during strenuous trekking days.

High-carbohydrate snacks
Dried fruits such as ready-to-eat apricots, prunes, figs, raisins etc are widely sold in Peru.
Muesli bars can be found locally or brought from home.
Energy bars, although nutritious, may not be to your taste, so try them at home before buying.
Licorice is a good source of iron, which helps in the making of red blood cells during acclimatisation.
Marzipan keeps well and is a good source of energy.
Chocolate bars contain a lot of fat, and some carbohydrate.
Powdered drinks are good to disguise the taste of water purifiers, and isotonic drinks and oral rehydration solutions help the body absorb water.

Don't get so carried away with the joys of eating that you consume risky food. Cold buffets served at upmarket hotels can be particularly dangerous because they have been sitting around for a while breeding a nice variety of bacteria. Be particularly careful to avoid mayonnaise and salad, and cold meat. You'll be safer eating freshly cooked food in the market.

Do-it-yourself meals bought at markets provide a welcome change and the chance to eat fresh vegetables and fruit. It is still better not to risk salad unless you can soak it for some time in purified water.

Everywhere in Peru and Bolivia you'll find a Chinese restaurant, a *chifa*. Food here is invariably good and cheap. In tourist areas restaurants have learned to cater to gringo tastes and provide yummy chocolate cake and pizzas and so on. They also provide menu translations which can leave you more confused than ever. What, for instance, is 'Bifstek with pickpocket sauce' or 'a small locust'?

CUY

In Cusco Cathedral (and in the cathedral of Ayacucho) there is a 17th-century painting of the Last Supper. The scene is traditional, but the main dish is startlingly different: as befits a meal of importance in Peru, Christ and his disciples are about to dine on guinea pig.

The domestication of the native guinea pig as a source of meat for special occasions would have been noted by the priests and Spanish artists who set out to save the souls of the Inca heathens by using images they could relate to. To this day the animals, known as *cuy* in Spanish (see page 16), are kept by the Indians of the high Andes.

Cuy takes hours to prepare for the table. After the neck is broken (no blood must be shed, since this is an important ingredient in cooking), the animal is plunged into boiling water to loosen the fur, which is plucked and finally shaved with a razor blade. All organs are carefully preserved, including the intestines, from which tiny sausages, *pepián de cuy*, are made. These contain minced innards and blood.

The method of cooking *cuy* varies by region. Generally, they are grilled whole over charcoal after the skin has been rubbed with herbs and garlic (an important step, since the skin is the tastiest part). In Arequipa fried *cuy* (*chactado*) is popular: deep oil is used and the *cuy* covered by a smooth river stone to flatten it during cooking so that it resembles Peking duck. Sometimes *cuy al horno* (baked guinea pig) is offered in the Cusco area, and in other mountain villages it may be casseroled in green (herb) or red (chilli and peanut) sauce.

While gringos fastidiously nibble at the scant meat on slender bones, locals crunch their way happily through head, brains and paws. One bone is carefully preserved, however: the *zorro*, a tiny bone from the middle ear said to resemble a fox. This is used for gambling. Wagers may be placed on the number of *zorros* collected in a given time, or the bone is placed in a glass of beer and the drinker challenged to swallow it with the beer (surprisingly difficult, because it tends to stick to the bottom of the glass).

Foreigners more used to seeing guinea pigs as cherished pets than culinary ingredients will be relieved to hear that the former role is not completely denied them in the Andes. A Peruvian friend told me his younger brothers and sisters refused to allow their pet *cuyes* to be dished up to an uncle in honour of his visit. It was three years before the uncle would speak to his family after this insult!

Local dishes – Peru

A classic Andean dish, guinea pig (*cuy*) is rarely served in restaurants but you will find it at street stalls during fiestas, since Indians save it for special occasions, and usually have *cuy* on birthdays (one for each person). Once pet-owning gringos see the little roasted animal lying whole on the plate and grinning at them, they lose their appetite.

The classic coastal dish in Peru is *ceviche*, raw fish or shellfish marinated in lemon juice with onions and red peppers. It is delicious but most foreigners have sensibly avoided it since the cholera outbreak.

The following are the items most commonly found on the menu:

Starters

Palta rellena	Avocado filled with chicken salad
Palta reina	Avocado filled with mixed salad and mayonnaise
Papa a la huancaina	Cold potatoes with a rich egg-and-cheese sauce
Rocoto relleno	Stuffed green peppers (often very hot)
Tamales or *humitas*	Ground maize steamed in banana leaves, filled with meat or cheese; sometimes they are served sweet, with sugar instead of meat
Sopa criolla	A creamy spiced soup with noodles and a little chopped meat
Chupe de mariscos	A very rich and creamy shellfish soup
Causa	A dish made from yellow potatoes, peppers, hard-boiled eggs and other ingredients

Main dishes
Meat dishes

Churrasco and Lomo	Fillet or rump steak
Apanado	Breaded meat cutlet
Chorrillana	Meat smothered in fried onions
Adobo	A Cusco speciality; chopped, marinated pork in a richly seasoned gravy, served only in the mornings
Piqueo	A very spicy stew with meat, onions and potatoes
Sancochado	Meat, vegetables and garlic
Lomo saltado	Chopped meat in a sauce containing onions, tomatoes and potatoes
Picante de ...	Meat or fish with a hot, spicy sauce
Parrillada	Barbecued beef, pork, sausage and viscera
Chicharrones	Chunks of pork fat, deep fried
Chaufa	Chinese-style fried rice
Cabro or *Cabrito*	Goat meat
Antichuchos	Baby beef-heart shish kebab
Pollo con papas	the ubiquitous chicken and chips
Pachamanca	Typical in the highlands, this is a delicious mixture of meat and vegetables cooked underground on hot stones.

Fish dishes

Corvina	Pacific sea bass
Pejerrey	Fresh-water fish
A lo macho	The main fish dish comes with a shellfish sauce
Trucha	Trout

Desserts

Mazamorra morada	Pudding made from purple maize and various fruits
Flan	Crème caramel
Picarones	Delicious rings of fried batter served with syrup or honey
Keke or *torte*	Cake

Drinks

Pisco	Grape brandy, very popular in the form of *Pisco sour* with lemon, sugar and egg-white
Chicha	Maize beer. This is an integral part of any celebration or communal work project in rural areas. In Andean villages look out for houses with flowers or coloured plastic tied to a pole above the door: this indicates that the householder sells *chicha*
Chicha morada	Unlike *chicha* not alcoholic, but a soft drink made from purple maize
Cerveza	Lager-type beer, which is very popular. There are several regional brands such as *Cusqueña* and *Arequipeña.*
Vino	Local Peruvian wines, which are worth tasting although very sweet by gringo standards. Tacama and Ocucaje are the best choices. *Tinto* is red wine
Agua mineral	Mineral water, which is mainly drunk by foreigners so not usually available in rural areas. You will need to specify *con gas* (carbonated) or *sin gas* (non-carbonated)
Mate	Herbal tea, which has become very popular. The best known is *mate de coca*, which is served to tourists on arrival in Cusco or La Paz to ward off symptoms of altitude sickness. Many other herbal teas such as *manzanilla* (camomile), *yerba luisa* (lemon grass), *yerba buena* (mint), and *inojo* (dill) are available. *Mate* is usually served after lunch.

Local dishes – Bolivia

Bolivian food lacks the variety of Peru's, most notably because the lack of a coastline means no fresh seafood. There are a few specialities, the most popular (with me) being *salteñas*. These delicious pasties are part of the Bolivian culture, being eaten in the mornings and advertised outside small restaurants that make and sell no other foods. The tough pastry casing encloses a runny mixture of meat, gravy, olives, potatoes, raisins and any other ingredients that take the cook's fancy. A good *salteña* virtually explodes at the first bite, spilling scalding gravy over your fingers and down your front. And it's worth every bit of the mess.

Here are a few Bolivian specialities not usually found in Peru:

Main dishes

Chuños	Tiny freeze-dried potatoes prepared in the high Andes. I've never acquired the taste for them (the experience is something akin to eating chalk, with a similar texture) despite the efforts of the cook to make them less revolting with the addition of egg or cheese
Sajta de pollo	Chicken with a spicy yellow sauce, onions and *chuños*
Fricase	Stew, usually pork
Saice	Mixed vegetable and meat stew

Drinks

Singani	The Bolivian brand of *pisco*, also distilled from grapes. As well as being drunk on all festive occasions it is splashed around the wheels of vehicles or the hooves of donkeys to ensure a safe journey
Pilsener	The most popular lager
Api	A thick, hot drink made from red maize, cinnamon, cloves and lemon. It is served at dawn on street corners and makes an ideal start to the day when you have a cold truck ride ahead of you.

BACKPACKING AND TREKKING IN THE ANDES
Where to go: an overview

Although some readers will be familiar with South America and can plan their itinerary from an informed position, the majority will have no idea what to expect and where to go. This summary will help you select areas that suit your interests and physical capabilities.

The Cordilleras Blanca and Huayhuash, Peru

This region in the north has attracted mountain climbers for over a hundred years and organised trekking since the late 1970s – one of the first places in South America to compete with the popular Himalayan routes. The appeal is the magnificent scenery with tightly clustered snowpeaks, many over 6,000m, numerous turquoise-blue glacial lakes and a large choice of trails. Distances to the trailheads are not great, and the variety of lowland scenery is an added bonus, with green, flower-filled valleys grazed by cattle providing contrast to the high, cold passes. Always there are stunning close-up views of the *nevados*, the snowpeaks.

This area, however, is not the Peru of tourist literature since the local people are *mestizo* (mixed blood) rather than Indian so you do not see the wonderful costumes and hats of the more traditional areas, nor do you see many llamas and alpacas, nor as much in the way of Inca remains as further south.

The Cordilleras Blanca and Huayhuash, therefore, are primarily for lovers of mountain scenery. The advantage of the Blanca is that it can be enjoyed by walkers of any age or level of ability (see *Geriatrekking*, page 63). Several roads built by an over-enthusiastic government in the 1980s lead over the *cordillera* providing access to vehicles. The Cordillera Huayhuash, by contrast, is one of the most challenging ranges in this book, and suitable for fit, experienced hikers.

The Cordilleras Vilcabamba and Vilcanota, Peru

The two mountain ranges near Cusco provide, between them, something of everything: Inca ruins, Inca roads, colourful Indians tending llamas and alpacas, thermal springs, snowpeaks and subtropical jungle – and plenty of other hikers.

The Cordillera Vilcabamba

The world-famous Inca Trail runs through this range, but there are several other choices, many of which descend into the densely forested valleys and along river gorges. Because the countryside is less open, there are not many opportunities to get off the beaten track and find your own route. This area is also unsuitable for llamas and alpacas so once you are hiking you are unlikely to see these animals. The chief attraction is the greenness of the scenery contrasting with the rugged snowpeaks, and the marvellous, and often quite remote, Inca remains that form the focus for many of the routes.

The Cordillera Vilcanota

This is an austere, challenging area of high, cold *altiplano* (the high plain) with low rainfall, sparse vegetation and mountain passes that test the fittest walker. Here the lives of the Quechua people can have changed little since the days of the Incas as they scratch a living from land that no-one else wants. Brightly coloured, hand-woven garments are worn by the women and some of the men, and in each community the women sport a different style hat. The people can be remote and seemingly unfriendly – the consequence of isolation. The grass is nibbled to its roots by large herds of llamas and alpacas. The Vilcanota is the 'real' Peru, and worth the effort for the stunning mountain views in the most remote areas. You cannot drive to these views, as in the Cordillera Blanca and, to a lesser extent, the Vilcabamba. You must walk there.

Other mountainous areas in Peru

The *cordilleras* mentioned above are the best known and the most popular for trekking and climbing, but that is not to say there aren't other mountainous areas good for trekking. There are. The northern highlands, in particular the areas around Chachapoyas and Cajamarca, have many trekking routes, and a rich pre-Inca and Inca history to be rediscovered. The Cordillera Central, easily accessible from Huancayo, is an extensive glaciated range of mountains that is relatively unexplored – itself a challenge. Then there are the snow-capped volcanoes of Southern Peru around Arequipa: the deep canyons of Colca and Cotahuasi and the Valley of the Volcanoes offer many beautiful routes through remote landscapes, relatively free of other trekkers.

The Cordillera Real, Bolivia

This is a super area for backpacking for two reasons: most of the trailheads are within a few hours' drive of La Paz, with plenty of llamas and alpacas in the high meadows and splendid views of snowpeaks, and most hikes end up in the Yungas (warm moist valleys that lead to the Amazon), a semi-tropical region with comfortable hotels; a deserved reward after all that effort. If you find going downhill difficult, however, this is not the region for you!

The Cordillera Apolobamba, Bolivia

This is the mountain range for adventurers and experienced hikers. Even getting there is a challenge and with no good maps available you are left largely to your own resources. The Apolobamba is wonderfully rewarding for those who dare, with dramatic scenery, high passes, and a fascinating local Indian culture.

Backpacking or trekking?

Broadly speaking, trekking differs from backpacking in that your gear is carried by pack animals (or, in the case of the Inca Trail, porters) and that some local organisation is involved in supplying tents, food, transport, etc. In effect, a trek is a package tour which leaves you free to enjoy the mountains without worrying about any of the logistics.

There are many advantages of trekking over backpacking, not least that all the hassle and anxiety of travel in rural Peru and Bolivia are taken out of your hands. For most trekkers there is no choice: for those with only three weeks' holiday a year, or who are disinclined to heave a 20kg/45lb pack around, or to cope with the uncertainties of arranging their own porters or pack animals, the only way to set foot in the Andes is with an organised group. Furthermore, it is only with pack animals that really long distances can be covered: most backpackers find a week's supply of food is all they can carry. Finally, with transport laid on, an organised trek can reach areas that are inaccessible to backpackers using public transport. Besides, it's often more fun (if you are with a compatible group) than doing it on your own.

In spite of this, the ultimate hiking experience, for most people, will be with one or two chosen companions, and all the effort and hassle of backpacking. For this is what exploring the wilderness is all about. Whatever the brochures say, with an organised group you are not exploring; on your own, even with a guidebook, you are. You are open to serendipitous events, you can stop when you are tired, go as far as you want, and choose the route that most appeals to you. And it will cost you about half the price of a packaged trek.

Organised trekking: choosing the right company

Trekking companies advertise in all the usual places: travel sections of daily or Sunday newspapers, travel magazines and walking and climbing magazines (and in this book). Some companies specialising in trekking in South America are listed on pages 36–8.

Care must be taken when selecting a tour operator. Read between the lines of the brochure to be sure that you can cope physically and mentally with the trek. Check the altitude gain each day, and find out the height of the highest passes and the number of rest days. Do not be beguiled by talk of 'verdant rainforests and glistening peaks'; the former will be hot and wet, the latter cold and exhausting. You can only enjoy the beauty if you can cope with the terrain. Check whether there are horses that can be ridden in an emergency. A good tour operator will happily put you in touch with someone who has done the trip, so you can get an unbiased account of what it's like. Remember that costs usually reflect the quality of the tour operator and the comforts lavished on you, so, unless you are very tough and adventurous, be wary of just going for the cheapest.

Organised trekking has been part of Peru's tourism since the early 1980s. Bolivia is now catching up, with many good local tour operators, but it still lags behind Peru in infrastructure and predictability. Bear this in mind when deciding between the two countries.

Trekking: the experience

If the trek is organised from your home country, the pampering should start shortly after you sign up, with pre-departure information giving you a good idea of what this particular company provides. Most likely they will deal with your air ticket, send you an equipment and reading list, and generally prepare you for what is in store.

In South America you will be met by your trip leader (or he/she may travel out with you) and will not have to think for yourself until you pass through passport control on your way out of the country! It's a wonderful chance for high-powered people to regress into complete dependency, and the happiest trekkers are often those who do just that.

All well-organised treks will have a built-in period of acclimatisation. In Peru, this is usually a few days' sightseeing in the Cusco area, or perhaps some gentle hiking around Huaraz. You will probably be agreeably surprised at how comfortable and well fed you are during this period. Then the tough part starts. Often you must travel in an open truck to the trailhead, because these are the only vehicles which can cope with the rough roads, and you will have to learn how to put up your own tent (or rather, the tent supplied by the local operator). With some of the very classy trekking companies your tent is put up for you, but the *arrieros* have so much to do anyway this only delays more important jobs – like preparing your supper.

You will be surprised at how many pack animals are needed – an average of one donkey per person. And you may likewise be surprised at the number of people taking care of your needs. A typical camp crew is led by a representative of the local tour operator who is both the guide and organiser. It is he who hires the *arrieros* (muleteers) or porters, buys the food, supplies the tents, decides where each night will be spent (pasture for the animals being the deciding factor) and deals with any crisis of a local nature.

Your own Fearless Leader's role is to keep you happy, healthy and well informed. Often there is a trip doctor who takes care of the healthy part, although his/her job is almost always limited to treating colds and diarrhoea (in

GERIATREKKING

When I decided to introduce my 77-year-old parents to the Andes I chose the Cordillera Blanca. For a couple who had been avid walkers all their lives but now looked for an adequate level of comfort and only a few miles of walking per day, this was an excellent choice. Huaraz has some good hotels and enough reliable tour companies to ensure that a driver and sturdy vehicle could be hired. Then it was just a question of selecting the most scenic of the new roads leading into the Cordillera.

Each day our driver took us high into the mountains, then drove back down the road to wait for us at a preselected place. We would walk downhill for a couple of miles, eat our picnic in meadows full of wild flowers and surrounded by the mighty peaks of the Cordillera Blanca, then continue walking down to the car. Thus were we able to see some of the finest scenery described in *Chapter 5*.

We also took an organised trip to the glacier of Pastoruri. The day tour first stopped at the grove of *puya raimondii* then continued on to the glacier, which, at almost 5,200m (17,000ft), is probably as high as you can get by vehicle anywhere in the world. You can climb on to the glacier (the tour company provides a rope for assistance), which my father managed despite his artificial hip. It was 51 years since he had been on a glacier – well worth the US$8 tour fee.

Some tour operators run treks for the over-60s. See pages 36–8.

the score or so treks I've led, there has been no case of serious illness or injury). All treks provide an impressive medical kit. Subordinate to the guide are the cook (plus helper) and the *arrieros* or porters. The cook generally works exclusively for that particular operator, whilst the *arrieros* are contracted locally, near the trailhead.

A typical day begins at dawn (about 06.00) with a wake-up call, although those sleeping near the camp crew (something you learn not to do) will have been woken long before by sounds of chattering and laughter as breakfast is prepared (the cook gets up at about 04.30 to start this chore). The concept of 'I'm not a morning person' seems to be exclusively Western: all South Americans are morning people! Some pampered trekkers find a bowl of hot water outside their tent. Otherwise, few take washing very seriously. With outside temperatures below freezing it's a question of putting on even more clothes and staggering out to the tea tent. The tea tent is one of the joys of trekking. It's big enough to stand and walk around in, and with fifteen tightly packed bodies can become quite cosy. Breakfast is a substantial meal. You will usually get porridge, eggs and bread, and sometimes even pancakes. The quality of food on a trek often comes as an unexpected pleasure.

MAKE THE MOST OF YOUR HOLIDAYS

Tearfund has outlined the following code of responsible behaviour for tourists:

1 **Find out about your destination** – take some time before you go to read about the cultural, social and political background of the place and people you are visiting.

2 **Go equipped with basic words and phrases in the local language** – this may open up opportunities for you to meet people who live there.

3 **Buy locally made goods and use locally provided services wherever possible** – your support is often vital to local people.

4 **Pay a fair price for the goods or services you buy** – if you haggle for the lowest price your bargain may be at someone else's expense.

5 **Be sensitive to the local culture** – dress and act in a way that respects local beliefs and customs, particularly at religious sites.

6 **Ask permission before taking photographs of individuals or of people's homes** – and remember that you may be expected to pay for the privilege.

7 **Avoid conspicuous displays of wealth** – this can accentuate the gap between rich and poor and distance you from the cultures you came to experience.

8 **Make no promises to local people that you can't keep** – be realistic about what you will do when you return home.

9 **Minimise your environmental impact** – keep to footpaths and marked routes, don't remove any of the natural habitat, and reduce the packaging you bring.

10 **Slow down to enjoy the differences** – you'll be back with the familiar soon enough.

While you are eating breakfast, the *arrieros* are rounding up the animals and starting to pack up. This is a long procedure, and you will get a head start, leaving camp at about 08.00 for the day's walk. In your daypack you will carry your picnic lunch, camera, sweater, raingear (however bright the day looks) and any other goodies you need. Your main luggage will not be accessible during the day.

Lunches tend to be rather dreary – there's not much that can be done with week-old bread – and most trekkers bring their own trail snacks. The group will spread out on the trail but assemble at lunchtime, generally at a pre-arranged spot. The day ends around 15.30 when the first walkers march into camp. There is a distinct advantage in not walking too fast. If you arrive before the pack animals and camp crew, you will have a chilly wait. If you struggle in at dusk, sobbing, at least someone will have put up your tent and tea will be almost ready. And tea is the most welcome 'meal' of the day; a chance to take your boots off and ease your aching limbs, and warm your hands round a mug of hot liquid while discussing your experiences. Supper comes at around 18.30 to 19.00. Meanwhile there is desultory or lively conversation, cards, Scrabble, jokes, boozing, reading, complaining, being a general pain to the Leader... depending on the disposition of the group. The evening meal is usually ample: three courses, often with fresh meat (chickens ride on donkeys, along with the luggage, and sometimes sheep join the trek – for a while), although vegetarians are catered for. Most people are in their sleeping bags by 20.00.

Some miscellaneous points

Most trek operators provide horses that can be ridden in emergencies, and these are often in use for ill or tired trekkers. If there are no horses (as in Bolivia), there is generally a rest day built into the itinerary which can be used as a sick day. Professional evacuation by helicopter is very rarely possible.

Most outfitters supply toilet tents, which allow for pit latrines to be dug, thus dealing with one of the major environmental problems caused by trekkers. It is a good idea to check on the situation before you start a trek and if necessary take your own trowel.

Washing soon becomes a non-priority. Even shower-twice-a-day Americans settle down to a quick dab every day or so when it's freezing outside and the shower comes from a glacier. In fact, hot water for washing yourself, your hair, or your clothes is often available on request. A plastic collapsible bucket is very useful for this. You soon get in the habit, on ordinary walking days, of bringing soap and so on for a noontime bath when the sun is hot.

Backpacking: the experience

Backpackers from North America, where areas of wilderness are set aside for recreation, are often surprised at the lack of solitude in the Andes. They tend to forget that the indigenous people cultivate fields and tend their animals at extraordinarily high altitudes, and some live just below the snowline. There are communities several days' walk from the nearest motorable road. The trails here are foot-roads, made and maintained by the *campesinos* who use them, and there is a constant traffic of people and their pack animals moving along them. Only in very remote areas will you be alone in the mountains.

The reception you receive in small villages depends a lot on how popular the trail is with gringos (see *Chapter 1*), but mostly the locals will be friendly and curious, and your chance to observe their way of life and make temporary friends without being obtrusive is one of the highlights of walking in the Andes.

Backpacking: practical considerations
Camping

Where to camp is governed by water supplies. The most idyllic camping places are near lakes or at the upper end of a *quebrada* (ravine, or narrow valley) where the water is unpolluted and the views exceptional. Often, however, you will need to set up camp near a village or small community, since houses are also built near available water (see *Village etiquette* on page 24 for advice on appropriate behaviour). The route descriptions in this book always indicate water supplies, but towards the end of the dry season some may dry up so it is wise always to carry water. Always treat the water you use, whether by iodine, filter, tablets or boiling – this is, unfortunately, essential.

Except in remote areas do not leave your campsite unattended, nor possessions outside your tent. Theft is common near villages on popular trails. If you can lock your tent it will protect your belongings from being pilfered.

Never leave food near your tent; animals will be attracted to it.

Livestock
Cattle and horses All the valleys are used as grazing land, and mostly for cattle and horses. You will find them as high as 4,500m. The cattle, even virile-looking bulls, are almost never aggressive and usually flee as people approach. Be wary, however, of approaching cows with newborn calves.

If you encounter cattle being driven along a trail, stand well back, preferably on the down-side of the track so if the animals spook they will run uphill (slowly), not down. However, if you meet pack animals stand on the upside of the trail to avoid being knocked over the edge by the projecting load.

Llamas It's a great treat for hikers to encounter a herd of ear-tasselled and laden llamas coming towards them on the trail. Everyone reaches for a camera and waits for the animals to get within photographic range. And the llamas stop dead or scatter. For the sake of their *campesino* herder move well off the trail so the herd can pass uninterrupted on their way.

Dogs Most families in the Andes have at least one dog for guarding the property or livestock. See page 93 for advice on dealing with vicious dogs.

Insects
They are not much of a problem at higher altitudes (above 4,500m), but in the low valleys small biting midges or blackflies can be a real pest (they are particularly bad around Machu Picchu). They tend to be near streams, damp green meadows and around cattle. Keep your tent closed and always carry insect repellent. At least they are not mosquitoes so are unlikely to carry diseases, but the bites itch like crazy. There are also horseflies, which bite painfully. Some solace comes with the fact that they are slow and easily killed.

Finding your own route
This is the most exciting sort of backpacking, and one which I hope all readers with sufficient time will adopt. Apart from the thrill of stepping into the unknown with only your map, compass and passing *campesinos* to guide you, finding your own trails will help prevent over-use of the popular ones. There

are thousands upon thousands of footpaths in the Andes, well used and passing through beautiful scenery, and only a very few of them have been trodden by gringos.

As well as the anticipation generated by not knowing what is over the next hill, you have the wonderful bonus of never being lost, because you never know where you are anyway.

The methods George and I used to find the trails described in our first books published in the 1970s can be easily adopted by other fit and adventurous people.

First we selected an area known for its natural beauty, or recommended by the locals, and with a population large enough to maintain trails between villages. No problem in the Andes. Then we tried to find a topographical map covering the area, preferably 1:100,000 or 1:50,000 scale. Again, usually no problem with the geographical institutes in Peru and Bolivia. Even with only a road map you can pick a likely looking area above the treeline, between two small towns, and be fairly confident that there will be a trail. Then we packed enough food to last the estimated number of days, plus two more, and additional emergency rations. And that was it...

Here are a few dos and don'ts for Andean explorers:

* **Do** carry a compass and know how to use it.
* **Do** carry and know how to read a topographical map.
* **Do** turn back if the route becomes dangerous.
* **Do** ask the locals for advice and directions.
* **Do** carry extra food.
* **Don't** plan a jungle trip without a guide.
* **Don't** underestimate time, distance, or weather conditions.

Guides, porters and pack animals

For independent travellers the reverse of finding your own route is to use local expertise to ensure a trouble-free trek. Guides, cooks, porters, muleteers (*arrieros*) and their pack animals – either donkeys (*burros*), mules (*mulas*) or horses (*caballos*) – are often hired by hikers to take the donkey work out of backpacking. You will not be allowed to hire the animal without its owner. Llamas are not usually available, although there is a company in Huaraz trying to introduce llama trekking and Bolivia sometimes uses trek llamas.

Arrieros and porters can be hired in most towns and villages next to the trailhead of popular routes. The charge in mid-2001 was US$10 a day for the man and US$5–8 for his donkey. These charges have only gone up a couple of dollars in the last four years, but they do vary a little, region to region. Remember you must pay for the *arriero* and his animals to return to the starting point. If he has done a good job a 10% tip can be added to the fee. A porter (*portador*) charges about US$6 a day (necessary on certain routes, such as the Inca Trail, where pack animals are not permitted, or on high passes and peaks where pack animals can't go).

In most well-known trekking areas, the *arrieros* have formed an association, and control the prices and conditions. This has done much to avoid

BROTHER CAN YOU SPARE SOME RICE?

George Bradt

I went to Cajamarca for a vacation, Hilary went to do some hiking. I slumped around eating and sleeping while Hilary scurried about organising a trek.

After two days of frantic activity, Hilary broke the bad news. 'George, you won't believe the wonderful hike I've plotted out for us. Out of bed, lace up your boots, put on your backpack and let's go.'

'Isn't it too late to start walking this afternoon?' I suggested hopefully.

'Isn't it too late still to be in bed?' she countered.

'OK. Where are we going, and how long is this gem of a walk?'

'Well, I asked a nice man if we could walk from Cumbe Mayo to San Pablo and he said it would only take a few hours.'

We reached the outskirts of town and I admired Hilary's new hiking style: she was walking on her heels like a penguin.

'What's this, the new Bradt Ergonomic Propulsion Technique?'

'No, it's athlete's foot, and I don't want to hear any jokes about it.'

Before we could pursue the subject further we heard the welcome sound of a vehicle climbing the hill behind us. A lift to Cumbe Mayo! We had plenty of time to look around the site with the archaeologist driver before finding a camping place and eating a lavish supper. I asked about food for the rest of the trip.

'No problem. There's quite a big village on the way so we can stock up with more food there.'

The next day in the village of Chetilla we met the mayor sitting outside a house. When he saw us he bustled over and asked our business. We told him about our walk and asked if we'd reach San Pablo that evening. He wasn't at all encouraging. Hilary looked nervous and asked directions to the village shops.

'There is only one, and it's closed.' As we continued through the village Hilary kept nipping off down side streets and asking for eggs or bread. No one had any, and this was the only village along our route. We ate our lunch in some fields. I was just reaching for a third roll when Hilary said 'George, two are plenty, why not save the rest for tomorrow?'

'OK, just fill me in on your supper plans then; you know, kind of give me something to look forward to.' Just as I was beginning to suspect, there would be no supper. In icy silence we walked down to the river valley. On the way, Hilary's search for local food became more vigorous. Braving the hysterically barking dogs, she asked at every hut we passed. No one admitted to having any spare food. We crossed the river at the bottom of the valley and had started up the other side when we met a man milking cows. We asked to buy a litre, and to our relief he agreed readily. After he had filled our water bottle with warm frothy milk he refused to accept payment. We continued in better spirits, but after four hours of climbing our legs felt like jelly.

We climbed, slower and slower, until just before sunset. 'After all, there's nothing to cook, so there's no point in stopping early,' said Hilary philosophically. Finally we found a good campsite, set up the tent, and tucked into 'supper'. Hilary swapped four peanuts for my share of the milk.

'If you're still hungry, George, you could walk over that rise and see if there's a village. I think I saw a soccer field up there from across the valley.'

'Me? Hungry? After hogging an entire roll and four peanuts? I'm full to bursting!'

'I'd go myself, but I don't think I can walk.' She'd taken off her boots and socks to reveal ten swollen, oozing toes with great raw areas where the skin had come off. Thinking that we were lucky to have survived this far, I sped up the hill, hoping to see a road. But there was no village at the top of the ridge, not even a house.

It was rather depressing to wake up to no breakfast, and even more depressing to climb uphill all morning and find how quickly we were drained of the energy we had accumulated overnight. Our food-finding efforts continued unsuccessfully. By this time Hilary was hobbling along like an old crone, her feet wrapped in an assortment of colourful rags. Eventually we came across a woman weaving, with lots of hens scratching about in the dust.

'Have you any eggs?' we asked as we casually waved a large bank note.

'Yes, I've got two', she said. Bliss, our salvation was at hand. She began weaving all the harder. Better check. Yes, we'd heard correctly, but she wasn't interested in getting them.

'You know, we're very hungry.' More weaving. 'We haven't eaten anything for three days.' Completely unmoved, even with my exaggeration. A day or two without food means nothing to these people. Then she saw someone hurrying towards us, and unhitched her backstrap loom immediately. She lifted a sitting hen, gave us the eggs, and took the money. The youth running towards us stopped and motioned us towards him. 'Why don't I cook those for you, and give you some rice as well?' We couldn't think of any particular reason why not, so followed him to a nearby hut. Very soon we were ploughing through two bowls of rice topped with a fried egg.

After watching us satisfy our initial hunger, he asked where we'd come from and where we were going. Then he asked the obvious question: 'But why didn't you bring any food with you?' We told him and he laughed long and loud. He kindly suggested we take extra rice with us in case we didn't reach San Pablo until the next day. But he assured us that even walking slowly, 'like fat ladies', we'd reach the town before sundown.

We'd stuffed ourselves so full of rice we could hardly get up, let alone carry our backpacks. But we liked the stuffed feeling better than the empty feeling. And we liked our arrival in San Pablo better than the journey.

This piece first appeared in the 1980 edition of this guide. Obviously things have changed in the Cajamarca region but as a reminder of what can happen to unfit, unprepared hikers it is worth keeping. Anyway, I like it!

exploitation by unscrupulous tour operators or individual hikers. Always go through the association, if there is one, not only to provide local employment and to encourage the maintenance of standards, but also to iron out any misunderstandings or problems that may arise.

Most *arrieros* are trustworthy, but you need to make your requirements clear, and to keep your valuables with you. When choosing an *arriero* try to get a recommendation from another traveller. That way excellence is rewarded. Take time to draw up a contract in writing. Discuss the price (only pay half up front, and the other half at the end of the trip), the duration of the trip, side trips, whether cooking is part of the deal, and whether you need to provide his food and/or sleeping equipment as well. *Arrieros* will have their own idea of how long a trip will take and it is almost impossible to shift them. Part of this seeming obstinacy is the necessity of camping where there is good pasture for the donkeys. Part of it is about making money, so you may end up paying more days than you need.

Despite what may appear to us as frequent cruelty to animals, *campesinos* are very solicitous over their general welfare: they need fit, healthy animals. So ask them how many days it will be, and agree on a total price for that time period.

Hiring local people is an important way for tourists to help the rural areas and bridge the cultural gap. However, for many hikers the freedom of walking alone outweighs the moral and practical advantages of using *arrieros*. A compromise is to hire someone for the first day to take your packs to the top of the first pass, and then continue on your own.

Minimum impact

As backpacking and trekking become increasingly popular in Peru and Bolivia, hikers must develop an awareness of their effect on the environment. Even the problems besetting the national parks in developed countries, such as erosion caused by over-use, are now seen here! Inca ruins that have withstood hundreds of years of the forces of nature have been damaged by the campfires of tourists, and flights of Inca stairs built for the light tread of bare feet have been worn down by the heavy tramp of hiking boots.

Environmental abuse, however, takes on a wider meaning since the foreign hiker is making his mark not just on the landscape, but on the local people. Ironically, of the two major problems, litter and begging, one is caused by imitating local customs and the other by ignoring them.

Litter

We should be truthful about litter. It offends the eye (and sometimes the nose) but does little permanent harm to the environment. However, it is so easy to put right, and so unpleasant when left, that we should do everything in our power to ease the problem. The quantity of litter and rubbish left on the popular hiking trails in Peru and Bolivia is horrifying. Some would have you believe that local people are the worst culprits but at least it is their country to mess up. Besides, few locals have Qantas airline baggage tags, Kangeroo matches, use water flavouring to remove the taste of iodine from river water, or smoke. Waste matter of all sorts, paper, fruit peel, plastic, and so on, is dropped on the highways and byways, rivers and creeks, and soon everyone joins in. Tourists, both gringo and South American (perhaps mostly the latter), are responsible for most of the litter on trails simply because the *campesinos* have so little to throw away. Tourist litter is so much more conspicuous: brightly coloured toilet paper, cans, dried-food packets, film cartons, Band-Aids, aluminium foil. It's hard enough to understand why visitors blow their noses on pink toilet paper and then drop it on the wayside, but why they also shit beside the trail, leaving a pile of turds and toilet paper, is almost incomprehensible! The culprits are unlikely to be readers of this book so it is a waste of space to preach about it. All I can say is try to clear up other people's mess as well as your own, unpleasant though it may be. And remember that orange peel is just as unsightly and alien as toilet paper, even though it is biodegradable.

Carry several roomy plastic bags and collect rubbish as you walk. Instead of ruining the entire walk with an obsessive hunt for rubbish, choose an hour or pick a bag and completely clean a section. It's tedious and tiring, but you'll feel noble (and if you do stoop to shit-paper you'll feel hypernoble) and will be doing something positive. Later you can burn or bury your collection. People are much more likely to throw rubbish in an area that's already littered – certainly don't add to it, and stop others doing it if you can.

Tell your porters or *arrieros* that you will pay them extra if they carry all the rubbish back to the main town, and help you clear up littered areas. This is a case where interfering with their culture is a good thing!

The preservation of the beauty of Peruvian and Bolivian hiking trails is up to you. Here are a few recommendations:

- Leave the trail and campsite cleaner than you found them. If you can't carry out other people's tin cans, bury them away from the trail.
- Defecate well away from the trail and water supply; carry a trowel and dig a cat hole approximately 15cm deep, or cover your faeces with a rock, and pack out or burn the paper carefully.
- Don't burn firewood needed by the local population. Cook on a stove. Uncontrolled fires cause major damage each year in Peru and Bolivia; don't become part of the problem.
- Don't contaminate streams. Pans and dishes can be cleaned quite adequately without soap or detergent, or use one of the biodegradable liquid soaps readily available. Use a bowl or pan to take water away from the stream for washing in so you are not putting any waste into the water.

Begging
Another indication that a trail is a popular gringo route is that children rush up to you and demand sweets or money. Before you offer a child such presents, reflect on the consequences of your action. You are promoting tooth decay in an area with no dentists, or you are teaching a child that begging is rewarding

RAFTING
Paul Cripps
Rafting In Peru
Another great way to get way off the beaten tourist trail is to take a rafting trip. Peru is home to some of the best whitewater runs on the planet, from extreme rafting through the world's deepest canyon to jungle float-trips through the Amazon rainforest. Using specially designed rafts and accompanied by experienced guides, you can access spectacular locations away from roads, villages and human contact whilst enjoying this exhilarating and adrenalin-pumping sport – this is the deepest darkest Peru of Paddington Bear fame (you may even glimpse one of his relations if you are lucky).

But before you jump on the first raft trip available it is worth bearing in mind that the very remoteness that makes these rivers so special also brings with it logistical and safety problems should anything go wrong. Every year accidents, including fatalities, do happen and you should be aware that your dream raft trip does hold with it certain inherent dangers. Don't be put off – there are all types of trips to cater for all types of people, but if it is extremes of adrenalin or wilderness you are looking for be sure to seek out the experts, as going with the wrong company can seriously endanger your life.

It is highly recommended to pre-book your multi-day rafting adventure before leaving your home country, as many of these expeditions have very infrequent departures and you could find yourself waiting for ages to get a group together. Prices vary dramatically, as do quality of equipment, food, experience of guides and safety records. Be sure to shop around. Day trips are easier to organise direct from Cusco.

Rivers to run
Cusco Río Apurímac, May–October, class 3+ and 5+, 4 days
One of the top ten rafting rivers of the world and the true source of the Amazon, the Apurímac run is rapidly becoming known as the best short whitewater-rafting adventure in Peru if not in the whole of South America. A short drive from Cusco into a 2,000m-deep canyon of spectacular rock formations, rare wildlife and outstanding whitewater, this is one trip not to be missed by lovers of adventure and wilderness.

Cusco/Arequipa Río Apurímac, April-May, class 1–2, 3 days
This rarely run section of the Río Apurímac high up in the Andes takes you through outstanding scenery and is ideal for the fun sport of inflatable canoes or duckys. You'll experience rare *Puya raimondii*, granite canyons and Inca ruins, plus wilderness beyond your wildest dreams.

Cusco/Abancay Río Charhuanca/Pachchaca, May–June, class 4, 3–5 days
A newcomer to river run. The first commercial descent is set for June 2002

on what looks like becoming another Andean classic for whitewater aficionados only.

Cusco/Puno/Madre De Dios Río Tambopata, July–September, class 3–4, 8–9 days
The Tambopata is home to over 800 species of birdlife, 1,200 species of butterfly and countless endangered mammals from rare giant otters to jaguars, black caiman to giant anteaters. Using a raft to access this area is the perfect way to experience a true rainforest adventure far off the beaten track. This trip ends near the world's largest macaw lick; it's a short flight back from Puerto Maldonado to Cusco.

Cusco Río Urubamba, all year round, class 2-5+, 1/2–3 days
Just out of Cusco and cutting through the heart of the Sacred Valley of the Incas, the Río Urubamba offers a variety of different runs, depending on time of year, to cater for the beginner to the adrenalin junkie. A great way to start the Inca Trail or enjoy a couple of days' tranquil canoeing and exploring the best ruins, the Urubamba is probably the most rafted river in Peru.

Arequipa Río Cotahuasi, June–July, class 4+, 8–9 days
Rafting the world's deepest canyon is a full-on expedition for expert rafters only, encompassing a rough 14-hour road, 2 days' desert hiking, 6 days of non-stop class 4+ whitewater, unexplored ruins and delicious freshwater shrimp. Amazingly, fewer than 50 people have ever run this river! Look out for the infrequent departures and definitely go with the experts.

Arequipa Río Colca, July, class 5–6, 6–8 days
Possibly even more extreme than the Cotahuasi, this even-less-explored river boast incredible scenery, huge portages and rock falls most afternoons.

Rafting in Bolivia
Rafting in Bolivia is very much in its infancy and has not yet reached its full potential, but if you like to go where few if any have gone before, way off the beaten track, then rafting in Bolivia might just be for you.

Río Tuichi, October–November, class 3–4, 14 days
The Tuichi valley, deep in the very heart of the Madidi National Park (the world's most biologically diverse national park), boasts some of the rarest tropical dry forest in the world as well as fun class 3–4 whitewater through a spectacular gorge, ending deep in the Amazon rainforest. A total expedition, rarely run but set to become a classic.

For details of running any of these rivers contact operators in Cusco (see listings *on pages 229–31).*

and that something can be got for nothing. Increasingly insistent demands irritate future trekkers and help widen the gap between gringo and *campesino*. (This subject is covered in more depth in *Chapter 1*.)

Adults, too, have been taught to beg. They usually ask for cigarettes or money and one's attempts at conversation or normal social interaction are thwarted.

This cultural erosion is reversible. If all trekkers and hikers stopped handing out unearned presents the begging would cease in a few years, and the *campesinos* would return to their traditional system of reciprocity, where presents and labour are exchanged, not given. So give a smile and a greeting instead.

Health and Safety

HEALTH
Co-written with Dr Jane Wilson-Howarth
Before you go
Inoculations

South America is not the hot-bed of disease you may imagine, but the following inoculations are recommended:

- Updated **diphtheria** and **polio**. Also **tetanus** or tetanus booster. These three are effective for ten years.
- **Yellow fever** (not effective until ten days after inoculation; not recommended for pregnant women). This is also effective for ten years.
- **Anti-malarial protection** (if going on a jungle trip; not needed for high-altitude treks). Peru has chloroquine-resistant strains of malaria and it is important that you follow the prophylactic regime carefully. Ensure that you consider avoidance of bites too and pack repellent, long, loose clothes and perhaps an impregnated bed net.
- **Hepatitis A** vaccine is available from British general practitioners free of charge and the course of two injections protects you for ten years.
- **Typhoid** vaccine is recommended by some doctors although it will not provide total protection and being careful about what you eat and drink is your best defence. It is given in two shots, four weeks apart, and lasts for three years. Unless at exceptional risk, people over the age of 35 who have received four or more courses of typhoid immunisation need no more.
- A pre-exposure **rabies** vaccination. Hikers are at risk from rural dogs, many of which carry rabies, and those venturing to coastal or rainforest areas could fall victim to vampire bats and other bats which are often rabid. The vaccine is essential for researchers or naturalists who will be handling wild mammals or for anyone entering caves (see also *Rabies* on pages 80–1) and for anyone who may be more than a week away from medical care.

Fitness

Being in good physical condition is an essential requirement for all hikers; lack of fitness is dangerous and will mar your enjoyment of the mountains. However, independent backpackers planning a long trip have very different fitness requirements from those of trekkers or others on a short holiday where

LONG-HAUL FLIGHTS

Dr Felicity Nicholson

There is growing evidence, albeit circumstantial, that long-haul air travel increases the risk of developing deep vein thrombosis. This condition is potentially life threatening, but it should be stressed that the danger to the average traveller is slight.

Certain risk factors specific to air travel have been identified. These include immobility, compression of the veins at the back of the knee by the edge of the seat, the decreased air pressure and slightly reduced oxygen in the cabin, and dehydration. Consuming alcohol may exacerbate the situation by increasing fluid loss and encouraging immobility.

In theory everyone is at risk, but those at highest risk are shown below:

- Passengers on journeys of longer than eight hours duration
- People over 40
- People with heart disease
- People with cancer
- People with clotting disorders
- People who have had recent surgery, especially on the legs
- Women who are pregnant, or on the pill or other oestrogen therapy
- People who are very tall (over 6ft/1.8m) or short (under 5ft/1.5m)

A deep vein thrombosis (DVT) is a clot of blood that forms in the leg veins. Symptoms include swelling and pain in the calf or thigh. The skin may feel hot to touch and becomes discoloured (light blue-red). A DVT is not

daily objectives must be achieved. The former will gradually get into shape on the trail, but the latter must make considerable efforts to get fit before they go.

Backpackers have the enviable advantage of being able to camp where they choose, and fatigue in the early stages of a long trip is almost an advantage since it encourages a very slow ascent, thus minimising the danger of altitude sickness. On the other hand, the weight of your pack at the start of the trail ensures that you go slowly and there's no point in letting lack of fitness add to your suffering!

Ideally, people signing up for an organised trek or expedition must start to get fit at least a couple of months before they leave. This preparation should as closely as possible resemble what they will actually be doing: hiking in the mountains. Therefore it is much better to walk briskly in hilly country than to run along level roads. Not all potential trekkers, of course, live close to suitable countryside, but everyone has access to flights of stairs and walking, then running, up an increasing number of stairs is an excellent means of getting fit for the Andes. Cycling is also a good way of preparing for trekking, since it involves most of the same muscles. Stepping up and down on a dining chair (leading 50 times with one leg then 50 times with another) is a daily exercise possible almost anywhere. This will strengthen the thigh muscles which in turn protect the knees.

dangerous in itself, but if a clot breaks down then it may travel to the lungs (pulmonary embolus). Symptoms of a pulmonary embolus (PE) include chest pain, shortness of breath and coughing up small amounts of blood.

Symptoms of a DVT rarely occur during the flight, and typically occur within three days of arrival, although symptoms of a DVT or PE have been reported up to two weeks later.

Anyone who suspects that they have these symptoms should see a doctor immediately as anticoagulation (blood thinning) treatment can be given.

Prevention of DVT
General measures to reduce the risk of thrombosis are shown below. This advice also applies to long train or bus journeys.

- Whilst waiting to board the plane, try to walk around rather than sit.
- During the flight drink plenty of water (at least two small glasses every hour).
- Avoid excessive tea, coffee and alcohol.
- Perform leg-stretching exercises, such as pointing the toes up and down.
- Move around the cabin when practicable.

If you fit into the high-risk category (see above) ask your doctor if it is safe to travel. Additional protective measures such as graded compression stockings, aspirin or low molecular weight heparin can be given. No matter how tall you are, where possible request a seat with extra legroom.

Common medical problems
This list of the most common health problems and their treatment assumes that you are not in easy reach of a local doctor. Even if the medical set-up isn't quite what you're accustomed to, remember that doctors in South America are well versed in diagnosing and treating local diseases. If you are unwilling or unable to see a doctor, pharmacists are accustomed to treating the local population for minor complaints, but check the expiry date on any medicines they prescribe. Many drugs, available only on prescription in the USA or Europe, may be bought – expensively – over the counter in South America.

'Filth-to-mouth' diseases and how to prevent them
Travellers' diarrhoea is common in Peru and Bolivia; it and a host of other diseases are caught by getting other people's faeces into your mouth. Contrary to popular belief, most of the diarrhoea-causing bugs get into you by way of contaminated food rather than via dirty water. Among the possible filth-to-mouth diseases that can be acquired in Peru and Bolivia is a particularly unpleasant larval tapeworm which can set up home in the brain and muscles where it is known as cystocercosis. Not surprisingly, this causes quite a serious – though curable – illness which is well worth avoiding. Cystocercosis seems

to be a particular problem where uncooked foods, especially lettuce, are irrigated with untreated sewage effluent. This happens in La Paz and parts of Peru where water is very scarce. Never eat lettuce, even in expensive hotels, and try to avoid all uncooked foods including *ceviche* (marinated raw seafood) and ice-cream and farmers' cheeses. PEEL IT, BOIL IT, COOK IT, OR FORGET IT.

Take the precaution of sterilising all water by boiling it (the best method bacteriologically), or treating it with iodine or chlorine or silver-based sterilising tablets. The latter are least effective but have the advantage of being tasteless. Iodine is the best chemical water steriliser; adding vitamin C after the period of sterilisation and before drinking improves the taste. Many people prefer water filters to sterilising tablets but up until now these have tended to be too heavy for backpackers. The new Aqua-pure Traveller (made by BW technologies) is lightweight and effective. Be careful to wash your hands after using the toilet (this is to wash off other people's germs; your own won't harm you). There are various hand gels on the market which are said to kill most germs within one minute and do not need to be rinsed off, so are ideal for trekking. Regular use, especially before eating, really does seem to work. Soap and water is also very effective.

Diarrhoea

Travellers' diarrhoea is caused by enterotoxigenic forms of the bacteria which everyone has in their bowel: *Escherichia coli*. The trouble is that each geographical area has its own strains of *E. coli*, and these alien strains cause diarrhoea. Everyone has his or her favourite remedy, and it is the subject of many a gringo conversation, but replacing lost fluids is the most important part of any treatment. The most sensible way to treat the problem depends on whether you are a backpacker on a leisurely trip lasting several weeks or months or a trekker on a brief holiday. The latter needs to feel better in a hurry, and he/she is advised to bring a supply of the antibiotic Ciprofloxacin. Take one 500mg pill twice a day for three days; this medication must be taken in conjunction with lots of fluids – aim for at least three litres per day.

If you are a backpacker and can rest up for a few days it is best to let your body expel the toxins and take no medication. 'Blockers', such as Lomotil or Imodium, will stop the diarrhoea by paralysing the gut, but leave you feeling ill. Drink plenty of fluids and eat bananas, papaya, crackers, mashed potatoes and/or boiled rice. If you don't feel like eating, don't eat. The body's ability to absorb fluids and salts is greatly improved by taking sugar at the same time; so, to counteract dehydration and loss of vital minerals, sip a solution of salt (1/2 level teaspoon), baking soda (1/2 level teaspoon), potassium chloride (1/4 teaspoon), and glucose, sugar or dextrose (four heaped teaspoons) dissolved in one pint (half a litre) of water. This 'electrolyte replacement' formula is effective and safe. Make up several packets before leaving home. Failing that, a pint of water containing four heaped teaspoons of sugar to half a level teaspoon of salt can be made anywhere. These rehydration solutions should taste only slightly salty – no more salty than tears. If you are travelling by public transport or are in other places where a dash to the lavatory is impracticable, some sort of chemical cork is required. Codeine phosphate (available on prescription) is a useful stopper as well as being a powerful painkiller; otherwise many people favour Lomotil, but if you are so sick that you need these powerful drugs you should also take them in combination with ciprofloxacin. Fluid replacement is the most important part of all the diarrhoea treatments: being dehydrated will make you feel a lot worse and slows down recovery.

Diarrhoea accompanied by a fever should be treated with Ciprofloxacin. Long-term and seasoned travellers will find they gradually build up a nice collection of South American *E. coli* in their intestines and will seldom suffer diarrhoea attacks. This does not mean, however, that they should be casual over hygiene and run the risk of getting other more serious filth-to-mouth diseases such as typhoid, cholera and hepatitis E.

Dysentery

If, in addition to diarrhoea, you have severe stomach cramps, pass blood or mucus with your faeces and/or run a fever, then you probably have dysentery. A doctor or a clinical laboratory (*análisis clínico*) should confirm the diagnosis before you take medication. Flagyl is effective for amoebic dysentery, as is tinidazole. Ciprofloxacin should cure bacterial dysentery. Antibiotics require a week-long course to be effective. Generally, while both kinds of dysentery cause blood to be passed, bacterial dysentery causes a fever and explosive diarrhoea while with amoebic dysentery there is no fever and the onset of the illness is more gradual.

Fever

If you develop a fever for any reason you should rest and take aspirin or paracetamol. But bring a supply of amoxycillin (convenient because you only have to take it three times a day) or erythromycin if pencillin-allergic (four times daily) with you since you could be struck by some infection in a hopelessly inconvenient place. Under these circumstances, take an antibiotic as prescribed, but not for longer than seven days without seeing a doctor.

Sores and skin infections

If the infection is serious (spreading redness, increasing pain, pus discharge or even fever) you will need an antibiotic, taken regularly for seven days, to clear it up. A slow-healing sore can be speeded on its way by applications of honey or papaya. A skin sore that won't heal over for more than a month needs a medical assessment; it could be leishmania or skin cancer, or just need proper medical attention. Athlete's foot can be a problem. Treat it before it cripples you. Tinactin or other antifungals in powder form are effective in the early stages (shake it into your socks each morning), but I (HB) needed a course of antibiotics because a bacterial infection developed as well. (Cloxicillin, 500mg six-hourly for seven days, is best – unless you are allergic to penicillin, when erythromycin is best.)

Colds and coughs

Respiratory infections are very common in the Andes. Perhaps the dramatic temperature changes are largely to blame: people go sightseeing in Cusco wearing only a T-shirt, and return blue with cold when clouds or the sudden dusk puts an end to the hot sun. Colds easily turn into coughs and even bronchitis in these conditions, so bring decongestants, and sore-throat lozenges. A soothing cough medicine can be made from equal parts of lemon or lime juice, honey, and (optional) *pisco* or other spirit in plenty of hot water.

Motion sickness

The local people are not the only ones to suffer from travel sickness on the rough roads in the Andes. Stugeron (cinnarizine 30mg) is recommended at least three hours before travel (or the night before); it does not make you drowsy. Remember that a full stomach is more likely to empty itself than a partially full one!

Snakebite

I include this not because it is likely to happen, but because people worry that it will happen. Fatal bites from venomous snakes are rare, even in areas where the reptiles are common, for a couple of reasons: snakes are timid creatures and will get out of the way when they sense the approach of a human, and even a potentially dangerous snake often fails to deliver the full amount of venom when it bites in self-defence.

Most of the hikes described in this book take you above the treeline where there are no snakes, but for the lowlands it is worth knowing what to do if you – or your companion – are bitten, just in case.

First forget everything you thought you knew about snakebite kits, tourniquets, sucking out the poison, etc. All are likely to cause worse problems. Snakebite experts now say that the only treatment should be to gently wash the surface of the wound to get rid off any sprayed venom which could subsequently enter the wound, and to bandage the wound itself and as much of the affected limb as possible with a crêpe bandage, tight enough to restrict – but not cut off – the blood flow. Keep the bitten part lower than the heart, and remain as calm as possible. If it is your friend who has been bitten, reassure him/her that the chances are very high either that it was a non-venomous snake or that it did not inject much or any of its venom. If you have had the presence of mind to kill the snake, keep it for identification so that an appropriate antivenom can be administered. Get to a hospital as quickly as possible.

Avoidable (but potentially serious) medical problems
Rabies

Rabies is a viral infection of the brain transmitted by infected animals. It is invariably fatal. In the less-developed countries vaccination of domestic animals for rabies is almost non-existent so the risk of contracting rabies from dogs and other animals is high. If you have not had the rabies vaccine before you leave home but are subsequently bitten by a suspect animal, take the following course of action and forget the conventional advice about capturing the animal and keeping it for ten days to see if it dies of rabies – this is simply not practicable in an Andean village:

1) Immediately *scrub* the bite for five (timed!) minutes under running water and with soap, followed by disinfection with iodine or, failing that, with *aguadiente* or other local spirit. Experiments have shown that this alone reduces the risk of contracting rabies by 90%.
2) Get an anti-rabies injection as soon as possible, but remember that the disease travels slowly along the nerves to the brain; it is only at this point, when symptoms appear, that the disease is incurable. Before that the rabies vaccine is effective, and the progress of the infection can take weeks or even months. Make your way to a clinic in a major town as soon as you can, but reassure yourself with the knowledge that if the bite is on your lower leg or foot you have time on your side.

Cholera

Cholera is a food- and water-borne bacterium that is spread through poor hygiene and contaminated foods. The cycle is reinforced by improper waste treatment, and the dumping of raw sewage offshore. In weaker people the bacteria cause major and immediate dehydration but those in good health rarely notice any symptoms at all; it is not a problem for normal travellers. The disease mostly affects the poor and malnourished. Preventive measures are the same as for diarrhoea — peel it, boil it, cook it or forget it — and beware of cerviche. Cholera vaccine is not recommended since it offers minimal protection.

Some rare Peruvian diseases

In the early part of this century, large numbers of labourers were brought in to build the Lima to Huancayo railway, and accounts of the project casually mention hundreds of deaths because of accidents and disease. The main ailment was *verruga* and I (JWH) have been asked how verrucae could kill so many men! *Verruga* is also the suggested cause of the unpleasant rashes depicted on some of the pre-Inca pottery displayed in museums in Lima. So what is *verruga*? It is an unpredictable disease which occurs from time to time in the Peruvian Andes at altitudes of between 500m and 3100m. Locals are usually immune to it, but if a large number of outsiders move into its territory it can cause outbreaks of a serious disease known as **Oroya fever** or bartonellosis. The labourers who built the railway were one such group of outsiders; the Inca conquerers were, perhaps, another.

Verruga is transmitted by the bites of minute sandflies which are so small that, when hungry, they can get through mosquito netting. Once bloated on blood, however, they cannot get out. Impregnating your mosquito net with permethrin will protect you. Sandflies are mainly active in twilight so insect repellents and long clothes will protect you at dusk. If the disease strikes it is usually caught at the end of the rainy season (March to May) but the risk to travellers is small and it responds to antibiotics. The first symptoms parallel those of numerous tropical diseases, namely fever, headache, aches and pains.

It is possible that the sores depicted on those pre-Inca pots were due to another, milder sandfly-borne disease which is also peculiar to the region. This is called *uta* or **Peruvian leishmaniasis**. The painless ulcers caused by *uta* usually heal without treatment. Peruvian leishmaniasis is almost unknown in travellers but it occurs most commonly amongst poor villagers who live between 1,200m and 3,000m in Peru and Bolivia. This form of leishmaniasis should not be confused with the more dangerous disease of the lowlands, locally called *espundia*. The sandflies that carry this leishmania are found on river banks and in humid forests, especially in the rainy seasons. The resulting sores do not heal and need medical attention.

Another disease that causes unnecessary alarm amongst backpackers is **Chagas disease**. This is a disease of poor lowland villages and is transmitted at night by the bite of the cone-nosed kissing or assassin bug known locally as *vinchuca*. These large insects live in the thatch and walls of wattle-and-daub type housing. Their bite is painful so you will know that you have been bitten. Some excrete the trypanosome organism in their faeces which are rubbed into the bite wound by the scratching of the victim. Afterwards there may be a raised lump at the site of the bite and in some people there is swelling of the eyelids. A blood test six weeks or more after a bite should show if the disease is present. However, if you are likely to be staying in rural huts, you can minimise the risk by sleeping in a hammock, not on the floor, and by using a mosquito net. If you are bitten, wash the wound under running water. Untreated, the disease shows itself in fever, heart disease, and enlarged organs such as the gullet and intestines, often years after the infection. Chagas disease is the main cause of heart failure in South Americans under the age of 40, but it is extremely rare in travellers.

Emergency medical treatment and blood transfusions

HIV which causes AIDS exists in Peru and Bolivia and so does the Hepatitis B virus which is spread in the same way but is much more infectious. Although transfusing unscreened blood is a well-understood route of transferring these infections, many developing countries do not have the resources to do this screening. It is possible to arrange insurance that covers sending safe, screened blood by courier (see addresses below). In case of an accident, ask local advice (your embassy should be helpful here) on the safest hospitals.

The problem in Bolivia no doubt parallels the situation in many developing countries; only about 30% of hospitals in the country screen blood and a recent survey found that 54% of blood was contaminated with Chagas parasites, Hepatitis B, syphilis, or HIV (in that order). The prevalence (47%) of Chagas parasites in the blood samples is alarming since, although easily cured in the early stages of the disease, it may not be recognised until a stage where treatment is difficult or ineffective. The good news is that the Red Cross are working to introduce a system of accreditation which will monitor hospitals which screen blood so it will be possible to pick a clinic or hospital where reliable screening is carried out. Presumably the situation is similar in Peru. (Thanks to Kate Cooper for this research.)

Mountain health

Paradoxically, backpacking in the Andes is both the healthiest and the most dangerous mode of travel. Fortunately the main killers (apart from accidents) – hypothermia, pulmonary oedema and cerebral oedema – can be avoided so read the section below carefully.

Injury

All the hikes described in this book take you well away from civilisation, but most are on good and well-frequented trails. Be careful and sensible. Remember that a badly injured person cannot easily be evacuated from the Andes, and that you may or may not be able to persuade local people to assist you. All backpackers should be conversant in first aid (preferably by going on a course), and should carry an appropriate first-aid booklet. There are some excellent ones specifically for mountain medicine.

Your medical kit should run the gamut from dealing with minor problems to coping with major situations like large wounds that would normally need suturing. Steristrips or butterfly closures are suitable for these. Zinc-oxide tape is useful for holding a dressing in place (non-stick Melonin dressings are good) and has many other uses as well. If you don't mind some funny looks bring panty-liners as multipurpose dressings: they are ideal, being sterile and water(blood)proof and the adhesive backing sticks to the bandage so they don't slip.

When compiling your medical kit (see end of section) bear in mind that medical supplies in the mountain villages are very poor or non-existent.

Sunburn

The combination of equatorial sun and high altitude makes sunburn a real danger to hikers in the Andes. Protect yourself with long, loose clothing and a really good suncream made for skiers or mountaineers, with a protection factor of 15. Lipsalve is essential to prevent cracked lips and should contain sunscreen, and remember how vulnerable your nose is. Wear a broad-brimmed hat and a long-sleeved shirt, at least until you have built up a protective tan and, if wearing a T-shirt, protect the back of your neck with a bandana or neckerchief.

Hypothermia

Simply put, this means that the body loses heat faster than it can produce heat. The combination of wind and wet clothing can be lethal, even if the air temperature is well above freezing. Trekkers and those on day hikes are more likely to have problems with hypothermia than backpackers, who, by definition, carry their requirements with them. So if you are only carrying a daypack, make sure you include a sweater or fleece, a windbreaker, and a waterproof anorak or poncho, however settled the weather looks when you set out. If you can include a survival bag or space blanket that's even better. Always carry some high-energy snacks, too. Your porters or pack animals may easily be delayed and you can get thoroughly chilled while waiting for them. Also, should you stray away from the group and become lost, the main danger to your life is taken care of. Backpackers should concentrate on keeping their warm clothes and sleeping bag dry (everything should be kept in plastic bags) and carry a space blanket or survival bag for emergencies. There are various ways of keeping warm without relying on heavy or expensive clothing. Wear a wool ski-hat, or *chullo*, to prevent heat loss from your head (although the oft-quoted statement that 40% of body heat is lost through the head is misleading since it includes heat loss through breathing!). Make sure heat can't escape from your body through the collar of your windbreaker; use a silk or wool scarf or a roll-neck sweater. Eat plenty of high-calorie trail snacks. Hot drinks have a marvellously warming effect. Have one just before going to sleep. Fill your water bottle with boiling water, put it in a sock and treat yourself to a 'hotty' at night (which also gives you sterilised, ice-free water in the morning). Always change your wet, sweaty clothes when you stop at the end of the day.

If a member of your party shows symptoms of hypothermia — uncontrolled shivering followed by drowsiness, confusion or stumbling — he/she must be warmed up immediately. Exercise is exhausting and eventually results in worse hypothermia. Conserve energy, raise the blood sugar with food, give hot drinks, and put the person in a warmed, dry sleeping bag under cover. If the condition is serious, climb (naked!) into the sleeping bag with him/her and use your own body heat as a radiator. And be prepared for your friend's astonishment when he/she regains consciousness.

Acclimatisation

Acclimatisation is the process of adjusting to the reduced oxygen pressure in the atmosphere at high altitude. This process differs for everyone and there are no rules as to who will suffer the effects of high altitude. Being in excellent physical condition does not aid in acclimatisation, nor does it make you less prone to altitude sickness; indeed, young fit men are often the most susceptible. If you have suffered from altitude sickness in the past you are likely to suffer again, but there can be a first time for everyone, sometimes after several trouble-free trips to high places. For most people it takes a week or two to become completely acclimatised, but there are some who never get there. So never compare yourself with another person, especially if travelling in a group, but respect the differing time needed for each person to be ready to proceed into the mountains.

On flying from sea-level to La Paz or Cusco, everyone feels the effects of altitude to a certain degree. The symptoms are headaches, breathlessness, feelings of dizziness or lightheadedness, insomnia, and loss of appetite. You can help alleviate it by drinking lots of water (or – better – coca tea), avoiding alcohol and heavy and hard-to-digest food, and above all by resting. Spend at least three days at an altitude of no more than 3,500m, then start doing some easy day-hikes. Allow at least five days to get used to the altitude before starting your backpacking trip (reputable trekking companies build a period of acclimatisation into their itinerary). Acclimatisation is achieved when the heartbeat is normal at rest, you can eat and sleep well and have no headache. If you experience any of the symptoms of altitude sickness while backpacking, try to rest for a couple of days. Then, if you don't feel better, turn back. Remember, too, that even a short visit to the coast will lose you your hard-won acclimatisation.

High-altitude sickness

This may be divided into three categories: acute mountain sickness (AMS), cerebral oedema and pulmonary oedema. All three are brought on by a too-hasty ascent to altitudes exceeding about 3,000m. The potentially fatal pulmonary and cerebral oedema can be prevented by acclimatising properly before the ascent and by climbing slowly; aim to ascend no more than 300m daily when over 3000m. Go even slower if a member of the hiking party shows any signs of AMS.

AMS, known locally as *soroche*, is the most common of the three variations. For the biochemistry of the problem, see pages 162–3. The symptoms of AMS, which usually develop six to 12 hours after exposure to altitude, are severe headache, nausea, and sleeplessness. If the victim is only mildly active and drinks plenty of liquids (three litres a day, if possible) for a day or two, these symptoms should moderate. Diamox (see below) can be used to treat the headache and nausea. Cheyne-Stokes respiration during sleep affects many people at high altitude. Also known as periodic breathing, it is characterised by the sleeper taking shallower and shallower breaths until he stops altogether; then comes a gasping deep breath and the cycle begins again. It is harmless, but disturbing both to the sleeper and his tent-mate.

The drug Diamox (acetazolamide) is an effective prophylaxis for AMS. Two 250mg pills are taken each morning for three days prior to the ascent (ie: when still at sea-level or thereabouts) and continued for two more days at altitude. Diamox can also be used as treatment for AMS: take 750mg (three tablets) for small adults or 1,000mg (four tablets) for big people, then 500mg per day for four more days. Since Diamox is a diuretic, take the pills in the morning to avoid being up half the night to pee. Another side effect can be tingling of the hands and feet. Missing out one dose will solve this problem.

Cerebral oedema is a more dangerous type of altitude sickness. Fluid accumulates in the brain, and can cause irritability, drowsiness, coma or death. The symptoms include intense headache or neckache, nausea, staggering gait, confusion, disorientation and hallucinations. Anyone showing signs of cerebral oedema should be taken down to a lower altitude – at least 500m lower – immediately. One of the symptoms may be denial – sometimes aggressive – of the problem, so a firm hand is often needed to persuade the person to turn back.

Pulmonary oedema is more common than cerebral oedema but equally dangerous. Fluid collects in the lungs, literally drowning the person if his ill-health is not recognised. He must be taken to a lower altitude immediately. The symptoms are shortness of breath when at rest, coughing, frothy bloodstained (sometimes) sputum, and a crackling sound in the chest. Each year climbers die in the Andes from pulmonary oedema because they have not taken the time to acclimatise and do not recognise the symptoms in time.

Many symptoms of AMS resemble those of other diseases but, if you are at an altitude of more than 3,000m and someone is clearly deteriorating, *descend*. If the symptoms are due to AMS their condition will improve and you will have saved a life. Do not wait overnight to see if they are better in the morning. Evacuating an uncooperative victim in the dark is no fun.

Medical kit
* water purifiers
* antiseptic (dilute iodine or potassium permanginate crystals)
* Vaseline (for cracked heels or lips)
* moleskin and adhesive-backed foam rubber (for blisters and sore feet)
* Steristrips or butterfly closures, panty-liners
* crêpe/ace bandage
* fabric Elastoplast/Bandaids (best is a dressing strip)
* ciprofloxacin and rehydration sachets; Lomotil or other diarrhoea blocker
* aspirins or paracetamol/tylenol
* amoxycillin or other broad-spectrum antibiotic. Take tetracycline or erythromycin if allergic to penicillin.
* thermometer (with a low-reading range). Remember that mercury may not be carried on planes
* cough and throat pills
* antifungal cream and powder

Medicinal plants
You'll come across a lot of traditional medicinal plants in South America, especially in the markets. They are the sole source of medicine for many people, so try to learn something about them. If you decide to use them as an alternative to Western medicine be warned that most vendors in the markets have no idea of how to use these plants and will sell you anything and everything. Get medical advice at one of the many local clinics where medicinal plants are used and bear in mind that the cure will tend to be slower than with Western medicine.

Also realise that just because it is natural does not mean that it is harmless – several killer poisons and drugs come from 'natural, herbal' sources. Herbal medicines have side effects and disadvantages too, and these can be less predictable since 'dosages' are more difficult to measure.

Western medicine and local people
One of the by-products of well-equipped trekkers permeating every mountain stronghold is that local people will beg medicines above any other

consumable. Even the most culturally sensitive trekker or backpacker feels that to deny them this easing of the harshness of their lives would be cruel, yet there are good reasons to say no. Apart from the risks to them of inappropriate dosage, it adds to the belief that Western medicine is good and traditional remedies are bad despite the advantages of the latter in availability and cost. In short, do not dabble in other people's health beyond perhaps offering a couple of paracetamol!

Travel clinics and health information

A full list of current travel clinic websites worldwide is available on www.istm.org/. For other journey preparation information, consult ftp://ftp.shoreland.com/pub/shorecg.rtf or www.tripprep.com

UK

Berkeley Travel Clinic 32 Berkeley St, London WIX 5FA; tel: 020 7629 6233.
The Blood Care Foundation PO Box 7, Sevenoaks, Kent TN13 2SZ; tel: 01732 742427; fax: 01732 451199; web: www.bloodcare.org.uk; or arrange membership through MASTA (see below) for screened blood in case of an accident.
British Airways Travel Clinic and Immunisation Service There are now only three BA clinics, all in London: 156 Regent St, W1B 5LB (no appointments); 101 Cheapside, EC1V6DT (tel: 020 7606 2977); 115 Buckingham Palace Rd, SW1W 9SJ (Victoria Station; tel: 020 7233 6661); see also www.britishairways.com/travelclinics. Also sell a variety of health-related goods.
Fleet Street Travel Clinic 29 Fleet Street, London EC4Y 1AA; tel: 020 7353 5678
Hospital for Tropical Diseases Travel Clinic Capper St (off Tottenham Ct Rd), London WC1; tel: 020 7388 9600; web: www.thhtd.org. Offers consultations and advice, and is able to provide all necessary drugs and vaccines for travellers. Runs a healthline (tel: 09061 337733) for country-specific information and health hazards. Also stocks nets, water-purification equipment and personal-protection meaures.
MASTA (Medical Advisory Service for Travellers Abroad) Keppel St, London WC1 7HT; tel: 09068 224100. This is a premium-line number, charged at 50p per minute.
NHS travel website, www.fitfortravel.scot.nhs.uk, provides country-by-country advice on immunisation and malaria, plus details of recent developments, and a list of relevant health organisations.
Nomad Travel Pharmacy and Vaccination Centre 3–4 Wellington Terrace, Turnpike Lane, London N8 0PX; tel: 020 8889 7014; travel health information (60p per minute): 09068 633141; email: sales@nomadtravel.co.uk; website: www.nomadtravel.co.uk. As well as dispensing health advice, Nomad stocks mosquito nets and other anti-bug devices, and an excellent range of adventure travel gear.
Royal Free Travel Health Centre Pond Street, London NW3 2QG; tel: 0207 830 2885; web: www.travel-health.co.uk. Immunisations, kits, aviation psychology and returning travellers' clinic.
Thames Medical 157 Waterloo Rd, London SE1 8US; tel: 020 7902 9000. Competitively priced, one-stop travel health service. All profits go to their affiliated company InterHealth, which provides health care for overseas workers on Christian projects.

Trailfinders Immunisation Centre 194 Kensington High St, London W8 7RG; tel: 020 7938 3999. Also at 254–284 Sauchiehall St, Glasgow G2 3EH; tel: 0141 353 0066.

Irish Republic

Tropical Medical Bureau Grafton Street Medical Centre, Grafton Buildings, 34 Grafton St, Dublin 2; tel: 1 671 9200. Has a useful website specific to tropical destinations at www.tmb.ie.

USA

Centers for Disease Control 1600 Clifton Rd, Atlanta, GA 30333; tel: 877 FYI TRIP/800 311 3435; web: www.cdc.gov/travel. The central source of travel information in the USA. Each summer they publish the invaluable *Health Information for International Travel*, available from the Division of Quarantine at the above address.
Connaught Laboratories PO Box 187, Swiftwater, PA 18370; tel: 800 822 2463. They will send a free list of specialist tropical-medicine physicians in your state.
IAMAT (International Association for Medical Assistance to Travelers) 736 Center St, Lewiston, NY 14092; tel: 716 754 4883. A non-profit organisation which provides lists of English-speaking doctors abroad.

Canada

IAMAT (International Association for Medical Assistance to Travellers) Suite 1, 1287 St Clair Av W, Toronto, Ontario M6E 1B8; tel: 416 652 0137; web: www.sentex.net/~iamat
TMVC (Travel Doctors Group) Sulphur Springs Rd, Ancaster, Ontario; tel: 905 648 1112; web: www.tmvc.com.au

Australia, New Zealand, Thailand

TMVC Tel: 1300 65 88 44; web: www.tmvc.com.au. 20 clinics in Australia, New Zealand and Thailand, including:
Auckland Canterbury Arcade, 170 Queen Street, Auckland City; tel: 373 3531
Brisbane Dr Deborah Mills, Qantas Domestic Building, 6th floor, 247 Adelaide St, Brisbane, QLD 4000; tel: 7 3221 9066; fax: 7 3321 7076
Melbourne Dr Sonny Lau, 393 Little Bourke St, 2nd floor, Melbourne, VIC 3000; tel: 3 9602 5788; fax: 3 9670 8394.
Sydney Dr Mandy Hu, Dymocks Building, 7th Floor, 428 George St, Sydney, NSW2000; tel: 2 221 7133; fax: 2 221 8401.

South Africa

SAA-Netcare Travel Clinics PO Box 786692, Sandton 2146; fax: 011 883 6152; web: www.travelclinic.co.za or www.malaria.co.za. Clinics throughout South Africa.
TMVC (Travel Doctor Group) 113 DF Malan Drive, Roosevelt Park, Johannesburg; tel: 011 888 7488; web: www.tmvc.com.au. Consult the website for details of clinics in South Africa.

Switzerland

IAMAT (International Association for Medical Assistance to Travellers) 57 Voirets, 1212 Grand Lancy, Geneva; web: www.sentex.net/~iamat

Further reading on travel health

Bezruchka, Stephen. *Altitude Illness – Prevention and Treatment.* The Mountaineers, Seattle. 1994.

Wilson-Howarth, Jane. *Bugs, Bites & Bowels:Travel Health.* Cadogan Guides, London and Globe Pequot, Ct; 3rd edition. August 2002. Contains a chapter on altitude and keeping healthy in the mountains.

Wilson-Howarth, Jane and Matthew Ellis. *Your Child's Health Abroad: A Manual for Travelling Parents.* Bradt Publications and Globe Pequot, Ct. 1998

SAFETY

Although the danger from the Shining Path (Sendero Luminoso) terrorists has abated, Peru is still a dangerous country for the unwary and particular attention should be paid to this section. Sadly, Bolivia is now as risky as Peru. Much of the advice below comes from the South American Explorers, who are excellently placed to know the security situation.

Peruvian police

In Peru there are three types of policemen:

- Police
- The private police (PIP), mostly plain clothes, who work with crime and terrorism
- Tourist police

Of the three, the traffic police are the most corrupt, but this rarely involves tourists. They do try to be discreet in their corrupt dealings with the locals! The private police are usually straight and can be very tough. They are mainly concerned that tourists are travelling legally in the country (ie: that visa requirements are adhered to) and that they do not deal in drugs. The tourist police are most helpful and we recommend you to contact them when you need help.

Unfortunately there are also some 'fake' police around; they will flash a reasonably plausible ID card and sometimes even wear a police uniform. If stopped by the police, always ask to see their ID ('*Su identificación, por favor*'). You have the right to do this so take your time. If they are not genuine police their nerve is likely to fail at this point. Providing you are not breaking the law, there is no reason to be intimidated by the police. The only hassle they can give you is checking your passport and visa. Always carry your passport (in a money belt or other equally secure place); if you get checked without it, the police have the right to throw you in jail for the night or even a few days.

Always be polite and friendly to the police, but put yourself on the same level and avoid giving them the feeling that they have any power over you. A firm handshake helps establish you on an equal footing.

Drugs

Dealing with drugs is a serious crime in both Peru and Bolivia and carries a heavy jail sentence. No one in their right mind wants to spend time in a South

American jail and I am assuming my readers are sane so will say no more about voluntary drug use. There are, however, cases where drugs have been planted on tourists, especially backpackers who fit the image of 'drug addicts'. Be suspicious of over-friendly locals and do not give the police an opportunity to plant drugs. If you feel as though you are being set up, just walk away.

Coca leaves

Someone once described coca leaves as having the same relation to cocaine as ivory has to elephants. The drug is derived from the leaves of the coca plant, which is grown in both Peru and Bolivia, but that is all. Chewing coca leaves is perfectly legal and has been part of the Indian culture for thousands of years (see page 26). Steady and prolonged chewing has a narcotic effect but few gringos have the perseverence to achieve this. Most use it to make a pleasant herb tea which seems to help alleviate altitude sickness.

It is illegal to take coca leaves out of the country, but coca tea bags are usually not questioned by your customs authorities. If you are hiking in coca-growing regions be aware that whites are mistrusted because of the US coca eradication programme. If you are not American it might be sensible to advertise this fact by sewing your country's flag to your backpack.

Theft

Theft is a major problem for travellers in Peru and Bolivia. Most theft is by deception and tricks, with the thieves working in groups. One thief gets your attention, the second grabs your belongings and throws them to a third, who escapes with them. Thieves are quick and clever, and most of the time you don't even realise what is happening. If you know the most popular tricks you can stay ahead of the game. The most dangerous areas for being robbed are crowded places such as markets, and bus and train stations. Basically theft falls into the three categories listed below.

Unguarded possessions

In risky situations (and that's any place where there are people around) your belongings should be either attached to your person or under lock and key. In a restaurant, never hang a bag over the back of your chair, or put it on the floor without wrapping a strap around a chair leg. One minute's inattention and it's gone. Other places to be particularly careful are in the waiting areas of bus and train stations, or in the trains and buses themselves. A chain with a combination lock is an extra safeguard.

At airports make sure you lock your luggage before putting it on the plane, and strap sticky tape around the bags. Protect backpacks by putting them in a strong canvas bag or flour sack. Airport thieves are looking for easily opened luggage that appears valuable. Never ask a stranger to watch your luggage for you.

Backpack pockets are a great temptation to young or casual thieves who have a brief encounter with your unattended luggage on public transport. It is best to have detachable pockets that you can keep inside your pack when travelling.

Don't leave stuff around, even if of little value. That includes your clothes, which should not be left on the hotel washing line overnight.

Thefts from the person

Handbag snatching, slashing and pickpocketing are very common, especially in Peru. Don't carry a handbag or a daypack in cities, unless you carry it in front of your body. If, like me, you can't bear to be without a handbag, make sure it is made from tough, hard-to-cut material. Never wear jewellery and don't keep a wallet in your pocket. Watches are often snatched from the wrist; wear a cheap one. When wandering around cities and towns, try to carry as little as possible with you. Most people tend to carry more than they really need. When you arrive in a new place leave your camera in the hotel and take it out the next day when you have got your bearings. Keep your money and passport in a money belt, neck or leg pouch. Do not put all your money in one place.

Never carry more than you can physically handle, especially if travelling alone, and always take taxis if you have too much to carry.

A scary new type of mugging is 'choke and rob'. Even small groups of tourists have been attacked by gangs who choke their victims until they pass out, then rob them. Particularly dangerous are market areas and quiet streets at night.

If you think you are being followed, turn around, stop and walk behind the person. If someone tries to rob you and you catch them at it, shout 'ladrón!' (thief!); passers-by are likely to come to your rescue.

The best protection is not to bring belongings that are dear to you, or that are expensive. Try to shed your consumer-oriented culture. The expensive camera takes better pictures, but what's more important, the pictures or the experience?

Theft by deception

It is particularly upsetting to be robbed by someone you thought was befriending you – and the hardest to avoid because visitors do not want to cause offence by being suspicious or hostile.

One of the most popular thefts by deception is the 'mustard on your clothes' trick. When you are walking in the street a well-dressed couple will approach you and point out that you have something nasty on your clothing or shoes. One of them helpfully produces a handkerchief to assist you in wiping it off. Meanwhile his/her accomplice is skilfully going through your pockets or handbag. These thieves are extraordinarily accomplished at their chosen trade, and generally you will not realise your wallet is missing until you get back to the hotel. Once you know about this practice you will recognise the set-up and briskly walk away.

There have been instances of foreigners accepting sweets or a drink from a friendly local and waking up some hours later minus all their possessions. Rare though this type of robbery is, you should be cautious about accepting food from strangers. You can avoid offence by offering some of your goodies instead.

Armed or violent robbery

Armed robbery is not as common as ordinary theft, but it does happen. If a robber threatens you with a knife, gun or other weapon there is little you can do but hand him what he wants, just as in any other place in the world – although the small stature of most Peruvians and Bolivians has given some tourists the courage to fight back. Avoid the same sort of places in South America as you would at home: impoverished slums and poorly lit streets after dark. Sometimes armed robbery takes place on buses or cars passing through remote mountain regions.

Tourist spots are more dangerous than areas that see few foreigners – thieves need a regular supply of victims. Generally speaking, your money and valuables are safer deep in your luggage in a locked hotel room than on your person.

Ways to protect your valuables

Take a taxi if you have a lot of luggage, at night, or in risky parts of the city. Ask your hotel to phone for a registered taxi.

- Use a money belt, neck or leg pouch or inside pocket for cash and passports. Or, better, all three so your valuables are not all in one place.
- Carry your passport with you in case you are asked to show your visa. However, a photocopy of the relevant pages of your passport will usually suffice when wandering about towns or when hiking. This photocopy will also help you replace your passport quickly should it be lost or stolen. Remember that it is illegal to be out without any form of identification.
- The safest place for valuables is in a hotel. Keep them in the hotel safe and get a receipt, or in cheaper hotels put them deep in your luggage and lock it before going out.
- Before you leave home, take photocopies of your passport information page, plane ticket, credit cards and any other vital information. Keep copies in a variety of places in your luggage, and at home with a friend. If you have credit card insurance, be sure to bring the help-line number with you.
- At most hotels you can store your unneeded luggage while you hike. Make sure it is locked, and that you are given a receipt.
- Emergency money in the form of a $100 bill is completely safe hidden under the insole of your boot. Or think of your own secret hiding place.

Remember, the point of all the above is not to make you paranoid, but to allow you to relax and enjoy the company of some of the millions of Peruvians and Bolivians who wouldn't dream of robbing you.

Safety on the trail

Mostly you will be safe on the trail, but unfortunately the number of 'rich' gringos trekking through the mountain villages has given the *campesinos* (peasant farmers) a new consumer awareness. Only a very few of the popular trails suffer from this problem. As a general rule it is safest to camp out of sight, or to stay with a family (or camp in their yard) thus gaining their protection. Keep valuables – and most of your money – at the bottom of your pack when hiking: even armed robbers are not going to rummage through your pack looking for them.

More dangerous than the people are their dogs. Most rural villages keep several underfed dogs which bark hysterically when they see a stranger, especially a strange-shaped one (with a backpack). Mostly it is just bravado, but, in a continent where rabies is common, don't take the risk of being bitten. If you are planning on doing a great deal of hiking, or are cycling, it would be worth investigating one of the anti-dog sprays on the market (your postman/mailman could probably advise you!). 'Daze', an ultrasound gadget, is said to frighten dogs away. Otherwise the most effective deterrent is a handful of stones. Most dogs will turn tail and flee at the very sight of you stooping to pick up a stone (if there are no real ones an imaginary one works) and actually throwing the missile – accurately – is highly effective. You can also carry a stick but dogs tend to jump at a stick, making the encounter more frightening.

Read up the section on rabies *before* you start hiking and carry the appropriate first-aid items (soap, scrubbing brush) where you can easily get to them. And don't worry: although the bite of these animals is certainly worse than their bark, an attack is relatively rare.

Take care to avoid accidents. Stop walking when you are very tired, don't venture off the trail without a compass and survival equipment, avoid hypothermia and AMS, and have access to basic first-aid supplies at all times.

Insurance

Be sure to get both medical and luggage insurance. Medical is most important and you should get cover for two million pounds. Check that you are covered for mountain sports (ie: backpacking), anything else you plan to do and declare any medical conditions before travel.

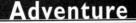

Part Two

Peru

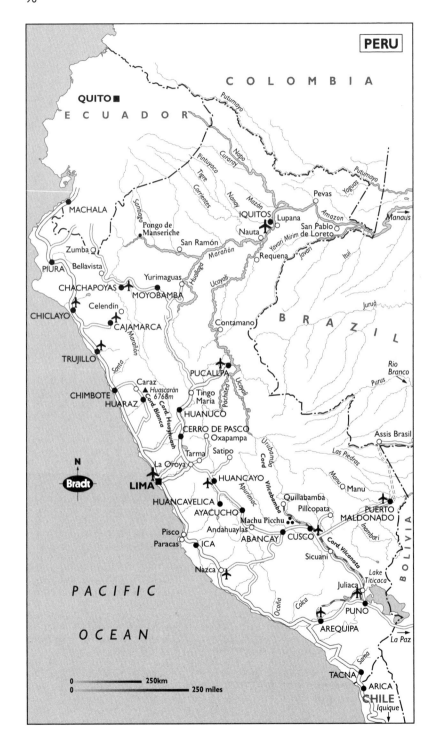

General Information

Peru was named by Francisco Pizarro who first landed in South America on a beach in southern Colombia. Nearby flowed the Birú creek, and this became the name of his newly discovered country. Or so legend has it. Peru is a country of contrasts, a place of extremes: desert and jungle, snowpeaks and sand-dunes, great wealth and grinding poverty.

Tourism here is based on special interests and adventure travel. This is not the country for someone who simply wants to lie on a beach: despite the long coastline there are few beaches one would want to spend any time on and no seaside resorts as such. What Peru does have is mountain scenery and trekking to rival the Himalayas, rainforest reserves full of animals and birds, the most impressive pre-Inca and Inca ruins and arguably the best museums in South America, and the Andean people, descendants of the Incas, with their dignity, colour and ancient customs.

Peru suffers all the problems of infrastructure and reliability that you would expect in a country emerging from economic catastrophe and still recovering from more than a decade of terrorism. Visitors who expect everything to run like clockwork will not be happy here. What surprises those who love Peru is how much *does* run smoothly.

THE COUNTRY
Physical and social geography
A cross-section of the country, from west to east, would reveal the following picture.

First there is the Pacific Ocean, teeming with fish and their predators, and bringing the cold Humboldt Current close to shore. The strong sun and the influence of the cold water create a mist, *garúa*, which blankets the entire 2,500km coastal strip for part of the year. This strip is desert, some of the world's driest land, which depends on meltwater from Andean glaciers for irrigation, drinking water and life itself. The width of this desert strip varies from 40 to 200km, across which over 50 rivers carry water to the Pacific ocean. Cotton, fruit and sugar crops are grown in irrigated valleys, and most of the nation's industrial sector is located along the coast, including Lima, the capital.

Crops don't really begin to grow without irrigation until a height of about 2,000m is reached on the western slope of the Andes. Corn, potatoes and sun-loving vegetables flourish up to about 4,000m, then cattle and general livestock take over, with mining and some grazing the only activities in the very high altitudes around 5,000m. There are 20 distinct mountain ranges in Peru, extending from central-northern Peru to its southern borders. They include two major glacial systems, the Cordillera Blanca north of Lima and the Cordillera Vilcanota in the southeast.

Crossing the continental divide, with peaks ranging from 2,500m to 6,768m, the descent begins to the Amazon basin. The change is noticeable immediately. Warm, moist air rising up from the jungle makes these slopes greener and wetter. At a height of about 3,000m dense rainforests begin, and continue uninterrupted to the Atlantic Ocean.

The population of Peru is about 23 million, nine million of whom are in Lima. Of the remainder, 50% live in the Andes at an average altitude of 3,000m. The rainforest, covering 60% of Peru, contains only about 10% of the population.

Climate

With three distinct geographical regions you have three distinct climates.

The coastal desert (*la costa*) The Austral winter runs from April until November when the coastal region is mostly cloudy, with daytime temperatures around 10–18°C, and a cold wind sweeps over the desert. It rarely rains but *garúa* (mist) hangs over the region from time to time. Lima suffers this fine drizzle throughout the winter, which, since it coincides with the sunny – and thus the tourist – season in the highlands, adds to the negative view of the capital.

Summer is from December to April. It's very hot with temperatures between 20° and 36°C – sometimes higher – and a warm breeze.

The mountain region (*la sierra*) In the Andean highlands there is a dry season and a rainy season. In contrast to the coast, it is dry and sunny from April to the end of September beginning of October. At 3,500m or over it is very cold (around or below freezing) at night and in the early morning and evening. It is cool on cloudy days – even the dry season is no guarantee of sunshine. Daytime temperatures range from 10° to 18°C.

The rainy season runs from October/November to late April/early May (when it is sunny on the coast). The mornings are mostly clear, but it starts raining in the afternoons and sometimes continues during the nights. It doesn't get as cold as in the winter dry season: daytime temperatures vary between 10° and 13°C and at night they drop to around 5–8°C (at 3,500m).

The jungle (*la selva*) The weather pattern is the same as the highlands. In the dry season it gets very hot in the rainforest (23–32°C during the day), and is not much cooler at night. There is an exception, however. During June, July and August a cold front, *el friaje*, may pass through from the south, pushing temperatures down to 8–10°C, which can come as a nasty shock to the unprepared traveller. It only lasts for a few days, however.

As you would expect, the rainy season in the rainforest is very wet indeed. The rivers rise – some are not navigable during this season – and road connections with the *sierra* can be closed by mud slides. Temperatures only drop about 5°C, but it feels chilly in the constant rain. During the fine spells it is very humid with lots of mosquitoes.

El Niño

El Niño is a warm ocean current which periodically flows south through the Pacific Ocean. Ocean temperatures heat up and storms ravage Peru's coast. Since it tends to arrive at Christmas, fishermen call it the Christ-child, although its effects are anything but beneficial. The warm water displaces the cold, nutrient-rich water of the Humboldt Current, driving the anchovy and other fish that fishermen and seabirds depend on to deeper, cooler waters, and the numerous species further up the food chain starve to death. The whole balance of nature is upset, with land animal species profiting from the burst of lush vegetation caused by the excessive rains, while the ocean shores are littered with the corpses of marine creatures. In 1998, during the worst *El Niño* for many years, a correspondent in *The Times*, David Lambert, pointed out that 'in the worst events so many fishes and seabirds die that their corpses produce enough gas to blacken ships' paintwork, a phenomenon wryly called, after Lima's port, the Callao Painter'.

HISTORY
Pre-conquest

The earliest cultures of any significance emerged around 900BC: Chavín de Huántar in the area now known as the Cordillera Blanca, and Sechín Alto, inland from Casma on the north coast. During the 700 years of their prominence they achieved some remarkable works of architecture, ceramics, textiles and metalwork, including gold, silver and copper. Around 500BC their powers declined and the Nazca culture emerged in southern Peru, lasting until about AD500. The textiles excavated from the tombs of Paracas, preserved by the dry desert, are arguably the finest ever found, and the Nazca ceramics are their equals in intricate and imaginative design. The famous Nazca Lines – vast 'line drawings' cut into the desert and easily visible only from the air – add weight to the awesome achievements of this culture, though little is known of the Nazca beliefs and way of life.

The Moche, on the other hand, left us a perfect record of their day-to-day concerns in the form of their wonderfully realistic pottery vessels depicting scenes from everyday life (including sexual activities). Many Moche achievements were echoed some 500 years later by the Incas: roads and other engineering feats, and irrigation canals. Their desert kingdom stretched from Piura to Casma, with Chan-Chán, later a Chumú city, their capital.

Around AD600 the power shifted from the north coast to the Andes and the Huari-Tiwanaku cultures. The Huari dominated the central highlands and the Tiwanaku had their religious centre around Lake Titicaca, but there was apparently friendly communication between the two. What we now think of as Inca achievements were further developed by these cultures with road-building, land terracing and irrigation being perfected, along with efficient administration and a labour tax.

When these civilisations collapsed, the Incas stepped in and completed what is widely considered the model of successful socialist government. The Inca dominance was short compared with its predecessors: about 300 years, from around the year 1200 to the Spanish conquest in 1533. In this period they developed from a small tribe in Cusco to the largest empire ever known in the Americas, stretching from the present-day Ecuador–Colombia border to the Río Maule in central Chile, and east to the Amazon. The story of its decline through civil war and its destruction by the Spanish conqueror Pizarro is told in the Cajamarca and Cusco chapters.

The impression is often given that Pizarro's conquest was the end of the Incas, but in fact they struggled to regain power through uprisings, with the last reigning Inca, Tupac Amaru, killed in 1572, and the last Inca noble, Tupac Amaru II, meeting his death in 1780.

Post-conquest

The Spanish also had to defeat groups that had largely resisted Inca domination. These included the Chimú in the north, whose capital, Chan-Chán, had fallen to the Incas a century earlier, and the Chachapoyas culture, with their main fortress at Kuelap (see *Chapter 6*).

A sea-going nation like Spain needed a port as its New World capital and Francisco Pizarro founded Lima in 1535. For the next 200 years the viceroys ruled throughout the Andean countries, retaining much of the old Inca system with Indian chiefs controlling large groups of natives. Quarrels among the *conquistadores* led to Pizarro's assassination in 1541, and constant uprisings by the Incas and later the Peru-born Spaniards made government of this valuable acquisition an unrewarding task. Finally, in 1821, José de San Martín proclaimed Peru's independence, even though the country was still in the hands of the viceroys.

The great liberator Simon Bolívar came to San Martín's assistance three years later, and the decisive battle of Ayacucho in 1824 led to full independence in 1826. Independent Peru was as turbulent as in the colonial era. In the 1830s Peru and Bolivia briefly united in a confederation, and in 1883 the two countries went to war with Chile; as a result Bolivia lost its sea coast and Peru lost much of its southern territory. Peru was under military rule from 1968 until 1980, but, most unusually, the junta in power in the early part of that era was socialist and instigated the agrarian reforms and redistribution of wealth that the country so sorely needed on moral grounds. Economically the reforms were a disaster, however, and the subsequent military rulers were right-wing. Peru was one of the first South American countries to move away from military rule towards democracy, and in 1980 presidential and congressional elections were held and Fernando Belaunde Terry was elected president. His successor was Alán García, who was elected with enormous enthusiasm in 1985 and rejected with equal enthusiasm in 1990 having failed dismally to deal with the rising economic problems and increasing terrorism. Alberto Fujimori was elected as president, entering national politics for the first time, and enjoyed early successes in dealing with the plague of inflation inherited from Alán García. In April 1992, Fujimori interrupted democratic rule in his controversial *autogolpe* (or self-inflicted coup) in which Congress was shut down and the constitution suspended. From 1992, the government drifted in a more authoritarian direction with Fujimori firmly in command. Elections were still held on a regular basis and there remained considerable freedom of the press. However, with the election of a 'rubber stamp' Congress in 1992, an absolute majority of which came from the president's *Cambio 90* party, and the narrow approval of a more conservative constitution in October 1993, more power was ceded to President Fujimori and the strength of Peru's political parties was undermined in the process.

In 1995, on the back of notable success with the economy and the fight against terrorism, Fujimori was re-elected in a landslide victory. But by the middle of his second term, his government was losing prestige both at home and abroad as evidence emerged of human rights abuses, government control within the judiciary, widespread corruption and excessive media controls. Also, ever more speculation arose surrounding the enigmatic Vladimiro Montesinos (Fujimori's chief security adviser) and his alleged involvement in illicit activities, including the drugs and arms trades.

The Fujimori juggernaut finally juddered to a halt in 2000, with dramatic and irrefutable video evidence of major corruption at the highest levels. The videos showed Montesinos bribing congressmen, owners of TV channels and media stars. While Fujimori tendered his resignation and called for elections in early 2001, Montesinos disappeared.

Valentin Paniagua's interim government oversaw the clean-up of corrupt institutions, as well as the pursuit and capture of Montesinos, whose ill-gained fortune was by now believed to be worth hundreds of millions of dollars.

A sense of unreality continued to pervade Peru's public life into 2001; Alberto Fujimori's flight to Japan to escape corruption charges seemed to confirm long-held suspicions that he'd been born in Japan and was not Peruvian after all; Montesinos languished in a top security prison with Abimael Guzman for a neighbour. And ex-President Alán García, exiled since fleeing Peru in disgrace in 1990, returned to fight the 2000 elections. He was narrowly defeated in July 2001 by Alejandro Toledo, whose rise from rural poverty to become Peru's first ethnic-Indian president, is the stuff of legend.

Although at the end of 2001 doubt still remained regarding the extent of Alberto Fujimori's involvement in the corruption scandal (some claimed that it was Montesinos who ran the show), Toledo's government continued to demand his extradition. Meanwhile, Peru's senior anti-corruption judge called for a life sentence for Montesinos.

By December 2001, Alejandro Toledo's government was being accused of incompetence and failure to fulfil its promises to end corruption, reduce poverty, decentralise government and reduce unemployment. Alán García waited in the wings.

GETTING THERE
Tour operators
If you are short on time or have a special interest, joining a group on an organised tour or requesting a tailor-made itinerary is a sensible option and there are many UK- and US-based tour operators that specialise in Peru and will be able to help you before you travel (see listings on pages 36–8). There are also many local operators in Peru, whose details appear in the relevant sections, that will be able to help you with localised information and operations.

Entrances and exits
Red tape
Visas are at present not required by western Europeans or North Americans, but rules change so check if you need one. Australians and New Zealanders do need a visa. Addresses and phone numbers of Peruvian embassies can be found at the website of the Ministerio de Relaciones Exteriores del Peru (www.rree.gob.pe).

In the UK, contact the Peruvian Embassy: 52 Sloane Street, London SW1X 9SP; tel: 020 7235 1917 or 020 7235 2545; fax: 020 7235 4463; email: postmaster@peruembassy-uk.com; web: www.peruembassy-uk.com

All nationalities are given a tourist card by the immigration authorities on arrival: a stamp and a little white slip of paper. Don't lose it, as you need it when leaving the country, and you may be asked to show it to prove you are in the country legally (attach it to your passport, and make a photocopy for extra security). If you do lose it, get a new one at the Immigration Department in Lima. All nationalities are automatically given a 90-day stay, although 30- and 60-day permits are also given so if you are staying for three months make sure you tell the authorities on arrival. You can renew this permit for a further 90 days (although you may only be given 30 days at a time) at the Immigration Departments in Lima and Cusco for US$20 for each 30 days. After that you need to leave the country before you can get another visa (spending one day across the border is enough).

Legally, you need to show a ticket out of the country when you enter. This, however, is not strictly adhered to and the authorities seldom check. Usually an explanation that you are travelling overland by bus will satisfy them, but failing that buy the cheapest bus ticket from one border town across the frontier to the next town (for example, Tacna to Arica).

Make sure you get an exit stamp when leaving Peru or the next country may not grant you entry. At most borders the departure/entry procedure goes very smoothly, but at some remote border crossings you will need to get your exit stamp in the last town that has an immigration office (for example, leaving Peru via the Amazon river into Brazil, you need to get an exit stamp in Iquitos).

Don't let your visa expire.

At the airport
When you choose your airline ask about the baggage allowance both to and from Peru. Some airlines allow two bags of 30kg each going out but only

25kg coming back. Others allow two bags (unlimited weight) each way or only 25kg in total.

The international departure tax is US$25, payable in dollars. The national tax is about US$4, payable in *soles*. The contact details for Lima International Airport are: tel: (01) 5751712 or 5745529; web: www.lap.com.pe.

CURRENCY

The currency in Peru is called the *sol* but has changed a few times over the years. Due to the high rate of inflation, from time to time the authorities lop off a few zeros and change the name. It went from the (old) *sol* to the *inti* in 1986 and to the new *sol* again in 1991. In August 1990 inflation was stopped in its tracks when Fujimori came up with the solution: hyper-inflation for one day! This shocked Peruvians, but brought the annual rate of inflation down from 3,000% to 60%. It is now a very respectable 7% – at least officially.

In May 2002 US$1 = 3.42 *soles*.

It is relatively easy to change travellers' cheques (but can be time consuming) in the large towns, and Banco de Crédito is probably the best bank. When changing into *soles* there is usually no charge (though the rate you get may not be great); changing into cash dollars will incur about 2–3% commission.

If you are changing cash dollars it is best (and safest) to do it in a *Casa de Cambio*. Unfortunately, you'll only see them in the bigger towns; in the smaller towns you may have to trust the street money-changers. Sometimes it's hard (or impossible) to change dollars, so plan ahead when heading off into the more remote areas of the mountains and take enough *soles*. Try to get small denominations of *soles*: no-one ever has change.

Because of inflation, prices are often published in dollars in the upper-range hotels, restaurants, and shops. Most of these places will accept credit cards, or you can pay with local currency using the exchange rate of the day, which is sometimes slightly lower than that offered by the *Casas de Cambio* and banks.

Never accept damaged dollar bills; you won't be able to change them back again. And beware of forged dollars or *soles*.

Note Controlling inflation means that Peru is no longer a very cheap country. Prices in this book (given in dollars) may have risen by the time you travel. Be sure to take adequate funds!

TOURIST INFORMATION
iperú

This is Peru's tourist-information and tourist-protection organisation (formerly Prom Perú and INDECOPI). It has a network of tourist information offices, unfortunately restricted to Lima (airport), Arequipa (airport), Ayacucho (Plaza de Armas), Cusco (airport and Plaza de Armas), Iquitos (airport) and Trujillo (Jr. Pizarro 412). It has a 24-hour phone service (tel: (01) 574 8000; email: iperu@promperu.gob.pe; web: www.peru.org.pe or www.rcp.net.pe).

Check out www.editoraperu.com for the latest news and political information.

South American Explorers

Excellent for all information and advice plus a whole host of other services (see page 53 for details).

Clubhouse addresses: Lima: Calle Píura 135, Miraflores; tel: 01 445 3306; email: limaclub@saexplorers.org; postal address: Casilla 3714, Lima 100. Cusco: Choque Chaca 188 no 4; tel: 084 245484.

Instituto Nacional de Cultura (INC)

The public body responsible for protecting, restoring and publicising all things cultural in Peru. Its website has information on the sites under its protection, organised events, museums and more. INC also has an office in the airport. If you are taking replicas of pre-Hispanic artefacts out of the country you will need a certificate from them. Contact Edificio Museo de la Nacion, 6th floor, A Javier Prado este 2465, San Borja, Lima; tel: (01) 4769900; email: inc@inictel.gob.pe; web: www.inc.perucultural.org.pe.

COMMUNICATIONS
Telephones

Peru's telephone company is called Telefónica and operates all over the country, even in small villages. The old system of using tokens has been phased out and almost all public telephones on the streets accept either coins or phonecards. You can buy Telefónica phonecards from vendors on the street or from Telefónica offices. There are other telephone companies in Peru. For example, Lima has Telepoint and Telecom but remember that their phonecards can only be used in Lima. It's better to stick to Telefónica, whose offices are at Carabaya 933 and also Tarata 280, off Avda Larco in Miraflores.

The following codes will access the overseas operator:

Belgium	0800 50330	Italy	0800 50040
Canada	0800 50290	Spain	0800 50050
Germany	0800 50320	Switzerland	0800 50140
Holland	0800 50340	UK	0800 50360
US: AT&T	0800 50000	MCI	0800 50010
Sprint	0800 50020	Worldlink	No direct access

Other useful numbers

Directory assistance	103
Emergency	105
International operator (for reversed charge calls)	108
National operator	109

Be warned that reverse charge (collect) calls to Europe or North America can be very expensive in Peru.

Electronic mail

Internet services are available in all large towns and there are literally dozens of internet offices in Lima, Cusco and Huaraz. Expect to pay US$1–2 per hour depending how remote you are. See *Useful addresses* in the relevant chapters.

Mail

Receiving If you want mail to be sent to you, American Express is more reliable than the post office, but you need to be a customer, with either Amex travellers' cheques or a credit card. For the post office, letters should be addressed to *Lista de Correo* or *Poste Restante*, followed by the town. Ask your correspondents to write your last name in capitals or underline it to avoid letters being filed under your first name (but when you call for your mail check your first name anyway). Letters are held for up to two or three months. A small collection fee is charged. Never risk having any money or valuables sent by mail unless they are registered.

Letters sent from the USA or Europe to Peru can take anywhere between eight days and three weeks.

Tell your nearest and dearest not to send you a parcel. Getting it through customs is an unbelievable hassle (at least a day is needed) and extortionate taxes are charged.

For this reason you will be doing no great service to your Peruvian friends if you send them a parcel.

Note In a Peruvian address, *Casilla* or *Apartado Postal* are not street names, they are the equivalent of 'PO Box'.

Sending Surprisingly, most letters sent from Peru reach their destination. To USA or Europe can take between five days and three weeks. Letters sent within South America always take longer than six days, and the post office is sometimes on strike. Be warned, postage is expensive.

Parcels sent home do get there, but set aside a day to do it and a fair amount of money for the postage. The post office requirements are exacting. Some shops will mail purchases for you. If you are desperate to get a parcel home you could use a courier such as UPS or DHL.

Air freight

This is a good alternative to the post office or couriers, particularly if you have more than 30kg of stuff to send home. The price is then about US$3–4 per kilo, plus about US$100 on paperwork and a day at the airport. It's reliable and they will deliver to your home address (though it's cheaper to have it picked up at the airport). Receiving an air-freight parcel is a different matter – it involves as much hassle, time and bureaucracy as receiving a mailed parcel. If this is unavoidable, for instance for a large expedition, set aside several days and expect to hire a 'fixer' at the airport.

Newspapers and magazines

The Lima Times An English-language paper, published sporadically, usually monthly. Topics cover the whole country, not just Lima, and it usually has articles of interest to visitors.

The Lima Herald An English-language paper published every Friday.

Peru Guide A tourist guide, available from many hotels and tourist offices (mostly in Lima). Very useful for listings of what's happening, restaurants, etc.

Cusco Weekly (web: www.cuscoweekly.com) A free English-language newspaper which is available in hotels, restaurants etc in Cusco. Contains a round-up of world news as well as local listings.

Caretas (web: www.caretas.com.pe) The best Spanish-language current affairs magazine (weekly).

Rumbos (web: www.rumbosperu.com) An excellent monthly geographical magazine with good photos.

El Comercio (web: www.elcomercioperu.com.pe) and *La Republica* (web: www.larepublica.com.pe) are the main daily newspapers worth reading.

Business hours

Siesta is rigidly observed all over Peru throughout the year, except in Lima. You might as well join them since everything is closed from 13.00 until 16.00. Business hours run from 10.00 to 13.00 and 16.00 until 19.00. Shops are open from 09.30 to 13.00 and 16.00 until 20.00.

Lima has the normal business hours, 09.00 to 17.00, closed one hour at lunch time. Government-run offices are mostly only open in the mornings. Some tourist shops stay open at lunch time. Banks in Lima are usually open from 09.30 to 18.00 and on Saturday morning. In other towns they follow business hours.

Holidays

At least once a month a saint has his or her birthday, which is lots of fun for the saint who gets to leave the church for a parade around town. It's an excuse for a fiesta (see page 27) and a national holiday. If the day falls in the middle of the week, it is automatically moved to the next Monday to make a long weekend. Remember that banks, shops and offices are closed on these days.

The national school holidays run from the end of December until the end of February. As at home – but worse – everyone wants to get out of town for Christmas so prices of hotels and transport double and all tickets on all means of transport are sold out days before. Avoid travelling at this time. The same problem occurs around Independence Day (July 28), bang in the middle of the tourist season, when school holidays start one or two weeks before the holiday and continue until mid August.

MISCELLANEOUS
Laundry

Laundries in posh hotels are very expensive, charging as much as US$3 per item. Fortunately the public *lavanderías* charge by the kilo: about US$2. You bring your laundry to the laundromat in the morning and it is ready in the evening.

Handicrafts

Peru has a wide variety of beautiful handicrafts and the artisans are proud of their work and its origin in their *tierra* (hometown): handwoven alpaca products from Huancavelica and Puno, ceramics from Cajamarca, Ayacucho and Cusco, carved gourds, silverware and weavings from Huancayo, tapestries from Ayacucho, wooden articles from Piura, and so on.

Lima is the main outlet for the sale and export of handicrafts, and it's also the refuge for many artisans of the *sierra* escaping poverty. So the range and quality is likely to be better in Lima than in the place of origin. The prices are also better.

The biggest and best craft market in Lima is situated along Avenida La Marina (from the 9th until the 12th block) in the suburb of Pueblo Libre. Spend some time looking around and examining the quality, and feel free to bargain. For top-quality goods it is better to go to a shop which only buys the best. Of course you will pay more, but it will be money well spent. The best shops in Lima are where the money is: Miraflores and San Isidro.

If Lima has the selection and quality, the tourist centres such as Cusco, Puno and Huancayo have the fun. You are probably buying direct from the maker here and, since handicraft sellers are part of the town scenery, you will not have to set out purposely to shop. Shopping for hand-made items is one of the ways that travellers can make a positive contribution to the local economy and well-being of the people and their culture. It encourages the continuation of traditional crafts and the development of new ones, and it helps prevent the drift to the cities. For this reason try to rethink the cliché that it is somehow shameful for a traveller to pay a little too much for an article. If it's not too much for you it certainly won't be too much for the vendor!

PROTECTED AREAS OF PERU

Peru is one of the most biologically rich countries in the world, ranking second in bird diversity, third for mammals and fifth for plants. Of the world's 114 life zones, 83 are found within Peru's borders.

Conservation of this unique natural heritage was officially begun in 1961 when Peru's first national park was established: Cutervo, in the Department of Cajamarca. Just over 15% of the country is now officially protected – almost 20 million ha in 53 protected areas. Conservation is under the control of the Instituto Areas Naturales Protegidos de Flora y Fauna Silvestre, a section of the Instituto Nacional de Recursos Naturales (INRENA). Their address is Calle 17, no 355, Urb Palmar, San Isidro, Lima. Tel: 01 224 3298. Open Monday to Friday, 08.30–12.00, 13.00–17.00. Contact them through their website for further details: www.inrena.gob.pe.

There are seven categories of protected area, the most significant of which are the following:

Parques nacionales (national parks)

Areas with complete protection and preservation of fauna, flora and nature. Special entry permits are required for visitors but the local people have the right to use resources if traditionally part of their culture. There are nine national parks in Peru, covering an area of 4,812,509ha.

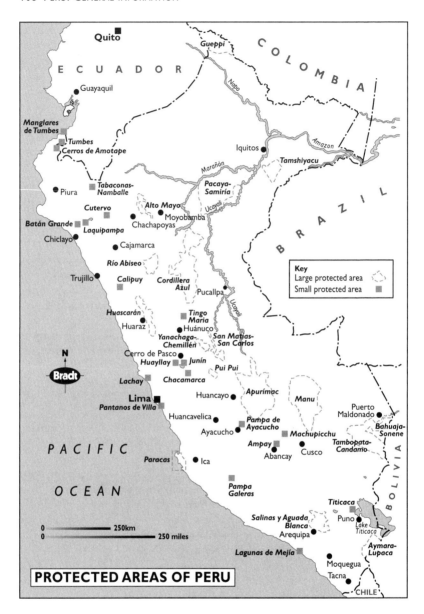

PROTECTED AREAS OF PERU

Name	Department	Date established
Bahuaja-Sonene (1,091,416ha)	Madre de Dios and Puno	2000
Cerros de Amotape (91,300ha)	Tumbes	1975
Cordillera Azul (1,353,190ha)	San Martín, Loreto, Ucayali, Huánuco	2001
Cutervo (2,500ha)	Cajamarca	1961
Huascarán (340,000ha)	Ancash	1975

Name	Department	Date established
Manu (1,532,806ha)	Madre de Dios	1973
Río Abiseo (274,520ha)	San Martín	1983
Tingo María (18,000ha)	Huánuco	1965
Yanachaga-Chemillén (122,000ha)	Pasco	1986

Reservas nacionales (national reserves)

Areas set aside for wildlife protection, but government-controlled culling is allowed, and the local people have the right to use the resources.

Name	Department	Date established
Calipuy (64,000ha)	La Libertad	1981
Junín (53,000ha)	Junín and Cerro de Pasco	1974
Lachay de Lomas (5,070ha)	Lima	1977
Pacayá Samiria (2,080,000ha)	Loreto	1982
Pampas Galeras (6,500ha)	Ayacucho	1967
Paracas (335,000ha)	Ica	1975
Salinas y Aguada Blanca (366,936ha)	Moquegua	1979
Tambopata-Candamo (1,500,000ha)	Madre de Dios	1990
Titicaca (36,180ha)	Puno	1978

Santuarios nacionales (national sanctuaries)

Here there is complete protection of fauna, flora and nature. Special entry permits are required and no-one is allowed to use resources.

Name	Department	Date established
Ampay (3,635ha)	Apurimac	1987
Calipuy (4,500ha)	La Libertad	1981
Huayllay (6,815ha)	Cerro de Pasco	1974
Lagunas de Mejía (69,060ha)	Arequipa	1984
Manglares de Tumbes (2,972ha)	Tumbes	1988
Tabaconas-Namballe (29,500ha)	Cajamarca	1988

Santuarios históricos (historical sanctuaries)

Areas of historical or archaeological importance, receiving complete protection, including fauna and flora. No use of resources is permitted.

Name	Department	Date established
Bosque de Pomac (5887ha)	Lambayeque	2001
Chacamarca (2,500ha)	Junín	1974
Machu Picchu (32,592ha)	Cusco	1981
Pampa de Ayacucho (300ha)	Ayacucho	1980

These are the best-known protected areas but this list is not complete. Also important are the *Bosques nacionales* (national forests) and *Zonas reservadas* (reserve zones). There are many national forests, but unfortunately they receive very little protection. Reserve zones are protected areas awaiting further scientific study, after which they will be categorised.

Conservation: entering the 21st century

John Forrest

Ten years ago, in February 1992, President Fujimori was invited to address an audience at Kew Gardens in their third annual environmental lecture. He began by highlighting poverty levels within Peru and argued that the Government could only prioritise environmental issues once the basic standard of living of the vast majority of people had been improved. He went on to propose the stimulation of international co-operation through environmental initiatives.

Peru did experience some relatively rapid economic growth in the mid 1990s but the economic performance of the country has since been variable and the ever-less predictable threat from *El Niño* can quickly wipe out any benefits to be gained from years of economic growth. Widespread poverty remains and will do so for the foreseeable future.

Consequently, the danger of severe environmental degradation on a large scale in the name of economic growth remains. Many peripheral regions experiencing some limited economic regeneration are those that are also most environmentally valuable and fragile and, consequently, at greatest risk. Over-fishing around the Paracas peninsula, incursions by loggers into Manu National Park, pollution affecting the lagoons of Mejia and mining in the high Andes are just some ongoing examples.

In a rare example of environmental concerns winning the day, permission to prospect for oil within the Pacaya-Samiria National Reserve, near Iquitos, was withdrawn after local and international protests in 1992. A few years later a similar campaign in the Tambopata region discouraged oil and gas explorations and led to the expansion of the recently declared Bahauja–Sonene National Park.

However, the new century brings many new potential environmental concerns, including the manner in which the vast gas reserves at Camisea, north of Cusco, will be exploited, how logging in northern Madre de Dios in to the territories of uncontacted native peoples might be controlled and, in the same area, what impact the proposed Transoceanic highway through to Brazil will have.

The concept of international co-operation through environmental projects was partially realised along Peru's border with Ecuador in 1995. As part of the package to resolve the 40-year-old border dispute both countries established new National Parks in the Cordillera del Condor overlapping the border zone. And, in southeast Peru, the Bahauja-Sonene National Park could, potentially, be linked through a joint management plan to the adjoining and equally isolated Madidi National Park in Bolivia.

All protected areas in Peru are severely underfunded and rely heavily on international aid to enable them to carry out at least part of their mandates. Even so, it took many years for Manu National Park, arguably the best-known protected area in Peru, to finalise a management plan despite receiving significant international funding. A national management plan for all protected areas exists but is not necessarily followed. In part this is because the Institute for Natural

Resources (INRENA), which includes environmental protection amongst its responsibilities, remains a department within the Ministry of Agriculture.

There is still much to be done to integrate local peoples in to the planning and administration of protected areas and to demonstrate that protected areas can bring benefits to local communities. Overall, attitudes towards the environment are changing as more Peruvians are able to travel and throughout the country more concrete conservation actions are being carried out both by individuals and some excellent local grassroots organisations.

Ecotourism
Ecotourism by responsible visitors who respect the rules and pay the required fee will help conserve threatened habitats in Peru, so do inform yourselves about the protected areas and make a point of visiting them. If you wish to help further, any of the organisations below would be pleased to hear from you

Conservation organisations
Fundación Pro Naturaleza Formerly known as the Fundación Peruana para la Conservación de la Naturaleza (FPCN), this organisation works closely with many foreign agencies such as the Nature Conservancy of the USA, IUCN, WWF and CI to protect viable, representative examples of each natural community or ecosystem in Peru and the biological diversity it contains. This is being achieved through the establishment and management of protected areas, by promoting the sustainable use of natural resources and by building environmental awareness. For more information contact Oscar Franco, Pro Naturaleza, Alberto del Campo 417, Lima 17; tel: 01 264 2759/2736; email: ofranco@pronaturaleza.com.pe; web: www.pronaturaleza.com.pe.

Asociación Peruana para la Conservación de la Naturaleza (APECO) This organisation is actively involved in environmental education and protection in many regions of Peru. Their main conservation efforts are concentrated on the national park of Río Abiseo and cloudforest in northeast Peru. They are also active in the buffer zone of Manu Biosphere Reserve where they are working with communities in environmental education. APECO is also working towards establishing a reserve in the Cordillera de Colan. Contact details: APECO, Parque José de Acosta 187, Magdalena del Mar, Lima 17; tel: 01 264 0970; email: apeco@datos.lima.peru; web: www.latinsynergy.org/apeco.htm.

International Society for the Preservation of the Tropical Rainforest Works hands-on with native villages and provides a free medical clinic, animal orphanage and education/conservation trips. Volunteer opportunities exist in different fields of the project. Contact details: Los Angeles office, Roxanne Kremer, 3302 Burton Avenue, Rosemead CA 91770; email: pard_expeditions@yahoo.com.

Sociedad Peruana de Derecho Ambiental (SPDA) This organisation investigates the legal implications and formulates Peru's standing in relation to intellectual property rights, pharmaceutical and gene prospecting, and the rights of indigenous peoples with respect to conservation initiatives. Contact details: Prolongacion Arenales 437, San Isidro; tel: 422 2720; web: www.spda.org.pe.

Asociación Peruana de Turismo de Aventura y Ecoturismo (APTAE) The Peruvian Association of Adventure and Ecotourism is made up of tour operators and individuals working towards sustainable ecotourism. If you are interested in taking a proactive role in supporting ecotourism in Peru, do contact them for more information: APTAE, Bajada Balta 169, Ofic. 203, Miraflores, Lima 18; tel/fax: 4460422; web: www.cenfotur.net.

Peru Verde This organisation is involved in several conservation and environmental education projects in the rainforest. Together with its partner group Selva Sur, it operates ecotourism lodges in partnership with local people. Contact details: Calle Manuel Bañon 461, San Isidro, Lima; tel: 01 221 7525/7512; email: proyecto@peruverde.org.

Survival International A worldwide organisation supporting tribal peoples, Survival International stands for their right to decide their own future and helps them to protect their lives, lands and human rights. It works for tribal peoples' rights in three complementary ways: campaigns, education and funding. Survival International works closely with local indigenous organisations and focuses on tribal peoples who have the most to lose, usually those most recently in contact with the outside world. Contact details: 6 Charterhouse Buildings, London, UK EC1M 7ET; tel: 020 7687 8700; fax: 020 7687 8701; email: info@survival-international.org; web: www.survival-international.org.

GIVING SOMETHING BACK
The main cause of habitat destruction in the developing world is poverty. By helping the people you will also help the environment.

Experiencing rural Peru on foot has a profound effect on many travellers, who would like to know of ways they can help – how they can repay the place and people that have given so much to them. By far the best way is to support one of the small, local charities. This ensures that your money is properly allocated to the people who most need it. The organisations below will all welcome your help. The South American Explorers can put you in touch with other local charities.

Cusichaca Trust Founded by archaeologist Dr Ann Kendall in 1968, this organisation has been active in restoring Inca canals to improve the agricultural practices of the descendents of the Incas living in the area around Cusco and the Department of Apurimac. The aim of the trust is to revitalise traditional agricultural practices, encouraging organic farming and income-generating projects, and to improve nutrition and health in general. Money donations to continue this work will always be needed. Contact details: Unit 2, Spinner's Court, 55 West End, Witney, Oxon OX8 6NJ, UK; tel/fax: 01993 709606; email: cusichaca@woden.com.

CAITH This project has been set up to help homeless or abused girls in the Cusco area. The girls are given a home, health care, education and are taught the skills necessary to help them find work. The project has just built a new building with good accommodation for tourists, long and short term, at US$15 per person per night (see page 226). Staying here is a good way to support the project which also welcomes volunteers. Contact details: Pasaje Sto Toribio 4 (just off Av Argentina), Uchullo Alto, Cusco; tel: 084 233595.

Hogar de Cristo, Escuela Especial 'Monte Carmelo' They work with women with mental health problems and are always in need of donations of money, clothes, shoes and medical supplies. Av Las Gaviotas 152, San Bartolo, Lima 28; tel: 430 8427/430 8071.

Posadita del Buen Pastor A residential home for children and mothers with AIDS. They welcome medical supplies, donations, and volunteer workers. Jr Espinar 260, Magdalena, Lima; tel: 01 263 4481.

CARE Peru They have an assortment of projects in various areas of Peru including Huaraz and Ayacucho. For more details check their website at www.careinternational.org. Huaraz office: Calle Simon Bolivar 791, Huaraz; tel: 044 722 854/924.

Remar A Spanish organisation that run homes and day-care centres for street-children in Lima, Tacna, Arequipa, and Trujillo. Visits should be arranged through their Lima office: Av Prol La Mar 779, La Victoria; tel: 01 324 7666; email: info@remar.org; web: www.remarperu.org.

Centro Ann Sullivan A day centre to teach children with severe learning difficulties. Calle Petronilla Alvarez 180, San Miguel, Lima; tel: 01 263 4880; email: annsullivan@tsi.com.pe.

Asociacion Benefica Prisma Work in health and nutrition nationwide. Calle Carlos Gonzales 251 Urb. Maranga, San Miguel; tel: 464 0490/0720; email: postmaster@prisma.org.pe; web: www.prisma.org.pe.

Fundacion por los Niños del Peru Run homes for orphaned children all over the country. Jr de la Unión 264 3er. piso Edificio Palacio; Lima; tel: 427 1951; email: gerencia@fpnp.org.pe.

Asociacion de Educacion para la Convivencia del Hombre y del Animal Also known as Sociedad Amigo de los Animales. An animal-protection society currently working on building a refuge for animals. They need money, books and volunteers. Contact Domingo Elías, 148 Miraflores, Lima; tel: 447 6030/242 1952; fax 446 6050; email: post@amigosdelosanimales.org.

The Yine Project This is a community-based ecotourism project with Pantiacolla Tours and the Yine indians of the Peruvian Manu Biosphere Reserve rainforest. The ten-year project, to build an eco-lodge and train the Yine people to run it, began early in 2001. In 2011, the eco-lodge will be handed over to the Yine. Over this period, the Project will welcome volunteers who can help with the various educational programmes. Contact Marianne van Vlaardingen, Calle Plateros 360, Cusco; tel: 084 238 323; fax: 084 252 696; email: pantiac@terra.com.pe; web: www.pantiacolla.com/yine/.

The Mountain Institute An America-based charity aiming to conserve the delicate ecology of the mountain areas around Huaraz. They work with local communities on a variety of projects to promote sustainable development. There are volunteer opportunities for biologists but also volunteer research assistants are sometimes needed. Lima Office: Av Petit Thours 4384, Miraflores, Lima; tel: 421 7579. Huaraz office: Alameda Grau 1028, Huaraz; tel: 044 72 1884; fax: 044 72 5996; email: tmiperu@wayna.rcp.net.pe or postmaster@tmi.org.pe; web: www.mountain.org.

Lima

Most people arrive in Lima by air. The drive from the airport to the suburbs provides their first glimpse of the city and they must wonder why on earth they came. Brown adobe slums on brown rubbish-strewn earth, and the occasional stiff body of a dead dog, line this scenic drive. Add to this the chaotic traffic which, with horns blaring, only marginally slows down for red lights. And all shrouded in the grey pall of Lima's winter *garúa*.

Actually it's not that bad. If you stay in one of the suburbs such as Miraflores, and indulge in some seafood eating, shopping and museums, you will not regret your time there. Each district has its own character: the centre with its Spanish-colonial buildings; Miraflores, the affluent commercial centre; Barranco with a Colonial Spanish flavour and attractive bars and little restaurants; and the fishing 'village' of Chorillos.

Tourist information is available at the *iperú* offices in the city centre and in Miraflores (see *Useful addresses*), and plenty of real information from the South American Explorers organisation (see page 53).

There are some useful publications, too. A free booklet, *Peru Guide*, is available from many hotels and the tourist office and contains much useful information on Lima and other tourist cities in Peru. The monthly English-language magazine *The Lima Times* is well worth buying; in addition to events around town it will give you a very good insight into the political and economic situation in Peru. *Rumbos* is an excellent locally produced glossy magazine with articles on all aspects of Peru.

TRANSPORT
From Lima airport

For newcomers to the developing world arriving in Peru can be a daunting experience. You emerge from the relative haven of the customs area to a mayhem of 'porters', taxi touts, hotel touts, and other *Limeños* intent on getting an early look in on your dollars. There is an airport bus that will take you to your hostel. It may take quite some time as it drops people off all over town, but this is a good and safe way to get to where you are staying. There are also dozens of *colectivos* going all over Lima from outside the

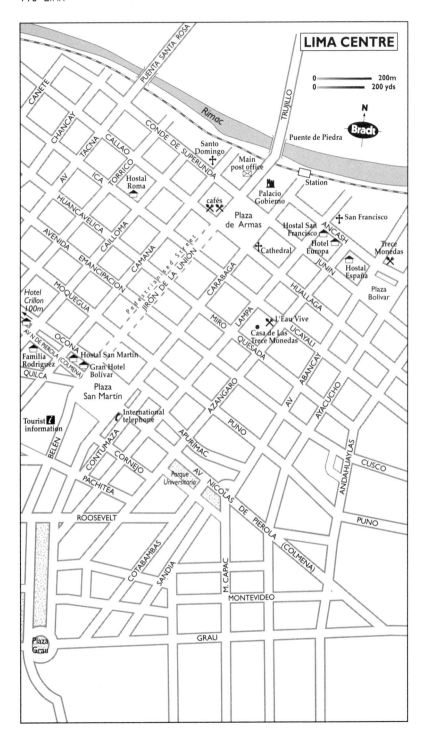

LIMA CENTRE

aiport. However, I would not recommend this form of transport until you know the city and never with luggage. *Colectivos* are always extremely cramped with just people squashed inside, there is certainly no extra space for bulky gringo rucksacks. You will probably have to resign yourself to taking a taxi. Knowing this, it is a good idea to join up with other passengers for a shared ride.

The easiest and most secure option is to order one of the official airport taxis at the desk as you come out of the customs area. It will be more expensive (about US$15) than taking your chance with the taxis waiting outside the Arrivals Hall with whom you can bargain. Official taxis also wait outside Arrivals; generally speaking, the nearer the taxi is to the door of the airport, the more expensive it will be.

You will be in a stronger position to bargain if you have *soles*. There are banks and ATM machines in the International Departures Hall.

The best hotels provide their own private buses so look out for the drivers holding up a sign with the name of the hotel. Check before travelling whether you will be met at the airport.

To get to the airport from the city (without luggage) take a *colectivo* from Miraflores to the entrance to the airport on the main road.

Buses

There is no central bus terminal in Lima as yet, so long-distance buses will deposit you at their depot somewhere in the city. It is best to take a taxi to wherever you are staying and avoid hanging round the depots, which are renowned for thieves.

City transport

Lima has an extensive bus, *colectivo* and taxi service. It needs it – the distances are huge. They run even on public holidays.

Buses

Fortunately the buses all list the main streets on their route on the front window. And they are very cheap. There are two types: private buses, painted different colours according to their route and usually in very bad condition, and the yellow, government-run buses, which are mostly new. Buses run between 06.00 and 24.00 daily, and on some routes run throughout the night, costing an extra 20% after midnight.

Colectivos

Private cars or minibuses running the same routes as the buses and with routes also listed on the front window. As a further aid the helper/money-collector will scream the main destination out from the window. *Colectivos* stop wherever the passenger wants to get off, or when they are hailed, so are more convenient than buses, and only a little more expensive. They run between 06.00 and 01.00 daily, and on some routes throughout the night, costing an extra 20% after midnight.

Taxis

Taxis are ubiquitous. Settle on the price before you get in; they rarely have meters. You should pay US$3–5 for most trips around the city. All taxis carry a taxi sign, but they do not need any legal documents to operate, and anybody can be a taxi driver. Be extremely wary late at night. Radio cars can be ordered by phone and are punctual and secure, but double the price of the normal 'street' taxis. It is always better to ask at your hotel for a reliable taxi, especially when travelling at night or with luggage.

SLEEPING AND EATING
Accommodation

There are several good guidebooks which keep an up-to-date listing of hotels and *hostales* – see *Further Reading* at the back of this book. Prices range from about US$5 per night to US$150.

The list below gives you the recommended backpackers' places, and a few mid-range hotels. Most backpackers stay in the centre of Lima because it has the cheapest accommodation and bus stations are close. Others prefer Miraflores, which is cleaner, safer and quieter. Watch the safety aspect particularly in the centre, take taxis if you need to move around with your luggage, and avoid walking around at night.

In the city centre

Recommended budget hotels with basic rooms, mostly without private bathrooms, or dormitory style. Prices range between US$5 and US$10 per person.

Hostal Roma Jiron Ica 326; tel: 01 427 7576; email: resroma@terra.com.pe. One of Lima's oldest gringo hotels. US$10/US$15. Recommended.

Hostal España Calle Azangaro 105; tel: 01 427 9196; email: fertur@terra.com.pe. Dorm rooms from US$3.

Familia Rodriguez Calle Nicolas de Pierola 730; tel: 01 423 6465; email: jotajot@pol.com.pe. From US$6 for a dorm.

Hostal Iquique Jiron Iquique 758, Breña; tel: 01 433 4724; email: hi758@blockbuster.com.pe. US$7/US$10 per room.

Hostal de las Artes Jiron Chota 1454 (nr Av España), Breña; tel: 01 433 0031; email: artes@terra.com.pe. Good central location. Dorm rooms from US$5 per person, private rooms with bath available. Airport pick up.

Mid-range hotels, rooms have en suite bathrooms with TV, phone, left-luggage facility and laundry; prices usually include breakfast. From US$15 per person.

Hotel Granada Jr Huancavelica 323; tel: 01 427 9033. US$20/US$25. TV, phone, left luggage, laundry.

La Posada del Parque Parque Hernán Velarde 60, Santa Beatriz; tel: 01 433 2412; email: monden@terra.com.pe. US$25/US$30.

Hostal Renacimiento Parque Hernán Verlarde 52; tel: 01 433 2806.

Hostal San Martín Av Nicolás de Piérola 882, 2nd floor, Plaza San Martín; tel: 01 428 5337; email: hsanmartin@goalnet.com.pe. Air conditioning, cable TV, breakfast included. US$33/US$50.

In Miraflores

Albergue Juvenil Internacional (youth hostel), Calle Casmiro Ulloa 328 (a side street off Av Benavides); tel: 01 446 5488. You do not have to be a YHA member. US$14 for non-members, US$10 for members.

Casa de Mochilero Jr Cesareo Chacaltana 130-A, 2nd floor, nr 10th block of Av Jose Pardo; tel: 01 444 9089; email: casamochilero@hotmail.com. From US$4 in dorm, US$9 for a double room.

Hostal De Ville Jr Chiclayo 533, Miraflores; tel: 01 447 4325. US$30/US$40. Very clean, central, quiet and friendly.

Pensión José Luis F Paula de Ugarriza 727; tel: 01 444 1015; email: hoteljl@hoteljoseluis.com; web: www.hoteljoseluis.com. US$12 per person, kitchen facilities, private bath, safe, quiet.

Pensión Yolanda Escobar Domingo Elias 230; tel: 01 445 7565. US$15/US$30, including breakfast.

Residencial El Castillo Diez Canseco 580; tel: 01 446 9501. US$12/US$24. Private bath, friendly.

Torreblanca José Pardo 1453; tel: 01 447 9998; email: hostal@torreblancaperu.com. $US45/US$60 with private bath. Includes airport pick-up, breakfast and welcome cocktail!

In Pueblo Libre

Marfil Guest House Parque Ayacucho 126 (Between 3 and 4 of Bolivar), Pueblo Libre; tel: 01 463 3161; email: yma25@yahoo.com. From US$6 per person. Kitchen and laundry facilities. Located in quiet, residential neighbourhood, not far from the centre, Miraflores and the airport.

In Barranco

Mochilero's Backpackers Av Pedro de Osma 135; tel: 01 477 4506/0302; email: backpacker@amauta.rcp.net.pe A new hostel in converted colonial mansion with dormitory accommodation from US$8 per person.

Restaurants

There are some excellent restaurants in Lima; seafood is particularly recommended. Be warned that an 18% government tax and a 13% service charge will be added to the bill in posh restaurants. For that final-day splurge the following are recommended:

La Rosa Naútica at the end of the pier at Miraflores; tel: 01 447 0057. The most expensive and probably the best restaurant in town. Great happy-hour cocktails. Very popular with groups.

Costa Verde Playa Barranquito, Costa Verde. International food.

La Trattoria Manuel Bonilla 106, Miraflores. Italian food.

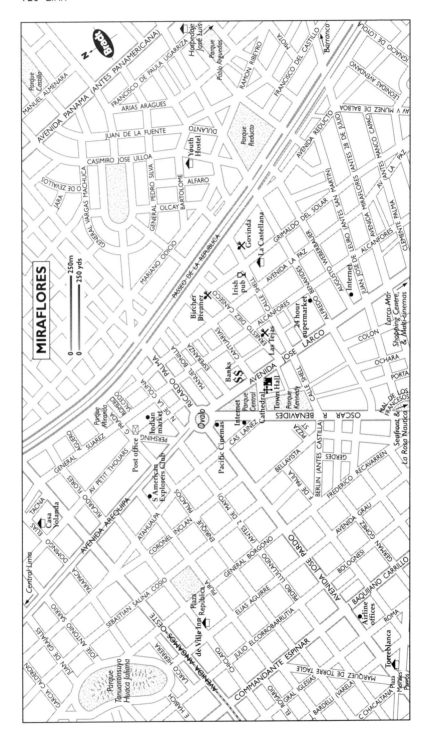

MIRAFLORES

Alfresco Malecon Balta 790, Miraflores (opposite Club Terrazas). Seafood.
L'Eau Vive Ucayali 370. Opposite the Torre Tagle palace in central Lima. Good food and the profits go towards helping the poor.
Pantagruel Calle Cantuarias 151, Miraflores (off Av Larco); tel: 01 242 8465. Peruvian food in elegant surroundings.

Cafés
Café Café Martir Olaya 250, Miraflores. Excellent coffee and sandwiches.
Mango's Cafe Ovalo Gutierrez 879l, Miraflores.
Millenium Calle Independencia 141, Miraflores.

Pubs
Bohemia Av Santa Cruz 805, Ovalo Gutierrez, Miraflores.
La Noche Av Bolognesi 307, Barranco.
Carlos & Charlie's Complejo Larcomar.
Sr Frogs Complejo Larcomar.
Hard Rock Cafe Complejo Larcomar.
Pub Irlandes Shell 627, Miraflores.

Entertainment
The best sources of information (if you read Spanish) are the local papers, *El Comercio* or *La República*. Look under the cultural section, and you will find a list of cinemas (English-language films are usually subtitled, not dubbed), music, and so on. *The Lima Times* lists (and reviews) English-language theatre or special film showings and concerts. For folklore shows or *peñas* try the tourist office or the *Peru Guide*.

Peña is typical Peruvian entertainment: a restaurant with live folk music and dance shows in traditional costumes. Not to be missed.

Maps
While in Lima take the opportunity to purchase all the hiking maps you need. The government-run Instituto Geográfico Nacional (IGN) is on Avenida Aramburu 1190, in the suburb of Surquillo. Open from Monday to Friday, 08.30–16.00. Take your passport with you. The IGN 1:100,000 topographical maps cover most of the country. Eventually the IGN plans to map the whole country, but they've been saying that for well over 20 years.

The IGN also publishes a good road map of Peru, departmental maps, satellite maps and satellite photos, a political map, a geographical map and others. It's worth a visit but check at the South American Explorers first. They sell some IGN maps and can tell you – in English – what's available at the IGN.

USEFUL ADDRESSES IN LIMA
Help!
Tourist police Jr Moore 268, Magdalena del Mar; tel: 01 460 1060/0965/0921
Tourist hotline If you have a complaint or problem to do with hotels, restaurants,

tour agencies, airlines or theft, phone 01 574 8000. English-speaking and helpful, this hotline functions day and night. Email: iperu@promperu.gob.pe.

Dirección General de Migraciones (Immigration), España 700 (corner of Huaraz), Breña, Lima. Open Monday to Friday, 09.30 to 13.00.

Cancellation of cards

American Express card Tel: 001 525 326 2660
American Express travellers' cheques Tel: 001 800 860 2908
Visa Tel: 001 800 428 1858
MasterCard Tel: 01 311 6000
Diner's Club Tel: 01 221 2050

Medical attention

Clínica Anglo-American Calle Alfredo Salazar 314 (3rd block), San Isidro; tel: 01 221 3656
Clínica Internacional Calle Washington 1475, central Lima; tel: 01 428 8060
Clínica San Borja Av Guardia Civil 337, San Borja; tel: 01 475 4000
Clinica Javier Prado Av Javier Prado Este 499, San Isidro; tel: 01 440 2000

National airlines

Aero Continente Av Pardo 651, Miraflores; tel: 01 242 4242/4260; email: aerocont@aerocontinente.com.pe; web: www.aerocontinente.net. Fly to: Cusco, Arequipa, Cajamarca, Trujillo, Chiclayo, Piura, Puerto Maldonado, Pucallpa, Iquitos, Tarapoto, Juliaca, Tacna.

Lan Perú Av Pardo 513, Miraflores, Lima; tel: 01 213 8200; web: www.lanperu.com. Fly between Arequipa, Juliaca, Puno.

Tans Av Arequipa 5200; tel: 01 213 6030 or 01 445 7107; email: comercial@tans.com.pe; web: www.tansperu.com. Fly between Piura, Arequipa, Juliaca, Tarapoto, Iquitos, Pucallpa,Tumbes, Cusco, Puerto Maldonado.

Aviandina Aeropuerto Internacional Jorge Chavez, Edificio Central Piso 8; tel: 01 447 8080/8700; email: aviandina@pol.com.pe. Fly between Cusco, Arequipa, Juliaca.

Taca Av Comandante Espinar 331, Miraflores; tel: 01 213 7000; email: reservasgt@grupotaca.com.pe; web: www.grupotaca.com. Fly between Cusco and Iquitos.

Aerocondor Juan de Arona 781, San Isidro; tel: 01 442 5215/5663; email: reservas@aerocondor.com.pe. Fly between Cajamarca, Trujillo, Huánuco, Ica, Juanjuí, Tarapoto.

Helicusco Av Arias Aragüez 369, Miraflores; tel: 01 445 6126: email: dfhr@amauta.rcp.net.pe; web: www.rcp.net.pe/HELICUSCO. Fly between Cusco and Machupicchu for approx.US$100.

Aeroica Jr Diez Canseco 480B, Miraflores; tel: 01 446 3026; email: aeroica@terra.com.pe. Fly over the Nasca lines.

Aeroparacas Calle Teodoro Cárdenas 470 Sta Beatriz; tel: 01 271 6941 or 01 273 0507; email: aeroparacas@wayna.rcp.net.pe; web: www.nascatravel.com. Fly between Paracas, Ica and Nasca.

International flights to Bolivia

Lloyd Aéreo Boliviano have daily flights, leaving late morning, from Lima to La Paz, which currently cost US$190. They also fly from Cusco to La Paz at US$110 with departures on Tuesday, Thursday and Saturday mornings. They are the only airline flying from Cusco.

Aero Continente fly from Lima to La Paz for around US$200 on Tuesday, Thursday and Saturday early afternoon (taking 2.5 hours).

Bus companies

There are dozens of bus companies in Lima, but as yet no central bus depot. Recommended companies are: **Cruz del Sur** (tel: 01 225 6163); **Ormeno** (tel: 01 427 5679); and **Civa** (tel: 01 426 4926).

Clubs/tourism

Comisión de Promoción de Perú (Promperu, main source of tourist information) Calle Uno Oeste No 50, Urb. Córpac, Lima 27. Edificio Mitinci; tel: 01 224 3279/3271/3395/3118; fax: 01 224 3323; email: postmaster@promperu.gob.pe; web: www.peru.org.pe.

Infotur (tourist office) Calle Belen (La Unión) 1066, central Lima; tel: 01 431 0117; email: postmaster@promperu.gob.pe. There is also a tourism booth in Parque Kennedy, Miraflores. Open 09.00–20.00;

Municipalidad de Lima Pasaje Santa Rosa 134, Plaza Mayor, Lima; tel: 01 427 4848. They organise tours of the city.

Peruvian Touring and Automobile Club Av Cesar Vallejo 699, Lince; tel: 01 221 2432/1050; fax: 4410531. Open Monday to Friday, 09.00–17.00.

South American Explorers Calle Piura 135, Miraflores; tel/fax: 01 445 3306; email: limaclub@terra.com.pe; web: www.samexplo.org. Open weekdays 09.30–17.00 (see page 53 for details).

Trekking and Backpacking Club Jiron Huascar 1152, Jesus Maria, Lima; tel: 01 446 3493.

Tour operators

There are numerous good tour operators in Lima. The following are personally recommended by the authors.

Aracari Av Pardo 610, miraflores, Lima 18; tel: 01 242 6673; email: postmaster@ aracari.com; web: www.aracari.com. Tailor-made tours with a cultural emphasis.

Ayllu Viajes Calle Elias Aguirre 126, Oficina 905, Miraflores; tel: 01 445 9639; mobile: 978 7060; email: aylluviajt@amauta.rcp.net.pe. A very helpful English-speaking travel agency; can organise flights, tours, hotel reservations and pretty much all other services in Peru.

Communications

The city phone code is 01.

Post office The main one (for *Lista de Correos*) is next to the Plaza de Armas in the centre of Lima.

Internet

Access to the Internet is booming throughout Peru, and Lima is no exception – there are dozens and dozens of places to email from, some of which are open 24 hours a day.

Cyberport Internet Public Booths Services Av Wilson 1282, Oficina 336, Lima. Open Mon–Sat 09.00–21.00.
Interaxis Café Calle Tarata 277, Miraflores. US$3 per hour.
Centro Cultural Ricardo Palma Block 6 of Larco, Miraflores. Open Mon–Fri 08.00–20.00. US$2 per hour.

Banks

Banco de Crédito Jr Lampa 499, central Lima; also the corner of Av Larco and Shell, in Miraflores. Open Mon–Fri 09.00–16.00. The best bank for changing travellers' cheques and cash from credit cards.
Banco Wiese Diagonal 1176, Miraflores. Travellers' cheques and cash from credit cards.
Interbank Jr de la Union 600. Good for using travellers' cheques and credit cards. Their Miraflores branch is at Larco 215.

Provisions

24-hour supermarket MASS, Calle Benavides/Calle La Paz, Miraflores.

There are also many other supermarketsthroughout Lima.

Museums

Museo Nacional de Antropología, Arqueología e Historia Plaza Bolívar s/n, Pueblo Libre; tel: 01 463 5070; fax: 01 463 2009; email: mnacional@perucultural.org.pe; web: mnaah.perucultural.org.pe. Open Tue–Sun 09.00–17.00. Well worth a visit for an overview of Peruvian history. Guides available in English and Spanish.
Museo Arqueológico Rafael Larco Herrera Av Bolívar 1515, Pueblo Libre; tel: 01 461 1312; fax: 01 461 5640; email: museolarco@tsi.com.pe; web: museolarco.perucultural.org.pe. Open Mon–Sun 09.00–18.00. Guides in English and Spanish on request.
Museo de la Nación Av Javier Prado Este 2465, San Borja; tel/fax: 01 476 9875. Open Tue–Sun 09.00–20.00. Guides in English, French and Spanish, café, bookstore and souvenir shop.
Museo del Oro del Perú y Armas del Mundo (Fundación Miguel Mujica Gallo) Av Alonso de Molina 1100, La Molina; tel: 01 345 1271. Open Mon–Sun 11.00–19.00. Guides in Spanish and English. Recent investigations have shown that the majority of objects in this museum are fake!

AN EXCURSION FROM LIMA
Lachay de Lomas

A day trip to this national park is recommended by Charles Davies who spent several months in Peru studying the cloudforest on the Cordillera de Colán.

The park is very rarely visited by foreigners though popular with Peruvians. This protected area of fog-desert lies 110km north of Lima, just before you reach Huacho. The bus will drop you off at the entrance. The park has good visitor facilities and footpaths.

The best time for a visit is from August to October, when the desert is in spring bloom, but any time of year is rewarding. The landscape has an other-worldliness about it, with gnarled trees and cacti, and you can see a variety of rare birds and mammals including the endangered desert fox.

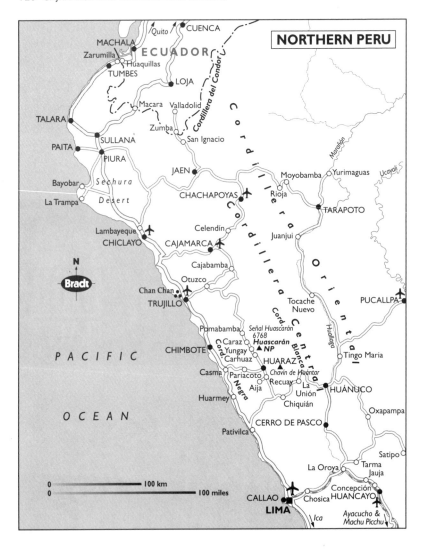

NORTHERN PERU

Cajamarca and Chachapoyas Regions

THE CAJAMARCA REGION

Cajamarca is one of Peru's gems. Situated at only 2,750m in the northern highlands of Peru, it nestles in a quiet, green valley surrounded by low mountain peaks.

The town has a colonial charm with lovely churches, and to this day the Indians have kept their traditions, fiestas and to a large extent their traditional costumes. It has a relaxing atmosphere, with open hospitality and excellent Andean food, and the surrounding green countryside is steeped in history. One attraction of Cajamarca is the Baños del Inca 6km outside the town. Thermal springs are channelled into a pool and private baths. A real treat, especially after a few days' hiking.

If you happen to be in this area around February (therefore in the wrong season for hiking) you will be able to take part in Carnival, one of the most colourful celebrations in Peru. In Cajamarca there is a marvellous display of costumes, music and dancing. The downside is that throwing water – and worse – at passers-by is a traditional carnival activity. Watch out for buckets containing the 'and worse' part.

History

Cajamarca was important long before the Incas established themselves here. Various pre-Inca sites have been found in the area and archaeologists are still making new discoveries. Any visitor who has read about the Incas will associate Cajamarca with one of history's great turning points: the conflict between Inca and Spaniard. The Incas had not been long in the area before the Spanish arrived: the estimated date of the Inca conquest of the local tribes is 1460. Cajamarca became an important place on the main Inca highway between Quito and Cusco. In November 1532 the victorious Inca Atahualpa rested for a few days in Cajamarca before marching down to Cusco to take control of the empire after defeating his half-brother in the civil war. At the same time, the Spaniards, under the command of Francisco Pizarro, landed on the coast of Peru.

Atahualpa agreed to a meeting with the Spaniards, was ambushed, and taken prisoner by Pizarro. In an attempt to secure his release his followers agreed to fill a room once with gold and twice with silver. But to no avail.

Their supreme ruler, the Sun God, was garotted and the empire died with him. Thus were 179 tired Europeans able to defeat an army of 6,000 or so and destroy one of the largest and best-organised empires the world has ever known.

Today little remains from the Inca period and these grim events are best held in the imagination. A visit to *El Cuarto de Rescate* (the Ransom Room) is worse than uninspiring; it cancels out your own mental picture.

The phone code for Cajamarca is 044.

Getting there and away
From Lima (via Trujillo) (856km)
By bus About 14 hours, US$16. Daily buses.

By air About 2 hours, US$70 one way with Aerocondor. The schedule is unreliable, but normally there are several flights a week. Less-frequent flights in the rainy season.

From Tumbes (via Chiclayo)(812km)
By bus Tumbes to Chiclayo about 10 hours, US$9. From Chiclayo to Cajamarca, about 7 hours, US$6. Daily buses.

By air No direct flights, but daily flights from Tumbes to Chiclayo, 1 hour, US$30 one way.

Sleeping and eating
Accommodation
The following are cheap backpackers' hotels, mostly with communal bathroom and cold water and costing around US$10–15 per person:

Hostal Sucre Amalia Puga 811, Plaza de Armas; tel: 044 822596
Hostal Plaza Amalia Puga 669, Plaza de Armas; tel: 044 822058. A rambling old building, with good atmosphere and restaurant.

Mid- and upper-range hotels, mostly with private bath and hot water:

Hostal Amazonas Calle Amazonas 528; tel: 044 822620. About US$15.
Hotel Cajamarca Calle Dos de Mayo 311; tel: 044 822532. About US$20.
Hotel Lago Seco Tel: 044 823149. A luxurious, country-resort-style hotel next to the Baños del Inca, 6km outside town. US$80/90.
Hostal Jusovi Amazonas 637; tel: 044 822920
Hotel Casa Blanca 2 de Mayo 446; tel: 044 822141. About US$20.

Restaurants
There's plenty of choice and good local food. Try the market on Calle Amazonas for fresh bread, fruit and vegetables. At the many *Tiendas de productos lacteos* you can buy the famous *Cajamarca cheese*, also *manjar blanca* (sweet caramel spread) and *galletas de maíz* (puffed corn biscuits).

Short hikes around Cajamarca
Half-day hikes
To Ayllambo, 3.5km, 1½ hours. A pleasant walk to the pottery village of Ayllambo. Leave from Avenida Independencia and walk south. Along the way you'll pass several craft shops selling the typical ceramics of Cajamarca. In Ayllambo there is a workshop, Escuela Taller, where pottery is taught.

To Cerro Santa Apollonia, the hill overlooking Cajamarca with a statue of Atahualpa on top. Leave from Calle Dos de Mayo, up the endless steps to the top.

To the Baños del Inca, 6km, 1½ hours. Follow Calle Inca from town.

A day hike through the countryside
Take a bus or walk 7km to Ventanillas de Otuzco from Avenida Arequipa. Visit this interesting pre-Inca cemetery, which consists of hundreds of funerary niches. From here you can walk 6km to the Baños del Inca. Ask the locals to show you the path which runs south to the river. It can be very muddy in the rainy season. Cross the river and follow the riverbank to your right. The local people are very friendly and often stop to have a chat.

Once at the Baños enjoy yourself! A huge private bath with all the hot water you want costs about US$1. Bring a towel. Clean and relaxed, continue your walk 7km along a dirt road to Llacanora, a typical country village, with an old colonial church on its little plaza. A walk up the valley from the plaza for 15 to 20 minutes brings you to a nice little waterfall. Another 15 minutes and you arrive at a larger one. Ask the locals for directions.

Continue the hike from Llacanora to La Collpa, about 7km. A dirt road connects these two places, running through flat farmland, but there are short cuts. Corn, wheat and barley are grown. La Collpa itself is a co-operative for cattle farming, and you can visit the Centro Ganadero and purchase cheese and *manjar blanca*.

From La Collpa it's a 2½-hour walk (11km) back to Cajamarca.

Cumbe Mayo
This is an extraordinary site, so even if you do not want to do the hike described below it is well worth taking a tour here. Even without the pre-Inca remains the area would be worth a visit for the 'forest of rocks' covering the bare hilltops. There are tall, thin rocks, enormous limestone faces cut deep by erosion, and isolated goblets. There is a cave decorated by pictographs showing the influence of the Chavín culture, and a remarkable aqueduct channelling water down to Cajamarca, carved into the rock with geometric precision. There are many perfect right angles, and dead straight stretches, as well as tunnels. It serves as a reminder that the Incas didn't invent the art of stone cutting. No-one knows the exact purpose of this aqueduct, but it certainly wasn't purely for agricultural purposes. It doesn't carry enough water and there are plenty of streams watering the valley anyway. Most likely it – and the cave with the pictographs – featured in some sort of water ritual.

Cumbe Mayo to San Pablo

This 3- or 4-day hike takes you through some lovely scenery and rural villages, beginning at one of the area's most important pre-Inca sites.

Distance	About 85km
Altitude	From 2,750m to 3,650m, descending to 2,365m
Rating	A comparatively easy walk, but with some steep ascents and descents
Timing	Four days. One day less if you get transport up to Cumbe Mayo
In reverse	Possible, but a long ascent
Start of the trail	Plaza de Armas in Cajamarca or Cumbe Mayo
Transport at the end	From San Pablo to Chilete, ½ hour, pick-ups, buses and trucks, mostly in the morning. From Chilete to Cajamarca, 3 hrs, buses and trucks.
Maps	IGN sheet *Cajamarca* (15-f)

Route description You may not want to walk all the way up to Cumbe Mayo. Sometimes you can catch a lift with a tour bus or private car going up to the site, or it may be worth organising a taxi. Another possibility is to sign up for a tour for the advantage of the lift up there and guidance round Cumbe Mayo (explain that you will not be coming back and check that they don't mind taking your luggage). It takes one hour by car.

Starting from the Plaza in Cajamarca, pass Cerro Santa Apollonia to your right. There is a short cut, a path well used by the locals, which goes straight up, from time to time crossing the road which curves its way up to Cumbe Mayo. It takes about 3 to 4 hours to get to the Cumbe Mayo pass (3,500m) where there are a few houses. The main footpath continues down into the valley, but you continue along the dirt road to your right, which works its way up the valley side to the second pass. After about an hour's hike (3km), you see a road going down into the valley to your left, with steep, rock-crowned slopes and a river below. Descend into the valley. The aqueduct lies in front of you at the foot of the narrow valley. It's still in a very good state, and is followed by a stone path that runs into the valley for about 500m.

The area is beautiful, with steep green hillsides, incredible rock formations and deep valleys. The locals who graze their sheep here are friendly, curious and anxious to have a chat with you. There are some great camping spots, but it gets cold and windy as soon as the sun disappears, so put your tent up in good time.

The easiest way to Chetilla, the next community, is to follow the dirt road up to the pass (3,900m). You can take a short cut by following the path up the

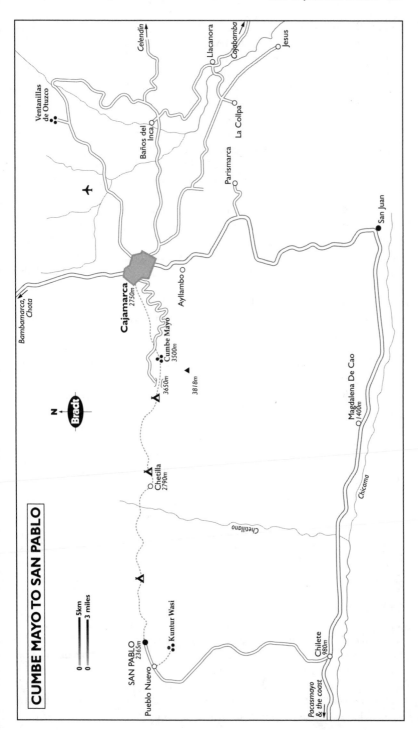

CUMBE MAYO TO SAN PABLO

mountain range to your left (ask a local to direct you as the path is not very clear). At the pass you get a great view over the valley.

Follow the dirt road for about 2 hours, descending into the valley, passing a few hilltops with crosses and the little *casario* of Jancate to your left. On the third hilltop (with three crosses), which you can reach via short cuts, you'll enjoy a good view into the valley in front of you. Descend into this steep valley, following the road for about an hour until you see a well-used stone path to your right. This leads to Chetilla (which the road bypasses). The walk takes about 3 hours through beautiful countryside.

Chetilla (2,790m) is an attractive little village with a few houses and a school – and about 800 friendly inhabitants who keep to their traditional way of life. Please respect that.

Continuing to San Pablo, the trail is part stone, part sand and part steps, which descend steeply down to the river. Cross this via the bridge and climb the steep hill on the other side until you reach green pastures with a few houses and a school, about 3 hours from the river. Sometimes the path fades away in the pasture but look ahead and you'll see the continuation; also ask the locals.

The path contours along the right slope of the valley, giving great views, and past subtropical vegetation splashed with little waterfalls. Then the path finally climbs up the mountainside, through pastures with a few houses, to the pass which is about 7 hours from the school. Here there's a little house with a gate on its left. Enjoy the view, it's the last one before you descend to San Pablo.

From the pass the path follows the mountainside, descending slowly, passing through the casario of Tamincha. From here it goes uphill, then descends to the river. Cross the bridge and take the steep short cut up the hill on your right. From here you can see the little picturesque village of San Pablo surrounded by green pampa. It's about a 5-hour hike from the pass/gate.

San Pablo is a typical colonial village, with its small streets and carved wooden balconies. The people are friendly and their culture intact. By the plaza at the lower end of the village is an attractive church with no fewer than three bell-towers. On Sunday there is a market on the main street and the locals from the surrounding villages come to barter or sell their produce. The village has one simple hotel and several well-stocked shops. You'll find a few basic restaurants so can indulge in the usual post-hike eating orgy.

The ruins of Kuntur Wasi

This was once an impressive pre-Inca site showing strong Chavín influence: the remains of a triple-terraced pyramid which once supported a temple. Unfortunately the ruins are now completely overgrown and anything of value has been removed. The entrance is marked by steps and you can still see the remains of a monolith carved with feline/human features. The area has been well explored by a Chinese expedition which studied the ruins for about two years, taking away some objects for further investigation.

The ruins are not really worth visiting unless you are a passionate enthusiast. To get there walk down the main road from San Pablo to Pueblo Nuevo (about 45 minutes). Here you'll find on the hill to your right a small path and a sign 'Kuntur Wasi'. Follow the path up to the top of the hill, where you'll see the ruins.

THE CHACHAPOYAS REGION
Updated by Tom Gierasimczuk

The northern department of Amazonas, with its virgin cloudforest and high rainforest, contains such plentiful ruins and ancient cities that it has been lauded as the richest archaeological zone in South America. Indeed outcrops of constructions on verdant summits and remains of roundhouses dating from the pre-Inca Chachapoya culture (AD600 to AD1500) will fascinate your inner-Indiana Jones.

Many structures – even entire settlements – are hidden under thick vegetation and camouflaged by epiphytes, vines and relentless undergrowth. Some sites, however, have been studied by national and international archaeologists, including such well-known names as Switzerland's Henri and Paula Reichlen, American Gene Savoy and Peruvian archaeologist Federico Kaufmann-Doig, director of the Instituto de Arqueología Amazónica in Lima. Various excavation projects live and die with the availability of funding. Many of the ruins are situated on or near trails that are still the only access into this area.

Local farmers know the ruins pretty well and are a good source of information, supplies, guides and mules. Remarkably, despite its attributes, the area is only now opening up to tourism – still obscure enough for adventurous backpackers looking to feel like Real Explorers. Known as *ceja de selva*, literally eyebrow of the jungle, the cloudforest here is particularly rich in orchids, bromeliads and other epiphytes, making it a rewarding area for botanists and natural-history enthusiasts as well as Lara Croft disciples.

Chachapoyas

The region's main town and provincial capital of 27,000 is a friendly place with whitewashed colonial homes and a traditional, provincial air. Improved road access from the coast and ongoing upgrades to hotels and restaurants are facilitating the growth of tourism.

There is a dilapidated museum at the INC (see listings), which has some Chachapoyan pottery and a few dishevelled mummies. It is worth visiting to see how *not* to care for millennia-old artifacts. There are plans to open another (proper) museum in the plaza in 2002.

The area telephone code is 044. Numbers have been changed from the prefix 074.

History

The Chachapoyas culture is one of the most enigmatic in ancient America. The Chachapoya appeared in modern-day northeast Peru sometime between AD300 and AD500. Over the next 300 years or so, they battled the Huari culture for the 25,000 square miles of territory flanked by the great Maranon River to the north and west and the Huallaga River to the east. The Chachapoya eventually won, establishing great centres like Kuelap (see below) that facilitated their dominance of this massive area (approximately the size of Taiwan). The empire wasn't an authoritarian regime like the Inca's. Instead, the Chachapoya existed as loose-knit chiefdoms, coming together for war but just as easily raiding each other's supplies when crops failed. The empire, it is believed, numbered almost 300,000 at its zenith, its roads, villages and fortresses – now so remote and solemn – all teeming with life. After successfully battling the expanding Inca empire, the Chachapoya were conquered around 1470, therefore losing identity at the hands of the Incas intent on weakening the cultural, as well as the military will of its opponents. The culture was thrown into further obscurity after the conquest, when, betrayed by the Spaniards who had initially helped them fight the Inca, the Chachapoya disappeared forever. With such historical ambiguity, it is easy to guess and culture has tickled the imagination, especially Inca and Spaniard descriptions of the Chachapoya as 'white and tall'. Since then, theories about their origin have run the gamut – everything from the lost tribes of Israel to Vikings who took a wrong turn.

Getting there and away

By air A few small airlines operate flights from Lima to Chachapoyas, although schedules are subject to change and flights may be cancelled at the last minute due to bad weather. Grupo Aereo Ocho sometimes flies from Lima to Chachapoyas and back between May and October on Tuesdays and Saturdays for US$55. Check and double-check at the airport in Lima. Other flights may start serving this increasingly popular area.

By road There are several relatively comfortable overnight buses from Lima that do the journey in 20–24 hours for US$17. Transportes Zelada runs throughout the week and leaves Lima in the late afternoon, arriving in Chachapoyas around the same time the next day. Transcarh and Civa run similar services. If you want to break the journey up, or if you're coming from Ecuador, direct overnight buses run to Chachapoyas from Chiclayo and back, with a one-way journey taking about nine hours, at US$7. Transervice Kuelap leaves Chiclayo at 17.30 and arrives in Chachapoyas early the next morning. If you start in Cajamarca, you'll need to change buses in Celendín – a 4-hour trip from Cajamarca. From Celendín a microbus runs to Chachapoyas on Thursdays, Fridays and Sundays. There are also trucks, but this is a 12–14 hour journey and the road is in poor condition. There is little in Celendín and most folks opt to access Chachapoyas via the daily buses from Chiclayo.

Getting around Like in most Andean towns, there is a reliable, albeit seemingly chaotic, network of minibuses that go just about anywhere, at least once a day. In Chachapoyas, this nerve centre exists on Jiron Grau, where it passes the market. From early morning until the late afternoon, transport of all shapes and sizes leaves for the nether regions of the Chachapoyas realm. Prices vary but expect to pay an average of US$1.50 for every hour travelled. Cabs will go anywhere as well and are handy if you missed the only transport that day. They charge about US$40 for the entire day for up to five people. Ask at the Café de Guias for recommended drivers.

Sleeping and eating

There is now a reasonable choice of accommodation and restaurants in and around Chachapoyas, as well as in Tingo, the gateway town for Kuelap and by the ruins themselves.

Accommodation.

Gran Hotel Vilaya Jiron Ayacucho 755, Chachapoyas; tel: 044 777664; fax: 044 778154; email: info@vilayatours.com. US$20–25. A new, highly recommended 3-star hotel that is the information centre for Chachapoyas. Glorious hot water. Home base for Vilaya Tours (www.vilayatours.com), a locally based adventure outfitter and guide service run by Englishman Rob Dover.

Hostal Amazonas Plaza Grau, Chachapoyas. US$7 double, US$4 single. The cheapest in town and a backpacker favourite.

Hostal Kuelap Amazonas 1057, Chachapoyas. A budget hotel and it shows.

Hotel El Dorado Ayacucho 1062; tel: 044 777047. Good value.

Hotelito Tingo Jiron San Juan, block M, lot 16; by the entrance to El Tingo. US$4 double. In the same area is **Albergue Leon**.

AROUND CHACHAPOYAS (SKETCH MAP)

Restaurants

Cafe de Guías Located in the Gran Hotel Vilaya. A recommended escape serving up maps, trip reports, trekking tips as well as local organic coffee, cocktails and fresh munchies in a mellow atmosphere. Occasional slide shows and talks.

Restaurant Chacha Plaza de Armas, Chachapoyas. Recommended for delicious regional and national food. Good, plentiful food at low prices. This popular local spot gets busy.

Restaurant Las Rocas Plaza de Armas, Chachapoyas. Recommended.

Restaurant Matalache Jiron Amazonas, Chachapoyas. Recommended for its large portions of traditional Peruvian food at low prices and its friendly service.

Outside Chachapoyas

INC Hostal Just below Kuelap ruins. Very basic. US$1.50. The guard, Gabriel, and his family have 20 years' experience at the site. The family prepares simple meals and sells drinks and snacks.

Choctamal Lodge Ideally located for a trek to Vilaya with a fantastic view of Kuelap clear across the valley. Owned by American Charles Motley. US$10 with sheets and dinner, US$5 with your own sleeping bag. Jacuzzi (tempting, but only use if heated by solar power, not firewood). Buses run there from Chachapoyas.

Hacienda Chillo 5km past El Tingo on the main road to Leimebamba. A rustic yet comfortable and charming *hacienda* run by local couple Oscar and Ada Arce, both well versed in local adventure information. Oscar built and designed the entire place himself and the *hacienda* itself is worth a tour. US$30–50 per person including a delectable dinner, breakfast and boxed lunch if you're on the go.

Hostal Laguna de los Condores Amazonas 320, Leimebamba. Owned by Julio Ullilen who may be reached via the village telephone 044 780209. US$6 for single room with shared bathroom. US$15 for double room with private bath. Ask to watch their various videos profiling the Chachapoyas realm.

Several other hotels have opened up in Leimebamba. Ask around.

Useful addresses and tourist information

Tourist office (ITINCI) Jr Amazonas 1037, Chachapoyas; tel: 044 778355. Will soon be moving to the Plaza de Armas.

Instituto Nacional de la Cultura Jr Ayacucho 675, Chachapoyas.

Rob Dover Jr Grau 624, Chachapoyas; tel: 044 777506; email: rob@vilayatours.com. This Englishman runs Vilaya Tours and has lived in the area for years. He offers day and multi-day trips and is very knowledgeable. Find him through the Café de Guias and the Gran Hotel Vilaya.

Jorge Luis Calle Puno 493, Chachapoyas; tel: 044 998542. A knowledgeable local archaeologist.

Charles Motley Runs Choctomal Lodge near Kuelap and has been visiting the area for years.

Martín Chumbe Jr Pivre 909, Chachapoyas. An experienced local guide who offers adventurous hikes. He charges US$25 a day, and can be found in Las Rocas restaurant (see listings) every lunchtime. He's loved by some, vilified by others.

The ruins of Kuelap

Kuelap was first discovered in 1843 but has remained in relative obscurity until recently, when adventure travellers and archaeology aficionados realised its sheer magnitude. It is dubbed the continent's largest stone edifice, dwarfing even Machu Picchu.

Kuelap lies about 37km from Chachapoyas and 189km from Celendín. More folks are able to enjoy Kuelap today now that roads have been improved and an Interpretative Centre and proper bathrooms built near the entrance. Local families sell drinks, snacks and even full meals so visiting the ruin isn't the expedition it was only a few years ago.

So just how big is Kuelap? The oval-shaped city stretches out for 600m in a perfect north–south trajectory on a ridge 3,100m above sea level. It is 110m wide and entirely enclosed by a massive defensive wall that soars up to 18m. The single structure covers six hectares. The two eastern entrances and one western entrance display an optical illusion of sorts. The massive limestone walls bottleneck and the approach gets steeper the deeper one penetrates the fortress, until eventually there's only room for one person to enter – making a spear and an affinity for blood the only prerequisites for defence. Even walking up the path today, you get chills thinking of all the blood that spilled down this corridor.

Once inside, you marvel at not only the view – of terraced plots of land resembling giant quilts and the distant Utcubamba River cradling the village of Tingo below – but at the mind-boggling Chachapoya city planning. Natural contours of the land are incorporated, not levelled, and the lack of hard angles gives the entire area an organic feel. The citadel is composed of an upper and lower town. This duality is common in ancient Andean centres as the nobles resided above the commoners – both literally and figuratively. The difference with Kuelap's high town is its design as a fortress within a fortress – complete

with bottlenecking entrance and soaring walls, designed to give the nobles one last shot at fighting should the first defence have fallen. Over 450 round houses – common buildings, kitchen buildings and armouries – are testament to the communal living practised within Kuelap. A peculiar conical building in Kuelap's southern end served, it is believed, as a solar observatory that kept track of the sunlight that indicated the wet and dry season – and therefore was an oracle of sorts for ancient farmers.

The general consensus among archaeologists is that Kuelap was built between AD600 and AD800 to support the thriving Chachapoya civilisation while it was still battling for territory against the pre-Inca Huari culture. The new empire grew within Kuelap's walls – with the citadel playing the role of market town, residence, solar observatory and sacred site. Agriculture on the surrounding fertile plains swelled the population to probably about three or four thousand in Kuelap proper, judging by the concentration of round houses that today pepper the site like decomposing mushrooms.

The fortified location's 360° view made attackers easy to spot. Indeed the entire colossal citadel was probably never conquered and was eventually abandoned by the Chachapoya, who settled in lower, warmer climes as rival tribes were defeated or moved on. The conquering Inca army didn't even mention Kuelap in their chronicles, perhaps confirming that by the mid 1400s the great city was just cheap housing for altitude fetishists.

Hiking and exploring the ruins
Climate
The only hiking time is in the dry season (April to November). In the rainy season the paths are too slippery and muddy, although some circuits are possible if you're prepared and sunny days in the wet season are not uncommon. Always be prepared for rain in the dry season. Don't forget you are walking in the cloudforest most of the time, which means dense vegetation, possible mud and difficult, unmarked paths.

Food and supplies
Bring everything you need with you; there is nothing for sale or to rent in the towns. Chachapoyas is the best place to stock up on food supplies. The local *campesinos* may trade some potatoes with you for bread, coca leaves, sugar, salt, and other food, but don't rely on it. Increasingly, even the smallest villages are stocked with soft drinks and snacks. Bring plenty of insect repellent and a well-stocked first-aid kit. Anti-malarial tablets are not necessary.

Guides, arrieros and mules
If you can't get hold of Rob Dover, Martín Chumbe or anyone through the Café de Guías (see listings), ask in Chachapoyas for recommended guides (who will charge anything between US$15 and $30 a day). *Arrieros* and mules you can find in almost any small village where you start your hike. An *arriero* will charge about US$8–10 a day for himself and his mule.

Maps and books

Good topographical maps are available in Lima and can be perused in Chachapoyas in the Café de Guias, along with recommended circuits and local information. Peter Lerche, a German ethnohistorian, has written a detailed guide to hikes in the Chachapoyas region. It has maps and currently is in Spanish only. The most useful IGN maps are sheet 1358 (13-h) *Chachapoyas* and 1357 (14-h) *Leimebamba*.

A must-read about the area is *Warrior of the Clouds* by Keith Muscutt (University of Mexico Press; web: www.chachapoyas.com). Accompanied by fantastic photography, Keith's vivid account of living and exploring Chachapoyas is as historically pertinent as it is poetic. The book *Antisuyo*, by Gene Savoy, is a great – although embellished – source of information if you can get hold of it (it is out of print). Useful, if you can read Spanish, is *Historia del Peru* by Federico Kaufmann-Doig, in two volumes. A number of works published by local archaeologists can sometimes be found at universities, the Instituto de Arqueología Amazónica in Lima, and the Instituto de la Cultura in both Chachapoyas and Lima.

Visiting the ruins of Kuelap

Timing	4 hours from Tingo up to the ruins
Altitude	From 1,500m to 3,050m
Rating	Steep ascent, often muddy trails
Starting point	The closest you can get is via the new road – a hike of 20 minutes from the car park up to the ruins. If staying at Choctamal Lodge you can hike up the road to the ruins in 5 hours. An alternative is the 2-hour walk from the village of Maria (daily minibuses from Chachapoyas).
Entry requirements	The fee to the ruins is US$3. Open 08.00–18.00. The gatekeeper lives in the last house before you get to the ruins, which also functions as a hostel (US$3).
Maps	IGN sheet 1358 (13-h) *Chachapoyas*

Route description and information The obvious trail starts at Tingo and works its way up to the ruins, short-cutting the newish road (constructed in 1990). The guardian to the ruins has the key, and is a great source of information.

Allow 4 hours of hard climbing up to the ruins from Tingo, 3 hours to look around the complex and 3 hours to get back down to Tingo. You can break the hike up into two days by staying at the Kuelap hostal. Doing so will allow you to see the citadel at sunset and sunrise, both magical spectacles in good weather.

Ruins and hikes beyond Kuelap

Various interesting ruins and hikes are situated beyond Kuelap, including the massive zone of Gran Vilaya publicised by Gene Savoy in 1985. The entire area is criss-crossed by ancient roads leading to and from, it is believed, up to 500 "lost" cities. Gran Vilaya is remote and isolated, though some *campesinos* cultivate land around here. They are a good source of information, and if you do one of these hikes you are recommended to take a guide. Always carry enough food and be prepared for rain. The Café de Guías and the book by Peter Lerche will give you plenty of inspiration plus the necessary maps (IGN sheet 1358 (13-h) *Chachapoyas*).

Organised tours of the area are provided by Vilaya Tours (see listings).

From Kuelap to Choctamal 5–6 hours' walk. Follow the road behind Kuelap to the village of Choctamal. Here you can stay with a family or there is a basic hotel; local families will cook you a meal. Some *campesinos* will happily work as guides, so ask around. You will need a guide to see the many ruins in the Choctamal area; there are many small paths and getting lost is easy.

From Choctamal to the top of Mount Shubert (3,700m) 5–6 hours there and back. Follow the main trail out of the village (west) until the junction. The right-hand path goes up the mountain and the left-hand one goes up to the pass of Abra Yumal. There are some ruins on top of the mountain, but it is the view that makes the climb worthwhile. It gets cold at the top, so take a jacket, food and water.

From Choctamal to the pass of Abra Yumal (3,500m) a 2-hour climb, with good views toward Choctamal and Kuelap.

From the pass of Abra Yumal to Tribulon 4–5 hours' downhill walking through the lush, although increasingly deforested, valley. Tribulon is a small community, with friendly people. Here you can stay with a family who will supply you with basic meals and guide you around the nearby ruins. All of the ruins are hard to get to, through dense cloudforest with no paths. Don't risk going without a guide. The following are the main ruins:

- Las Pilas. A small site with an unusual water system.
- Machu Llaqta. 1½–2 hours' walk. A large and impressive site.
- Santa Cruz. 30 minutes from Machu Llaqta. These ruins are situated on top of a ridge with great views down to the valley.
- Pueblo Alto. Ruins from an unknown culture.
- Ojilcho.
- Santa María. An impressive fortress.

The return route from Tribulon to Choctamal takes 6–7 hours.

Other hikes and ruins near Chachapoyas

From the pass of Abra Yumal to Vista Hermosa 7–8 hours. A steep, difficult path through lush cloudforest. The small community of Vista Hermosa offers basic accommodation and meals with a family. Nearby are the ruins of La Plazuela, a steep climb up from Vista Hermosa, and a bit further on are the ruins of La Mesa and La Pirquilla. You also pass an impressive well-preserved Inca staircase that rivals anything in Cusco. You need a guide to visit these sites. The return to Tribulon will take 4–5 hours.

From Vista Hermosa to Chachapoyas. Allow two days for this hike. You'll be passing through the community of Shipata, where you can admire the *sarcófagas* situated on the mountain slope called Karajia, outside Shipata. Just before getting to Chachapoyas, at the village of Luya (1½ hours away from Chachpoyas by *combi*), you can hike for 1½ hours to the ruins of Wangli. Here there are impressive tombs, petroglyphs and funeral niches. Take the frequent *combis* that travel from Luya to the sister town of Lamud (10 minutes) for even more trekking opportunities (see Lamud below).

And further afield

Yalape, near Levanto César Torres Rojas, of the Instituto Nacional de la Cultura in Chachapoyas, recently supervised the clearing of these ruins. The site was probably a residential complex and includes many well-preserved examples of typical Chachapoya architecture. Some beautiful friezes have survived. This is another massive ancient city.

To get there take a truck or taxi early in the morning from Chachapoyas to Levanto, which takes about 2 hours, or – better – do it on foot, 3–4 hours along a pleasant but steep path. Take plenty of water. Leave from the plaza in Chachapoyas, down Jirón Amazonas for two blocks and then turn left down Santo Domingo. Generally speaking, for the first 2½ hours take each left fork you come to. After you cross a small field, near the end of the walk, you'll see a stone path leading off to the right. Take it and continue turning right until you arrive at Levanto. Ask for directions frequently from the *campesinos* because it is easy to get lost. Or get a guide in Chachapoyas.

Levanto is a small, friendly mountain village. Chachapoyas was actually founded here by the Spaniards in 1538, before it was moved to its present location. The town was an important Chachapoya settlement and was used by the Incas as an administrative centre. Not satisfied with proving their superiority on the battlefield, the Incas reconstructed their version of the Chachapoya roundhouse just southwest of Levanto. The site, called Colla Cruz, was reconstructed again by Morgan Davis, a Canadian architect, in the early 1990s. To see the site, follow the Chachapoyas road for 5 minutes and then take a left at the first large path (flanked by houses to the left). If in doubt, just ask for Colla Cruz. There are two new hotels styled after Chachapoya roundhouses. Prices range from US$5–10, depending on the season. You can also get accommodation with a family if you ask around, or you can camp. Basic meals are available at the small shops or with a family.

Lamud Situated 37km northwest of Chachapoyas, a 2-hour ride along a good, yet heart-stopping road. The new hotel Kuelap (US$6) is cosy and the area is rife with little-known archaeological gems. A worthwhile day hike takes you to the San Antonio *chulpas* (pre-Columbian funeral towers) some 5km from Lamud, a 45-minute walk each way. In Lamud, ask for Jose Espinoza to guide you. He's got a bit of a reputation as a grave robber but he knows the area well. Just remember that it is illegal to buy artefacts anywhere in Peru and Bolivia!

Pueblos de los Muertos North of Lamud, about a 3-hour walk from town through unusually barren pasture lands. This is an impressive site with mummy casings, caves and cliff dwellings overlooking the stunning Utcubamba River from 2,250m. Gorgeous scenery makes trudging along the narrow path worth it. Get a guide in Lamud as it is easy to get lost.

Purúnllacta This site was named Monte Peruvia by Gene Savoy. It is 40km east of Chachapoyas on the road to Mendoza, and a 2½-hour walk from any public transport. Here are hundreds of stone houses with staircases, temples and palaces. The site is pre-Inca but was probably also used by the Incas. The massive site may very well dwarf even Kuelap in size when excavation is finished. Clearing and studies are currently being done by Chachapoyas-based archaeologist Jorge Ruiz.

Puente de Conica, 8km from Purúnllacta, has some pre-Columbian burial figures in niches on the cliff side, known as the Purumachus de Aispachaca. Catch a van from Chachapoyas to Cheto and then ask for directions or take a guide. It's about a 3-hour climb up muddy trails through lush foliage to access this impressive summit city.

Hiking in the Leimebamba region

Leimebamba is a gorgeous and friendly lush Andean town blessed with a myriad of archaeological sites and hiking opportunities. The town gets its name from the Quechua term *Raymi Pampa*, Field of Festivals, after the conquering Inca army defeated the Chachapoya here during their Festival of the Sun.

Buses and trucks run to Leimebamba from Chachapoyas at noon, taking about 4 hours. The recommended hotel is Hostal Laguna de Los Condores (see listings) but there are others.

Rob Dover writes 'There are many hiking possibilities starting from Leimebamba including a well-preserved Inca trail going south. Also Leimebamba is the starting point for a trek to the Laguna de los Condores – a beautiful and mysterious lake where over a hundred mummies were found in 1997. This trek takes 8–10 hours and permission to walk there must be granted beforehand from the INC in the village.'

An impressive museum opened in 2001, 3km south of Leimebamba, to house the Laguna mummies and the more than 5,000 artefacts recovered from the site. Tucked among a verdant valley and built completely by hand, the museum is one of the prettiest in Peru. Guides are available to show you around and a US$3-per-person gratuity helps fund the ongoing studies at the museum.

There is also a 2½-hour hike from Leimebamba to the ruins of La Congona, a Chachapoya site. There are three sites here, originally on hills or mounds, two of which have now been levelled. A conical mound remains, with 30 decorated round stone houses and a watchtower. The ruins are covered in brambles and thick undergrowth, but the views are wonderful. Get clear directions before setting out from Leimebamba. Or use a guide. The trail starts next to the police station, levels out and contours the mountain before dropping down into a little valley. The ruins are above the cliff, but to reach them you have to climb the adjoining, higher hill rising above the cliff. There is no trail here; head straight up for 20 minutes. At the very top the ruins are clustered in a small area, impossible to see until you are right above them.

Leimebamba had the foresight to develop a guide co-operative a few years ago so guides are as knowledgeable as they are plentiful. They charge US$8–10 per day and can arrange horses for longer treks for US$6 per day. Nixon Rivas is a personable, oft-recommended guide around Leimebamba and even speaks a bit of English. Be advised that you need to register with the INC office and be accompanied by a guide from town on multi-day hikes (this includes the Laguna). IGN map sheet 1357 (14-h) *Leimebamba* covers this area.

From Leimebamba to Laguna de los Condores (2,800m) 8–10 hours in the dry season, not recommended when it is raining. Follow the main trail out of the village (south) through the annex of Dos de Mayo, following the short cuts towards the museum. The path follows a mule track and intersects the Leimebamba–Celendin highway before passing behind the museum. Follow the wide trail past some farms for about 45 minutes. After dropping down into lush cloudforest, you'll immediately cross a bridge and see a sharply climbing path on your left. Take it. An ascent of 700m follows before the path levels off somewhat. There is no trail to follow as you work your way southeast so a guide from Leimebamba is essential. The path alternates between steep climbs and level ground before you come to a windswept plain with gorgeous rock outcrops. Be especially careful as the path is riddled with cavities (read: holes) in the porous limestone. Keep your eyes on where you step. After 1½ hours of fending off Mother Nature's booby-traps, you're rewarded with a 700m climb of a 3,900m pass before dropping down into the stunning lush forests surrounding the lake. The descent to the lake is slippery, with exposed rocks as the only working trail. There is a lodge at the edge of the lake (US$6) where you can sleep. They can prepare food but be sure to bring at least some of your own. The next day is spent exploring the lake and overlooking cliff tombs. These are the same tombs that yielded incredible artefacts to the Peruvian archaeological team and their partners from the Discovery Channel in 1997. Staring out from the cliffs onto the remote, cloud-shrouded lake, it is easy to see why the Chachapoya chose this place to immortalise their royalty. You return to Leimebamba on the third day.

The Cordilleras Blanca, Negra and Huayhuash

This is an incredible hiking and climbing area, with fascinating flora and fauna and the remains of several pre-Inca cultures and also some Inca remains. The focal point – or rather line – of the area is the Callejón de Huaylas, the name given to the Río Santa valley, which separates the Cordillera Negra (west) from the Cordillera Blanca (east) in the department of Ancash in Peru's northern highlands. The department capital, Huaraz, is at the southern end. A paved road runs through the length of this valley, linking the villages and providing spectacular views of the Nevados Huandoy and Huascarán.

THE CORDILLERAS

There are three *cordilleras* (mountain ranges) in Ancash: the Cordillera Negra, the Cordillera Blanca and the Cordillera Huayhuash. The Cordilleras Negra and Blanca face each other across the Río Santa, and the Cordillera Huayhuash lies about 50km to the southeast of the Cordillera Blanca. All three are excellent for hiking and draw enthusiasts from all over the world.

As its name implies, the Cordillera Negra is not snow-covered (although 'black' is an exaggeration). Nevertheless it is still a good area for hiking, if only for the stunning views of the Cordilleras Blanca and Huayhuash.

The Cordilleras Blanca and Huayhuash are the highest of the country's astonishing total of 20 glaciated mountain ranges. The largest concentration of tropical-zone glaciers in the world is found in the Cordillera Blanca, including Peru's highest mountain, Huascarán, at 6,768m (22,206ft). The second highest mountain, Yerupajá (6,634m, 21,759ft), is in the Huayhuash.

The *campesinos*, who cultivate land up to about 4,000m and graze cattle and sheep almost to the snowline, are mainly *mestizos*, although they speak Quechua as their first language. The Indian culture is still alive, but less than in the Cusco area, perhaps because this was never an Inca stronghold. Not many Inca ruins of importance are found in this area, the main exception being Huánuco Viejo in the department of Huánuco, on the eastern side of the Cordillera Blanca, and not far off the road between Huaraz and Pocpa in the Cordillera Huayhuash. One of the principal Inca Trails connecting Cusco and the northern parts of the Inca Empire passes through this area. The pre-Inca site from the Chavín culture is important and warrants a visit, and archaeologists are constantly finding more pre-Inca remains throughout the Cordillera Blanca.

Cordillera Negra

Because few hikers want to spend much time in this snowless range we have given it short shrift. This doesn't mean, however, that you should not investigate the trails yourself – the best views of the whole Cordillera Blanca range are from the Cordillera Negra. It is worth exploring this range while acclimatising in Huaraz. Hikes are fairly easy, the highest pass being around 4,500m and the highest peak 5,187m (Rocarre, in the northern part of the range).

If you hike in this area be sure to carry plenty of water; there are few streams. Watch out for dogs. A few carefully aimed stones usually keep them away.

Cordillera Blanca

This is Peru's best-known mountain region. Only 100km from the Pacific Ocean, and 180km long, it provides a barrier between the desert coast and the wet Amazon basin. On the west side of the Cordillera Blanca the Río Santa drains into the Pacific, while on the east side the Río Maranon drains into the Atlantic. If you count the multi-peaked mountains, 33 peaks rise above 6,000m (19,686ft), crowned by Peru's highest peak Huascarán (6768m). The range is an important hydrological reserve, much of the extremely arid coastal area directly to the west depends on glacier meltwater, from some of its 722 glaciers, for survival. The range includes seven life zones, which gives it great biodiversity (almost 800 species of flora, 112 of birds, 10 of mammals) and over 30 pre-Inca archaeological sites have been found in the area.

The glaciers are retreating and rarely extend much below 5,000m; the valleys below are grasslands, *puna*, usually grazed by cattle. There are very few llamas in this region. As the range is quite narrow all the hiking areas are easily accessed from roads. Most hiking routes run from west to east, crossing the *cordillera* at a high pass and descending to a road. These trails were created centuries before the arrival of recreational hikers, being the main thoroughfare for the Andean inhabitants. Some of the trails have recently been made into roads for vehicular traffic.

The rural population living around the park speaks Quechua and still maintains many aspects of traditional Andean culture.

We have described the best-known hikes in the Cordillera Blanca, but of course there are plenty more. You can discover your own personal trek or even walk the complete length of the Cordillera Blanca from north to south.

Cordillera Huayhuash

This compact range is just under 30km in length from north to south, and yet it has seven peaks over 6,000m (19,686ft), the highest of which is Yerupajá at 6634m (21,759ft). Many hikers consider it even more spectacular than the Cordillera Blanca, and it is certainly more remote and challenging. The peaks all seem to have towering, vertical ice-covered faces on all sides! The major town and traditional starting point for hiking is Chiquián. (There are other options for getting into and out of the Huayhuash area.) The classic hike described here is a complete circuit of 164km around the Cordillera Huayhuash.

PARQUE NACIONAL HUASCARÁN

Huascarán National Park was established in July 1975, rewarding the efforts of Peruvian journalist and mountaineering expert Cesar Morales and Huaraz politician Augusto Guzman Robles. These men had been urging the government to declare this exceptional area a national park since 1960, but it was only after the attention of the world was drawn to the area by a catastrophic earthquake in 1970 that the authorities took notice. In 1985 UNESCO declared the park a World Natural Heritage Site.

The park includes the whole area of the Cordillera Blanca above 4,000m, with the exception of Nevado Champará at the extreme northern end of the range, and covers in total 3,400km². Conservation and sustainable development are the main goals of the park administration; it sometimes seems that development is winning, with roads being constructed through some of the most beautiful areas. Tourism is growing rapidly in Peru, especially adventure tourism, so the pressures on Huascarán National Park are ever increasing. The most popular areas for conventional tourism are the Lagunas Llanganuco and the Pachacoto Valley, where tours visit the Pastoruri Glacier. The most popular trekking route is the Santa Cruz–Huaripampa–Llanganuco circuit, and the most popular mountains to climb are Alpamayo, Huascarán and Pisco. The most important economic activities in the park and the valleys around it are agriculture and raising livestock, with mining and tourism increasing in importance.

The park office is on Av Raimondi, block 13, in the building of the Ministerio de Agricultura (tel: 044 722086), open Monday to Friday 08.00–13.00. All visitors to the park should register at one of the park offices and pay the entrance fee of US$20 per person. Unfortunately, there is still only a control (where you pay) at Llanganuco, and at the Pastoruri sector, so most visitors don't bother paying. This is a shame; the fee would – or should – help with conservation projects. Details of the Huascarán National Park Recreation and Tourism Plan are on the Mountain Forum website: mfsupport@mtnforum.org

In common with national parks throughout the world, there are regulations to stop tourists damaging the place they've come to enjoy. Sadly, these are often ignored:

* Don't leave garbage; carry it all out
* Don't make fires
* Don't harm the flora or fauna
* Don't pollute the streams and lakes
* Don't fish in the lakes during the spawning season from May to September

Even if you do not plan to go hiking, try to visit the park's most spectacular living thing: the *Puya raimondii* (see page 7). These incredible plants grow in the valley of Pachacoto, 57km south of Huaraz and in the Cordillera Negra near Caraz. You may not be lucky enough to see them in flower, but even so they are an unforgettable sight. Get transport to the village of Pachacoto (see *Getting there and away*) and hike up the valley to the park station (2½ hours). You'll find the *puyas* up the road from there, to your right. Organised day tours go to this area, and then on to the glacier of Pastoruri.

Safety

There have been some scare stories about the safety of hikers in this area. Yes, there have been robberies and even deaths, and because of the terrorist threat the Cordillera Huayhuash was closed to tourism between 1990 and 1992, with many people staying away from the Blanca as well. The danger from the Shining Path terrorists has now disappeared, which leaves only the occasional robbery to worry about. This happens from time to time on the most popular trails, but robbery can happen from time to time anywhere. Be sensitive to the attitude of the locals, ask permission to put up your tent, and if people seem hostile do not camp near their village.

HUARAZ

Situated at 3,050m (10,007ft), this thriving small town has a lovely climate and lively atmosphere. It exudes energy: there's a bustling market, some discos, and all the gringos you meet here are either planning a hike or have just returned from a hike, so it is easy to get information. There are lots of travel agencies, shops, hotels, restaurants, night-life, and all the attractions designed to persuade the visitor to stay as long as possible.

The telephone code for Huaraz is 044.

History

The problem with Huaraz is that visible historical remains keep disappearing under landslides. From time to time the water levels build up in the high mountain lakes, causing them to breach. When an avalanche lands in a lake, or rather when an earthquake dumps half the glacier there, a huge wall of water, mixed with snow, ice, mud, rocks and other matter, breaks the weak morraine wall of the lake, and flows down the mountain taking everything with it. Since 1702 there have been more than 22 catastrophic events resulting from ice avalanches in the Cordillera Blanca area. There have been three disasters this century: in 1941, an avalanche in the Cojup valley landed in Laguna Palcacocha, broke its banks, and inundated Huaraz; in 1962, a huge avalanche came down from Huascarán and destroyed the town of Ranrahirca; the most recent and worst catastrophe was in 1970, when a massive earthquake devastated much of central Peru and the town of Yungay in the Santa valley was completely buried. Evidence of this disaster is still to be seen throughout the valley.

A government organisation, INGEMMET (Instituto Geológico Minero y Metalúrgico), has been formed to control the lakes, most of which are now dammed, to try to avoid future disasters of this kind. This seems to be successful as there haven't been any destructive floods as a result of glacial lakes breakouts since the early 1970s in the Cordillera Blanca.

Getting there and away

The information below is comprehensive enough to get you from Lima to Huaraz, and to the surrounding villages and trailheads.

From Lima to Huaraz (400km)

There are no flights so bus is the only option. The journey takes 8 hours and costs US$8–12. The road is paved all the way, though landslides may be a problem. This road is used by several mining companies taking ores to Lima, so is generally kept in good condition. Recommended bus companies are Cruz del Sur and Móvil (both of which offer a normal service and a more luxurious slightly more expensive option, with no stops). Try to travel during the day, and sit on the right side of the bus, to enjoy the beautiful scenery.

From Chavín to Lima (438km)

14 hours/US$12. One or two buses daily and some trucks.

From Chiquián to Lima (353km)

10 hours/US$8. Buses leave daily, morning and night.

From the north of Peru

Huaraz may be reached from the northern coast via three routes. They are all rough and time-consuming, but the visual impact of approaching the *cordilleras* this way, particularly in an open truck, is unforgettable.

Casma to Huaraz (150km) 6–7 hours.

Chimbote – Río Santa Valley – Huallanca – Cañón del Pato – Caraz – Huaraz (185km) 10 hours (longer in the rainy season). This formerly terrible road was surfaced in 1997.

Local transport through the Río Santa valley

Colectivos run the 66km between Huaraz and Caraz daily, between 07.00 and 20.00. They leave whenever they fill up, every 15 minutes or so, from their departure point on block 1, Avenida Centenario (the main road leading out of town over the bridge). The full journey takes about two hours, but they stop at every village along the way: Monterrey (20 minutes), Marcará (45 minutes), Carhuaz (1 hour), Mancos (1½ hours) and Yungay (1½ hours).

Going south

From Huaraz to Recuay (27km) 1 hour; **on to Catac** (11km) 20 minutes; **on to Pachacoto** (9km) 15 minutes.

From Huaraz to Chiquián (111km) 3–4 hours. There are several companies running daily buses. Most of the route is now on good, tarmaced road. 'El Rápido' (tel: 044 726437) leaves from Mariscal Caceres at the back of the market. There are a couple of other companies in nearby streets. Buses usually leave at 06.00, 13.00 and 19.00. US$3 approx.

Routes to the eastern side of the Cordillera Blanca
These are all dirt roads going over the high passes of the *cordillera*. In the dry season trucks and some buses run daily. In the rainy season, road conditions are poor and there's little transport.

From Macará to Vicos (7km) 1½ hours by *colectivo*.

From Carhuaz, up the Ulta valley and down to Chacas (75km) 7 hours. Trucks daily in the morning. Occasional buses from Huaraz. The road is often closed in the rainy season.

Huaraz to Chavín (110km) 4 hours. Several buses a day. Chavin Express, Calle Mariscal Caceres goes at 07.30, 08.30, 11.00, 14.00. US$3.

From Yungay, up the Llanganuco valley and down to Yánama (58km) 4 hours. Daily vehicles at 09.00. Most transport continues on to **San Luís** (61km) 3 hours.

Huaraz to Huari (148km) 6 hours. Via Chavín.

Huaraz to Piscobamba (157km) 8–9 hours. Buses at 06.30. Transportes Los Andes from Calle 13 de Diciembre 201. US$5.

Piscobamba to Pomabamba 1 hour. Los Andes buses leave from Huaraz, 13 Diciembre 201.

There are also frequent minibuses from Yungay that run to the **Lakes of Llanganuco** in the tourist season; 1½ hours.

From Caraz to Cashapampa (22km) 2–3 hours. Daily trucks (mornings).

From Huaraz to Pitec Pick-ups leave from the corner of Calle Caraz and Calle Comercio, daily, whenever they fill up (about every 30 minutes), between 06.00 and 18.00. They go as far as **Llupa**; 40 minutes. Ask the driver to drop you off at the footpath up to Pitec. From there it's a 1½-hour walk to Pitec.

From Huaraz to Olleros (7km before Recuay) Either get off at the junction on the main road and walk the 2km up a dirt road, or catch a truck from Calle Frigorífico in Huaraz, going all the way to Olleros, 29km. 45 minutes.

From Catac to Chavín (98km) 3½ hours. Buses and trucks daily. **On to Huari** (38km) 2 hours, and **on to San Luís** (61km) 3 hours. Several trucks and buses a day serve this route.

From Huaraz to Huallanca (140km) 4 hours. Daily buses do this route (depart 06.00), bus companies in Mariscal Caceres. From here there is transport on to La Unión (1 hour) and Huánuco (4 hours).

Sleeping and eating
Accommodation
The following are cheap, backpackers' places, all for about US$5–8 per person. It is definitely worth booking in advance if you are in Huaraz during July and August.

Alojamiento Soledad Jr Amadeo Figueroa 1267, Huaraz; tel: 044 721196; email: ghsoledad@hotmail.com

El Albergue de Casa de Guias Parque Ginebra; tel: 044 721811. Small dorm rooms, above the Casa de Guias. Café downstairs.

Galaxia Jr de la Cruz 638; tel: 044 722230. Popular with climbers and trekkers, can provide information and also has an equipment-rental shop.

Hostal Churup Pedro Campos 735, directly below the Iglesia Soledad; tel: 044 722584; email: churup@hotmail.com. From US$4 per person per night. Welcoming, lively place, informative, and recently very popular, 15 minutes' walk from centre.

La Casa de Zarela Julio Arguedas 1263, Soledad; tel: 044 721694; email: zarelaz@hotmail.com. Popular with climbers and trekkers, private house, plenty of information available.

La Quintana Jr Mariscal Caceres 411. Just off the main street. From US$4 per person.

Mi Casa 27 de Noviembre 733; tel: 044 723375; email: bmark@ddm.com.pe. Family-run guesthouse in the centre of town.

Olazo's Guest House Julio Arguedas 1246, Soledad; tel: 044 722951; email: info@andeanexplorer.com. Family house in a safe, residential area.

A little more comfortable, about US$10–12 per person, with private bathroom:

Edward's Inn Calle Bolognesi 121; tel: 044 722692. From US$10 per person, 15 minutes' walk from the centre. Helpful with information, and also organise treks and climbs.

Hostal Montañero Parque Ginebra (next to Casa de Guías); tel: 044 721811

Hostal Yanett Av Centenario 106; tel: 044 721466

And as a treat:

Casablanca Hotel Av Tarapaca 138; tel: 044 722602; email: cashotel@telematic.edu.pe. Central, clean and comfortable. Also organises treks. From US$30 a double.

El Patio On the main road in Monterrey; tel: 01 437 6567. Bungalows. Double about US$50.

Hotel Andino Pedro Cochachin 357; tel: 721662. Terrific ambience and service. US$50–90 per person, depending on the room.

Hotel Colomba Jr Francisco de Zela 278; tel: 044 721501/721241; fax: 044 721501; email: colomba@terra.com.pe; web: www.bed42.com/hotelcolomba/. US$30–40. A characterful *hacienda* with accommodation in bungalows, a large garden full of plants, 15 minutes' walk from the centre.

Hotel Real. Tel: 044 721717. A few kilometres out of town, next to the (public) hot thermal baths. An old and characterful hotel with all comforts. Double about US$40.

Restaurants

There are dozens of restaurants in Huaraz. For those whose stomachs have already adapted to local food, check out the market for variety and excellent value (06.00–18.00 upstairs). There are many restaurants in the streets near the market offering great value.

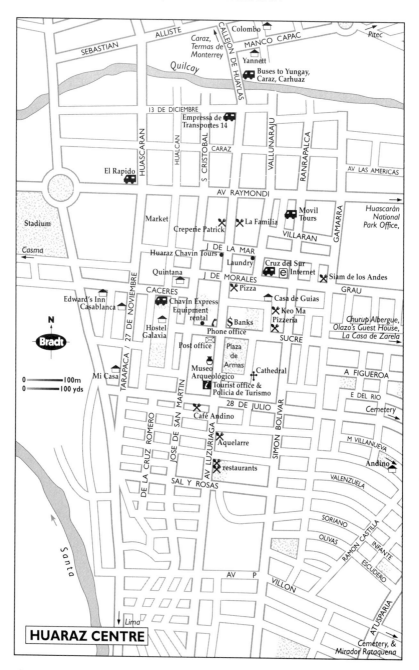

HUARAZ CENTRE

Brasa Roja On Luzuriaga, two blocks south of the Plaza de Armas. Deservedly one of the most popular restaurants in Huaraz, with locals and tourists alike. Basically chicken and chips, but of good quality and with plenty of other options.

Restaurant Pizzeria Luzuriaga 672, upstairs. A variety of excellent veggie dishes and pizzas.

El Encuentro On the corner of Gamara and 28 de Julio. A good quality, friendly, fun place.

Chifa Min Hua Av Luzuriaga 424b. Great Chinese food, cheap and lavish helpings.

Sala de Kushuru Simón Bolívar 926. Serves real local specialities such as *kushuru* (algaes), *ceviche de chocho* (lupin seeds) and *cuy* (guinea pig).

There are several tourist restaurants if you feel like some more upmarket food. Most are whole or part owned by expats:

Bistro de Los Andes Julian de Morales 823. Serves an excellent vegetable stir-fry, also steaks and pastas. One of the less expensive, and very tasty, tourist places.

Siam de Los Andes On the corner of Jr Julian de Morales and Av Gamarra. A Thai restaurant operated by climber/cook Naresuan. Great food but not cheap.

Crêperie Patrick Av Luzuriaga 424. French cuisine with good crêpes and desserts. Moderate to expensive prices.

Monta Rosa Av La Mar, block 6. A good pizzeria, with moderate to expensive prices. Great coffee, and also has a small mountaineering shop.

Casa de Guías Parque Ginebra. Does good muesli, yoghurt, pizzas, soups and salads at moderate prices. Open for breakfast and dinner.

Campo Base Av Luzuriaga 407. Serves good gringo food at a reasonable price.

Cafés and entertainment

Café Andino Jr 28 de Julio 562. Offers good coffee, good chat, and a book exchange.

Keo Ma A pastry and bread shop opposite Casa de Guias, with good coffee and very tempting cakes.

El Tambo Calle La Mar, block 7. A popular gringo disco, busy towards the end of the week, which sometimes has folk groups and dancers.

Amadeus Parque Ginebra. A local disco.

Las Kenas Pub Jr Gabino Uribe (off block 9 of Luzuriaga). A popular local and gringo disco.

Useful addresses

Tourist police Just off the Plaza de Armas, in Pasaje Tiburios. Open 08.00–13.00 and 16.00–19.00 daily. Friendly and helpful. Some English spoken. Contact them if you are robbed or in the event of an accident in the mountains. When closed go to PNP Police on Calle Sucre, block 5 (off Luzuriaga, opposite Plaza de Armas).

Museo Archaeológico Just off the Plaza de Armas, is also the Oficina de Turismo Cultural. Open Monday to Friday until 18.00, and Saturday morning. Friendly staff and helpful information on conventional tours, and Huaraz. Some books and maps are available here and the museum is worth a visit. It has a collection of videos, including a harrowing one of the 1970s' earthquake.

Spanish School Sierra Verde Lucar y Torre 538; tel: 044 721203; email: svlc@qnet.com.pe

Communications
Telefónica Block 6 of Av Luzuriaga. Telephone and internet.

There is a profusion of internet offices. Try in Parque Ginebra near Casa de Guias, or along Av Luzuriaga.

Tour operators
The reliable ones have been there for years; others come and go. Recommended tour companies include:

Casa de Guias Parque Ginebra. See below.
Chavín Tours/Trek Andes Av Luzuriaga 502; tel: 01 442 1514 (Lima), 044 721578 (Huaraz); email: chavin@telematic.edu.pe
Montañero Andean Experience Parque Ginebra 30-B, Huaraz; tel: 044 726386; email: andeway@terra.com.pe; web: www.trekkingperu.com
Milla Tours Av Luzuriaga 528; tel: 044 721742
Pablo Tours Av Luzuriaga 501; tel: 044 721145
Pyramid Adventures Av Luzuriaga 530; tel: 044 721864; fax: 044 722525. Works with UK and US tour operators.
Santa Cruz Expeditions Contact Hernando Oropeza through the Casa de Guias or tel (mobile): 49 487428; email: info@santacruzexpeditions.com; web: www.santacruzexpeditions.com. Extensive range of mountaineering equipment for rent and some for sale. Also operate climbing trips , and treks.
Sky Line Adventures San Martin 637; tel: 044 682774; email: skylineadventures@hotmail.com. US-run agency. Free coffee while you discuss trekking, climbing or snow-school options.

Day tours to Chavin, Pastorori and Llanganuco are recommended if you're short of time. Day tours can be cancelled if not enough people sign up, which is sometimes the case out of the main season. It is recommended that you use responsible operators, such as those mentioned above. They are definitely more reliable than some of the many cowboy operators that have proliferated in the last few years.

Casa de Guías
Parque Ginebra 28-G; tel/fax: 044 721811. Open 09.00–13.00, 16.00–20.00. Home to the Peruvian Mountain Guide Association. This is the best place in Huaraz for information on trekking and climbing, local or private transportation, prices, guides, cooks, porters, *arrieros* and mules. They can also advise you on organised trips, weather conditions, and a place to meet up with other hikers. They have a hostel, a rescue team and their qualified mountain and trekking guides are registered members of the association. They have a small library of hiking books for reference, and some books and maps for sale. Don't head for the mountains without visiting them.

OUTSIDE HUARAZ
Callejón de Huaylas
There are several villages in the Santa valley, which offer a good alternative to staying in Huaraz. The villages are the access points for many of the treks described below, and you will find them friendly places with lively markets and less used to gringos than Huaraz.

Carhuaz
La Casa de Poncha is on the road to Hualcan, US$18 including meals, organic farm produce; **Hostal La Merced** is on the Plaza (singles about US$6); and **Hostal Residencial Carhuaz**.

Yungay
Hostal Gledel is along the main road. A friendly, family-run place. Singles about US$8.

Caraz
Caraz is about 67km north of Huaraz. At an altitude much lower than Huaraz, this pleasant, untouristy town has a warm climate and welcoming atmosphere. There are plenty of really nice places to stay and some good options for day trips as well as easy access to Cashapampa and Hualcayan for trekking.

There are daily buses/pick-up trucks from the market mid-morning to Cashapampa and Hualcayan.

Day walks or mountain biking in the Cordillera Negra
There are several possibilities, all of which will give great views across to the highest peaks in the Blanca. One of the best is to visit the Puya Raimondi in the Winchus sector. Ask locally for details. Take a *colectivo* to Pamparomas and get off at the Pass of Winchus (42km from Caraz) or take a guided day tour with one of the local agencies (see listings). From the pass you can see the Pacific Ocean to the west and about 140km of Cordillera Blanca to the east, and spread below you Caraz and its surrounding colourful fields and the River Santa. From the pass it is a 3km walk to see *Puyas*. Take a *colectivo* back to Caraz.

While waiting for an ill friend to recover enough to set off on a trek I found a walk straight out of town up the hillside on the east, towards a large antenna. The views are spectacular, but few gringos walk here and the locals are happy to stop and chat. Once high up the hillside follow a clear path in a southerly direction. The path descends to the valley again after a few kilometres, from where you can take a *colectivo* back to Caraz.

Also recommended is the quiet and interesting hike Pueblo Libre to Caraz, which has plenty of cacti and great views over the Cordillera Blanca. It is approximately 9km, 3–4 hrs, with a short climb of some 200m.

Sleeping and eating
The better places to stay are:

La Alameda Av Noe Bazan Peralta 262 (at the junction with Jr Sucre); tel: 044 791177; email: laalameda@huarazonline.zzn.com. New rooms with private bath and TV. US$12, more basic rooms from US$2. Includes breakfast. Run by three pleasant elderly spinster sisters.

Los Pinos Lodge & Camping On Plaza San Martin (on Jr Daniel Vilar, 6 blocks from main square); tel: 044 791130; email: apuaventura@terra.com.pe. Old casona, with a variety of rooms or camping. Great location on a quiet square with views. The owner Luis (a former Inca Trail guide from Caraz) has also opened the agency **Apu Aventura** (tel: 044 792159) next to Banco de Credito on Vilar.

Pony's Lodge and **Pony's Expeditions** Jr Sucre 1266, Plaza de Armas; tel/fax: 044 791642; email: ponyexp@terra.com.pe; web: www.ponyexpeditions.com. Rooms from US$9 per person. Lots of information available; food served from 08.30. Run by outdoor enthusiast Alberto Cafferata. Organises trekking, climbing and mountain biking. Camping gear for rent.

Perla de Los Andes Plaza de Armas; tel: 044 792007. From US$8 per person. New and clean.

Alojamiento Caballero Jr Daniel Villar 485; tel: 044 791637. From US$4 per bed, shared bathroom with hot shower. Laundry facilities, tourist information.

Restaurants

Restaurant Esmeralda Jr Alfonso Ugarte, right behind the church. Serves good *comida criolla*, and a great-value set meal.

Cafe de Rat Pizzeria Jr Sucre 1266, Plaza de Armas (upstairs). Breakfast, muesli, salads, vegetarian food, pizza and pasta, book exchange, dart board.

HIKING
Weather

Although the dry/wet season pattern is more reliable than the weather in temperate climates, you should not be surprised to have rain, hail or snow in the dry season (mid June to mid September), nor some bright, clear weather in the rainy season (early October to late May). Bear in mind that in bad weather it is unrewarding and even dangerous crossing the high passes, which will be cloud-covered, and you may get caught in a blizzard. Even in the dry season always carry good quality, waterproof camping equipment, warm and waterproof clothing and extra food just in case you need to wait out the bad weather somewhere in the mountains.

Acclimatisation

Read the discussion on this subject in the Health section in *Chapter 3*, and spend at least two or three days in Huaraz before doing any hiking trips, then do a few practice day hikes.

Guides

There is no shortage of guides in Huaraz, but only a few are really experienced and reliable. The Casa de Guías will advise you; they have a list of all the qualified guides. It is also worth getting recommendations from other hikers. In the high season there is a set price of US$50 per day for one to three people for trekking guides, or US$60 per day for a group of four or more. In the low season prices are slightly lower. It is normal practice to write up a contract between yourself and your guide. However, you do not need a guide for the hikes described in this chapter. If you decide to attempt the trekking peak of Pisco you will definitely need a guide unless you are an experienced mountaineer. In general the trails are clear, and if you do get lost it's no great disaster assuming you are carrying sufficient food. You are not lost, you are exploring, and after a while you'll meet a *campesino* who will put you right. Nevertheless, you should carry – and know how to use – a topographical map.

Arrieros **and their animals, porters and cooks**

Many hikers use mules or *burros* (donkeys) to carry their camping equipment and food. The advantages are great; you can walk with just a day-pack (which you will appreciate on those long uphill stretches to the passes), and you can take more food and clothing, both of which help considerably with the strenuous days and cold nights. A good *arriero* knows the route and the possible variations, and thus serves as a guide. He will also help bridge the gap with local people that you meet along the way, help you buy food where possible, even fish for you, and could be invaluable in the case of an emergency. *Arrieros* are ideal for groups, who can get one or two animals to carry the heavier stuff. *Burros* and mules may only be hired with their owners, the *arrieros*, who lie in wait for hikers at the trailheads, so don't worry about finding one before you leave Huaraz. The *arrieros* have organised themselves into an association, and the prices are set: at the time of writing an *arriero* costs US$10 per day and a *burro* US$5 per day. A horse costs US$7. Plus you are responsible for providing all meals for the *arrieros* and their helpers, and should check that they have shelter for the nights, otherwise you may need to provide that as well. Settle all conditions beforehand (in writing if both you and they can read/write Spanish) and pay half at the start of the trip and the other half at the end. If you are planning on going above the snow line or on some of the treks where passes are too rocky for donkeys you may need to hire porters. Porters and cooks in this area generally charge US$15–25 per day.

Entrance to the valleys

Most of the valleys where the trails start have locked gates at their entrances. This is to stop thieves from stealing the animals that graze in the valleys. The *campesinos* who own the animals and usually farm the land at the foot of the trails operate a toll system for hikers with *burros*. You have to pay for the gate at the start of the trail to be opened; and, if returning the same way, you will have to pay to exit. If you have an *arriero* with you he will deal with this. Make sure you discuss this in advance as gatekeepers may need advising of your plans ahead of time. The fee is expensive – from US$5 to US$15 – but does not apply to backpackers who can climb over the gate. For further information check at the Casa de Guías.

Renting equipment

All trekking, climbing and general camping equipment – boots, clothing, tents, stoves, ropes, ice-axes, helmets, crampons etc – can be rented in Huaraz, at reasonable prices, eg: sleeping bag US$2–3 per day, stove US$1.5–2 per day. There is an increasing number of hire shops in Huaraz, and fortunately there seems to be increasingly better quality equipment around. However, during peak season demand is high and you may not find any equipment of good quality. Most is the discarded gear of other hikers, so if you are planning a long trip, it's still preferable to bring everything you need from home.

The best rental places are: Mountclimb on Avelino Caceres; Montañero, Plaza Ginebra; MonTrek, Av Luzuriaga 640; and Santa Cruz Expeditions (see page 154).

Food and supplies

Huaraz is the best place to buy food for your trip. In the smaller towns in the valley you can get fresh food from the market, but the choice is limited. Up in the mountains, you might be lucky to find a *señora* who wants to cook a meal for you, or you might find very basic food at some tiny shop. You cannot rely on this, however – mostly the *campesinos* have barely enough to feed themselves – so bring enough for the whole trip, plus some extra. The market in Huaraz has a good selection of trail food, and on the corner of Avenida Luzuriaga and Calle Raimondi there is a pretty good supermarket.

The local fuel is what Americans call white gas, and Brits know as stove alcohol. This *bencina* may not be top quality, but it burns and is widely available in hardware stores and pharmacies for about US$1.5 per litre. Kerosene/paraffin (*kerosina*) is sold at the petrol/gas stations and hardware stores. And the butane canisters (Camping Gaz) are widely available, though not cheap, at some equipment-rental places and travel agencies.

Maps

You are advised to take a map if you are hiking independently. Fortunately there is a good selection.

Cordilleras Blanca y Huayhuash by Felipe Diaz is readily available in Lima and Huaraz (US$5). This useful map shows the routes and roads in the valleys, giving you an overview of the whole area with enough information for the popular hiking trails.

Topographical maps of the Cordilleras Blanca, Negra and Huayhuash, at a scale of 1:100,000, are published by the Instituto Geográfico Nacional (IGN), but the full range of these is only available in Lima (US$6 each, payable in local currency). They are useful and interesting, but only really necessary if you are finding your own route. The entire Cordillera Blanca is published in six sheets (so you need to have decided beforehand which areas you are visiting) and the Cordillera Huayhuash in two. The Austrian Alpine Club published a new edition of their Cordillera Blanca North map in 2000. This is now available in shops in Huaraz for $12. When planning a new route bear in mind that the glaciers have receded a lot since the area was surveyed.

The South American Explorers has published some useful black-and-white maps of the most popular treks: Llanganuco to Santa Cruz, Honda Valley, and Huayhuash. These cost US$2 or so – much cheaper than the US$6 needed for the IGN maps.

The Parque Nacional Huascarán is planning to publish a series of 24 maps covering trekking and climbing routes.

Perú Trek (Av Luzuriaga 504) has produced a large map of the whole Cordillera Blanca and another of the Huayhuash. This is a good overall map, but it does not show contours in detail. This map is for sale at their office or the Casa de Guías.

HIKING ROUTES IN THE CORDILLERA BLANCA

The following hikes have been selected for their views, their variety, or because they are relatively easy. We begin with an acclimatisation hike near Huaraz, and then describe the longer treks beginning at the northern end of the range and working south:

* A day-hike outside Huaraz
* Los Cedros: Hualcayan or Cashapampa to Pomabamba or Vaquería
* The Santa Cruz Trek: Cashapampa to Vaquería or Colcabamba
* The Lagunas Llanganuco and Laguna 69
* Pisco
* Quebrada Ulta to Colcabamba
* Quebrada Honda to Chacas
* Huari to Chacas
* Quebrada Ishinca
* Quebradas Churup, Shallap, Rajucolta and Quilcayhuanca
* Pitec to Collón via Quebrada Cojup and Quebrada Ishinca
* Olleros to Chavín.

A day hike outside Huaraz

This is an easy hike outside Huaraz, so ideal for acclimatisation and to enjoy the views of the city, and the Cordilleras Blanca and Negra. However, there have been many instances of armed robbery on the hill so try to get local reassurance before doing this beautiful walk.

Distance	6km
Altitude	Between 3,150m and 3,650m
Rating	Easy
Timing	3–4 hours
In reverse	Possible
Start of trail	Plaza de Armas in Huaraz
Map	IGN sheet *Huaraz* (20-h)

Route description Head south from the Plaza de Armas on Avenida Luzuriaga until the intersection with Avenida Villón. Turn left and walk up Avenida Villón until the cemetery, then right and left again and follow the obvious dirt road uphill then curving to the right. Follow this road all the way to the pass, taking short cuts where possible. The road drops into the valley on the other side of the pass, with some spectacular views. Stay on this side of the valley, following the footpath which goes along the mountain ridge and finally drops down in the direction of Huaraz again. The path meets up with the start of the trail at the cemetery.

Los Cedros: Cashapampa to Pomabamba or Vaquería

This is one of the toughest and longest hikes of the Cordillera Blanca, so don't attempt it unless you are fit and properly acclimatised. There is no escape route once you are over the first passes, so altitude sickness would be serious. The rewards are awesome scenery, varied hiking conditions and a great feeling of accomplishment.

Distance	About 83km
Altitude	Between 2,800m and 4,850m
Rating	Difficult, only for the well-acclimatised hiker
Timing	6–10 days (depending on side treks)
In reverse	Possible
Start of trail	Cashapampa at 2,900m; transport available early morning from Caraz. Or Hualcayan, daily transport from Caraz.
Maps	IGN sheets *Corongo* (18-h) and *Pomabamba* (18-1) or *Cordillera Blanca Nord Alpenvereinskart.*

Route description The starting point of Cashapampa has a small shop. *Arrieros* and *burros* are available for hire if you want to take the donkey-work out of the long trudge up to the pass. The first destination is Cholín, an old *hacienda* just before Hualcayan, 8km north of Cashapampa. There is a small shop here, which sometimes sells bread. Many paths lead in that direction, so check with the locals to find the main trail. Follow it for 3–4km, passing the Baños de Huancarhuas (disappointingly more like a footbath). From here the trail continues to Cholín, 2,850m. Camping spots are available, with a good water supply nearby, although it is hard to find a level area. Ask permission to camp in this area. This is the last place with water for 12km. Beware of the dogs!

Note If you take transport from Caraz direct to Hualcayan, 3,100m, this will shorten your trek by 8km. *Arrieros* and donkeys or horses are usually available for hire. From Hualcayan take the path that heads straight out of the village up the hillside.

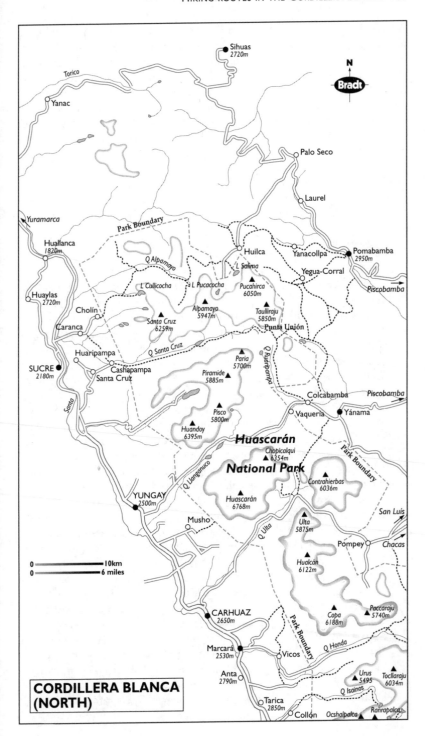

CORDILLERA BLANCA (NORTH)

After Cholín, the long, hard climb to Laguna Cullicocha begins, with an altitude gain of about 1,800m (5,904ft)! This will take 5 or 6 hours. There is good camping before you begin this climb. Follow the red dirt trail that climbs steeply north from Cholín to the top of the Inca terraces. After passing through a flat area you'll come to the start of a long series of switchbacks, which you'll think will never end. The trail crosses the remains of a 1970 earthquake landslide, then climbs slowly past two dry (most of the time) creeks, and comes to a meadow atop a little hill. This is a possible camping place, with great views. A newly constructed canal provides water. It is another 7km of moderate climbing to Laguna Cullicocha. Continue up the switchbacks, passing a creek, before the trail goes up a ridge where you get the first glimpses of the *nevados* (snowfields). The trail climbs to the right and comes to a fork. Here you're at about 4,450m and 14.5km from Cholín.

HIGH ALTITUDE TREKKING
Dr Chris Fenn

People live in an astonishing range of environments, where external temperatures may be tropical or below freezing. Our bodies make the appropriate adjustment so that we are able to maintain an internal temperature that only fluctuates by a few degrees. An altitude of 5,820m (19,094ft) seems to be the limit at which humans can live for any length of time. The guardians of the Aucanquilcha mine in northern Chile work at an altitude of 5,985m (19,636ft), but return to slightly lower levels to live. It is, of course, possible to climb higher, but your body cannot sustain the changes it needs to make in order to survive. Although we can cope with the intense cold, it is the thin air at high altitudes that we cannot cope with. It forces our lungs to fight for oxygen. It is not the amount of oxygen that changes as you go higher, it is the pressure at which the oxygen molecules are forced into your lungs. At sea level the atmospheric pressure is 1 atm. Take a hike up to 5,500m (18,045ft) and the atmospheric pressure is about 50% less. Essentially the air has fewer particles per cubic inch or, in scientific terms, has a lower density at higher altitudes. With less oxygen being forced into your lungs, your body sets about making a few adjustments that will improve this situation. Firstly, the sensors in your neck detect the reduced oxygen level in the blood and stimulate an increase in breathing rate. This is noticeable at altitudes above 3,500m (11,483ft), but is only a short term measure to ensure that the body is supplied with enough oxygen – it can't be kept up for long. Anyone who climbs above 8,000m is able to survive the summit attempt by hyperventilating. The highest breathing rates ever recorded were in climbers on Mount Everest, at 6,340m (20,800ft). Their average respiratory rate was 62 breaths per minute, which has the effect of shifting 207 litres of air every minute. Imagine their rate of breathing

The trail to the left goes to Laguna Cullicocha (called Laguna Atuncocha on the IGN map) and the one straight ahead to Laguna Yuraccocha, at the foot of *nevado* Santa Cruz. There is an ElectroPeru hut nearby. If you need shelter for the night ask the guardian if you can sleep there. If you want to take a side trip to Laguna Yuraccocha, it is 9km with little change in altitude.

The trail to Laguna Cullicocha continues climbing to 4,650m, about 3.5km from the trail fork. There is another, higher, lake, Rajucocha, but it is difficult to reach. The best campsites are found at the little Laguna Azulcocha, just north of the outlet from Laguna Cullicocha.

Now head towards Alpamayo. The trail starts about 40m below Laguna Cullicocha, crosses some granite rock, and climbs up to the pass of Osoruri (4860m) and then a second pass, Los Cedros at 4,800m, about 3km from the lake. You can camp between the first and second pass – there is water here.

on the summit at 8,796m (29,028ft)! This puts a heavy burden on the intercostal muscles (found between your ribs), and working these muscles just to keep breathing at high altitude accounts for 10% of the oxygen you need – simply at rest.

In order to make use of every precious molecule of oxygen that comes into the body, polycythemia (marginally easier to spell than pronounce!) also occurs. This is the increase in red blood cell manufacture and is considered to be one of the classic and most rapid responses when you take your body trekking in thin air. With a greater number of red blood cells, the oxygen-carrying capacity of the blood is improved. However, so is the stickiness of the blood and its tendency to clot, so if you have a history of heart disease or stroke, it may be wise to enjoy trekking at sea level.

Despite these efforts by the body to supply the blood with enough oxygen, the brain and central nervous system are particularly sensitive to a reduced oxygen supply and don't function quite as well as usual. At extreme altitude (5,500m, 18,054ft), climbers complain of strange goings on in terms of hallucinations, tunnel vision, lack of co-ordination, memory loss and mood swings. Even simple tasks, like tying your boot laces, need far more attention and concentration than usual.

A lack of oxygen to the brain also affects co-ordination and balance. Trying to walk, heel to toe, along an imaginary straight line is one of the tests for acute mountain sickness. If you sway off your path your brain and body are struggling to adapt to the high altitude environment. This activity may look amusing, but suggests you have acute mountain sickness (AMS), not much fun. Surprisingly little is known about why some people suffer from mountain sickness and others don't. Even within the same person, there is a variation with repeated exposure to altitude.

The symptoms of AMS and treatment are covered in *Chapter 3*.

FARMING IN THE CORDILLERAS
Roberto Arévalo

In the Cordilleras Blanca and Huayhuash the pastures are administered by local communities, principally for the grazing of animals: cattle, sheep, donkeys, mules and horses, in order of importance. Grazing is extensive; a rotation system is practised whereby during the rainy season (January to April) animals are moved to lower pastures, and during the dry season (May to November) they are grazed in higher areas. This allows the grass to rejuvenate and maintains the quality of grazing. While the animals are being grazed on higher ground, some of the villagers will move up with them and spend several weeks at higher altitudes watching over the animals. They will usually stay in simple stone houses with ichu roofs, known as *tambos*.

Ecologically the high forests and scrublands help to collect and store the water from rainfall and glacier melt water, as well as conserving the soil, and inhibiting erosion. In the dry season, the stored water is of vital importance for the lower regions, for agriculture and for village water supplies.

The biggest problem faced in the *Cordilleras* in terms of conservation of grass and shrub lands is overgrazing and burning by local farmers. The *ichu* grass is burned every few years to stimulate new growth and produce a softer plant for livestock to eat. Burning has a high impact on all the plants in the vicinity, decreasing the amount of seeds available, and reducing the fertility of the soil, often destroying trees and shrubs, thereby preventing forest regeneration. Overgrazing prevents adequate plant re-growth leaving soil exposed to erosion.

From the pass a long descent begins into the Quebrada de los Cedros via a series of switchbacks. Near the bottom the trail forks. The trail to the left continues down to the hamlet of Alpamayo, and the main trail (yours) to the right crosses a stream and descends to the east to meet the river where there are some indeterminate ruins and terraces. Quebrada de Los Cedros is at 4,000m, 10km from the pass. There are lots of good camping spots here, but it's best to move on up the Quebrada Alpamayo to Lake Jancarurish for the superb views of Nevado Alpamayo. This pyramid-shaped mountain was voted the most beautiful mountain in the world by a German climbing club back in 1966.

If you are still full of boundless energy you can make a side trip from here. It is a 10.5km climb of about 500m from the valley to the base camp used by climbers of Alpamayo (5,947m) and Santa Cruz (6,259m).

The regular trail continues to the pass of Safuna – also known as Caracara – (4,830m), crossing the streams below Laguna Jancarurish, and climbing north to the right of two creeks to some small lakes. Continue up the slopes of loose rock towards the pass (on the right side of the crag at the top). The trail is faint until higher up on the moraine. Take great care in bad weather

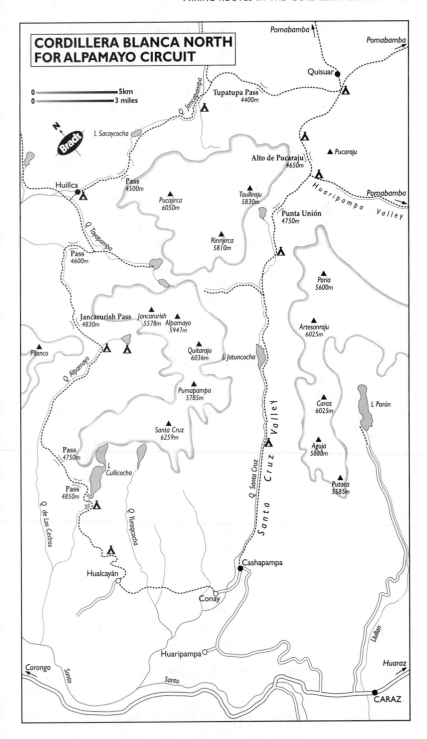

when it may be difficult to find this route. In good weather the views behind are inspiring, looking over the moraines to the immense glaciers and peaks of Alpamayo, Jancarurish (5,578m), Quitaraju (6,036m), Pumapampa (5,785m) and Santa Cruz.

From the pass it's a steep descent into Quebrada Mayobamba, but on a much better trail. This is a beautiful *quebrada* (canyon), reminiscent of Scotland, with many good camping spots.

Continue towards a ridge on the east side of the valley. A faint path goes to the top of the ridge at a small pass (4,600m) then descends into Quebrada Tayapampa. You can turn right (south) here if you want to take a side trip to the Lagunas Safuna just below the multi-peaked Nevado Pucahirca (6,040m is the highest) on the far side of the valley. Laguna Baja lies at 4,250m with good campsites. Laguna Alta is 1km further on and has no campsite.

From here you can walk 5.5km to Laguna Pucacocha, which lies at 4,500m. To reach it take the trail that leads to the middle of the canyon, passes tiny Laguna Kaiko, and comes to a crude cabin above Laguna Pucacocha. Above the next moraine you find Laguna Quitaracsa, directly below Nevado Alpamayo.

From Laguna Safuna, the trail follows Quebrada Tayapampa to the small community (2 hours!) of Huilca at 4,000m. It's about 5.5km from the lake. If you camp here keep an eye on your belongings.

To Pomabamba

Now there are two possible routes to Pomabamba. The first is via the village of Laurel. Follow the road, with several short cuts, along the Río Collota down to the valley which runs to the northeast of the village. It's about 3km. From here the road climbs up to a small pass at 4,300m. Coming down the other side you'll see some small lakes, about 12km from the Río Collota valley. At this point the road and the trail separate. The road continues to Palo Seco and the trail goes southeast to Laurel. The trail descends about 6km through a narrow valley to Laurel at 3,500m. From Laurel you can find buses to Pomabamba, or continue to the north and return to Huaraz via the Cañón del Pato.

The second choice is longer, via Yanacollpa, but goes direct to Pomabamba. The trail climbs steeply from Huilca, heading northeast, to the first pass at 4,280m. You'll see Laguna Shuitococha ahead. The trail continues east to the second pass at 4,350m. It's about 6.5km from Huilca. From here it drops down into Quebrada Yanacollpa, passing a few small lakes. Here you are faced with another choice of two routes. If you decide to go to the village of Yanacollpa, continue down through the meadows to the stream. Follow this on its left bank until a bridge where you can cross the stream, and descend to Yanacollpa (3,700m). It's about 8km from the pass. To continue to Pomabamba you then drop down to the river and look out for an irrigation canal. Follow this all the way (about 2hrs) to the well-used track which leads to Pomabamba. The distance from Yanacollpa to Pomabamba is about 12km.

The alternative route from the small lakes is via Quebrada Jancapampa. At the small lakes you can see a path going up the slopes to the south; follow it until the pass at 4,350m, from where it goes steeply downhill on a faint path

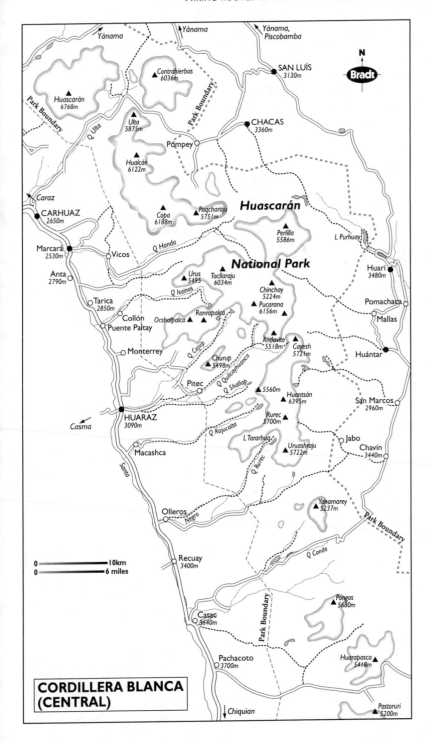

CORDILLERA BLANCA (CENTRAL)

until the upper end of Quebrada Jancapampa, just below the Nevados Taulliraju and Pucajirca. From here it's an easy descent (10–12km) over the meadows to the start of the *quebrada*, following an aqueduct. Continue down to the Río Shiulla and thence to Pomabamba.

Pomabamba is a nice little town with friendly people. You can stock up on some supplies here, find accommodation, and give yourself a good feed in one of the basic restaurants before returning to Huaraz by bus.

To Vaquería

The trail heads southeast from Huilca, a steep climb taking you to the next pass at 4,600m, from where you look down over wooded slopes of *quenual* forests to the picturesque Laguna Sactaycocha far below. Pucajirca towers above the pass. A beautiful long descent brings you to the vast flat open valley of Jancapampa (3,500m) at the foot of Taulliraju (5,830m) and Rinrijirca (5,810m). There are plenty of camping places in this dramatic spot, glaciers above, waterfalls cascading to the valley and farming communities dotted around the slopes below. The following day cross the broad grassy *pampa* (meadow) heading south, towards the houses of Pishgopampa on the far side of the valley. From here continue to climb out of the valley, heading southwards, towards the pass of Tupatupa (4,400m), one of the most stunning viewpoints on the trek. The Cordillera Blanca spreads out before you. The views stay with you as you descend to the village of Quisuar (3,800m), a good camping spot for the night.

From Quisuar head west, a gentle start up the valley towards the Pucaraju pass. Leave Lake Huecrococha to your left. The climb steepens considerably as you near the pass at 4,650m, but the spectacular panorama of snow-capped peaks spread before you, makes all that climbing worthwhile. There may even be condors soaring in the Quebrada Huaripampa below. The jagged top of Taulliraju (5,830m) is impressive to the west. Ahead of you both peaks of Huascarán fill the view. From here it's all downhill. Carefully descend the steep and loose zigzag path to join the Huaripampa valley. There are camping places in the valley bottom at Tuctubamba (3,800m). The final day is a gentle stroll down the valley to the road at Vaquería.

The Santa Cruz Trek

This is the classic trek of the Cordillera Blanca and the most popular – deservedly so, but it does become very crowded in the peak season. An idea of just how crowded is given by the number of *arrieros* currently working out of Cashapampa: well over 70. Nevertheless, nothing can diminish the impact of the spectacular views as, following the route clockwise as described here, you hike gently up Quebrada Santa Cruz where giant, snow-covered peaks tower above you on both sides of the valley.

Opinion is divided on which is the best direction to do this hike. Starting in Cashapampa gives you the gradual acclimatising ascent on the first day which suits unfit trekkers. Backpackers using public transport may, however, prefer the counterclockwise direction because there is a daily bus from Huaraz to Vaquería that allows sufficient time to walk to the campsite on the first day, thus giving you a good start on the high pass the following day. Then, at the end of the trek, it is easy to hike out by midday and catch one of the early afternoon *colectivos* from Cashapampa.

You should have no problem reversing the directions for Cashapampa to Vaquería below, but take care at the beginning of the trail if you want to bypass Colcabamba. From the bus stop at Vaquería drop straight down to a creek, cross it, and follow the path, taking the left-hand trail over a small hill/pass and descending into the next valley. Here you follow/cross the river up to the park boundary.

Cashapampa to Vaquería or Colcabamba

Distance	45km
Altitude	Between 2,900m and 4,750m
Rating	Moderate
Timing	3–4 days (without the side trips)
Start of trail	Cashapampa (2,900m), accessible by micro (1½–2hrs) from Caraz. Several buses run each day.
Maps	IGN sheets *Corongo* (18-h) and *Carhuaz* (19-h); trekking map *Llanganuco to Santa Cruz* from the SAE.
Arrieros	Muleteers have formed a collective and charge a flat rate of US$5 per animal and US$10 per *arriero* per day. You must also pay for them to return to Cashapampa at the end of the trek.

Route description The trail starts just outside the village of Cashapampa where you can hire *arrieros* and *burros* or horses if you need them. If you need accommodation in this village, try the Hospedaje Alpamayo. There is camping in a grassy field near the start of the trail (for a small charge) and a kiosk where you can buy soft drinks and basic supplies.

Note that there are now established campsites and pit toilets at regular intervals (every 3–4 hours) along the route. These reduce the damage to the environment and should be used. It is a steep, gravelly climb up the Quebrada Santa Cruz, following the right bank of the river along a narrow path, crossing some landslides higher up. The path is pretty obvious, but not easy, taking you all the way up to the first *pampa* (meadow), about 6km from the village, which makes a suitable camping place for the first night, being 4–5 hours from Cashapampa. This campsite is known as Llamacorral and you will see the first of several toilets that have been constructed along this trail.

The next day continue up the Santa Cruz valley, with spectacular mountain views on both sides, until you reach Laguna Chica and, a bit further up,

Laguna Grande at 3,900m. This lake is about 11km from Cashapampa, and some 3–4 hours from the *pampa*. Continue along the main trail for 40 minutes, and where the path splits, a signpost indicates the trails. There is an interesting side trip to the Alpamayo base camp from here. To visit the base camp take the path climbing steeply to the left (northwest). You don't have to come all the way down again to continue the main trek, but can cut across the valley side traversing round to the campsite at Taullipampa.

The main trail continues along the left bank of the river, climbing gently. In May 1997 a lake breached the wall of the terminal moraine on the south side of the valley, depositing a massive amount of sand and boulders into this valley. Cross the river on a small bridge an hour after the junction, arriving at the meadows of Taullipampa beneath the peak of Taulliraju (5,830m). There is a toilet block here and plenty of space to camp. There are wonderful views of glaciated peaks and an interesting glacial lake, Taullicocha, worth an afternoon walk. From the camping area it's a steep and long climb up to the pass of Punta Union at 4,750m, about 15km from Laguna Grande and a 7–8-hour walk from there, or 3 hours from the Taullipampa campsite. The view from the pass, looking back at the Santa Cruz valley, is one of the finest in Peru. The majestic peak of Taulliraju guards the pass, its glaciers calving into the turquoise lake of Taullicocha. Further down the valley the snows of Chacraraju (6,112m), Huandoy (6,395m) and Huascarán (6,768m) form the backdrop.

After gazing at the view, prepare yourself for the steep, slippery descent into the valley on the other side, keeping to the right and passing the Lagunas Morococha on your right, with the peak of Nevado Pucaraju (5,028m) ahead of you. The trail makes a right turn, descending into Quebrada Huaripampa, a lovely valley of meadows and small lakes. Keep to your right, following the river, until you reach the junction of Quebrada Pária, (named Q Vacaria on some maps) about 11km (3–4 hours) from the pass. There are plenty of excellent camping places here, with the glaciers of Artesonraju (6,025m) providing a spectacular backdrop.

The energetic can take a side trip up Quebrada Pária and, further down, up Quebrada Ranincuray. Both are on your right, and get you closer to those magnificent mountains. Continuing down the valley turn right to descend to the river and cross. On the far side the path splits, the left fork going on down to the village of Colcabamba. Here there are the rewards of a small village including basic accommodation and meals. There is a path leading up to the road from Colcabamba, for transport back to Yungay and Huaraz or to Yánama and San Luís. Alternatively take the right fork, climb a few minutes over the ridge, down the far side, cross the river and summon your energy for a final steep, hot ascent to the road. Enjoy a cold drink at the bar in Vaquería. From here there is transport to Yungay and Huaraz or to Yánama and San Luís. There is transport throughout the day, though it can be somewhat infrequent.

The Lagunas Llanganuco and Laguna 69

The valley of Llanganuco is spectacular for the views of Chopicalqui (6,354m), Huascarán (6,768m and 6,655m) and Huandoy (6,395m). A dirt road runs from Yungay up and over the pass (Portachuelo de Llanganuco) to Yánama on the eastern side. This carries trucks, buses and *colectivos* of locals and trekkers heading to the start of the Santa Cruz trek at Vaquería. There are also several *colectivos* a day from Yungay, during the tourist season, that only go as far as the first of the Llanganuco Lakes, Chinancocha. They are specifically for tourists and after driving up, hang around for an hour or so to give you time to visit the lakes, and then head back to Yungay. The jumping-off point for walking to Laguna 69 is a few kilometres beyond this, so if you are going that way either ensure you get a *colectivo* that is going on over the pass or negotiate with your driver to take you to Cebolla Pampa. The walk from Cebolla Pampa to the unimaginativeley named Laguna 69 is not tough and gives wonderful views. There is even a hut near Laguna 69, so you can spend the night in this beautiful area without carrying a tent.

To Laguna 69

Distance	About 10km (each way) from Cebolla Pampa
Altitude	Between 3,840m and 4,450m
Rating	An easy hike, not steep, with beautiful scenery
Timing	2–3 days total. 3–4 hours each way from the road
Start of trail	At Yungay, get transport up the Quebrada Llanganuco
Maps	IGN sheet *Carhuas* (19-h), *Cordillera Blanca Nord* 1:100 000 Alpenvereinskarte

Route description Below the lakes there is a park office check point; where you have to pay an entrance fee. A day ticket is US$2 (payable in *soles*), and if you plan to stay longer you have to pay US$20 regardless of the number of days.

It is possible to walk from the park office on up the valley, but most buses will be going higher up. A trail climbs up to the Llanganuco lakes from the park control. Take the short cuts along a footpath, not the dirt road. It's about 6km, 2 hours to the lakes. First you'll pass the smaller Laguna Chinan Cocha, and then the bigger Laguna Orcan Cocha. It's best to cross the stream at the upper end of the Lagunas Llanganuco where the path continues up the valley, crossing the road several times. Don't forget to look back on the superb views. About 3km above the lakes at the first major bend in the road a path descends to the meadows of Cebolla Pampa beside the stream in the Quebrada Demanda (4,200m). This is a good camping spot, with excellent views of the nearby peaks of Huascarán Norte and Chopicalqui. There are a couple of toilet blocks at the site, which by the end of the season inevitably end up extremely disgusting. Responsible camping is essential.

This is the start of the trails up to Pisco base camp and Laguna 69. For Laguna 69 follow the trail up Quebrada Demanda on the right of the river. The path is obvious and the scenery is beautiful. You will pass some huts and then the trail peters out. Stay on the right side of the valley until you cross a stream coming down from your right. Follow the path up the far side of this stream and then up the steep zigzags on the valley side. As you climb high above the valley you look down on open pasture and have a beautiful view of a large waterfall over on the left. The path takes you round and above this waterfall, passing a small lake before dropping into an open meadow. You can camp here but the inquisitive cows can be irritating. They have a penchant for eating clothing left out to dry and knocking over stoves.

Continuing across the plain you will find a sign indicating that Laguna 69 is 3km away toward the left (north) and that the Cabaña Glacier Broggi is 2km ahead (east). Both trails are obvious.

To reach the *cabaña* continue up Quebrada Demanda. The hut is located at the edge of Laguna Demanda in the shadow of Chacraraju (6,112m), the summit off toward the left (northeast), above Laguna 69. Recently it has been cleaned up and it is now well maintained. Take care of it or it could revert to it's dirty, trash-strewn state. The hut has a new door and windows. It offers protection from the wind, and if you don't have a tent but want to do an overnight hike, this is a great option (you will need a sleeping bag and food). You are serenaded to sleep by avalanches breaking off the mountain face. If everyone takes away their rubbish and tries to keep it clean, it will be a nicer place for the next hiker. The lakes near the *cabaña* provide water, but it should be purified: there is plenty of human waste in the area. Don't make this any worse. This is one of the base camps for the mountain of Yanapaccha.

After a night in the hut you can walk back to the junction in the meadow, then hike the 3km up to Laguna 69. Returning to the road you have several options: continue walking on the path that stays to the right of the road over the pass (Portachuelo de Llanganuco, 4,767m) and head for Colcabamba or Yánama (there is plenty of morning transport to Yánama if you don't want to walk); complete the Quebrada Santa Cruz circuit by swinging north at Vaquería or Colcabamba and up to Punta Union; or return the way you came to Yungay.

Pisco

This trekking peak is the most popular in the Cordillera Blanca, and although it is non-technical it should not be attempted by inexperienced mountaineers unless fully equipped (crampons, ice-axes, harness, rope) and accompanied a fully qualified mountain guide. Contact the Casa de Guias in Huaraz for recommendations and help in organising this trip.

From Cebolla Pampa cross the river and head northwest steeply up the valley side on the path signed to Pisco. It's a good 3-hour trek up to base camp, with a full backpack. Donkeys can usually be hired at the bottom to help, and at just US$5 per animal and US$10 a day for an *arriero* this is a small price to pay to make the climb a bit easier. The views of surrounding peaks improve as you climb, and from base camp itself the panorama is superb. There is a large mountain refuge at Pisco base camp (US$10 a bed), and plenty of space for camping, with fresh water from a spring. Book your bed through the Casa de Guías in Huaraz.

Quebrada Ulta to Colcabamba

This isn't a popular hike, which is one of its big advantages. It has plenty of other things going for it: marvellous views of the snowpeaks looming above the valley on either side of the *quebrada* and some great side trips. There's also the opportunity to be terrified as you come over one of the Cordillera's most dramatic, nerve-racking passes. If you are scared of heights don't do this one – there's an alternative (and less stressful) route to Chacas.

This trek provides one of the best opportunities in the Cordillera Blanca for seeing condors.

Route description There is a road all the way up the Quebrada Ulta and down the other side to Chacas, but it carries relatively few vehicles because of the difficulty in getting over the pass. At least this road can be used to save you some climbing, and it does nothing to destroy the superb views. There are plenty of camping possibilities in the valley, but be careful never to leave your belongings unattended.

From Shilla follow the main footpath to Llipta; it crosses the road several times. After about 7km of path and road beyond Llipta, you come to the entrance of the Quebrada Auquiscocha to the right. There is a possible side trip up this *quebrada* to its lake at 4,300m, about a 3km walk from the entrance of the valley. There are not a lot of camping possibilities at the lake, but a large cave hidden behind the underbrush just to the right of the outlet stream will give you shelter.

The main trail continues climbing up the valley until the Portada de Ulta (the entrance of the valley) at 3,600m, about 3.5km from Quebrada Auquiscocha. Quebrada Huallcacocha leads off to your right, and there's another possible side trip up this to Laguna Huallcacocha, 4,350m, about 3.5km from the *portada*.

The main route splits into several trails running from the *portada*, through the meadow and up the valley. The snow-covered summit of Chopicalqui appears to the left and on your right you'll see the Quebrada Cancayapampa (Matará). There are some super campsites in the meadows of this Quebrada at 4,350m, about 4km from the entrance of the *quebrada*. The massive cliffs of Nevados Huascarán (6,768m) and Chopicalqui (6,354m) loom above.

You have a choice here: if you can't face the drama of the Yanayacu pass, there is an easier route which follows the road to the right up to the pass of Pasaje de Ulta. It climbs to the right of a little ridge, crosses the pass, and brings you down to Pompey and then Chacas.

The more adventurous trail to Yánama continues north towards Nevado Contrahierbas (6,036m) at the head of the *quebrada* at 4,100m, just under 2km from the Quebrada Matará. It passes above the shallow Laguna Yanayacu (possible campsites, and the last water for 8km), turns up the valley to the east, and climbs to the pass of Punta Yanayacu at 4,850m, about 8km from the start of the *quebrada*. This is the dramatic one. The narrow path is cut into the side of the mountain, with a rock cliff on one side and a sheer drop on the other. Having survived this, you descend to a very high and cold lake full of icebergs, below the glaciers of Contrahierbas. If you are well equipped for freezing conditions, this is a marvellous campsite, with rumbling avalanches during the evening and night. The path continues down the valley and soon reaches the valley floor and good campsites.

Keep to the left side of the stream, crossing it near the lower end of the valley, and you have reached the junction of the Colcabamba trail and the Yánama road at 3,350m, about 10km from the pass. Take the left trail to Colcabamba, which climbs steeply for about 500m. Then it levels out and traverses the ridge before dropping to the village of Chaullua. Here it meets the Colcabamba–Yánama trail. Take this to the left, making a short climb to where the trail splits; the upper trail leads to Quebrada Morococha and the Portachuelo de Llanganuco, and the lower trail to Colcabamba, about 6km.

Note Don't camp close to the villages in this area, and watch your belongings.

Distance	About 42km
Altitude	Between 3,050m and 4,900m
Rating	Generally easy, except for the passes, which are tough going
Timing	4 days (excluding side trips)
In reverse	Possible, and can be done as an extension to the Santa Cruz trek
Start of trail	Quebrada Ulta
Maps	IGN sheet *Carhuas* (19-h)

Quebrada Honda to Chacas

This is a nice easy walk up the Honda valley. Even though a new dirt road has been constructed here, it is still a great hike with some very interesting side trips. Locals are very friendly and eager to have a chat with you. The pass gives excellent views and good possibilities to see condors, the valley on the other side is green and beautiful, and Chacas is still an unspoiled, picturesque mountain village.

Route description From the little village of Vicos at 3,050m, a dirt road has been constructed all the way to the end of the Quebrada Honda. Follow the footpath, which provides a short cut and is more interesting than the road. First you'll pass the Portada de Honda, the gate to the entrance of the valley at 3,600m, about 9km from Vicos. There are good campsites just after the gate.

The first side trip is shortly after the *portada*. A disused road branches off to the left, and runs to about halfway up Quebrada Paccharuri. Then a path

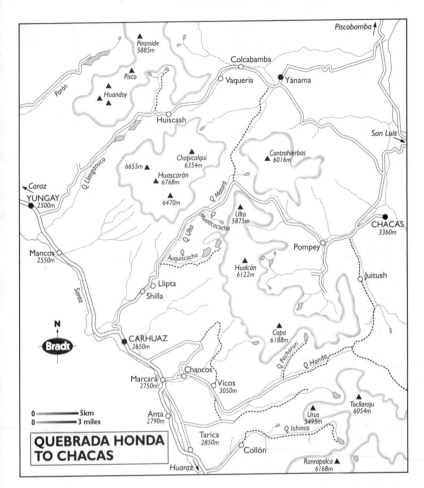

QUEBRADA HONDA
TO CHACAS

continues to Laguna Paccharuri (4,450m), which is situated below the majestic bulks of Nevados Copa (6,188m) and Paccharaju (5,751m) at the head of the canyon, about 9km from the entrance of the valley.

The main hike continues up the Quebrada Honda and is pleasant and easy, following the dirt road along the river, passing through farming land, steep canyons, and green meadows, until the end of the valley; this area is called the *rinconada*, and if you left Vicos in the morning you should reach it by the end of the day. If not, there are camping places before the *rinconada*. The route is well travelled and you'll probably be accompanied by local *campesinos*. It's about 10km from the *portada* to the *rinconada*, which lies at 3,850m.

From here there is a possible side trip to Laguna Pucaranracocha: a trail leads southeast up the Quebrada Vinoyo or Pucaranra, crossing a bridge, and climbing past a mighty waterfall. At 2km past the falls you'll see the Quebrada Escalón on your right. Continue along the river, across the meadows and up the moraine at the head of the canyon. A short, faint spur to the right leads to

Laguna Pucaranracocha at 4,400m, about 9km from the *rinconada*. A trail beyond the lake continues to a mine (which is the reason for the Quebrada Honda road).

Back to the main trail. Leaving the valley floor at the *rinconada*, you have to look for the start of the trail climbing up the left side of the valley; it is not easy to see.

The climb to the pass is steep, but the views are great (the surrounding peaks are Chinchey (6,222m), Palcaraju (6,274m) and Pucaranra (6,156m), and this is a well-known spot to see condors). The turn-off to the Portachuelo de Honda pass (4,750m) is located about 200m beyond a stone shelter on the left side of the road before the road switches back to the left of a prominent waterfall about 7km (3 hours) from the *rinconada*.

Distance	47km
Altitude	Between 3,050m and 4,750m
Rating	Moderate, with a steep pass
Timing	3–4 days (excluding side trips)
In reverse	Possible, dramatic and easier to follow the trail.
Start of trail	From Marcará get transport to Chancos and Vicos
Maps	IGN sheet *Huari* (19-i)

A steep descent brings you into the Quebrada Juitush, and meets the dirt road on the left-hand side of the valley, after passing through lush green meadows and farmland with good campsites everywhere. The little settlement of Juitush lies about 9km from the pass (3 hours) at 3,800m. After Juitush, the trail forks at a new irrigation control structure. The left-hand trail crosses a bridge and runs up the other side of the valley, which is the route to the village of Pompey, about 9km away. There you could get a truck or hike over the Pasaje de Ulta and back to Huaraz. The right-hand trail continues to Chacas, 12km (3 hours) from Juitush.

Chacas is a little village at 3,350m. There is now a basic hotel (rather overpriced at US$12) and other cheaper (unmarked) accommodation in addition to some small shops, a market and trucks leaving in the morning and early afternoon to San Luís. There is also a bus to/from Pomabamba.

Huari to Chacas

We discovered this trek after waiting in vain for transport up the eastern side of the *cordillera* to Pomabamba. The route passes through two beautiful, peaceful and mainly uninhabited green upland valleys, crossing a pass of 4,500m from where there are good, though brief, views of the peaks north and west of Chacas. More impressive though, besides the tranquillity, are the contorted bands of rock.

Distance	About 34km
Altitude	From 2,700m (Huari) to 4,500m
Rating	Moderate; some steep sections
Timing	2–3 days
In reverse	Possible (see page 178)
Start of the trail	Huari (served by bus) or Chacas (bus from Pomabamba)
Maps	IGN sheet *Huari* (19-i)

Route description

From Huari Leave the lower (cathedral) plaza by the steps climbing from the lower left-hand corner, to meet the higher of two roads which leave Huari to the north. Follow the road round for 2km to the town of Ulia. Just after passing through Ulia plaza with its church, you cross a river. Immediately afterwards take the path which climbs steeply up to your left. This is the most direct route up to Laguna Purhuay, which you will reach in about 1½ hours.

Alternatively you may prefer to follow the rough road, which zigzags up along the bottom of the Río Purhuay valley and forks left a little further on. Both road and track join before you reach the tranquil Laguna Purhuay. Here you may like to pause and catch a few trout for your supper – the lake seems well stocked with them. Rest at least: from here your route is steep and ever upwards.

As soon as you reach the southern end of the lake, look for a fork to the left. This is not very clear in its lower part, but from the lake shore it is clearly visible higher up where it passes a small group of eucalyptus trees. Whatever happens, don't follow the lake shore beyond the first small valley and stream to enter the lake from its western side. Once on the path, you'll find it easy to follow, taking you up and round into Quebrada Asnoragra. There's a good picnic spot where you cross the stream which is a rare source of water.

Once across the stream the path continues steeply up through the scrub and bush, eventually emerging in open *puna*. On the crest, the path forks, the main route continuing left and upwards whilst a smaller path goes straight on. Less than 100m more of climbing, at a more gentle angle now, brings you round on to a high level path above and to the south of a deep *quebrada* unnamed on the IGN map. It will take 3–4 hours from the lake to here.

The next 3–4km are a pleasant high traverse, with several camping possibilities and plenty of side streams for water, although these dry up from time to time so it's safer to carry water. If it has been a long hot day and you want a private pool and jacuzzi, continue until the path drops down the valley, running along the left-hand side close to the main stream. There are plenty of camping opportunities here.

The path now remains in the valley bottom and climbs steadily, crossing the stream from left to right where the main valley bends to the right. Little water is available once you leave the valley bottom until you drop well down the other side of the pass, so it's a good idea to fill up your water bottle when you cross the main stream. As you round the bend in the valley the top of the pass comes into sight some 3km ahead. The cross on its summit cairn is clearly visible. Unlike most routes in the *cordillera* the climb to the pass is gentle and relatively painless, and another hour or so will see you crossing the ridge between rock bands and traversing around the top of a high valley dotted with small lakes.

From the summit the path drops steeply down, entering the valley of the Río Arma via a side valley. You may decide to camp at the junction of these two valleys. If not there are one or two small sites amongst the trees before the path crosses the side stream in Quebrada Tayanchocha, some 2.5–3km further on, otherwise you will be forced to continue all the way down to Chacas (another 4–5 hours' walk) or pitch in a farmer's field lower down the valley.

There is only one obvious path down the left-hand side of the Río Arma. This climbs up and to the left to cross the tributary stream coming from Laguna Patarcocha by a splendid little bridge. Turn right across the bridge and continue along the path high up on the left-hand side of the valley. Eventually this will bring you to the small group of houses, the village of Cochas, and, beyond these over a slight rise, the town of Chacas.

From Chacas To do the route in reverse (which has the advantage of a higher starting point: Chacas is at 3,350m), go out of Chacas at the top end of the plaza and, after two blocks, take the track leading to the left, up over a low ridge, to the village of Cochas. Passing through Cochas keep on the main, high track which leads round to the right and will bring you out high above the Río Arma on the right-hand side of the valley. Follow this up to the bridge over the side stream from Laguna Patarcocha. Cross the bridge and take the path to the left which curves around the end of the spur between this tributary valley and the main valley of the Río Alma. Continue along the path up the right side of the Río Alma, crossing the Río Tayancocha by an earth bridge. The path leaves the valley of the Río Alma by the next *quebrada* up, and is then the only obvious path to lead up and over the pass.

Similarly the descent at the other side is by the only path along the valley bottom. After the valley bends to the left, cross the main stream and keep to the path down the right-hand side of the valley bottom, traversing round to the right and staying high as the valley falls away more steeply. The route from here should be obvious and needs no further description.

Quebrada Ishinca

This is a beautiful one-way hike up the valley of Ishinca, with an interesting side trip to the Ishinca glacier. There are great views all the way, and the hiking is easy. This is the route for climbers going up to Ishinca, Uros or Tocllaraju. Ishinca and Uros are trekking peaks that can be climbed by suitably equipped trekkers (crampons, ice-axe, harness, rope) with a qualified guide. Ask the Casa de Guías for details and recommendations.

Distance	19km
Altitude	From 3,200m to 4,950m
Rating	Easy to base camp, a steep climb to the lake
Timing	2 days from Collón to Ishinca moraine camp
Start of trail	Get private transport (taxi or pick-up) from Huaraz to the small village of Collón. You can take transport along the Callejon de Huaylas and get off at the junction to the dirt road to Collón. If you're lucky a truck will take you up to the village (3,200m) or you can hike there in 2–3 hours (6km)
Accommodation	A refuge has been built in the valley at Ishinca base camp by Italian Catholic missionaries. A second refuge is being equipped at Ishinca moraine camp, 2 hours above the main one. Ask at Casa de Guías about booking a bed.
Map	IGN sheet *Huari* (19-i)

Route description Walk on the road out of Collón for a half hour to where a rock is painted red with 'Ishinca' and an arrow. Follow the trail to the right for 2 hours to the *portada*, the entrance of the Quebrada Ishinca, at 3,850m, about 7.5km from Collón. Campsites can be found here.

The trail continues through a series of meadows to the head of the valley. Good campsites abound. A clear path passes by a waterfall on the south wall, and after an easy climb of 2km it crosses the stream and reaches the Ishinca climbers' base camp, at 4,400m, about 8km (4 hours) from the entrance of the valley. There is a large refuge here, and plenty of camping spots.

Beyond the base camp the trail begins to climb the south wall, at times quite steeply, before passing a swampy meadow and making the final climb to Laguna Ishinca, at 4,950m. This is about 3.5km (2 hours) from base camp.

From here it takes about an hour to the Ishinca glacier, following the moraine on the right side of the lake.

From Ishinca base camp there is a possible 1½-hour side trek up to Laguna Toclla, below Nevado Tocllaraju (6,034m). An alternative side trip is to the base camp for Nevado Urus: a trail climbs up from the head of Quebrada Ishinca to this small base camp at 4,980m, about 2½ hours. There are a few small camping spaces and beautiful views of the Nevados Ishinca (5,530m), Ranrapalca (6,162m) and Ocshapalca (5,888m).

Return the way you came.

Quebradas Churup, Shallap, Rajucolta and Quilcayhuanca

All these routes are close to Huaraz, making them ideal warm-up hikes for something more ambitious. Some are short hikes from Huaraz, like Churup, and some are spectacular valleys where you can spend a few days and do some side trips.

The start of most of the hikes is Pitec (3,850m), east of Huaraz. You may be able to get transport all the way there, or just part way (to Llupa) and then walk along the obvious path. Pitec is not a village, just a few farmhouses.

To Laguna Churup

Distance	3.5km each way from Pitec
Altitude	From 3,850m to 4,600m
Rating	A steep climb, sometimes off trail
Timing	3 hours from Pitec to the lake if acclimatised (not advisable on the first two days in Huaraz)
Maps	IGN *Recuay* map (20-i) and *Huari* (20-h)

Route description The simplest and most direct route from Pitec to the lake is to follow the obvious path along the left side of the long ridge (moraine) heading up behind the national park information board at the Pitec car park. The path is obvious for the first two hours, then it splits in two. The path to the right goes round the hillside to a flat area with a waterfall ahead. From here the last 40 minutes or so are a real scramble up the left of the waterfall. Tree roots and boulders provide plenty of hand and foot holds, but in wet conditions the route can get slippery and be quite intimidating. You will need to use some basic rock-climbing techniques so don't go this way if you don't feel confident about a bit of scrambling. There is also a route up the right side of the waterfall, but it is also extremely steep and can be slippery. If you take the left hand fork back at the junction, continuing on up the ridge, although you end up climbing considerably higher than on the other (right) path, you avoid the scrambling altogether.

Churup is a jewel of a lake, deep blue in colour and half encircled by Nevado Churup (5,495m).

To Laguna Shallap

Distance	10.5km
Altitude	From 3,800m to 4,300m
Rating	Easy to moderate
Timing	About 5 hours from Pitec to the lake

Route description From Pitec, you'll see the valley of Shallap to your right. It first descends to the Quilcayhuanca bridge, and then climbs the opposite bank, crosses a plateau, turns left, passes the community of Cahuide, and starts up the Quebrada Shallap. The Shallap bridge is down a path to the right of the corrals, just past Cahuide. Another bridge is 400m further and the trail ascends through the boulders and thick brush, to the *portada* marking the entrance of the Quebrada Shallap at 4,000m and about 4.5km (2 hours) from Pitec. The president of Shallap has the key to the gate. Ask at the Casa de Guías if you are travelling with pack animals and need the gate to be opened.

The path ascends the valley, through some pleasant meadows and past waterfalls, until the lake's moraine. Pass the old INGEMMET hut and you reach Laguna Shallap at 4,300m. This is 6km (3 hours) from the *portada*. It lies just below Nevado San Juan (5,843m). There are some exposed campsites at the lake; better camping is found in the *quebrada*, although the cows can be annoying.

To Laguna Rajucolta

Distance	17km
Altitude	From 3,800m to 4,250m
Rating	Easy/moderate
Timing	8 hours from Pitec to the lake
Start of trail	Macashca. Buses run there from Huaraz (corner of Caceres and 27 Noviembre/Tarapacá).

Route description This is an exceptional hike because of the way Nevado Huantsán dominates the view so you hardly notice the cliffs and waterfalls en route. A correspondent writing in 1997 described his visit enthusiastically, not only for the exceptional beauty of the area but because, in August, there were no other tourists.

From Macashca follow the river up to the first gate (about 5 hours), crossing to the left bank (north) of the river within the first hour. About 10 minutes beyond the gate is excellent camping. The next day continue on to a second gate and then to the base of the canyon wall, where you follow the path along the stream and up to the lake. Laguna Rajucolta lies at 4,250m, a perfect glacial lake backed by the majestic Nevado Huantsán (6,395m). It is about 6.5km (2–3 hours) from the *portada* to the lake.

To return you can either retrace your steps, or take the route to Pitec, via the community of Janco and Quebrada Shallap. For better transport out, modify the route by heading north after the gate but before you reach Pitec go left and head down the *quebrada*. Pick up a trail across the river, which will bring you to the road at Llupa where there are *colectivos* to Huaraz.

Up the Quebrada Quilcayhuanca to the Lagunas Tullpacocha and Cuchillacocha and Quebrada Cayesh

Distance	19.5km to the lakes
Altitude	From 3,850m to 4,650m
Rating	Easy to moderate
Timing	4 days

Route description The dirt road from Pitec continues to the Portada de Quilcayhuanca, at 3,850m, about 3km from Pitec. Go through the gate or climb over it and follow the trail up the valley on the left hand side. This is an easy hike to the head of the valley, through green, marshy meadows with lots of cattle, ascending slowly. The distance is about 8.5km, 3½ hours, to 4,050m. There are plenty of camping places.

The *nevado* in front of you is Andavite (5,518m), the valley to your right is Quebrada Cayesh and the one to your left is the continuation of Quebrada Quilcayhuanca, which brings you to the Lagunas Tullpacocha and Cuchillacocha.

If you want to go up Quebrada Cayesh – and you should, for a closer view of the dramatic *nevados* – look for the little bridge over the river, hidden to your right. Cross and climb up the small ridge to the meadow. Across the meadow is another stream. Cross at a shallow place, and enter Quebrada Cayesh. The first part is green meadow; cross to your left, where you'll find a path bringing you to the head of the valley, passing through *queñoa* forest. Distance: 8km, 2½ hours. Good campsites (but look for a dry place) and great views of the needle-like Nevado Cayesh (5,721m) to the left, Maparaju (5,326m) in front of you, and San Juan (5,843m) and Tumarinaraju (5,668m) to your right. For an even better view climb up the mountain slope to your right. There are remains of an Inca path up here if you can find it. It leads up to the Maparaju glacier, about 2 hours ahead.

To reach the lakes in the Quebrada Quilcayhuanca, from where the two valleys join you'll see a well-marked path heading north. After 15 minutes on this path you reach a long grassy meadow, Llupanapampa. The path fades but continue in the general direction you're going, aiming for the top end of the *pampa*. The trail to Laguna Tullpacocha heads up through the bushes, curving around to the right, passing the old INGEMMET hut, and continuing up the small canyon until it reaches Laguna Tullpacocha, at 4,300m, about a half hour's walk from the start of the trail. The lake is right underneath Nevado Tullparaju (5,787m), which feeds the lake with its calving icebergs.

To reach Laguna Cuchillacocha take the path back from Laguna Tullpacocha past the huts and continue until you cross a stream (Cuchilla). You'll clearly see the path you're aiming for on the mountainside ahead, climbing steeply up the ridge in a series of switchbacks to the top of the ridge. The path was once used by workers from INGEMMET (the government agency responsible for the glacial lakes) so is well worn. After an hour you'll reach the meadow of Cuchilla Pampa, where there are a few small stone

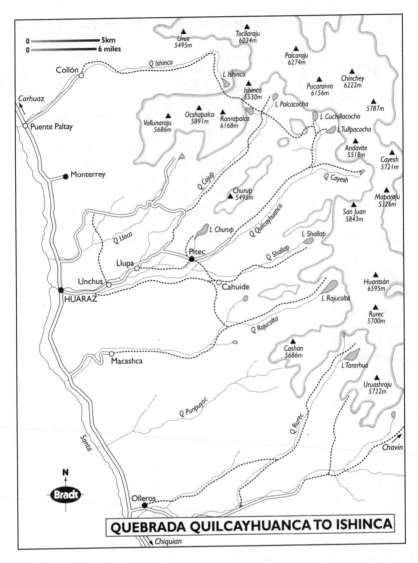

QUEBRADA QUILCAYHUANCA TO ISHINCA

circular constructions, good for shelter. If you look to your right you'll see a path climbing up the slope, making a few switchbacks, until it reaches a little meadow with the old INGEMMET camp. It takes around 40 minutes to get up to Laguna Cuchillacocha at 4,650m, about 500m from the start of the trail.

The head of the valley provides good campsites and super views of Nevados Huapi (5,530m) and Pucaranra (6,156m) in front of you, with Chinchey (6,222m), Tullparaju (5,787m) and Cayesh (5,721m) to your right.

For even better views, climb up the mountain slope on a rather sketchy path (some cairns appear every now and then) to your left (as you face the mountains) until you reach Laguna Paqsacocha in about 1½ hours.

Pitec to Collón via Quebrada Cojup and Quebrada Ishinca

Distance	Approx 67km from Pitec to Collón, via Ishinca valley
	25km from Pitec to Laguna Paqsacocha
	23km from Laguna Paqsacocha to Ishinca base camp
	19km from Ishinca base camp to Collón
Altitude	From 3,850m to 5,100m (Huapi pass), 5,350m (Ishinca pass)
Rating	Moderate to difficult
Timing	4–5 days Pitec to Huaraz via Cojup valley (moderate)
	8 days Pitec to Huaraz via Ishinca valley (difficult, requires crampons and ice-axes)

Follow the directions for Laguna Paqsacocha given above. If you are already acclimatised this takes two days walking from Pitec. The path goes up to Laguna Paqsacocha southwest from the *pampa* below Laguna Cuchillacocha. There are a few cairns if you look carefully, but it's a bit of a steep scramble for 30 minutes, then becomes slightly easier as the gradient levels slightly. A further 45 minutes, following the cairns, will bring you out to a spectacular plateau, with two small lakes (Laguna Paqsacocha) at the base of the *nevado* Huapi (5,421m). There is a 360° panorama from here, one of the best views of the Cordillera Blanca from anywhere. You can see Pucaranra (6,156m), Chinchey (6,722m), Tullparaju (5,787m), Andavite (5,518m), Cayesh (5,721m), Maparaju (5,326m), San Juan (5,843m), and Huantsán (6,395m). This plateau is a good spot to camp, though pretty cold. There is nowhere else above this suitable for tents, and over the pass it's a long way down the other side until you find any flat land. It takes an hour and a half from the lake camp to reach the pass (5,100m). It's mostly boulders with no clear path, just sporadic cairns to mark the way. The route becomes unsuitable for donkeys, so if you are organising porterage of equipment you'll need porters from here on. There are unsurpassable views from the pass of a dozen peaks. As well as those mentioned above you can see Ranrapalca (6,162m), Ishinca (5,530m), Palcaraju (6,274m) and Huapi (5,421m).

From the pass there's no path down the other side, just sections of animal track, steep and rocky in places, muddy and slippery in others. Care is required, walking sticks definitely help the knees. Aim for the building of Electro Peru about 3 hours below. You can camp nearby or sleep in the hut if it's open. From here it's a 4-hour walk out down the Cojup valley to Llupa, where you can pick up a bus to Huaraz (40 minutes).

Cojup to Ishinca

The pass (5,350m) on this trek is permanently glacier covered. Only take this route if you have suitable equipment (ice-axe, crampons, rope) and experience of crossing glaciers (or are with a qualified guide). From the hut of Electro Peru it's a steep 4–6 hour climb up to the next pass between the peaks of Ishinca and Ranrapalca. Head up the valley side on animal tracks, zigzagging up steep grassy slopes. Look out for cairns to give you some guidance, but generally aim upwards (north) and above Lake Perolcocha, until you reach two small lakes after 2–3 hours. From there a further 2 hours pretty much straight up the rocky moraine of the valley headwall, keeping to the right of the stream, brings you to the ice just below the pass. Ranrapalca looms large to your left and Ishinca to your right. A few minutes on the ice will bring you to the pass. If you look down the other side to your left you can pick out the path on the wall of the moraine below. That is where you are heading. Watch out for crevasses as you descend the glacier. A 15-minute descent brings you out on to the moraine, from where you can follow the path down to Ishinca moraine camp, 2 hours below. Some stretches of this path are vertiginous so care should be taken, especially on wet rock. There is a basic refuge just above moraine camp, and a few spots to camp by Laguna Ishinca at the base of the mountain.

Ishinca is a relatively easy trekking peak, and can be climbed by fully equipped trekkers with a qualified mountain guide.

From the moraine camp it is a long walk out to the village of Collón, where you can find transport back to Huaraz. Follow the path down to base camp for 2 hours and then on down the valley for another 4 hours.

Olleros to Chavín

This is an underrated walk which consequently sees few tourists. It has some excellent views and exciting pre-Inca stone work. It also takes you to one of Peru's most interesting archaeological sites, Chavín de Huantar. Some people attribute this trail to the Incas, because of the stretches of fine stone paving, but it almost certainly pre-dates the Inca empire. The trip is made much more exciting and dramatic by taking two extra days and visiting Laguna Tararhua, tucked in between three glaciated peaks.

Route description From Olleros (3,420m) go past the plaza and after 100m take a clear track (actually a dirt road) downhill to the right and across the river. The trail goes straight up the valley to the right of the Río Negro at first passing through clusters of adobe houses with characteristically blue-painted doors. After an hour of walking the track leaves the settlements and passes through open fields. Where the driveable track doubles back, continue on indistinct footpaths staying to the right and above the Río Negro. Soon the trail joins a well-worn pre-Inca road, which is severely eroded. You pass the entrance to Quebrada Rurec after 3 hours of walking. The trail drops into a long plain – marshy in the wet season. About 8 hours from Olleros you reach the head of the plain where there is a shallow lake dammed by a low moraine with some good campsites. Here you will be faced with three valleys; the one

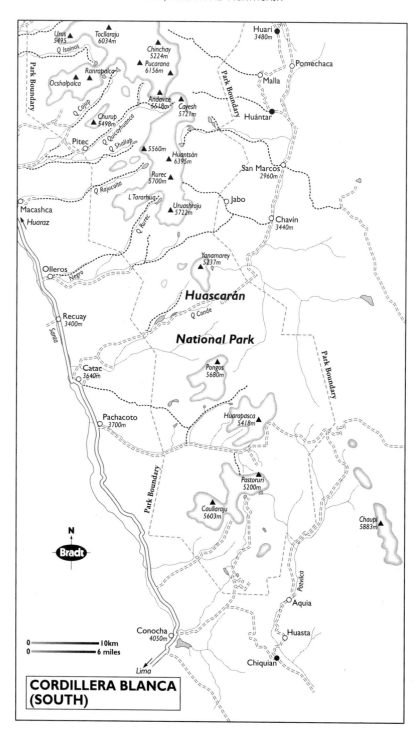

CORDILLERA BLANCA (SOUTH)

Distance	37km
Altitude	Between 3,200m and 4,700m
Rating	Moderate
Timing	2–3 days
In reverse	Possible, but a more difficult, steeper climb from Chavín. More dramatic views.
Start of trail	Truck to Olleros or hike in from the main road. There is a an established *arriero* in Olleros who charges US$5 per day for his mule and US$10 per day for himself.
Map	IGN sheet *Recuay* (21-i)

to the far left has orange and black vertical rock layers, the one in the centre has well-developed scree slopes and the one straight in front of you is hummocky and rocky. This is the valley you want. The main trail may be difficult to find but head up the right side of this valley and you will soon encounter an obvious and wide pre-Inca trail.

This rises steeply with good views of glaciated peaks opening to the north. There are several lakes and two false passes before you reach Punta Yanashallash at 4,700m, about 14km (4–5 hours) from the moraine lake at the bottom of the valley. From the top of the pass the pre-Inca road switchbacks down on well-preserved stone abutments. Look out for an interesting upright stone with stonework around the base, also for a seemingly inaccessible small ruin on the opposite side of the river canyon on a cliff about a half hour from Chavín. This was probably a lookout station for the ancient city of Chavín.

To Laguna Tararhua Quebrada Rurec, about 9km from Olleros, is easy to find because that's where the road crosses the river. The 25km, full-day trip to Laguna Tararhua takes you up the *quebrada* on a good trail. Follow the right bank of Río Rurec to the *pampa* and the entrance of the valley where there are a few houses. Beware of dogs! Continue along the path to Laguna Tararhua at 4,500m, set below the glaciers of Nevados Rurec (5,700m) and Uruashraju (5,722m), about 3 hours from the entrance to the valley.

To return to the eastern section of the main trail (at the marshy area) it should be possible to skirt the sides of Uruashraju, and hike due south across country. However, I don't know anyone who's tried it.

Chavín

This is a rather dreary small town, made exciting by its ruins. Chavín is quite popular with Peruvians, and many buses a day come from Huaraz.

There is a phone service here and about seven hotels. The Hostal Chavín (US$10) on a side street about 100m from the main square is recommended because it has private bathrooms. The quainter Hostal Inca has not got en suite facilities. If you feel you've earned a good meal try one of the rather expensive restaurants near the ruins. In the centre of town the restaurants all serve a very basic meal, and there's a little market.

The ruins

The ruins and museum are open from 08.00 to 17.00, with an entrance fee of about US$2. The guard is knowledgeable and will usually act as a guide. Bring a torch for exploring the dark underground chambers.

Experts vary in their estimate of the age of the Chavín culture, but most agree that it flourished between 1300 and 400BC, spreading from the coastal areas to the northern highlands, and reached its zenith around 500BC, when the temple at Chavín de Huantar was built. Chavín appears to have been a predominantly religious culture with various animalistic deities. Highly stylised feline forms are a common feature of the sculptures and carvings, along with eagles or condors, and snakes. It's a fascinating place. The enormous and enigmatic stone heads and finely carved reliefs have a strength and beauty unrivalled by the Incas, who left little in the way of representational art. The seven underground chambers have the finest stone work and an impressive sacrificial stone placed in the middle of the complex. There is electric lighting, but your torch will help pick out the details.

THE CORDILLERA HUAYHUASH
Chiquián

Chiquián is a thriving small community, lying at 3,400m, which makes its living from agriculture and the hikers and climbers who visit the Huayhuash.

Getting there and away

Chiquián can be reached from Lima in 10 hours by Cavassa bus (Jr Ayacucho 942, Lima) or Transfysa bus. Buses run three times a day from Huaraz, operated by El Rápido (Mariscal Caceres 312), at 06.00, 13.00 and 19.00.

Eating and sleeping

There are several simple hotels and restaurants.

Hostal Los Nogales Comercio 1301; tel: 044 747121. From US$4 per person. A colonial place, clean, with big rooms around a courtyard full of flowers.
Hostal Huayhuash Jr Figuerado Amadeo; tel: 044 747049. From US$5 per person. (Also the office of the bus company El Rápido. Buses depart from Chiquián at 05.00 and 14.30; 3 hour journey)
San Miguel Calle Comercio 233. From US$3 per person. Also recommended.

In Cajatambo
Hostal Tambomachay Tel: 044 244 2046; (Lima) 01 564 5584.

Pack animals

You can hire *burros* here for about US$5 per day (US$7 for a horse) with US$10 per day for the *arriero*. Remember you must pay for the *arriero* and his animals to return to the starting point. If he has done a good job a 10% tip can be added to the fee. If you hire an *arriero* make sure he really does know the route and that he has adequate camping equipment. Ask at the Casa de Guías in Huaraz for recommendations.

Hiking the Huayhuash circuit

This hike circles the entire range, and is probably the most scenically exciting hike in Peru. The most dramatic scenery of the walk is around the east side of the *cordillera*, where a chain of trout-filled lakes reflect the towering white peaks. The whole circuit involves 160km of walking between altitudes of 2,750m (9,020ft) and 5,000m (16,400ft), which represents a serious and difficult endeavour, so this is only recommended for hikers in excellent physical condition or who plan to take at least 12 days to complete the circuit. Of course it is not necessary to do the whole thing: you can hike for a few days and backtrack, or leave the trail at Cajatambo (a 7–8-day hike) from where there is transport to Lima. Side trips are mentioned in the route description.

The route is fairly obvious most of the way, although a well-worn trail is not always present. This is a remote area, so you should carry (and know how to use) the IGN maps. Because of the popularity of this circuit, garbage and other human waste is beginning to mar the enjoyment of some camping areas. Don't add to it, and better still help clean up after other people. Also do not make campfires since there is very little wood left in the area.

Alternative starting and finishing points. Consider coming into Huayhuash from the east side via La Unión and Queropalca, or from the north via Huallanca (my favourite entry point). You could travel by bus to La Unión, visit the fantastic Inca site of Huanuco Pampa, and then get transport from Huallanca to the Cuncush pass, and walk down from there to Matacancha to start the circuit. It is also possible to join up with the Inca trail as described by John Pilkington (see pages 209–14).

Distance	164–186km for the full circuit (depending on whether you do side treks)
Altitude	Between 2,750m and 5,000m
Rating	Difficult, with more than 6,000m (19,680ft) of climbing
Timing	7–8 days (if you leave at Cajatambo), 12 days for the circuit (without side trips)
In reverse	Possible
Start of trail	Chiquián
Maps	IGN sheets *Chiquián* (21-i) and *Yanahuanca* (21-j) or The *Cordillera Huayhuash* from the SAE. The map *Cordilleras Blanca y Huayhuash* by Felipe Diaz is excellent and widely available in Huaraz.

BIODIVERSITY IN THE CORDILLERA HUAYHUASH

Translated and adapted from Spanish, originally written by Roberto Arévalo of The Mountain Institute in Huaraz

An initial study of biodiversity in the Huayhuash has identified 272 species of plants, grouped into 148 genera and 55 families. There are 61 species of birds, 14 mammals, two amphibians and two fish. Ten species of bird threatened by extinction have been identified. These include ash-breasted tit-tyrant (*Anairetes alpinus*), Zárate's cotinga (*Zaratornis stresemanni*), giant conebill (*Oreomanes fraseri*) and tit-like dacnis (*Xenodacnis parina*). There is often a close dependence between the bird and the forest: the giant conebill finds its food supply of insects among the flaking bark of the *Polylepis* tree.

There are five ecological zones in the Cordillera.

Riverside woodland (Bosque ribereño)

This type of vegetation consists of a mix of trees, shrubs and grasses. It is generally found near water, along the edges of rivers, and up to altitudes of 3,500m. Typical plants include willows (*Salix humboltiana*), and pepper trees known as *molle* (*Schinus molle*), as well as a diversity of shrubs dominated by species of *Baccharis*, *Calceolaria* and *Lupinus*, many of which have thorns and partially lose their leaves in the dry season (between May and November). This vegetation protects riverbanks from erosion, is a source of plant material for local residents, and also acts as a protected corridor for wildlife to pass through.

There are also many epiphytes and lithophytes including *Tillandsia* species and orchids as well as a variety of mosses, lichens, ferns and fungi. This is the favourite habitat of the skunk, *zorrillo* (*Conepatus rex*), and opossum, *zarigueyas* (*Didelphis marsupialis*).

Scrubland (Matorral)

This zone is characterised by dense scrub and cacti. Typical in this zone also are small trees such as *mito* (*Carica candicans*), a wild papaya with aromatic, edible greenish-yellow fruit; pepper trees, *molle* (*Schinus molle*), whose leaves are used as insect repellent, and the agave, *la penca* (*Agave americana*), a rosette-shaped plant with a sharp spine at the end of each leaf. These are frequently used as protection around small fields, and the leaves were used in pre-Hispanic times for making rope.

Scrubland and puna grassland (Pajonales y Césped de puna)

The high scrublands (*pajonales*) are areas of vegetation composed principally of species of tussocky bunch grass known as *ichu*. They occupy open areas above the tree line at 4,000–4,600m. It is a mixture of grasses of the genera *Festuca*, *Stipa* and *Calamagrostis*. There are few shrubs at these altitudes, just some wild lupins (*Lupinus weberbaueri*), and some heather-like brush of the genus *Baccharis*. This vegetation constitutes most of the grazing land found in the highland *puna*. Is it the best grazing for llamas, and the shrubs provide a home to the partridge, *perdice*, and ornate tinamou (*Nothoprocta ornata*).

This is one of the best habitats for seeing the Andean condor. It is home to some of the larger Andean mammals, such as the puma (*Puma concolor*) and the Andean fox (*Pseudalopex culpaeus*).

Mountain forest (Bosques de montaña)

In the Cordillera Huayhuash there is some high woodland between 3,800m and 5,000m, most of which consists of the species known locally as *queñual* (*Polylepis weberbauer*). There is a total of 1,500ha of this forest, largely on the west side of the range.

The genus *Polylepis* (Fam. *Rosaceae*) includes 14 species of trees, of which 12 are found in Peru growing in the Andes above 1,500m and sometimes even over 5,000m. This is one of the few angiosperms growing at such high altitudes.

Queñual forests are generally found on steep rocky slopes, on glacial moraines, clinging to the sides of gorges, and occasionally fringing streams and lakes, such as at Laguna Carhuacocha and Jahuacocha. It is thought that the current distribution, small isolated patches of trees, is attributable to human influence, and that in the past the forest was much more widespread. Early Andean cultures may initially have been responsible for the removal of forests, as they cleared areas for terracing, cultivation and grazing. Today's landscapes are very much man-made, with cultivated habitats and human-influenced species distribution. It is estimated that less than 3% of the original forest has survived colonisation by man.

The *Polylepis* woodland in the Cordillera Huayhuash is of great importance in terms of biodiversity. Approximately 25 species of birds use the forest for one thing or another. As well as the birdlife, the trees offer protection to a number of animals such as the Andean deer, *tarugo* (*Hippocamelus antisensis*).

Peatlands and lakes (Los bofedales y lagunas)

Peatlands, known locally as *oconales*, are formed through bad drainage; for most of the year they are completely underwater. They are commonly found around lakes and on valley bottoms in high Andean glacial valleys.

More than 20 plant species are found in peatlands, including the attractive *Gentiana sedifolia* (Andean gentian) and cushion plants such as *champa estrella*, *Plantago rigida* and *Aciachne pulvinata*.

These habitats are characterised by their diverse bird life. The most representative is the *huallata* or Andean goose (*Chloephaga melanoptera*), *yanavico* or puna ibis (*Plegadis ridgwayi*), *pato andino* or puna teal (*Anas puna*), and *gaviota andina* or Andean gull (*Larus serranus*).

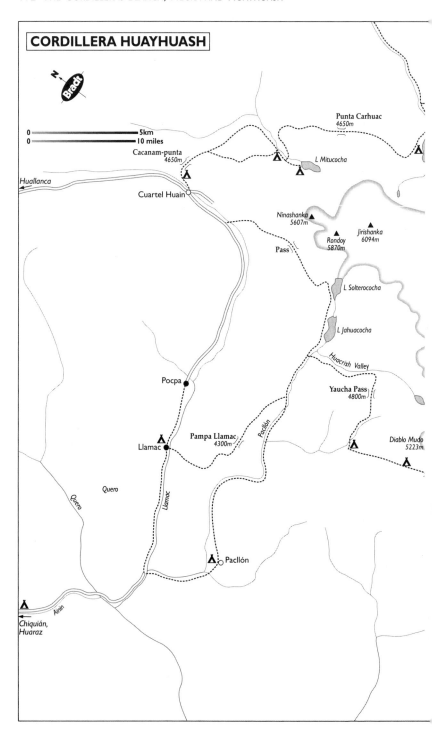

CORDILLERA HUAYHUASH

Bradt

0 ————— 5km
0 ————— 10 miles

Huallanca

Cacanam-punta
4650m

Cuartel Huain

Punta Carhuac
4650m

L Mitucocha

Ninashanka
5607m

Rondoy
5870m

Jirishanka
6094m

Pass

L Solterococha

L Jahuacocha

Huacrish Valley

Pocpa

Yaucha Pass
4800m

Pampa Llamac
4300m

Pacllón

Diablo Mudo
5223m

Llamac

Quero

Quero

Llamac

Pacllón

Ainn

Chiquián,
Huaraz

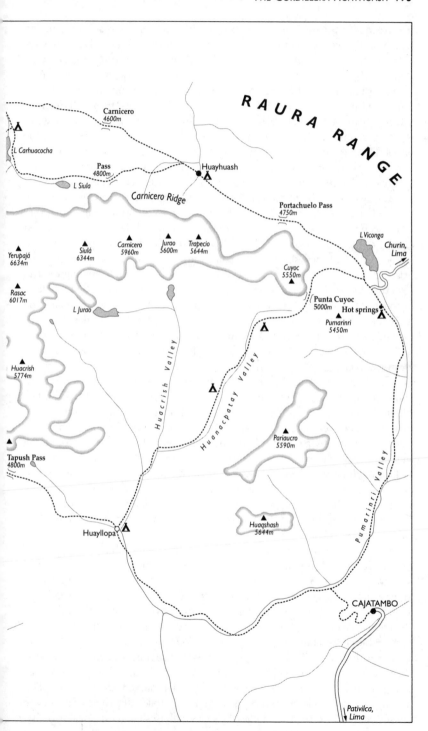

Route description There is a considerable amount of road construction going on the west side of the Huayhuash, which may influence your starting and finishing points. A new road has been constructed from Huallanca via Matacancha to Pocpa. Plans are to extend it as far as Chiquián. There is also a new dirt road from Chiquián to Pacllón. It is not yet being used by vehicles, but could be by late 2002. It is a hot, dusty 9-hour walk from Chiquián to Llamac (part of the walk being along this new road) so fill up with water whenever you can. Until you get above Llamac there are lots of nasty biting black flies to contend with. If you wear shorts (tempting in the heat) make sure you have plenty of insect repellent on, especially around the ankles.

Follow the footpath from the north side of the cemetery in Chiquián, eventually descending to the Río Pativilca where you meet the road; about 1½ hours. Cross the Río Pativilca on a beautiful old stone bridge where the river narrows into a gorge, turn right and follow the route of the newly constructed dirt road (the path down the right bank of the river has been completely washed away). There are a few short cuts avoiding the corners on the long zigzags of the road. Continue down the left bank of the river for 1½ hours, crossing the Río Quero, which comes down from your left, on a small and rather fragile-looking wood and adobe bridge. (It is possible to follow the Quero Valley, rejoining the route described below after 2 days, at Matacancha. Ask locally for details.)

The path then curves round a spur and turns left up the Pacllón valley; then follows this valley. To begin with you walk on the new dirt road, which is destined to carry traffic to Pacllón. Sections of the road have been washed out, so it could be some time before it is in use. Stay left following the Río Llamca when the Pacllón road goes off to the right. Your path crosses the river after about 2 hours of climbing, continuing on to Llamac (3 hours from the valley bottom). This lies at 3,250m and is about 21km from Chiquián. There are good campsites along the way, better perhaps than in Llamac where your large audience may get on your nerves. If you do camp in Llamac, ask permission before pitching your tent. There is a small fee for camping on the football pitch. It is not recommended to drink the river water, which is now contaminated by the mine workings. It is better to ask for water in the village. There is a hostal at the bottom end of the village with six rooms costing US$3 per person. Another is being constructed.

Llamac is a small community where you can make a refreshments stop even if you don't spend the night; the shops sell some soft drinks and basic supplies. If you are leaving the Cordillera at Cajatambo it is well worth taking the longer route via Laguna Jahuacocha, the epicentre of the Huayhuash as far as most visitors are concerned. Take the path south from Llamac (ask in the village for directions). About 10 minutes from the edge of the village the path rounds a spur and doubles back, climbing diagonally to the left towards an obvious cleft in the mountain horizon. Climb steeply up the eroded mountainside to a false pass, then for a further hour (enlivened somewhat by an Inca wall) to the real pass, Pampa Llamac (4,300m), which is on the right of a round, loaf-shaped hill. The ascent is a real struggle, but it really is worth it. You follow the route of the newly constructed water pipe, that supplies the valley with fresh water from Jahuacocha.

I experienced one of my moments of purest exhilaration on the pass. In front lies the western face of the Cordillera: giant dragon's teeth of glistening white – Rasac, Yerupajá, Jirishanka. As a further reward, the trail turns into a proper Andean path, winding gently through *queñoa* trees and lupins, past waterfalls and rocky overhangs to the valley below. In another 2 to 3 hours (if you haven't decided to camp on the way) you will arrive at Laguna Jahuacocha. A local family may offer to cook you trout and potatoes, or to sell you Coca-Cola.

When you are ready to leave the lake and rejoin the main trail, take the path along the left (north) side of the lake, which then swings to the left and begins to go uphill. Fill up with water before you start on the pass – there are no streams for several hours. It should take 3 hours to reach the top, but it took our group 4 hours; not because it was so difficult, but because it was so beautiful. We had to keep stopping to gaze. You seem to be almost on top of Rondoy's glacier, and look down into a milky, blue lake. The serious business starts below a long scree slope: the pass is to the right of a set of jagged grey teeth, obvious on the skyline above you. The path goes directly to the left of the teeth, then traverses across to the 4,750m pass. To descend, it is probably best to go down to a small lake at the foot of Rondoy/Ninashanka and follow the *quebrada* to the valley floor. Or traverse the hillside on the left, but keep low for a much more interesting route. In all events, you will reach Río Llamac, at the bottom of the valley, after 2–3 hours descending, and the new road built for mining operations in the area.

Hikers taking the direct route from Llamac will continue along the trail running east from that town, heading for an hour up the valley to the smaller community of Pocpa, at 3,450m, an easy 45-minute walk, with good camping spots before Pocpa. The climb continues up the valley (the new road making the walk easier, though still hard on the feet), passing another small community called Palca, the mine camp (3 hours from Pocpa), and finally you arrive at the entrance of Quebrada Rondoy at 4,000m, about 11km (5 hours) from Pocpa. From here you get the first glimpse of snow-capped mountains, and there are some good camping spots.

Side trip *If you want to get closer to those snowpeaks, an enjoyable hike can be made to the lake at the end of Quebrada Rondoy, below Nevados Rondoy (5,870m) and Ninashanca (5,607m).*

The trail to the first pass of Cacanampunta (4,700m) is hard to find. It is a good half-hour walk above the Quebrada Rondoy. The most obvious reference is where the road makes a sharp left turn crossing the river; here is where your path starts. There are a couple of houses just below the bridge where the road goes over the river. Sometimes you can buy delicious cheese here. The path runs up the valley just above the river (on it's east (right) for 100m, then strikes up the valley side, heading above and to the left of a couple of stone houses and round sheep corrals). If you scour the hillside above you, you should be able to make out the route you need to follow. You should reach the pass about 3 hours after leaving the road. From the pass, the trail drops down through a wide marshy valley to the junction of two rivers (2 hours). Continue to the right, up the Río Janca for about 1½ hours to Laguna Mitacocha (4,300m), where there are fantastic views and plenty of camping places.

Side trip *From Mitacocha you can continue up the valley to Laguna Ninacocha, at the foot of Jirishanka Chico (5,446m). It's a steep climb, but not difficult, over a moraine. It takes about 1½ hours each way.*

Your route continues from Janca, half an hour below lake Mitucocha, up the valley to the southeast, passing the corrals of Mayas, to the pass of Punta Carhuac, at 4,650m, 7km (3 hours) from the start. Beware of aggressive dogs in the valley on the way down. On the descent follow the river to the Laguna Carhuacocha (2 hours) at 4,100m. This is a gorgeous place with some marvellously scenic campsites, one of the best being above the lake on the *pampa* with fantastic views of the east sides of Yerupaja and Siula. There is a little community situated below the lake at the top end and another at the bottom end. You can camp near either. You may be greeted by Sr Wenseslau-Simeon Flores, who sells drinks and provisions including trout. Sr Flores (or one of the other locals) can also guide you over the dramatic high-altitude pass beneath the snowpeaks. Carhuacocha to Huayhuash takes 7–8 hours (described below).

Side trip *Up to the Lagunas Siula, at 4,300m (4km/2 hours) and Quesillacocha, which lie nestled below the towering east face of Nevado Siula Grande (6,344m).*

Alternative route *Carhuacocha to Huayhuash. Warning: This route is not recommended unless a local goes with you to show you the way. There is no path, it is vertiginous, and is easy to get lost, especially in low cloud. There have been several accidents here over the past few years.*
Walk along the southern edge of Lake Carhuacocha and then along the east side of Lake Siula and Lake Quesillacocha (2 hours). At the top of Quesillacocha, pass a waterfall coming down from the left, and after a few minutes start to climb steeply, on a narrow zigzagging path. Continue to climb steeply for an hour before the gradient flattens out. The views behind of three glacial lakes and sharp snowpeaks are astounding, some of the best on the circuit. Cross a flattish grassy corrie and then climb steeply again up the rocky slope ahead for 45 minutes to reach the pass. You will see a cairn from below. There is no path down the other side. Stay to the left of the lakes ahead and below. It's boggy; 2–3 hours will bring you onto the normal path to Huayhuash, and your camp.

Continuing along the main route you will need to find a fording place across the river below Laguna Carhuacocha since there is no bridge. The easiest place is where the river flows out of the lake, and there is a whole line of stepping stones. Cross carefully. Follow the Carhuacocha valley down for 20 minutes then climb steeply up the Carnicero valley to your right (south), passing dry lakes and a good chance to see *vicuñas*, to the pass of Carnicero, at 4,600m, about 8km (3–4 hours) from Laguna Carhuacocha. The trail, clear all the way, comes down between the two Lagunas Atocshaico, at 4,500m. Good campsites but cold nights. The trail continues its descent, passing a little settlement, to the community of Huayhuash, at 4,350m, 4km from the lakes. The village is situated on the bottom of the valley, with a junction of another valley to the right. This is a popular camping spot. It can get quite dirty by the end of the season. It is also renowned for robbery, so keep a careful eye on your belongings and on your donkeys.

The trail continues up the valley (south), with good camping places and some small lakes at the right, to the pass of Portachuelo de Huayhuash, 4,750m, 5km (3–4 hours) from Huayhuash. Ahead are spectacular views of the Cordillera Raura. The trail drops down from the pass to Laguna Viconga, 4,500m, 5km (1 hour) from the pass. If you decide to stop the night here, camp above the lake. The path continues to the lower end of the lake, where there is a dam and a building for a hydro-electric project.

This is the point where you can leave the Cordillera via Cajatambo; the town lies at 3,400m, about 22km (8–9 hours) from the lake. On this trail, after about an hour, you'll come to a small thermal, concrete-lined pool. Not the best hot springs in Peru, but after six nights camped above 4,000m you are not going to be fussy! You need to fill the tanks by opening or closing the water flow from the springs above. Beware: the water flow of the river is controlled by the dam on Lake Viconga and when the water is released it is virtually impossible to cross the river. In 2001 water was released during the day and the flow stopped at night. There is basic accommodation in Cajatambo and buses to Lima every other day (check the latest timetable with the SAE club before leaving Lima). There is little alternative transport.

The main route continues from the dam and climbs up the valley to your right to the pass of Punta Cuyoc at 5,000m (making it the highest pass on this hike), a good 4 hours from Laguna Viconga. The pass lies quite a bit above and to the left of the ridge's low point below Nevados Cuyoc (5,530m) and Puscanturpa Sur (5,442m). A steep, slippery trail descends to the *pampa* on the far side where there are good campsites, then down the narrow valley of Quebrada Guanacpatay to Río Huayllapa, 4,000m, about 12km (4–5 hours) from the pass. As you reach the end of the Guanacpatay valley the path divides. If you are planning to go directly to the village of Huayllapa, the left bank of the river is better (extremely steep, somewhat vertiginous and not passable for *burros*, which should go down the right side). If you wish to take the side trip to Lagunas Jurau and Sarapococha, stay to the right of the river. There is a dramatic (300m) waterfall just before Quebrada Guanacpatay meets the Río Huayllapa, which makes a wonderful shower.

Side trip *Up to the Lagunas Jurau (4,350m, 7km, 3–4 hours) and Sarapococha. Take the trail heading up the right bank of the Río Huayllapa to the base of the moraine in front of Laguna Jurau. Some steep, rocky trails climb to the right of the outlet stream to the barren, beautiful lake lying below Nevados Jurau (5,600m) and Carnicero (5,960m). It is easy to cross the stream near the lake and take the path across the moraine heading toward Sarapococha. Another small lake, Ruricoltau, lies to the right directly below the face of Nevado Sarapo (6,127m). You can descend back to Río Huayllapa from Laguna Sarapococha. This side trek will take one day.*

PERU ON HORSEBACK

Jane Barnett and her friend Julie decided to buy horses and explore the Cordillera Blanca. Clothing and equipment were much the same as for a backpacking trip – warm sleeping bag, rain gear, waterproof boots, water filter and repair kit. Plus: 'At a village market we purchased a huge Thermos for keeping sugary milk tea hot all day. That Thermos was a real blessing during cold days at high altitudes, as was handcream, without which our skin would have been rubbed raw.' Jane takes up the tale:

Purchasing horses proved more difficult. Eventually, we found Alberto Cafferata at Pony Expeditions in Caraz. Alberto is fluent in English and a gracious source of information about the area. Upon his recommendation we headed up to Cashapampa, where mountain ponies accustomed to high altitude and severe weather were being brought down from their winter pastures. The people were generally friendly and honest, but business is business, and selling a horse to gringas is a chance to make big money. We had to be assertive. A post-sale libation of Coca-Cola (our treat) soothed any ruffled feathers our tough girl act and accidental cultural improprieties might have caused.

For riding gear, we went local style. Among other things, we bought saddles, sheep skin saddle pads, traditional saddle bags, ponchos, and sombreros. From a distance we blended in. The reality of our undertaking sunk in when we bought a very large, sharp knife for killing an injured horse.

For some, taking a guide might make for a more enjoyable, less stressful trip. There are plenty of guides available in the area. A fellow did escort us for the first two days of our trip as we headed towards his village to buy a third horse. He taught us cargo loading tricks, mountain horse handling techniques, and many uses of the all-purpose poncho. This was helpful. On the other hand, the addition of a local male definitely changed the energy of our group. According to him, we cut our vegetables wrong, cooked with too much garlic, picked bad campsites, and so on.

We more or less rode a big loop. We began with the well-known Santa Cruz trail, riding from Cashapampa to Colcabamba. From Colcabamba we made our way to Pomabamba, our mid-way point, where we could rest up and restock the food supply. Then we headed to Laguna Safuna via Yanacollpa. To get to Alpamayo without having to cross high passes covered in snow, we took a long detour through the beautiful Collota Valley and over

The main trail descends alongside Río Huayllapa, passing the entrance of the long Quebrada Segya which leads to Laguna Caramarca below Nevados Rasac (6,017m) and Tsacra (5,548m), which can be another side trip, to the small village of Huayllapa, at 3,600m. In the village you can find accommodation (ask at the shop) and meals and even stock up on some basic foods.

two somewhat treacherous, rocky passes. From there it was a two-day ride back to Cashapampa. We spent a good deal of time poring over topo maps trying to work out where we were. The landscape varied from wide-open pampas to icy peaks, and glacial lakes to wooded river valleys. Being on horseback freed us from the backpacker view of our own feet, and every moment was a vista moment.

On day six a small, bony, golden puppy began tailing us. That evening he joined a horde of children as they encircled our tent and stared at our supper. When pup settled down for the night on our pile of saddles, we knew we'd found our guard dog. There are some problems with folks stealing horses by night, so we were pleased to have him. With just two friends, three horses, and a puppy together out there ñ all of us dwarfed by the majestic terrain, it was easy to get attached to the little fellow. Puppy came to the USA to live with me.

A 'town' on the map was often no more than a mud or stone hut with a small corral. Tiny dots of colour in the distance transformed into women quietly spinning wool and watching over their flocks. Sometimes I didn't know people were there until we were practically face-to-face. Such was the case when I took advantage of a sunny moment between hailstorms to bathe in a river, unaware I was being watched until there was giggling on the hillside above.

On occasion people approached us asking for medical supplies or milk for their children, but they weren't bothersome. They were generous, bringing us potatoes for dinner or inviting us into their home during a storm. One sweet man spent hours pursuing our horse, Charlie, when he took off after a wild mare and disappeared into the distance, taking our cargo with him. During our mid-way stop in Pomabamba, the family Alajandro Via took us in as if we were family. In the town of Alpamayo, boys watched our tent so we could canter to see the nearby famous peak.

The trip wasn't easy. But the maxim 'you get out of it what you put into it' held true. All the hard work was worth it for just one cowgirl moment of being bundled in a warm poncho sipping hot tea, watching the sunrise reveal a backdrop of snowy peaks behind our grazing horses.

Two UK tour operators offer horse-riding trips in Peru and Bolivia:
Roxton Bailey Robinson Worldwide (UK) (tel: 01488 689700; email:
richard.laker@rbrww.com) and VentureCo (UK) (tel: 01926 411 122; email:
mail@ventureco-worldwide.com).

From Huayllapa you have another chance to leave the Cordillera via Cajatambo.

The main route continues north up the valley to your left as you climb back out of Huayllapa (right if coming down from Quebrada Huayllapa and a 10-minute hike above the village), climbing up to the *pampa*, where there are good campsites, in about 2 hours. From the *pampa* stay on the left-hand side of the valley until a high valley appears to your left after about an hour. That's the route up to the next pass of Punta Tapush, 4,800m, 8km (5 hours) from Huayllapa. From the pass the trail descends, passing two small lakes (good camping spots, though cold) to a valley junction (a valley comes down from your right), about one hour from the pass.

The trail straight ahead goes to the village of Pacllón, but most people want to make the diversion to Laguna Jahuacocha. This trail climbs east up the right-hand valley for about 2½ hours to the obvious pass of Yaucha at 4,800m. From the pass the trail descends to the left (north) into the Río Huacrish, and along the river to its junction with Río Achín, just below the southern shore of Laguna Jahuacocha, 4,050m (12km, 4 hours from Punta Tapush). If you are brave enough to swim, there is a lovely pool here at the foot of the waterfall. It's a 10-minute hike up to the lake from the river junction. The lake is the focal point of the Cordillera Huayhuash, and the many visitors have left far more than footprints. Make sure you leave the place cleaner than you find it.

The trail back to Llamac and Chiquián goes down the north bank of the Río Achín below the lake. It's not a clear path to begin with, but stay on the right, passing the settlement of Jahuacocha. Follow the path from the village, along the top of the covered irrigation channel, then, where it splits not long after the village, gradually begin to climb. This is a good path, winding gently through *queñoa* trees and lupins, past waterfalls and rocky overhangs up the valley side for about 2 hours until you reach the pass. Cross the pass, have a good last look at the view of the Huayhuash peaks, then head down the steep gravelly path until you reach Llamac in about 2 hours, following the pipeline of water. An alternative, easier route out of Jahuacocha is to follow the irrigation canal all the way. Donkeys aren't allowed to take this route and must go over the top. This water channel provides water for irrigation to the village of Llamac.

It's another 6 hours' hike from Llamac to Chiquián.

Alternative route Jahuacocha to Pacllón. *Follow the path that leads right down the valley from the lake. This is a hot day's walk, not too long, mostly following a river. You can camp at the village of Pacllón, where you can buy basic supplies and even make a phonecall. From Pacllón you have a 4–5 hour walk back to Chiquián. The route you take is that of the road being built between these two villages.*

Alternative route Jahuacocha to Matacancha. *If you have arranged transport out of Matacancha, or are prepared to walk on up the Palca valley towards Huallanca, you can avoid the hot dusty trek back to Chiquián. There are daily colectivos from just below the far side of the pass to Huallanca, and occasional mine vehicles and pick-up trucks, but I wouldn't depend on being able to get a lift. From Matacancha to the pass is 5km. Follow the route described above, which brings you out in the Quebrada Rondoy. This is a beautiful mountain pass and avoids some of the less pleasant parts of the trek. In the future with the road from Chiquián to Llamac functioning and the Palcpa Huallanca road also likely to have more traffic, this will be a better way to go into and out of the Huayhuash than starting and finishing in Chiquián.*

The Central Andes

This part of Peru covers the departments of Huánuco, Cerro de Pasco, Junín, Huancavelica and Ayacucho. Having emerged from the awful shadow of the *Sendero Luminoso*, most of whose thousands of victims came from this region, it is all set to become Peru's new gringo destination, having many of the attractions of Cusco with none of the hassles brought on by huge numbers of tourists. This area is still well off the beaten tourist trail. Go there now, before its secret is out. If you are thinking of heading into remote areas take care: terrorism has not completely disappeared. You should check the current situation with the South American Explorers in Lima or locally, in Huancayo, with one of the agencies there (see below) before planning adventurous excursions into the Central Andes, especially in the remoter parts of the department of Ayacucho.

HUANCAYO

The region's capital is a large town spread out across the fertile Mantaro Valley. It has a definite and interesting centre, dominated by the once-famous market where Avenida Huancas meets Avenida Ica. Before the *Sendero Luminoso* did so much damage to the town's economy, Huancayo and its market were on every tourist itinerary (the currently unoperational 'Highest Train in the World' from Lima being part of the attraction). Here you can buy everything you can think of, plus a lot more that you hadn't thought of. Huancayo merits a stay of several days, using the town as a base to explore the interesting nearby villages and for treks into the Cordilleras Central and Huaytapallana.

The town has a disadvantage. I remember from the 1960s that Huancayo had some of the most competent thieves in Peru. Apparently they have lost none of their expertise!

Getting there and away

Huancayo lies directly inland from Lima. The road from Lima is paved and in good condition. Cruz del Sur Imperial buses (Jr Quilca 531, Lima; tel: 01 424 1005) are very comfortable; cheaper is Mariscal Caceres (Avenida 28 de Julio 2195, Lima; tel: 01 427 2844) and there are others (ETUCSA, Paseo

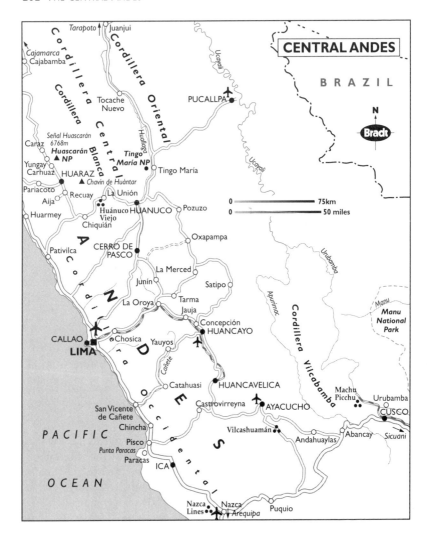

de la Republica, 646 or Grau 699, Lima; tel: 01 426 0561 and Ormeño, Carlos Zavala 177, Lima; tel: 01 472 1710). The journey takes about 7 hours.

The 207-mile railway line from Lima, closed since 1991 following attacks by the *Sendero Luminoso*, was briefly back in service between July 1998 and June 1999, but is once again out of service.

You can get away by train to the pretty small town of Huancavelica. (It runs at 06.30 each day.)

Accommodation

Casa de la Abuela Av Giraldez 691; tel: 064 223303; email: travelinfo@incasdelperu.org. From US$5 per person, includes breakfast. 10% discount to carriers of this book and students. Secure parking for vehicles and luggage can be stored while you are trekking.

Alojamiento Aldo y Soledad Huánuco 332 y Real; tel: 064 232103. US$15 double. English-speaking, safe, popular.

Hotel Presidente Real 1138 y Huánuco; tel: 231736. US$40 double. Safe, parking, café, solar energy, hot water.

Hotel Baldeón Amazonas y Giráldez. Cheap, safe, friendly.

Hotel Kiya Plaza de la Constitución. US$25 double.

Hostal América Jr Trujillo 358

Restaurants

Chez Viena Puno y Ferrocarril. Café, good cakes, also alcoholic *calientes*.

Chicharronería Cuzco Cuzco y Amazonas. Really excellent *chicharrones* (fried pork ribs). Basic but cheap and delicious.

El Otro Lado Next door to above, serves breakfasts, trout dishes and snacks during the day.

El Viejo Madero Paseo la Breña, near Plaza Constitución. Good chicken and chips.

Juliette Av Giraldez 594. An excellent coffee shop just off the main square.

Koki´s Great café/bread shop with good coffee including cappuccino.

La Cabaña Av Giraldez 652. Bar, *peña* and restaurant, traditional food and pizzas. Live folk music.

Los Maderas Pizzeria Jr Puno 599. Good-value pizzas.

Restaurant Nuevo Horizonte. Vegetarian. Don't be put off by the menu that quotes meat dishes – they are all prepared with vegetarian ingredients.

Entertainment

Galileo Breña y Libertad. Up-market bar with live music.

Karaoke Torre Torre Plaza de la Constitución. Good Pisco Sours.

Useful addresses
Spanish classes and activities

Incas del Peru Av Giraldez N, 652; tel: 064 223303; fax: 064 222395; email: luchoh@yahoo.com; web: www.incasdelperu.org; postal address: Apartado Postal No 510. Language courses in Spanish and Quechua. Also weaving, natural dyes, Peruvian cooking, and traditional musical instruments (panpipes, flute, charango).

Katia Cerna Rivera Av Huancavelica 612; tel: 064 225332; email: katiacerna@hotmail.com. Spanish classes for US$5 per hour, long-term courses available, lodging with local families US$6 per day.

Lucho Hurtado (same address as Incas del Peru). Will organise trekking in the area, especially the Mantaro Valley, the Huaytapallana area and to the cloudforest of Chanchamayo. Also mountain biking. At the weekends there is a chance to join cultural or outdoor trips with the language-course students.

HighLand Tours Av Huancavelica 612; tel: 064 225332; email: karis_cer@LatinMail.com. Karina Cerna Rivera organises excursions and treks into the surrounding area.

Medical clinics

Clínica Ortega Run by Dr Felix Ortega. He speaks some English.
Doctor Gustavo Llanos Tel: 064 608186
Dentist Lucho Mendoza Calle Real, past Plaza Huamanmarca on left, 2nd floor, next to Bata shop; tel: 064 239133
Optician Óptica Santa Lucia Ricardo Traverso, Calle Real 775

Money

Money Gram Calle Real. Good travel agent (Velitours) and will change travellers' cheques, give cash advance on credit cards and change dollars for 3% commission.
Banco de Crédito Plaza Constitución. Visa, ATM.
Western Union Ancash y Lima
Casas de cambio Several on Real near Plaza Constitución.

Internet

Service is always faster early in the morning or late at night. US$1 per hour. Several internet places in town, mostly near Plaza Constitución on Real and Giráldez.

Shopping

Casa del Artesano Plaza Constitución. A good selection of all local crafts under one roof.
Markets Huancayo has a famous Sunday market (Feria Dominical) with everything from antique sewing machines to grapefruits. It is an extension of the craft market. The craft market functions every day and is on Av Huancavelica.

Miscellaneous

Stove alcohol *Benceina blanca* available from Union Ferretera SA, Calle Arequipa 333.
Post office Serpost Plaza Huamanmarca
Laundry at Paseo la Breña y Real. Quick.

PLACES OF INTEREST NEAR HUANCAYO

The neighbouring villages, none of which is more than an hour from Huancayo, each specialise in its own crafts. Cochas Chico is known for its carved gourds, Hualhuas for weaving, San Jeronimo for silver work, Viques for belts. Ingenio is great for local trout dishes. Jauja is a good base for day walks, and the monastery at Santa Rosa de Ocopa is worth a visit.

THE CORDILLERA CENTRAL

John Biggar

The Cordillera Central, which lies inland and south of Lima, is an excellent trekking destination. The trekking routes are much quieter than the popular treks in the Cordillera Blanca and Huayhuash to the north, and the weather is generally better too. The dry season runs from May to September and this is the best time to trek. The highest peak in the Cordillera Central is Ticlla, 5,897m (19,460ft), and a circuit trek around this dramatic snow-covered peak is described here. A brief description is also given of a much shorter variation along an interesting bit of Inca Road.

The Ticlla Circuit

Highlights of this circuit include some exceptionally beautiful high altitude lagoons, interesting wildlife and very friendly local people. The easiest place to start this trek is from the village of Miraflores at the southeast corner of the range, but a similar route could be followed by starting from Ayaviri to the west or Tanta to the northwest. Being a circular trek, it would also be quite feasible to do this walk in reverse.

Distance	About 80km
Altitude	From 3,650m to 5,050m
Rating	Moderate to difficult
Timing	5 or 6 days
Start of trail	Miraflores, occasional public transport from Huancayo
Maps	IGN sheets *Huarochiri* (25-k) and *Yauyos* (25-l)

Getting to the trailhead There are two main ways of approaching Miraflores. These are either from the inland city of Huancayo or from the coast at Cañete.

Approaching from Huancayo has a big advantage for acclimatisation because of the altitude of this city. From Huancayo travel via Angasmayo and San Jose de Quero to reach Miraflores; in 1998 there was reported to be a bus on Sundays only, otherwise you will have to arrange private transport – it's a 5-hour drive on a reasonable road. From Cañete travel via the town of Yauyos, from where you may need to hire a private vehicle.

The village of Miraflores is a friendly place at an altitude of 3,650m. There are only a few very small and basic shops. Accommodation, donkeys and any other basic tourist facilities can usually be found here. For all of these try asking at the mayor's office on the southwest corner of the square or just sit and wait in the square and ask the locals who come past.

Route description From Miraflores cross back over the river and walk up lanes on the south side of the deep Quebrada Tomapampa valley. There are lots of nice flowers and cacti in this valley. It is possible to camp in high pastures at Ancacucho near the head of the valley after 3–4 hours. There are good views of the dramatic southeast face of Ticlla from near here. From Ancacucho make the short climb over the pass of 4,750m to the west and then descend steeply to the long Laguna Huasacocha (4,250m) under the south slopes of Ticlla (2 hours). There are good campsites at the near (northeast) end of this scenic lake.

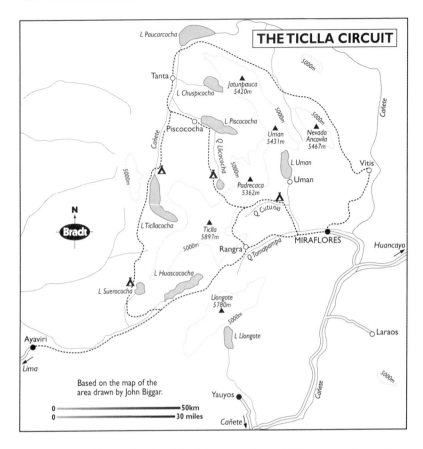

THE TICLLA CIRCUIT

Based on the map of the area drawn by John Biggar.

Walk down the south side of the lake to the far end. Then cross the outflow stream and begin gradually ascending the hillside on the north side of the valley of the Río Ayaviri. This leads up and round into the Quebrada Suero and a short walk up this valley to the scenic Laguna Suerococha, where camping is possible (3-4 hours).

From Laguna Suerococha climb the grassy slopes to the northwest and cross a pass at about 4,800m. Go down the valley on the other side of this pass until it begins to steepen and then traverse rightwards on animal tracks over open slopes to the head of the Quebrada Pichahuacra (2 hours). Climb a steep side valley to the north and a pass of 4,750m with views of the beautiful curving Laguna Ticllacocha. It is a steep 2-hour descent to the north to reach the campsites at the outflow stream of this lake.

A worthwhile side trip from here if you have time is to walk up to the end of the valley on the north side of the lakes to the spectacular mountain cirque under the northwest side of Ticlla. From the campsites at the outflow walk down the headwaters of the Río Cañete to the north for about 7km (2 hours) until another wide valley joins from the right. From this junction it is possible to walk to the small settlement of Tanta, just an hour to the north. You can start or leave the trek at Tanta, though it might be difficult to arrange transport (the only public transport is reported to be a once-a-week *colectivo* to Jauja). In Tanta you can purchase some basic supplies.

Going back to the main description, from the valley junction turn into the right-hand valley and walk up the broad, sometimes swampy valley bottom to a small settlement at the west end of Laguna Piscococha. Continue (3 hours) on a trail along the hillside immediately south of the lake. There are nice campsites at several points on or near the south shores. From the far end of Piscococha walk for 2–3 hours up the swampy Quebrada Llicococha to the south (there is a good path on the right-hand side) to the blue-green waters of the scenic Laguna Llicococha. Just beyond this lagoon the path climbs steeply up and over the highest pass of the circuit, at 5,050m, then descends steeply to the Quebrada Cutunia at 4,600m (2–3 hours). This section of trail is very well made and may be of Inca origin.

Walk out down the Quebrada Cutunia probably passing many herds of llamas, to the small settlement of Uman at the valley junction. From here there is a worthwhile side trip along to the impressive Lagunas Uman to the north (2 hours including return), where you may well see flamingos and *taguas* (giant coots). From Uman the valley drops slowly southwards then suddenly descends the steep and narrow Quebrada Huayllacancha by a rocky path, which bends and twists amongst boulders and beautiful *queñoa* trees on the right-hand (west) bank of the stream. You rejoin the original route out of Miraflores for the last hour. It will be a total of about 4–5 hours from the Quebrada Cutunia to Miraflores.

A short trek from Miraflores

If you don't have so much time this short two or three day trek is a great alternative to the Ticlla circuit. Follow the description above out of Miraflores and up the Quebrada Tomapampa. Just before the Ancacucho camp (Rangra on the IGN map) look for a trail heading up the north side of the valley. This takes you over a 5,000m pass with great views of the huge east face of Ticlla. Keep to the left here and the trail soon turns into a spectacular and well-made trail high up on the north side of the Quebrada Cutunia. This trail joins the trek described above just below the Llicococha pass. Its worth going up to the pass for the view. Then follow the description above down to Miraflores.

OTHER PLACES OF INTEREST IN THE REGION
Cordillera Huaytapallana

The Cordillera Huaytapallana (from Quechua, meaning place where flowers are collected) is a beautiful, and still very unexplored glaciated range which forms a part of the Cordillera Central. It lies just 30km east of Huancayo and has 12 snow-covered peaks, with a glaciated area of around 35km^2. The highest peak in the range is the Nevado Lasuntay at 5,720m. Treks are organised by local companies (see listings) into this area, and there is great potential for exploring trekking routes.

Cerro de Pasco
A chilly, high town with some interesting hikes in the surrounding mountain areas.

Tarma
A typical mountain village, situated in a beautiful valley. There are some exceptional hiking possibilities in the surrounding mountains, with ruins, lakes and caves.

Huancavelica
A very pretty mountain town with good crafts and local festivals, and some interesting hiking possibilities in the surrounding mountains.

There are various hotels in Huancavelica including:

Hostal Camacho Jr Carabayo 481. Hot water, clean and well looked after. US$4–6.
Hotel Tahuantinsuyo Jr Carabaya 399. Well-lit rooms with tables and chairs. Shared and private showers. US$3–4.
Hotel Ascencion Plaza de Armas. Hot showers, shared and private rooms. US$3–10.

Ayacucho
Until recently this was more famous as the birthplace of the *Sendero Luminoso*. Now it is regaining its prominence as an important centre with notable crafts and festivals. There are plenty of hiking possibilities in the surrounding mountains, with some interesting ruins.

Ayacucho is becoming an increasingly popular stop-over place for travellers taking the eastern route to Cusco. It is a beautiful and dramatic 12-hour bus journey from Huancayo.

Huancayo to Ayacucho There is a regular bus service between these towns (12 hours) but a popular route is to take the train from Huancayo to Huancavelica and then catch various local buses/trucks from there to Ayacucho. The whole trip should take 2–3 days and is highly recommended. The train leaves Huancayo from Estación de trenes de Chilca (Libertad; tel: 064 217724) Monday to Saturday 06.30 and 13.00, Sunday 14.00 only (all services 6 hours or more). Tickets can be bought on the day, an hour before travel. Executive class (US$4) is recommended as it is less crowded although not particularly 'executive' and luggage is less likely to get stolen.

From Huancavelica There is a bus service to Lircay (2½ hours), where you can ring Fico (tel: 064 758078) (friend of Lucho Hurtado), who will let you stay in his house for a small fee. From Lircay, take a bus to Julcamarca (3 hours) and from there another bus to Ayacucho (3 hours). An alternative route is on more of a main road by bus to Santa Inés and truck to Ayacucho.

THE INCA ROYAL ROAD
This hike gives a wonderful insight into Andean rural life as it passes through many small farms and villages. What makes it special, however, is that it

follows what was once the principal highway of the Inca empire. Soaring and diving for 2,500km along the spine of the Andes, this was the greatest road in the medieval Americas. Castillo to Yanahuanca is one of its finest stretches, and halfway along the walk you'll come upon the extraordinary Inca citadel of Huánuco Viejo, a major archaeological site, which has the added bonus of being visited by very few tourists.

Castillo via Huánuco Viejo to Yanahuanca
Ann Spowart-Taylor and John Pilkington

Routefinding is generally easy – the Inca road stretches out clearly before you – but you should carry a compass in case of poor weather, together with the IGN sheets listed in the box below. The walk divides into two roughly equal parts with an opportunity to rest and re-supply at the small town of La Unión, just off the route in the valley of the Río Vizcarra. Water is readily available except on the 6km and 7km stretches noted in the route description. It is sometimes of dubious quality, so carry a means of purification and fill up where possible at the cleanest sources.

Distance	About 160km
Altitude	Between 3,200m and 4,470m
Rating	Moderate
Timing	10 days including a rest day at La Unión
Start of trail	Taxis and occasional trucks and minibuses from Huari
Maps	Essential: IGN 1:100,000 sheets *Huari* (19-i), *La Unión* (20-j) and *Yanahuanca* (21-j). Optional: sheet *Recuay* (20-i).

Conditions/what to take As usual in the Andes this walk is best done in the dry season between May and October. During these months you'll enjoy mostly blue skies but you should be prepared for rain at any time, especially on the two high passes where you'll also need protection from the cold. Food supplies are available in Huari, La Unión and Yanahuanca but the choice is limited; anything out of the ordinary should be brought from the cities of Huaraz, Huánuco (not to be confused with Huánuco Viejo) or Cerro de Pasco.

Getting to the trailhead If you do the walk from north to south you'll make your approach via Huari, a small town perched on a ledge above the valley of the Río Huari. There are several *residenciales* including the recommended El Dorado at Bolívar 341. There's also a tiny indoor market for last-minute supplies. The quickest way to reach the start of the walk in the village of Castillo (3,200m) is by taxi for US$13. Trucks also leave occasionally for Huachis via Castillo; or you could take one of the regular minibuses to Masín

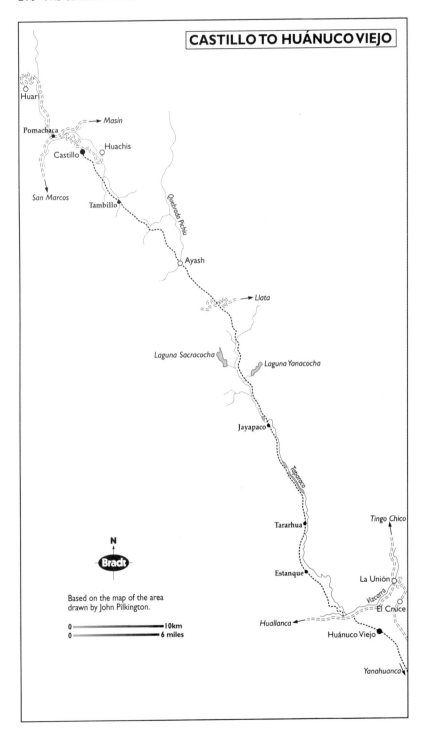

CASTILLO TO HUÁNUCO VIEJO

Huari

Masín

Pomachaca

Huachis

Castillo

San Marcos

Tambillo

Quebrada Pichiu

Ayash

Llata

Laguna Sacracocha

Laguna Yanacocha

Jayapaco

Taparaco

Tararhua

Tingo Chico

Estanque

La Unión

El Cruce

Vizcarra

Huallanca

Huánuco Viejo

Yanahuanca

N

Bradt

Based on the map of the area
drawn by John Pilkington.

0 ▬▬▬▬▬▬ 10km
0 ▬▬▬▬▬▬ 6 miles

and ask to be dropped at the Castillo turnoff by the river. (The last option will leave you with a stiff 5km climb.)

Route description Despite the recent arrival of streetlights, Castillo is a village with an old-fashioned feel. Walk up the main street and turn left at the top. This path becomes the Inca road and climbs steadily uphill for several hours to the first pass. From time to time there are fine paved stretches, and as you gain height splendid views open up back to Huari and the mountains to the north. Four hours from Castillo the valley opens out at a place called Tambillo – there's good camping here and also beyond the pass. The route crosses the river and then climbs steeply and stonily to the pass at 4,400m, from where it descends gently on the southwest side of a valley. After making a brief detour up a side valley it climbs to a second pass at 4,100m, before turning south and descending steadily past a school and small farms to the village of Ayash on the banks of Quebrada Pichiu.

If you're using IGN sheet *La Unión* (20-j), note that the Inca road is wrongly marked between Quebrada Pichiu and the next pass. The correct route descends into Ayash on magnificent Inca paving, then climbs to a conspicuous nick before resuming its southeasterly course up a steep side valley. After 2 hours the valley opens out into broad upland meadows. There's good camping here and for most of the way to La Unión.

The track climbs gently past prominent crags, keeping first to the right and then, after crossing the gravel road to Llata, switching to the left. The crossing is technically a pass at 4,400m. Don't be tempted to follow the gravel road, but instead continue on a course slightly east of south. The Inca road now maintains its altitude across rolling uplands to the broad headwaters of the Río Taparaco.

Walking down this valley is delightfully easy. The Inca road, in places 6m wide, is grassy and leads steadily downhill, keeping to the left of the river. High above are two lakes, large but unseen. The road goes straight through a farm and the valley then narrows, forcing the track to the river's edge until suddenly the scenery opens out again at a left-hand bend. Wade across here to the huts of Jayapaco and the start of a superb section which follows the river's right-hand bank for the next 12km. You'll pass through a large village with a school and 30 minutes later will come to the last really good campsite, on the riverbank. It's 4 hours from here to the Río Vizcarra and the road to La Unión. After 15 minutes the village of Tararhua is reached from where the road climbs steadily up the right-hand valley side, giving spectacular views of the river below. Eventually it levels off, passes through a village called Estanque, and 4km further on begins its dramatic descent into the Vizcarra valley. Look out for the ruins of Huánuco Viejo, just visible across the valley in the middle of a plain.

A couple of minutes beyond the Vizcarra bridge you'll come to the Huallanca–La Unión road, with regular public transport to the easy-going riverside town of La Unión 7km downstream. This makes a good stopover. There's accommodation at the basic Hostal Gran Turístico, Comercio 1300, or the even more basic but friendly El Domaino, Dos de Mayo 359. Soothe your aching limbs in the hot baths at Tauripampa, 3km up the valley. This is a perfect base for exploring the sprawling ruins of Huánuco Viejo, one of the most important cities of the Inca empire. The site boasts superb stonework and its crowning glory is a huge *usnu* or ceremonial platform in the middle of a vast central plaza. North and east are temples, dwellings, military barracks, storehouses and a palace for the visiting Inca, approached through a sequence of fine stone arches.

The ruins are on a high plain south of La Unión, a tough 2-hour walk away. Take the steep path starting behind the market and climb towards a prominent cross; then continue through a village on a wide path. Ahead and to the right you'll see the corrugated iron roof of what turns out to be a chapel, with the ruins beyond. Alternatively you can take an Iscopampa minibus and get off at El Cruce from where it's a level 30-minute walk.

No trace is left of the Inca road shown on the IGN map between the Río Vizcarra and Huánuco Viejo. If you'd like to prove this for yourself, leave the main road 1km east (downstream) of the point where you joined it and pick your way up the ancient scree slope spilling out from a narrow side valley. Although steep the route isn't difficult, and as you enter the valley you'll find yourself on a clear path which leads all the way to the top. The entrance to the ruins is 2km east-southeast from here, an easy walk across the level plain. Allow 1½ hours from the main road.

From Huánuco Viejo, by contrast, the Royal Road is almost continuously clear and easy to follow as far as Yanahuanca, four days' walk away. Start from the east gate of the ruins and head up a prominent valley, keeping the stream on your left. Pass through a farm and under a power line, then cross the stream and climb steadily up the left-hand valley side, first across open land and then through a field. This is one of the few sections where the route isn't obvious, but it levels out to the right of the power line. After picking it up again you'll pass above the village of Iscopampa, then climb gently to 4,000m before dropping down to Quebrada Tambo where there's good water and a place to camp.

The road undulates for the next hour to the hamlet of Huacarcocha where there have been landslips; ask local people to guide you through. A little further on it begins a long descent to the Río Nupe at 3,350m where waters from hot springs have been fed into a couple of rough open-air baths. The first of these is close to where you join the main valley road; the second is 300m downstream, near the river. The Inca is said to have bathed regularly in the latter during his journeys along the Royal Road.

Only a crumbling abutment remains of the original river crossing, so to continue south you have to make a detour to a suspension bridge downstream. Walk northeast along the main road for 1½km, then follow a broad footpath down to the river. You'll rejoin the Inca road at a log bridge across Quebrada Tingo; this is known locally as Puente Huascar after one of the last Incas.

Now begins a fabulous section, climbing steeply alongside Quebrada Tingo before heading across a high plain and finally climbing again to 4,050m. In the dry season, after crossing a stream where the road begins its final ascent, there'll be no further water until you reach Laguna Tambococha 6km ahead.

This beautiful lake lies in a broad marshy valley which in the rainy season presents a serious obstacle. John Pilkington recommends wading the river just below the outlet. 'The ooze spread for miles in both directions, so I chose what looked like the narrowest bit and waded in. It was rather scary to be up to my waist at one point, flailing about and sinking; but I managed to extricate myself somehow and emerged dripping and gooey on the other side. The Inca road crossed this marsh on a causeway which has sunk without trace.' John adds reassuringly that he made the crossing in April, at the end of the rainy season. From June onwards it shouldn't be too bad.

Your reward for these tribulations comes less than 1km further on in the shape of the eerie Inca ruins of Tunsucancha, also known as Tambococha. Many *tambos* or staging posts have been found on the Inca road network but this seems to have been rather a special one, having three long barrack-buildings as well as accommodation for the *chasquis* or relay runners who carried the king's messages.

Continue south, joining a dirt road which climbs a ridge before passing through the village of Gashapampa at just under 4,100m. There's little evidence of the Inca road here but it picks up again after the village, keeping to the left (east) of a broad plain. Don't be tempted to follow the dirt road which contours round the west side of this plain. The route descends, first gradually and then more steeply, into the deep gorge of the Río Lauricocha, which is finally reached after a breathtaking section round a rocky buttress. Tunsucancha to the river is about 4 hours.

The river is wide and the Inca bridge has long since disappeared, but getting across isn't as difficult as it might seem. Follow a tiny path downstream for just under 2km to where a huge boulder provides a natural bridge. Although the river roars underneath you can hop across here without difficulty. To continue south don't take the path by the river, which is a dead end, but instead head steeply uphill to some fields on a ledge and then pass left of a small hill to rejoin the Inca road high above the river. It's worth detouring to see the stone staircase leading back down to the original crossing.

Now begins a steady climb to a minor summit at 4,250m, followed by a drop into another valley and a long, gentle ascent which finally steepens to culminate in the spectacular 4,470m pass known as Inka Poyo or 'Inca's Resting Place'. This is a high point in every sense of the word, with distant views to the snow-capped Cordillera Huayhuash in the west. But beware! After the prominent stream 1km before the summit the route enters a limestone area and there's no more water for 7km.

From the summit the terrain falls away into a huge basin studded with rocky outcrops. The Inca road descends its left flank, passing farms and crossing minor ridges to reach, after 5km, one of the most perfect limestone pavements to be found anywhere in the world. The whole landscape here is surreal, with great sinkholes to the west and cliffs ahead towering over what proves to be the precipitous gorge of Quebrada Huarautambo. A truly special place, and luckily after a dizzying 20-minute descent down an Inca staircase you'll find a perfect campsite where the road joins the valley floor.

The final stretch to Yanahuanca is idyllic. The Inca paving is stunning and soon you'll reach a beguiling multi-spanned Inca bridge across the ever-growing *quebrada*. Oddly the Inca road doesn't cross the bridge but remains on the left bank of the river, descending steadily to the prominent village of Huarautambo where it eventually gives out in the village square. A stone water spout and trough here may be of Inca origin, and there's a beautifully preserved Inca building with eight niches 50m to the north. Villagers will point the way.

From Huarautambo a road of recent origin zigzags down a narrowing chasm to the valley of the Río Yanahuanca, and unfortunately its builders seem to have destroyed what was left of the Inca road. You can avoid the zigzags by following a path, first left and then right of the river. At the bottom you'll be just 20 minutes from Yanahuanca and the end of the walk. But before you saunter down the valley road we recommend a small diversion. Walk a few hundred metres up the Río Yanahuanca, cross the bridge, and return the same distance to a riverside cliff through which has been hewn an impressive pedestrian tunnel. Although just off the Royal Road this may well be of Inca origin; local people certainly think so. There are commercial baths fed by hot springs near the bridge.

Getting back Yanahuanca is a small but lively town with basic accommodation in and around the main square. Buses and minibuses leave daily for Huánuco and Cerro de Pasco. If you have a day or two to spare you could explore more of the Royal Road, climbing steeply south from the tunnel to a village called Chiripata from where a well-preserved section follows first Quebrada Ranracancha and then the Cerro de Pasco road for 14km to the village of Tambopampa, before striking out across the vast, lonely Plateau of Bombón.

Cusco and Vicinity

Cusco lays claim to being the oldest continuously inhabited city in the Americas. It was the religious and administrative capital of the far-flung Inca empire, and the equivalent of Mecca for the Inca's subjects: every person of importance throughout the empire tried to visit Cusco once in his lifetime.

Tourists feel the same way. Cusco is indisputably the most beautiful and interesting town in Peru, and one of the finest on the whole continent. Nowhere else do you find the combination of splendid Inca stonework and elegant Spanish colonial architecture, Quechua and *mestizo*, traditional and modern. The tourist boom that started in the 1980s has ensured that homesick gringos can munch their way through chocolate cake and pizza as well as *cuy* and *papas*, and luxuriate in top-quality hotels as well as backpacker *hostales*. And as one who remembers Cusco from 1969 I cannot say the town has been spoilt by tourism. For one thing it smells a lot better!

HISTORY OF THE INCAS

The Inca legend tells us that Cusco was founded by the son of the sun, Manco Capac, and the daughter of the moon, Mama Occllo, who materialised on the Islands of the Sun and Moon in Lake Titicaca and journeyed together to Cusco, 'the navel of the earth'. The Incas built their empire on the achievements of earlier cultures: the coastal peoples that they conquered have left an artistic legacy richer than the Inca's. It was in the field of conquest and social organisation that the Incas really excelled. At the time of the conquest the empire stretched from the present-day Ecuador/Colombia border to the River Maule in southern Chile, bounded in the east by the Amazon jungle and in the west by the Pacific Ocean.

Expansion began around 1438 with the Inca ruler Pachacuti (Pachacuti Inca Yupanqui), who was largely instrumental in defeating the Chanca, long-time enemies inhabiting the region northwest of Cusco. His son Topa Inca continued to extend the empire and his efforts were consolidated in the next generation by Huayna Capac. The Inca conquered and ruled by a combination of conciliation and force. Nobles of the conquered groups were given important positions, and officials from the Cusco area settled in the remote reaches of the empire to teach the Quechua language and customs.

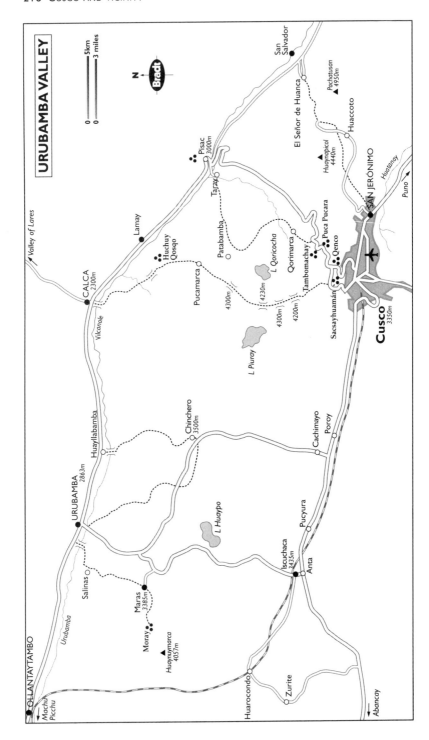

The empire was in decline before Pizarro reached Cajamarca. Before Huayna Capac died he divided the unwieldy empire in two: his son Atahualpa was to rule the north, whilst the south was under the control of Huáscar. Rivalry between the two half-brothers exploded into a civil war, which Atahualpa eventually won around the time that the Spaniards reached the Peruvian coast. The story of what happened when they arrived in Cajamarca is told in *Chapter 5*.

The Inca empire was called Tawantinsuyo, meaning the four quarters of the earth. Cusco was the heart of it, and its exact centre was considered to be the main plaza of the city. To the north lay the Chinchaysuyo, to the west the Condesuyo, to the south the Collasuyo and to the east the Antisuyo. The name Andes comes from the original inhabitants of this region, the Antis.

The victorious Spaniards marched into Cusco and began to destroy it although, according to the chroniclers, they marvelled as they smashed. Gold was stripped from the walls and the great stones were broken up to be used for Spanish buildings. What the *conquistadores* began, rebellion and natural disasters completed. An insurrection by Manco II left much of colonial Cusco in ruins, and a devastating earthquake in 1650 finished the job. The combined forces of man and nature, however, could not destroy the great Inca stone walls, which stand to this day.

Subsequent centuries were punctuated with uprisings against Spanish rule, the most important one being led by the *mestizo* rebel Túpac Amaru II in 1780. Peru gained independence in 1826.

With the discovery, in 1911, of Machu Picchu by Hiram Bingham, Cusco was back in the limelight again and overseas visitors began to arrive to admire the mysterious ruins. Cusco was added to the list of the world's cultural heritage by UNESCO, which has been instrumental in conserving the visible remains of that great empire.

FESTIVALS

The area is well known for its traditional celebrations, with most of them having an Inca/Spanish mix. It is worth visiting one if you happen to be in the area.

- January 6, Ollantaytambo. Festival of the Magi, with dancing and parades.
- January 14, Pampamarca. Festival and market.
- January 20, Cusco. Procession of saint effigies in San Sebastián district.
- Easter Monday, Cusco. Parade of the Lord of the Earthquakes.
- May 2 and 3, at all mountaintops with a cross on them. The Vigil of the Cross.
- June, the Thursday after Trinity Sunday, Cusco. Corpus Christi. Saint effigies from all the churches of Cusco are brought to the cathedral to 'sleep' with the other saints, and paraded the following day.
- Early June, Qoyoratí. The 'Star of the Snow' festival at a remote mountain site near Tinqui, north of Ausangate.
- June 17, Raqchi. The festival of Viracocha.
- June 24 and several days on either side, Cusco. Inti Raymi, the Inca festival of the winter solstice, celebrated at Sacsayhuamán.

INCA STONEWORK

'How *did* they do it?' is the question most frequently asked by tourists admiring the perfectly cut and fitted stones that constitute the empire's most famous legacy. The seeming impossibility of cutting and dressing lumps of granite without the use of metal tools has provoked some fanciful theories. The explorer Colonel Fawcett speculated that the Incas knew of a substance that would soften the stone to a clay-like consistency, thus facilitating a perfect fit. More serious archaeologists have suggested that discoveries of parabolic mirrors of gold and silver indicate that the Incas used amplified rays of sunlight to cut stone. In the 1980s, however, Jean-Pierre Protzen, an architect at UC at Berkeley, demonstrated that using only materials available to the Incas it is not difficult to cut and position stones to the highest standards. He built his own 'Inca' wall to prove it.

Protzen selected a quarry of andesite rock that had not been worked since Inca times for his researches. Evidence showed that stones were selected out of rock falls or prised out of a rock face. The Incas had no metal tools, so used simple river cobbles as hammer-stones. These, although of the same hardness as the andesite being worked, do not shatter on impact. Protzen used a 4kg hammer-stone to shape a block of andesite. He found that it was necessary only to drop the hammer-stone at the required angle, letting gravity do the rest. Using this technique it took only 20 minutes to dress one side of the stone. Protzen then turned his attention to creating a hole through stone, such as those used to secure the roofs at

- July 18, Paucartambo. Fiesta del Virgen del Carmen. Typical dances.
- July 28. Independence Day.
- August 14, Tinta. Festival of San Bartolomé.
- September (date changes every year), Cusco. Huarachicoy festival at Sacsayhuamán. A re-enactment of the Inca manhood rite, performed in dancing and Inca games by the boys of the local schools.
- September 8, Chumbivilcas. Bullfights and horse races.
- September 14, Huanca. Religious pilgrimage to the shrine of El Señor de Huanca.
- November 1, All Saints' Day. Celebrated everywhere with bread dolls and traditional cooking.
- November 4, Combapata. Local festival.
- December 24, Cusco. Santo Rantikuy, 'the buying of saints', a massive celebration of Christmas shopping in Cusco style.

CUSCO

You will see various spellings, Cusco, Cuzco or Qosqo (the Quechua spelling), but they all mean 'navel of the earth' or – more prosaically – centre of the empire. Some historians say that the Incas built Cusco in the

Machu Picchu. Hiram Bingham speculated that the Inca stonemasons bored holes by rotating a bamboo between the palms of their hands, using sand as an abrasive, but Protzen believes that they were pounded out from each side; the conical shape at each end of the hole supports this theory.

The Incas generally cut the top face of each stone to receive the shape of the stone to be laid above it, so that the upper courses of stones project into the lower course. Protzen proved that, through trial and error, it was possible to achieve a perfect fit. The Incas had an abundance of manpower and time, as chronicled by the Spaniard José de Acosta in 1589. '[The stones] fit together with incredible precision without mortar. All this was done with much manpower and much endurance in the work, for to adjust one stone to another until they fit together, it was necessary to try the fit many times, the stones not being even or full.'

Visitors to Ollantaytambo marvel at the way huge rocks were transported across the Río Urubamba. Again, this seemingly mighty feat was in fact relatively easy if the great stones were slid over the small stones on the river bottom. With enough people working together almost anything is possible. The Inca Pachacuti, under whose rule the greatest buildings were created, imposed a labour tax to supply this manpower.

Many of mankind's greatest works have this in common: they were constructed for the glory of God. The Incas were no exception. Without their worship of the Sun and absolute obedience to his deputy on earth, the supreme Inca, the awe-inspiring temples and fortresses that draw us to Peru would never have existed.

shape of a puma, with the River Tullumayo (which now runs underground) forming its spine, Sacsayhuamán the head, and the main city centre the body.

Visitors should spend at least two days here getting used to the altitude (3,350m). Make the most of it – there is something for everyone: excellent shopping for handicrafts, the best Andean music, good food, fine colonial buildings, and of course the awe-inspiring Inca stonework. The crisp air, hot sun and clear blue sky of the winter dry season make it an ideal town for pottering around and there are plenty of coffee shops and juice bars to collapse into when you get tired.

The city telephone code for Cusco is 084.

Getting there and away
By air
Flights are heavily booked and more expensive around school holidays (January/February and July/August) and national holidays, especially around Independence Day and Christmas.

The airport tax is US$4. Airport information, tel: 084 222611 or 222601. Always reconfirm flights with the airline or through a travel agent.

Aerocontinente and Aviandina Portal de Carnes 254; tel: 084 243031/243032
Tans San Agustin 315; tel: 084 242727/254545/251000
Lan Perú Av El Sol 627-B; tel: 084 255552/255553/255554
Lloyd Aéreo Boliviano Santa Catalina Angosta 160; tel: 084 222990/224715.

To Lima 1 hour. Prices always change, so check, out of season there are often special offers. Daily flights with Aero Continente, Aviandina and Lan Perú.

To Arequipa Half hour. Daily flights with Aero Continente and Lan Perú from US$60.

To Juliaca No flights at the moment.

To Puerto Maldonado For the Tambopata reserve (see boxes on pages 246–7 and 252–3), daily flights.

To La Paz 1 hour. Lloyd Aéreo Boliviana has three flights a week, Tuesdays, Thursdays and Saturdays, for US$110. Currently it is the only airline flying to La Paz from Cusco. Lloyd also has daily flights leaving late morning from Lima to La Paz, currently around US$200.

By road

Cusco has a new bus station, *terminal terrestre*, in Prolongacion Pachacutek; tel: 224471. This makes land transport a much easier business as most buses leave from and arrive here.

To Juliaca (344km) 5–6 hours on newly tarmacked road. Daily buses and trucks, mostly at night. On to Puno (44km), 45 minutes. There is a good *colectivo* system between the two towns.

Imexo Tel: 084 2291276, upmarket service, costs US$7, departures at 08.30 and 21.30.
Transelva Tel: 084 238223, costs US$4 with departures at 08.00 and 12.00.
Civa Tel: 084 229762, US$4, departures at 20.00 and 23.00.
Power Tel: 084 227777, US$4, departures at 07.30, 08.30 and 12.30.

On to La Paz (Bolivia) 6 hours. *Colectivos* leave from Puno daily in the morning.

To Arequipa (521km). 14 hours (longer in the rainy season). Buses leave in the late afternoon.

To Abancay (195km) 4 hours (longer in the rainy season). Several buses and trucks a day. On to Andahuaylas (135km), 6 hours (longer in the rainy season).

The following companies run this service: Ampay (tel: 084 227541), Civa (tel: 084 229762), Abancay (tel: 084 224447), and Wari (tel: 084 247217), with departures at 06.00, 13.00 and 20.00. Costs US$5.

On to Ayacucho (252km) 10 hours (longer in the rainy season). Poor road conditions.

THE CENTER FOR TRADITIONAL TEXTILES OF CUSCO

One of the highlights of my 2000 visit to the Cusco area was a weaving demonstration at the Center for Traditional Textiles of Cusco (supported by Cultural Survival in America) which took place in an adobe-built compound not far from Calca. Our guide was the dynamic director, Nilda Callañaupa, who grew up in Chinchero so has seen for herself how traditional weaving practices are giving way to synthetic materials and less time-consuming methods. The history and diversity of weaving in Peru is astounding. Some designs and techniques date back over 2000 years, and each Andean village has its own favoured patterns. Collecting and documenting these is one of the goals of the centre.

Our visit began with a talk by Nilda explaining the spiritual significance of weaving to the descendants of the Incas, as well as their traditions and techniques. The weavers, dressed in the traditional clothing of their villages, were kneeling on the ground (a position that I would find agonising after a few minutes!) in front of their looms. The intricate designs grew in front of our eyes and I shot a roll of film in a few minutes. In a corner were a group of men knitting *chullos*, the traditional hats of the region. Their big, stubby fingers manipulated the tiny needles with enviable dexterity. Peruvian weavers use the indigenous backstrap loom (modern, pedal-operated looms are not used in the Andes), either working on broad textiles to make ponchos or *mantas*, or creating narrow belts, or beautiful tubular 'ropes'.

Before we left there was some serious shopping to be done. It was good to know that we were helping to support the work of the centre, as well as purchasing a particularly beautiful souvenir.

Our visit was organised by Aracari (see page 123) but most tour operators should be able to arrange it. For more information see the website www.incas.org, or write to Cultural Survival, 96 Mt Auburn St, Cambridge, MA 02138, USA; tel: 617 441 5400; email: csinc@cs.org.

Note Always check the political situation in the Central Andes before travelling by road through these areas.

By train

Peru Rail are currently running all passenger train services in the southern (Cusco and Arequipa) part of Peru. Their central office is in Arequipa, Avenida Tacna y Arica 200; tel: 054 215640. For the latest times and prices check their website at www.perurail.com; for reservations email them on reservas@perurail.com. In Cusco tickets are available from travel agents or direct from the Wanchaq station: Estación Wanchaq, Av Pachacutec s/n; tel: 084 238722/221992.

The service is supposed to have improved following the privatisation of the railway services in 2000, and at the top end of the market this may be

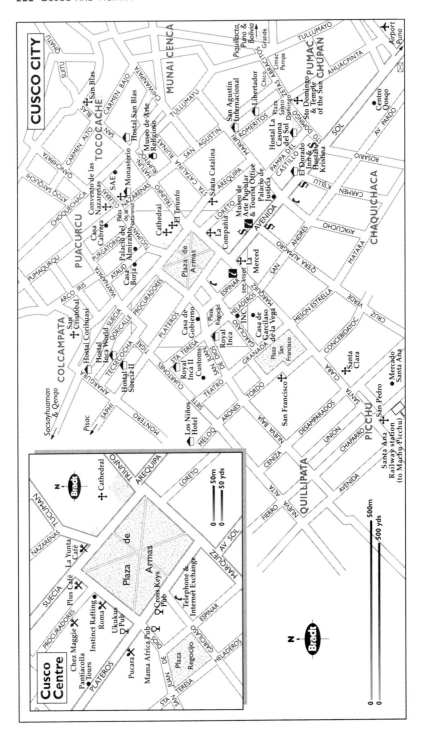

the case. However, options for backpackers have been reduced as tourists are no longer allowed to travel on the local train. The classes available now are a posh 'Inka Class' with reclining seats and a meal, Autowagon class and Ferrostal class, where you get special panorama-style windows and a free snack and the Backpacker Express, apparently a no-frills service at a cheaper (but still expensive) price. Unfortunately the colourful local train is no longer an option for visitors. Peru Rail say this service is designed as a social service for local residents only. They ask for identification when buying tickets.

To Machu Picchu Everyone takes the train (or walks) since the site is not accessible by road. Trains depart for Machu Picchu from San Pedro Station in Cusco. The station is next to the San Pedro church and market, in an area which used to have a bad reputation for theft. Security has been much improved recently, but be wary.

Inka class costs US$70 return, Autovagon US$73, Backpacker US$35.

The **autovagon** leaves Cusco at 06.00, arriving at Machu Picchu around 09.30 (return service departs Machu Picchu 15.00, arrives Cusco 18.40). The **Inka class** leaves Cusco at 06.10 and arrives at Machu Picchu around 10.00 (return service departs 15.15, arrives 19.10), The **Backpacker** train leaves Cusco at 07.30 and arrives at Machu Picchu around 11.25 (return service departs 16.30, arrives 20.45).

Ollantaytambo to Machu Picchu Between Ollantaytambo and Machu Picchu there is the option of Ferrostal for US$55 or Backpacker Cerrojo for US$30.

The **Ferrostal** trains leave Ollantaytambo at 06.30, 09.30 and 15.50, arriving at Machu Picchu just over an hour later. Trains from Machu Picchu to Ollantaytambo depart at 08.00, 14.00 and 17.30.

The **Backpacker Cerrojo** leaves Ollantaytambo at 10.45, arriving at Machu Picchu at 12.10. Trains from Machu Picchu to Ollantaytambo depart from 18.30 to 20.05.

To Juliaca and Puno Cusco/Puno/Cusco (The Titicaca Route): Trains depart from the Wanchaq Station in Cusco (Peru Rail reservations office). This service also stops in Juliaca. Inka class costs US$30 one way, tourist class US$19 one way. At Juliaca the line splits, one part going to Puno and the other to Arequipa. The train station is at the end of Avenida Sol, opposite the Hotel Savoy. There are trains on Monday, Wednesday, Friday and Saturday from Cusco to Puno (08.00 arrives 16.45), and Puno to Cusco on Monday, Wednesday, Thursday and Saturday (08.00 arrives 16.45).

To Arequipa Puno/Arequipa/Puno, with a stop at Sumbay in the Colca Canyon (The Blue Sky Route): Sumbay is 3.5 hours from Arequipa and 6.5 hours from Puno. Trains stop at Juliaca on request. Fares: Inka class US$30 one way; tourist class US$9 one way.

Arequipa to Puno: Sunday 21.00 (arrives 07.00), Wednesday 07.00 (arrives 17.00) Saturday 08.00 (arrives 18.00)

IN CUSCO FOR GOOD

Titus Bovenberg and Jolanda van den Berg, from the Netherlands, were typical backpackers. They travelled independently, as cheaply as possible, with the goal of seeing the pink dolphins of the Amazon. Stuck in Cusco for a few days, they at first resented this delay to their plans. The Inca ruins were fabulous, of course, but it was another aspect of the city that caught their attention. 'We had seen them before, of course. Children trying to sell us things at traffic lights, wanting to shine our shoes, carrying loads which looked too big for an adult, cute little girls and boys, always snotty-nosed, always dressed in dirty, torn clothes. But all of a sudden we saw only children...'. Titus and Jolanda bought more postcards than they could possibly write, had their shoes shined twice a day, and started playing with the kids, drawing pictures with them, kicking a football around, trying out a few words of Quechua.

At six o'clock one morning they attended Mass in the cathedral in the Plaza de Armas. At that hour they were the only gringos. The service was in Quechua, the temperature in the great building close to freezing, but the atmosphere of spirituality was overwhelming. For nearly an hour afterwards neither of them spoke, then Jolanda said quietly 'I'm going to do something for those children.'

Two days later the backpackers flew to Iquitos and swam with the dolphins. But their thoughts stayed in Cusco. Back in the Netherlands friends and family reassured them. 'You'll get over it. That's how it goes with holidays. You want to help but you can't change anything.' Jolanda thought otherwise, and six months later she was back in Cusco alone, in a rented room. Within a month she had two street boys living with her. Then four more. To support them Titus established the Niños Unidos Peruanos Foundation in Holland, and when the number of children reached 12 he flew out to Cusco to join his partner.

The boys were mostly 11- and 12-year-olds except for little Oscar who was three. 'We had to take Oscar. His mother was in jail for the murder of Oscar's father. Self defence.' Apart from the obvious lack of food, shelter and education, the street kids of Cusco were poor in something else: self esteem. They were aggressive and often violent. Karate lessons

Puno to Arequipa: Monday 09.30 (arrives 19.30), Thursday and Sunday 07.00 (arrives 17.30).

Note Time schedules change frequently (as do prices), so check.

Accommodation

You are spoilt for choice in Cusco, from luxury hotels to the basic backpackers' places. Prices are lower outside the tourist season and good deals can be expected at the upper- and mid-range hotels around that time. Most prices became as important a part of their day as school attendance and helping with the chores.

Jolanda and Titus wanted to open a hotel in Cusco. They saw it as a way of giving financial support for their project and at the same time providing employment for the older children. A benefactor came up with the money and a beautiful colonial house was purchased. It took almost a year to convert it into a hotel but the two-star Niños Hotel opened in 1998. It was an immediate success.

I was shown around the spotless rooms, glimpsed a vase of arum lilies in one of the loos before being led into the kitchen to admire a pile of steaming loaves of crusty bread. Celso, the oldest boy, has become a dab-hand at bread-making and takes a pride in supplying the hotel's requirements. As the boys become older they will play a larger part in running the hotel. At present they need to catch up with their missing childhood. They need play more than work, and they need schooling. Titus and Jolanda now employ two teachers to help with homework.

The success of the hotel has enabled the couple to open a Niños Restaurant. A hundred of Cusco's poorest children get a free hot meal each day. Close co-operation with the schools helped Jolanda to select the most deserving kids. Tipped off that two sisters were living in a derelict building, Jolanda went to collect them for their first meal. The two girls were tense and anxious, but agreed to come. Then Jolanda became aware of a snuffling sound in the corner. A little girl of six was stiffling her sobs. Seeing her sisters about to disappear she burst into noisy crying 'What shall I eat? I don't know how to cook!'. The teachers had forgotten about little Olga and her older sisters didn't dare mention that there were three of them. So Olga came too.

The Niños project is growing. The children receive regular health checks, daily showers (both a treat and a source of embarrassment to the dirtiest children), education and discipline. Titus and Jolanda would like to hand over the running of the Cusco hotel to local people so they can turn their attention to other cities in other countries. 'It's such a workable idea!' says Titus. 'Sometimes we visualise it as a world wide movement. Wherever there are tourists there can be childrens' hotels. And all because we wanted to see pink dolphins!'

include taxes, but always check, and remember that prices given here are a guide only; they are likely to have gone up.

Top-of-the-range
Libertador-Marriot In a colonial building on Calle San Agustín 400; tel: 084 231961. US$168 double.
Royal Inca I and II Plaza Regocijo; tel: 084 231067/234221. US$54/US$78.
El Dorado Inn Av Sol 395; tel: 084 231232. Single/double US$80.

Mid-range

Hostal Kristina Av Sol 341; tel: 084 227251. US$25/US$30.

Hostal Loreto Pasaje Loreto 115, one block off the Plaza de Armas; tel: 084 226352. US$25/US $35.

Hostal Monarca Calle Pumapaccha 290; tel/fax: 084 226145. Double US$35.

Hostal Corihuasi Calle Suecia, block 4; tel: 084 232233. US$15/US$23.

Orquidea Real Calle Alabado 520; tel: 084 240671; email: orquidea@telser.com.pe. Double US$39.

CAITH (Centro de Apoyo Integral a la Trabajadora del Hogar) Pasaje Sto Toribio 4, Uchullo Alto, off Av Argentina; tel: 084 233595. An NGO project, which provides a home and training for orphaned or abused girls, and has a new, clean tourist hostel above. Not in the centre of town but a 5-minute taxi ride away. A project worth supporting. Private rooms, some shared bathrooms, US$15 per person, longer stays negotiable.

Budget

Hospedaje Cassana Av Don Bosco A–7; tel: 084 261177. US$14 double. Friendly, with breakfast, laundry and luggage storage.

Hostal Rumi Punku Choquechaca 339; tel: 084 221102. From US$11 per person. Central, clean, good value.

Hostal Suecia II Calle Tecsecocha, block 2; tel: 084 239757. US$9/US$12 (cheaper without bathroom).

Hostal Inca World Calle Tecsecocha (opposite Suecia II). US$10/US$15.

Hostal Residencial Las Rojas Calle Tigre 129. US$7/US$10.

Hostal Familiar Calle Saphi 661. US$6/US$8.

Hostal Luzerna Av Baja 205; tel: 084 237597. A base for organising trekking in Ausangate (see page 281).

Albergue Municipal Kiskapata 240; tel: 084 252506. US$7 per person.

Niños Hotel Calle Meloq 442; tel: 084 231424; email: ninoshotel@terra.com.pe; web: www.targetfound.nl/ninos. US$12 single, US$24 double (communal bathroom), US$32 double with private bathroom. A 20-room hotel, which helps train the street children of Cusco in tourism skills. Each room is named after a child and will be decorated by his or her paintings or stories. All profits are put back into the charity Niños (see box). What a wonderful opportunity for readers to give something back!

Restaurants

Most backpackers will want to try typical Andean dishes rather than international fare although the taste of home is sometimes welcome after a long trek. I have included some of my favourites.

Al Grano Santa Catalina Ancha, 398. Central location with good Asian dishes, excellent coffee, central and tasty desserts.

Ayllu Portal de Carnes 208, Plaza de Armas. Open all day, popular with locals, great fruit drinks, apple pie and all sorts of other snacks. Great location for writing postcards and people-watching.

El Buen Pastor Cuesta San Blas 579. Excellent café and bakery. Project to help girls from disadvantaged backgrounds.

El Truco Calle Regocijo 225, Plaza de Cabildo; tel: 084 235295. Popular with groups because of the live folk music, so quite expensive. Good food.

El Tumi Portal Belén 115, Plaza de Armas. Great location for people-watching, and some really good food.

Govinda Espaderos. Hare Krishna vegetarian restaurant. Slow service but good value, especially the menu of the day. Their wholemeal bread survives trekking for a few days.

La Garanja Heidi Cuesta San Blas 525; tel: 084 233759; web: www.geocities.com/naturefood. Extremely good natural/organic food, including yogurts and cheesecakes. Good-value lunches.

La Tertulia Procuradores (upstairs on left). Delicious wholemeal buffet breakfasts.

La Yunta Portal de Carnes 214, Plaza de Armas. A café with a good variety of cheap dishes.

Macondo Cuesta San Blas 571. Popular pub/restaurant with inventive food; great hangout.

Mesón de los Espaderos off the Plaza de Armas on Espaderos and Plateros. Meat place, *cuy* sometimes available, expensive but good quality.

Pizzeria Chez Maggy Procuradores, and Plateros. A cosy pizza place with a wood fire.

Planet Sur Plazoleta in San Blas. Jazz bar.

Plus Café Portal de Panes, Plaza de Armas (upstairs). Especially recommended for coffees and snacks.

Pucara Plateros 309; tel: 084 222027. Japanese owned, good local dishes at highish prices. Excellent homemade chocolates. Good-value fixed-price lunch.

Quinta Eulalia Choquechaca 384. Popular with the locals. A nice courtyard so best for lunch. *Cuy* is usually available. Open 12.00–1800.

Quinta Zarate Totora Paccha 763, at the end of Tandapata in San Blas. Peruvian food, good views.

Roma Portal de Panes 105, Plaza de Armas; tel: 084 245041. One of the original Cusco restaurants. A good varied menu, though quite expensive. Has folk music.

Entertainment

As you'd expect in the tourist capital of Peru, there is plenty of choice. *Peñas* (nightclubs with folk music) include **Peña Americas** (Block 1, Av de la Cultura) and **Los Incas**, on the Plaza de Armas, and nightly folklore shows at **Centro Qosqo de Arte Nativo**, Av Sol 604 and **Teatro Inti Raymi**, Calle Saphi 605. The **Teatro Municipal**, Calle Mesón de la Estrella 149, shows plays, music and dancing on most nights.

The English-run **Cross Keys Pub**, on the Plaza de Armas, is an ever-popular hang-out for tourists and a few locals. Amongst the other night-spots is **Ukukus**, on Plateros, which is a very lively disco/club with live music at around 22.45 every night except Monday. It is always packed with locals and gringos. Several groups play there, a sometimes strange fusion (typical in Cusco) of traditional Andean music with injections of rock, reggae and salsa. **Los Perros** on Calle Tecsecocha has Sunday night jazz sessions. **Rosie O'Grady's** offers a variety of music, different styles on different nights, **Eko** is a new and popular club, also with a mix of music.

There are several places for watching films in Cusco – great for entertainment on a day off. Programmes are put up on notice-boards outside the following: **Andes Grill** Portal de Panes, Plaza de Armas; **Peliclub** Tecsecocha 458; **Sunset Café** Tecsecocha 2; **Ukukus** Plateros 316.

Useful addresses
Help!
Tourist police Sapphi, block 2.
Immigration office Av Sol, block 5. Open: Mon–Fri 08.00–13.00.

Licensed taxi firms
Okarina Tel: 084 247080
Aló Cusco Tel: 084 222222

All taxis, whether licensed or not, cost 2 *soles* for all daytime fares within the city and 3 *soles* after 22.00; if you call a licensed taxi to your hotel, it will cost slightly more.

Hospitals and doctors
Hospital Regional Av de la Cultura; tel/fax: 084 227661; emergencies: 22369; clinic: 084 239792. Clinic consultation US$12.
Private doctors Dr Oscar Tejada Ramírez; tel: 084 233836. Dr Jaime Triveño; tel: 084 225513
Clínica Pardo Av de la Cultura 710; tel: 084 240387. 24-hour service, some doctors speak English. Highly recommended, with quick test results. Consultations US$10. Specialist consultations throughout the day, normal consultations 17.00–2030.
Clínica Panamericana Av Infancia 508; tel/fax: 084 249494; emergencies: 651888; email: clinicapanamericana@tourcusco.com; web: www.tourcusco.com/. Clínica Panamericana represents International Companies of Travellers Insurance. It has a network of medical services in Cusco (Machu Picchu, Sacsayhuaman, etc), offering vaccinations, antiofidic serum, malaria prevention, air and terrestrial ambulance, repatriation, laboratory analysis, and clinic.
Clínica Paredes Calle Lechugal 405; tel: 084 225265. Consultations US$30. Open Mon–Sun 24 hours.

Dentist
Dr Virginia (Vicky) Valcarcel Velarde, Portal de Panes 123, Office 206, Plaza de Armas; tel: 084 231558. Consultation US$15. Speaks some English, and has modern equipment.

Chiropractor and therapeutic massage
Ayni Chiropractic Clinic Av La Cultura 102, Santa Fé Building, Office 207; tel: 084 651906/623850. Dr Ilya E Gomon offers spinal diagnostic and low-force therapeutic methods. Open Mon–Sat 10.00–12.00 and 16.00–19.00.
Massage English holistic practitioner offers excellent therapeutic massage and other treatment. Very relaxing after a long trek. US$20–25. Tel: Lorena Alcock 084 248528.

Clubs and tourism

Automóvil Club del Perú Av Sol 349; tel/fax: 084 224561

OFEC (Visitor's Tickets) Av Sol 103, Office 106; tel: 084 226919/227037. Mon–Fri 07.00–18.00, Sat 08.30–12.30. Tickets US$10 (students US$5).

CONSETUR (Bus service to Machu Picchu) Santa Catalina Ancha 336, Interior B; tel: 084 252959/222125. Mon–Fri 07.00–18.00, Sat 08.30–12.30.

Ministry of Tourism (Dirección Regional de Turismo) Av de la Cultura 734, 3rd floor; tel: 084 223701; fax: 084 223761; email: Cusco@mitinci.gob.pe; web: www.dritcusco.gob.pe. Mon–Fri 07.15–13.00 and 14.00–16.00. Information offices at the airport, bus station and Calle Mantas 117A.

Universidad Nacional San Antonio de Abad Av de la Cultura 735; tel: 084 222271/228661/232398

Tourist Office Calle Mantas 117A, just off Plaza de Armas. The 'visitor's ticket' can be bought here, which covers the entrance fees to the main (but not all) churches, museums and ruins for US$10 (half price for students) with a validity of 10 days.

SAE Cusco Choquechaca 188, no 4; tel: 084 245484; email: cuscoclub@saexplorers.org; web: www.saexplorers.org. Mon–Fri 09.30–17.00. The clubhouse offers an excellent travel advice and information service to members. It also has a book exchange, books and topological maps for sale and is a friendly, relaxed place to hang out where you will met other travellers. The Cusco clubhouse is often in need of volunteers, so if you can spare a week, a month or more email or drop in. For membership details see entry in *Chapter 5*.

English-language newspaper

For information on what's happening in Cusco (and the rest of the world) with listings of hotels, restaurants, clubs, shops, etc, check out *Cusco Weekly* which is widely available (and free) in the city.

Adventure tour operators

There are dozens of travel agents in Cusco. The following are some of the better-known ones. They should be able to provide a good service with professional guides and reasonable equipment. Many of these companies have joined up to form the Asociacion Peruana de Turismo de Aventura y Ecoturismo (APTAE), which theoretically at least, promotes protection of the environment and works towards improving working conditions for its staff. Don't sign up for tours on the street, and do make sure you get a proper contract of services and receipt.

Amazonas Explorer PO Box 722; tel: 084 227137 (UK: 01437 891743); email: sales@amazonas-explorer.com; web:www.amazonas-explorer.com. Specialists in rafting and trekking expeditions. Fixed departures for the rivers Apurímac and Cotahuasi in Arequipa.

Andean Life Calle Plateros 341; tel: 084 221491; email: andeanlife@terra.com.pe; web: www.andeanlife.com. Treks and tours of Peru.

Aventours (also known as **Ecoinca**) Av Pardo 545, Cusco; tel/fax: (5184) 224 050; email: info@aventours.com; web: www.aventours.com. Has been the leader in Peruvian trekking for over 20 years.

MOUNTAIN BIKING IN PERU
Paul Cripps

A great way to get off the beaten track in Peru is by taking to two wheels and exploring the maze of Inca trails, mule paths and dirt roads that criss-cross the Andes. Monster downhills, lung-bursting uphills, some of the best technical single tracks in the world, incredible scenery and friendly locals are just some of the joys of cycling in the Andes.

To really get away from it all you need to bring your own bike, as local hire bikes are of highly varying quality. Also consider hiring a guide – there are an increasing number of local guides who know the area well and can choose the right trip for you that you'll almost certainly never find on your own. If you are planning for an extended trip consider joining an organised tour, as your guide should have an in-depth knowledge of the best routes, plus you'll have the peace of mind of a support vehicle to carry all your camping gear, plus cooks, spare bikes and of course yourself – should you get tired.

There are countless trails and routes available in and around the Cusco Valley – from a 3-hour road ride around the ruins to amazing off-road loops that visit rarely explored ruins and will challenge the very best of riders.

Further afield a ride to Pisac is a great option with its huge downhill on tarmac or, for those in the know, a wicked single track. Possibly the

EcoAmazonia Lodge Calle Garcilaso 210, Office 206; web: www.ecoamazonia.com.pe. Operates daily tours to its jungle lodge.

Eric Adventures Plateros 324; tel/fax: 084 228475; email: cusco@ericadventrues.com; web: www.ericadventures.com. Rafting.

Explorandes Av Garzilaso 316 A, Wanchaq; tel: 084 238380; email: postmaster@explorandes.com; web: www.explorandes.com/. Up-market operation offering private tours and treks.

Helicusco Calle Triunfo 379, 2nd floor; email: dfhr@amauta.rcp.net.pe; web: www2.rcp.net.pe/HELICUSCO/. Daily helicopter flights from Cusco to Machu Picchu: US$100 each way, 24 people per flight, 25-minute flight time, departs Cusco 08.30, returns from Machu Picchu 15.00.

Instinct Procadores 50; tel: 084 233451; fax: 084 238366; email: instinct@protelsa.com.pe. Rafting trips.

Manu Ecological Adventures Plateros 356; tel: 084 261640; fax: 084 225562. Tours to Manu.

Manu Expeditions Av Pardo 895; tel: 084 226671/239974; fax: 084 236706; email: adventure@manuexpeditions.com; web: www.manuexpeditions.com. Up-market company owned by ornithologist Barry Walker; part owner of the Manu Wildlife Centre, trips into Manu, specialises in birdwatching.

Manu Nature Tours Av Pardo 1046. Top end of the market trips into Manu.

Mayuc Portal Confituras 211, Plaza de Armas; tel/fax: 084 232666; email: chando@mayuc.com; web: www.mayuc.com. Rafting trips on the Urubamba, most famous ride in the region is Chincheros–Moray–Maras–Urubamba – easy to get lost but mainly downhill on a great mix of dirt road, single track and mule trail. This ride offers awesome views of the Sacred Valley and the chance to visit the cool circular ruins of Moray and the even cooler Saltmines of Maras. It is a great day out and doable by most fairly fit cyclists. A beautiful road ride along the Sacred Valley of the Incas is also possible.

Even further afield the dirt roads behind Ollantaytambo, Calca and Pisac provide a variety of multi-day options up and over the final passes before a monster descent into the Amazon jungle. There are also many single tracks that join these routes, hard to find but rated as some of the best off-road mountain biking in the world – go with the experts.

Finally, a favourite route of mine has to be the 550km 'TransAndean Challenge' of Cusco to Puerto Maldonado. Far from a holiday, this is more a total mission, but one that can only be descibed as fantastic when finished. This 9-day event takes places once a year in October and is for serious bikers only.

And for those who are looking for something totally wild, there is 'mule biking'. This latest craze involves attempting to find the most outrageous descents in the Andes by putting bikes on mules and trekking many of the routes described in this book, cycling the downhill parts as fast as possible. Maybe best not mentioned in a book like this!

Apurímac and Tambopata, some trekking.

Pantiacolla Tours Plateros 360; tel: 084 238323; fax: 084 252696; email: pantiaco@pantiacolla.com; web: www.pantiacolla.com. Recommended for Manu.

Peruvian Andean Treks Av Pardo 705; tel: 084 225701; fax: 084 238911. Upmarket tour operator.

Peruvian Safaris Plateros 365; tel: 084 235432; email: safaris@amauta.rcp.net.pe; web: www.peruviansafaris.com/. Owns and operates Explorer's Inn lodge, 58km up the Tambopata River from Pto Maldonado, which, as well as being a tourist lodge, is also one of the main research centres for scientific work in the Amazon basin.

Q'ente 2nd floor, Plateros 365; web: www.qente.com. Treks, including daily Inca Trail departures.

Rainforest Expeditions Calle El Triunfo 350; tel: 084 232772; email: rforest@perunature.com; web: www.perunature.com. Operates tours to its two lodges in the rainforest of Tambopata – the Posada Amazonas Lodge and the Tambopata Research Center (TRC).

Tambopata Jungle Lodge Av Pardo 705; tel: 084 225701; fax: 084 238911.

United Mice Plateros 348; tel: 084 221139; fax: 084 238050. Daily departures for the Inca Trail.

Vilca Expediciones, Plateros 363; tel/fax: 084 251872/244751; email: MANUVILCA@terra.com.pe; web: www.cbc.org.pe/manuvilca. Recommended for trips into Manu.

Communications

Post office Av Sol, block 5. Open Mon–Sat 08.00–19.00.
Telefónica Calle Garcilaso (off Plaza de Armas). Open 06.00–23.00 daily. Av Sol, block 2. National and international telephone calls and also internet.

There are also dozens of internet offices, all over town.

HIKING INFORMATION
Climate
The weather here is typical for the Central Andes, with a dry season (April to October) and rainy season (November to March). If you can only visit in the rainy season don't be downhearted. Apart from the really wet months of January and February you are likely to have some sunny days, and mornings are often fine. Most days are clear and sunny in the dry season but you should still be prepared for rain or – more likely on the high passes – snow.

Acclimatisation
Adjusting to the altitude is no hardship here. Take time to see the marvels of Cusco and the Urubamba valley before you set off for the mountains.

Guides, *arrieros* and pack animals
You do not need a guide for most of the trails described here and in *Chapter 10* (they are popular and quite easy to follow) but if you are venturing off the beaten path you would do well to hire one or some other local staff, as much for security reasons as to find the way. There is plenty of choice, so try to get a recommendation from a reliable local person or another traveller. Clarify all details before you set out, pay half the money in advance, and sign an agreement.

Pack animals can be organised in Cusco through a trekking agency, but if you speak Spanish it will be cheaper to do it yourself in the village at the trailhead. Around Cusco, as elsewhere, most *arrieros* are members of an organisation and there are set prices: *arrieros* US$10 a day and *burros* US$5–8. Remember you have to pay for their return journey also. Prices can vary from area to area and may well have gone up by the time you read this. For the Inca Trail, recent changes mean you have to go with an organised group, or at least a guide. Most agencies do not include porters for your personal belongings in the cost, but you can hire porters for an extra cost (see *Chapter 10*).

Renting equipment
It is best to bring your own equipment if you can because what's available in Cusco is limited and not of great quality. Several trekking agencies in Cusco rent out camping equipment and there are some dedicated equipment rental shops (try Soqllaq'asa, Plateros 365). Generally speaking the quality is poor, so check all items carefully before paying your deposit. Prices per day: tent US$3, sleeping bag US$2, stove US$3.

Food and supplies

Buy all your trail food in Cusco as variety is extremely limited in trailhead villages. Between the markets and supermarkets the selection in Cusco is very good. Start your search down Avenida del Sol. Buy sufficient extra supplies for your *arriero* if you are hiring pack animals or using porters.

Maps and books

The Instituto Geográfico Nacional (IGN) is a reliable source of hiking maps. There is a map of the Department of Cusco (scale 1:400,000), which is some help in planning, and topographical maps (1:100,000) for the area from Calca, Cusco and to the south. The best maps for the Cusco area are *Urubamba* sheet 27-r for Lares, Ollantaytambo, Urubamba and the start of Inca Trail; *Machu Picchu* sheet 27-q for Machu Picchu, Salkantay and Choquequirao treks; sheet 27-p for Espiritu Pampa; and *Ocongate* 28-t for the Ausangate trek.

Many tour operators sell a small map of the Inca Trail, but the best map of this trail is from the South American Explorers (SAE) in Cusco or Lima. The SAE also publishes a good map of the Ausangate circuit. The SAE in Cusco has most of the IGN topological maps of Peru. If you didn't buy the appropriate map in Lima they may allow you to take a photocopy.

Cusco has a couple of good bookshops (Special Book Services, Av Sol 781; tel: 084 248106; email: sbsperu@amauta.rcp.net.pe. Try also on Plaza de Armas and Calle Heladeros, and at the SAE clubhouse), where you should be able to purchase the most informative and best-written guide to the area: *Exploring Cusco*, by Peter Frost. Other books that include sections relevant to Cusco are listed in *Further reading* in *Appendix 2*.

HIKING ROUTES AROUND CUSCO

The area around Cusco is a delight for hikers. Here you can step back in time and see a rural way of life that has hardly changed for 400 years: women spin as they walk along the trails, carrying babies in their brightly coloured woven mantas; herds of llamas and alpacas peer at you curiously; donkeys and mules are driven round and round over the freshly cut wheat or barley to separate the grain from the chaff; and the earth is still dug using the ancient Inca foot plough.

In the valleys near the thatched huts of the descendants of the Incas, and high on the hills far from human habitation, are the marvellous remains of that mighty empire: stone walls and temples of a grace and strength unique in the Americas and backed by a range of snow-covered mountains.

The hikes detailed are just a beginning and there are lots of other possibilities. If you do go out exploring by yourself, please respect the culture, make contact with the local people and ask permission when you want to camp on their land. Do not be the instrument of change, environmental or social. Your responsibility is to keep these places as they are. The following hikes are described:

- Inca ruins around Cusco
- Tambomachay to Pisac
- San Jerónimo to Huanca

- Cusco to Calca via Huchuy Qosqo
- Calca to Cusco
- Tipón

Chinchero–Urubamba Valley hikes:

- Chinchero to Huayllabamba
- Chinchero to Urubamba
- Chinchero to Maras (ruins of Moray), Salinas and the Urubamba River

The Valley of Lares:

- Huaran to Lares and Paucarpata

Inca ruins around Cusco

For most people Sacsayhuamán and the nearby ruins are their first introduction to Cusco's Inca past – and the breathtaking effects of its altitude. To do the full distance would be too much for a new arrival: until you are fit and acclimatised, limit yourself to sections and take it slowly, both to appreciate the ruins and to ease your breathing.

Route description Sacsayhuamán is a massive Inca temple-fortress overlooking Cusco. It's a steep half hour's walk to the site, beginning at Calle Suecia which runs from the upper corner of the Plaza de Armas by the cathedral. Keep going uphill, taking the track rather than the road, until you reach the gigantic walls that are Sacsayhuamán.

Everything that is 'known' about the origin and purpose of Sacsayhuamán is pure speculation. Every tourist guide has a different story. Some claim that it is pre-Inca, others that it is very early Inca. As in all matters pertaining to Cusco, I find Peter Frost's *Exploring Cusco* the best short account, though serious students of the Incas should read one of the experts, such as John Hemming. To the casual visitor, it scarcely matters why the massive zigzag walls (attributed to defence – in the event of an attack the enemy would expose his flank – or to the deities of lightning or the puma) were built. They are one of the wonders of Peru, and the most accessible example of massive Inca stone masonry. Climb to the top of the mound to see the 'reservoir' or astrological structure, built in a circle with 12 radiating 'spokes'. Most likely this was the foundation of a tower, with an underground system of water channels. Opposite the giant walls, across the 'parade ground' which is now used for the spectacle of Inti Raymi on June 24, are naturally eroded rocks, some with Inca carvings. This is popularly known as the Inca's Throne, and the rocks make good slides for young Inca descendants and gringos alike.

Women bring their llamas for a highly profitable graze in the Parade Ground. They are extremely photogenic and well aware of their current worth. Bring plenty of change, and don't be conned into paying more than the equivalent of 50 cents (1 *sol*) or so for a photograph. Sometimes there is a condor here too, tied on a rope, forcibly posed for tourist photos. Don't support this cruelty, and make a point of complaining about it to the tourist-complaints office in town.

From Sacsayhuamán hike up the hill (east) to the statue of Jesus, and then follow the road to the sign for Qenco (Kenko). A path to the right will bring you to this unusual site. Qenco is a huge limestone rock, naturally eroded, and skilfully carved both on top and within its caves. It is full of enigmas, too. The rock monolith in front could have had a phallic significance (unlikely, as the Incas seem not too impressed with the phallus as a symbol of power), or could be a desecrated carving of a puma … or what you will. The delicate zigzag carvings on top of the rock were probably ceremonial channels for *chicha*, and the beautifully carved cave must surely have been associated with Pachamama, Mother Earth.

Distance	20km (10km if you find transport back to Cusco)
Altitude	Between 3,500m and 3,900m
Rating	Easy
Timing	One day
In reverse	Possible, and easier (downhill)
Start of trail	Plaza de Armas, Cusco
Safety	Robberies have happened in and around the ruins. Try to go in a small group. If alone, don't carry any valuables – leave them in the hotel safe.

From Qenco continue east along the trail for about 15 minutes and you'll reach Cusillyuioc (Temple of the Monkeys) although you will be puzzled by the name as you explore the caves and tunnels. Continue east for another 15 minutes to Salumpunku, another carved rock. There are usually children around who'll be delighted to show you the main features: a carved cave and altar, a very eroded puma shape and a sundial. Salumpunku lies about 1.5km from the road to Pisac (to the east) via a dirt road.

Follow the road to the ruins of Puca Pucara, about 6km from the junction with the dirt road; you'll see the sign to your right. This site is unimpressive, but across the road lie the Inca Baths of Tambomachay which are well worth seeing. Inca 'baths' were to do with ritual bathing rather than washing, and this is an excellent example of the Inca fascination with water and their ability to direct it where they wanted. Water is channelled through three stone outlets and is pure enough to drink.

If you are tired, there should be buses or *colectivos* to take you back to Cusco. Otherwise you can return the way you came.

Tambomachay to Pisac

Tambomachay marks the end of one hike but the beginning of another. You cross the mountain range behind Cusco, dropping down the other side to Calca in the Urubamba Valley. The varied sights and scenery include an Inca ruin, typical villages and traditional agriculture.

Distance	25km
Altitude	From 3,500m to 3,900m, then down to 2,930m
Rating	Long in distance but fairly easy hiking apart from the steep descent to Pisac.
Timing	1–2 days
In reverse	Possible, but more difficult, with a steep climb up from Calca.
Start of trail	Tambomachay. Take a tour which culminates in Tambomachay, or the bus or colectivo towards Pisac, leaving from Cusco's Avenida Tacna. Get off at the ruins – about 45 minutes from Cusco.

Route description The trail starts about 100m down the road from the ruins. Take the well-marked trail up the hill, then through farmland passing a few farmhouses, and climb the slope to the pass, admiring the views of Cusco from the top. This should take you about 1 hour.

Follow the path to the right, along the mountain slope, passing through two valleys and climbing to a ridge above the little village of Qorimarca below – about 45 minutes. The path descends into the valley, with an aqueduct to your right. Pass through Qorimarca and continue down the valley, following the main road until you reach a concrete bridge over the stream to your left in 45 minutes or so. The main road continues down the valley and connects with the paved road from Cusco to Pisac.

Cross the concrete bridge. Your goal from here is the top of the mountain range. You have several options, so get your bearings:

1 Up the left-hand valley A road has been constructed all the way to the pass to service the pipeline that supplies Cusco with water from Laguna Qoricocha up in the mountains. Take the direct route to the top, following the footpath which crosses the road several times until you reach the edge of the lake. Pass the lake to your right and continue climbing to the highest point of the mountain range in front of you. From here you can see the village of Patabamba on the edge of the *pampa*. It will take about 4–5 hours from the bridge to here.

2 Up the middle valley Start up the left-hand valley following the road and taking short cuts, until a smaller valley, with a stream, opens up to your right. Follow the path up to the highest point of the mountain range in front of you, keeping first to your right and then up the mountain ridge to your left. At the top you get a great view over Laguna Qoricocha, and can see Patabamba below. It takes about 4 hours from the bridge to the top.

3 Up the right-hand valley Make a right turn after the bridge and hike up through the village to the valley furthest to the right, which has the advantage of leading

THE POTATO
Kathy Jarvis

Hundreds of years ago the upland regions of the Andes were one of the seven major centres of crop domestication, but the plants from there are still little known. In the past 20 years a few far-sighted agronomists have begun to take an interest in the under-exploited crops of Peru. These include grains (amaranth, quinoa, canihua), legumes (tarwi and nunas), fruits (chirimoya, naranjilla, pepino, passionfruit, tree tomato) and roots.

The Inca farmers were some of the best in the world. On slopes at altitudes up to 5,000m and in climates ranging from tropical to polar they cultivated as many species as the farmers of Asia. Without money, iron, the wheel or written language they terraced and produced food for the vast Inca empire, which reached from southern Colombia to central Chile. Silos and storehouses overflowed with grain, roots and dried meat. The Spanish conquerors, when they came, were interested only in gold and looting and not in the advanced agricultural systems. As a result of this, much traditional farming was abandoned and European grains were planted. However, some Indians today still grow the crops of five centuries ago.

The potato, an Inca staple unknown outside the Andes, proved popular with the Spanish conquerors, and was carried to Europe later to become one of the 20 major food crops of the whole planet. But the Spanish left behind several species of cultivated potato, and hundreds of wild potatoes. Collectively these are adapted to a wide array of climates and contain a wealth of diversity and disease resistance. Peruvian Indians have some 200 words for describing sizes, colours and textures of potatoes. Some potatoes are bitter, turning sweet after freezing, some are black, some yellow, some withstand the extreme cold; all have distinctive flavours and are more nutritious than our white potato.

Most of these potatoes produce small tubers but have considerable commercial potential. A few are immune to pests. There are two species of Bolivian potato whose leaves are a minefield to insects. The smallest insect crawling over a leaf breaks open tiny four-lobed hairs that cover the leaves. This releases a sticky substance, trapping the insect, and catching leaf-eaters by the jaws. Although this potato is unsuitable for eating, it is being interbred with other cultivated potatoes to improve pest-resistance.

to the lowest pass. Start climbing to the top of the ridge, keeping to the right of the stream. At the top the area flattens out and you'll walk through farmland. Hike up to the highest point of the mountain range, where you can enjoy a great view and the sight of Patabamba below you.

From this point there is only one possibility. Descend to Patabamba and continue through the village to the edge of the ridge (stay to the right and ask the locals for the path to Taray and Pisac). You'll see the Urubamba Valley far below you. Give your knees a pep-talk and start the descent. To add to your misery fine sand from the soft white rock of the mountainside covers the trail and makes it slippery. Learn from the crab: sideways may be safer. At some point stop to admire one of the Inca's most amazing feats: canalising the Río Vilcanota so it runs dead straight for over 3,000m, probably to conserve the farmland on the sides. Once the trail levels out, continue up the valley towards Pisac, passing through the small village of Taray. It takes about 2 hours from Patabamba to Pisac.

San Jerónimo to Huanca

The destination for this hike is one of the landmarks of the Sacred Valley. Tour groups from Cusco often ask their guides about the large, red-roofed church which stands, seemingly alone, on the mountainside. This is the Sanctuary of El Señor de Huanca, and pilgrims have been coming here since 1674 when Our Lord made a miraculous appearance before an Indian miner. For good measure He appeared again in 1713, this time shrewdly choosing a rich landowner as witness, hence the handsome church that commemorates the event.

Around September 14 there is a pilgrimage to the Sanctuary. The faithful walk through the night to Huanca in order, it seems, to have a thoroughly commercial time bartering their goods at a huge fair set up for the day.

This is a long day-hike (if you don't want to bother with camping gear) or two days if you want to be more leisurely and are getting acclimatised for trekking. The trail is clear, but steep and rough in places. It's best to stay the night at Huanca since transport back to Cusco is erratic. Always carry plenty of water.

Distance	15km
Altitude	From 3,300m to 4,250m and down to 2,950m
Rating	Easy
Timing	7–8 hours
In reverse	Possible
Start of trail	San Jerónimo, a town to the east of Cusco. Colectivos run there every 10 minutes from the corner of Avenida Sol and San Miguel, near the post office in Cusco. The journey takes an hour. A taxi will cost around US$5.

Route description Leave early if you want to do this hike in one day. A road has been constructed from San Jerónimo all the way to the pass (eventually it will run all the way to Huanca) so if you are in a taxi and want to cheat a bit, have the driver take you to the top. The road does take away some of the beauty and remoteness in this mountain area, but mostly you will be following the footpath, which only crosses the road a few times.

If you are hiking up from San Jerónimo, start from the plaza on the right-hand side of the church, following the street and turning left at the first opportunity. Follow this road to the end of the village, making a right turn at the end, and continue on the footpath which goes slowly uphill through eucalyptus groves. Ask the locals if you're not sure. The path is an old Inca road, passing some *tambos* (Inca rest places) and following an Inca aqueduct up the mountain ridge. It takes about 2–2½ hours to the top of this plateau. You can see a few farmhouses to the right, and the road winds its way up the mountain to the right. After the houses on your left the footpath climbs up in the same direction as the road, but passes the highest point on the left.

At the first pass at 3,700m, which you will reach in about half an hour, you can see the village of Huaccoto on the other side of the valley. Descend into the valley and towards the village; a further half hour. Walk through this small, typical Quechua village, taking the well-marked path (with loose stones) up the hill to your right. The path makes a left turn, winding around the mountainside above the village. Soon you reach the top, which has a cross on it. An open *pampa* stretches in front of you. Continue up the *pampa*, keeping left, until you reach the pass and the highest point on this hike at 4,250m – about 2½ hours from Huaccoto. The pass gives a spectacular view over the Urubamba Valley. The mountain to your right is called Pachatusan (4,950m). Just a few metres below the pass on the other side, on top of a cliff, you'll see the remains of an Inca building which probably served as a guard post overlooking the Sacred Valley.

As you descend you'll see the church roof below you on the right. A well-marked path descends along the steep slope. The descent takes about 1–1½ hours. Take time to visit the church and its painted rock, which commemorates the first miracle and is now part of the altar.

From the sanctuary to the village of Huanca it's a half-hour walk with a further half hour to go to San Salvador. From here you can get transport back to Cusco via Pisac – a 2-hour journey.

Cusco to Calca via Huchuy Qosqo

This is a treat of a walk, taking you through lovely countryside and over the mountains just outside Cusco, with spectacular views and interesting and seldom-visited Inca ruins, then down the Urubamba Valley.

Distance	31km
Altitude	From 3,350m to 4,350m and down to 2,930m
Rating	Moderate, with four high passes.
Timing	2 days
In reverse	Possible (see next hike)
Start of trail	Cusco

Route description Hike or take a taxi up to the ruins of Sacsayhuamán, passing the site on your left and following the path up to the road, where you turn right. After about 150m, just before the house, turn left following a small footpath up the valley. This widens as you climb. Continue up, passing a radio mast, until you come to a dirt road. You can see the Cusco–Pisac road to your right. Cross the dirt road and continue hiking up the hill for a while along the fairly obvious trail which parallels with the Cusco–Pisac road.

Follow this trail all the way up to the first pass at 4,200m – 3 hours. Go down the valley along the left-hand slope until you come to the stream at the bottom. The path splits going up on the other side: it doesn't matter which one you choose, they both lead to the second pass at 4,300m, from where you'll see the small Laguna Quellacocha lying in the valley in front of you. Descend on the high trail round the north end of the lake, ignoring the path that leads off to the left. Climb east to the third pass at 4,250m (about 3–4 hours). From the top you can see Laguna Qoricocha to your right. There are campsites in both this valley and the next one. Continue along the trail leading northeast over the next ridge and on to the fourth pass at 4,300m. Descend into the valley ahead of you, keeping to the right. Get directions from the *campesinos* whenever possible – the trail disappears in places.

After a while you'll see the village of Pucamarca. Below it the valley forms a steep ravine, and on the right is a platform with Inca walls. Cross this and find a steep, well-preserved Inca stairway descending into the ravine. At the narrowest part of the ravine, cross to the left bank. The trail traverses around the mountainside (west) for a spectacular view of the Urubamba Valley. The path leads through an Inca gateway: the entrance to the ruins of Huchuy Qosqo.

Huchuy Qosqo means 'Small Cusco' in Quechua. Little is known about this extensive and mysterious site, although Charles Brod in his book *Apus and Incas* quotes John Hemming's theory that these buildings may have been built as a tribute to the conquering Inca Viracocha by the local tribe, and could have been used by the Inca lord as a 'country retreat' from Cusco. Brod writes:

> As you enter into the ruins you can see a small reservoir that is choked with weeds but still functions... The main buildings are grouped around a walled-in, sunken area that may have served as a swimming pool, though no water channel is apparent. Located in a far upper corner of the complex, a stone enclosed by high walls and large niches is reminiscent of the pinnacle at Qenco, but its sacred function has been lost to time.
>
> At the main plaza, a long building with six doorways stands above the terrace wall. This is a *kallanka*, a large building that once had a peaked roof covering it. These structures were constructed around the main plazas in the principal towns of the empire to house soldiers, labourers and other transient people. It was from buildings like this one that Pizarro and his men made their desperate charge on the Inca Atahualpa at Cajamarca, capturing him and massacring thousands of his Indian troops.

From Huchuy Qosqo you have a choice: take the old trading route to Chinchero, which is apparently a short walk, or continue on to Calca. For the latter, cross the stream to the left of the ruins when facing the Urubamba Valley (ask the caretaker at the ruins for directions). Follow the path up to the mountain ridge, passing a farmhouse. From the ridge it's an obvious, but steep and tiring, zigzag path down into the Urubamba Valley. Be careful; it can be slippery on the loose gravel. On the valley floor the trail turns left along the base of the cliffs to the dirt road. It follows the river, passes a small building (the mineral-water baths of Minas Mocco) and continues to a bridge, which you cross to reach Calca.

Calca to Cusco

Sarah Booth hiked the previous trail in reverse and found it, in general, easy to follow. The advantage of doing it this way round is that the ruins are easy to find and for the last part of the walk – the confusing bit – you have a clear destination (Cusco) and plenty of *campesinos* of whom to ask directions.

The first leg from Calca to the ruins takes about 4 hours. From Calca cross the bridge and turn left. A valley lies ahead and the zigzag trail up the opposite side is clear to see. Follow the flow of the water in the concrete irrigation channels to find the reservoir and ruins of Huchuy Qosqo. From here the trail is clear to the village of Pucamarca (2½ hours). From the village follow the stream into a valley for half an hour until you reach a junction with another stream. This is a good place to camp. The next morning resist the temptation to follow the new stream to the right, but continue up to the pass, keeping close to the original stream bed (which will probably be dry).

At the top of the pass Sarah and her companion took the wrong trail and, though they arrived at Cusco safe and happy, she advises that you make sure you don't walk too far south. Your visual aid is Laguna Quellacocha, a small lake. You need to pass to the right (north) of it, picking up a trail that will take you over two passes beyond the lake. From the second path you can either join the Cusco–Pisac road or continue on to Tambomachay or Sacsayhuamán. This second day will take you 5–6 hours walking. Wherever you end up you will find transport into Cusco.

Tipón

This extensive Inca site is easily accessible from Cusco, and well worth a visit. It is relatively unknown and hence not overflowing with other tourists. It is also a good starting point for day walks up into the hills above. There are several tracks that climb the hillside above the site, just pick one and follow it. Tipón is 4km off the main road running to Sicuani from Cusco (21km from Cusco). Take any of the buses heading south along this road and ask for Tipón. Tipón was an important Inca site, thought to have been dedicated to the veneration of water. It is extensive, with a series of stone-walled *andenes* irrigated by a beautifully channelled stream of water, originating from a spring high on the mountainside. To the west of the terraces lie the remains of a settlement, with various buildings of typical Inca stonework, including an *intihuatana*. The terraces, similar to those at Moray, may have been some sort of agricultural experimentation centre.

Chinchero–Urubamba Valley hikes

Chinchero is on the tourist route, but is a perfect example of the resilience of the Andean Indian to outside influences. The Sunday market is still amazingly colourful, full of traditionally dressed women in the regional cartwheel hats, and geared as much to the villagers' needs as to those of the milling tourists. Women sit in groups by their produce, fry fish, or serve *chicha* from earthenware pots. Others sell handicrafts.

Chinchero is well worth visiting, even on a weekday, for the impressive Inca stone wall forming one side of the plaza, and some wonderful terracing with very fine stonework. The town used to be an important Inca centre and there are many examples of their stone carving. If you walk down the Inca stairs, which start behind and below the church to the left of the terraces, you'll come to the main trail going down the valley. There are two large rocks near the path, with carved stairs, seats and water channels.

Before you leave Chinchero take a look inside the Spanish colonial church, built on Inca foundations (the side chapel has an Inca well and water channels from the temple that once stood here). The church dates from 1607 and has a wonderful painted ceiling and walls. The main figure is of St James, patron saint of the *conquistadores*.

These walks are three of several which take you into the Urubamba Valley with its many Inca sites and transport back to Cusco. At the high point there are lovely views over the Cordilleras Vilcabamba and Vilcanota.

Leave Chinchero by noon at the latest (preferably earlier) to be sure of reaching the valley floor before dark. Always carry water on these hikes; the valley is pretty dry and hot, especially in the dry season.

Chinchero to Huayllabamba

This trail is a fine example of an Inca road, with the ruins of a *tambo*, an Inca posthouse, half way.

Distance	8km
Altitude	From 3,500m down to 2,760m
Rating	Easy
Timing	4 hours
In reverse	Possible, but a steep climb from the valley so it will take longer.
Start of route	Chinchero

Route description From the plaza of Chinchero you can see the trail on the opposite hill, climbing up to the right (north). Follow the trail up the slope, heading northeast. It makes a turn around the slope and starts descending, staying to the left of the Quebrada Urquillos and dropping steeply to the small village at the bottom. From here continue along the road leading down the valley to the village of Huayllabamba, a few kilometres away (note this is not the same Huayllabamba as on the Inca Trail). At Huayllabamba a bridge crosses the river and puts you on the main road through the Urubamba Valley.

Chinchero to Urubamba
A pleasant hike through a patchwork quilt of farmland, with good views of the *cordilleras*.

Distance	10km
Altitude	From 3,500m down to 2,865m
Rating	Easy
Timing	3–4 hours
In reverse	Possible, but hard work and longer.
Start of the trail	Chinchero

Route description Follow the old Chinchero–Urubamba dirt road, which leads off to the left when leaving Chinchero. Ask the *campesinos* if you're not sure. The dirt road makes its way over the *pampa*, crossing the paved road, and continues until the edge of the valley. From here the route drops into the valley, following a pretty obvious trail, although it does fade away in places. It's hard to get lost, however, as you just need to head down the valley until you reach the river. Here you join up with the paved road again, which crosses the Urubamba River by a bridge and takes you into Urubamba.

Urubamba is a pleasant place to spend the night (there are several hotels) and is a good base for exploring the Sacred Valley, where there are numerous walks.

Chinchero to Maras (ruins of Moray), Salinas and the Urubamba River
Thanks to Peter Frost for information from his book Exploring Cusco.
This is a longer hike than the others. It takes you through interesting countryside and Quechua villages, but its outstanding feature is the three very different but equally impressive ancient sites visited en route.

Chinchero has already been described: a classic of traditional imperial Inca stone walls and terraced farmland, with a small colonial church thrown in for good measure. Moray is quite different: unique, in fact. It is not the ruins of a city or a fortress, but an earthwork. The ancient peoples of the region took four huge natural depressions in the landscape and sculpted them into agricultural terraces that served, hundreds of years ago, as an experimental agricultural station for the development of different crop strains. Recent investigations have shown that the terraces are organised into sectors, with significantly different temperatures in each level. Much of the terracing survives intact, leaving regular concentric layers flowing harmoniously into the land. The largest of each of the circular structures has a diameter of 150m, is 150m deep, and is formed by seven of the above-mentioned concentric rings. The interest here is more subtle than the massive walls of the Inca sites; it is a place more for contemplation than admiration.

Salinas, as the name suggests, is a village of salt. A salt river runs down the mountainside, partly underground, and since pre-Hispanic times salt has been collected here in hundreds of artificial salt pans, using a natural process of evaporation.

Distance	27km
Altitude	From 3,760m up to 4,057m and down to 2,865m
Rating	Easy walking, but a long day unless you take a car for the first part.
Timing	8–9 hours
In reverse	Possible if you find transport for the last stretch into Chinchero; otherwise not feasible in one day because of the steep climb.
Start of trail	Chinchero

Route description Leave Chinchero in the direction of Urubamba and follow the paved road until the turn-off to Maras after about 11km. If you want to avoid the long road-walk, catch a ride with one of the many buses or *colectivos* on this route. From the turn-off follow the gravel road to Maras (3,760m), about 4km. This is a colonial town, which used to thrive on mining the salt deposits in the cliffs to the north. Now it is smaller and you can only expect to buy basic supplies here.

The trail to Moray (Huaynuymarca) leads westwards, away from the town in roughly the same direction you followed from the paved road, at right angles to the main street. Ask the locals for directions as the path is hard to find.

Follow the path until you reach the first ravine (6–8m deep), cross it on a log bridge, and continue until the second ravine (about 30m deep). Cross the bridge again. Don't continue along this main trail up the slope to the right. Take, instead, the path that climbs to the left, almost straight up the slope, passing a farmhouse and two small ponds; you'll be able to see a large signboard in the distance bearing the name of the site. Aim for that, crossing the third ravine (about 15m deep), to arrive at Moray, about 7km/1½ hours from Maras. Here, as well as the earthwork and terraces described earlier, there are the remains of an irrigation system.

A dirt road connects Maras to Salinas (3,385m), about 5km/1½ hours away. Approaching Salinas from above like this is ideal: it is an astonishing and extremely photogenic site. The pans look like a giant white honeycomb, with the small bee-like figures of Indians bustling around the rims harvesting their 'crop'.

To finish the hike follow the trail down the left side of the valley from Salinas to the Urubamba River. If you turn left when you reach the river you'll come to the picturesque village of Pichinjoto. Nearby are caves – some of which are inhabited. Turn right here and you'll soon reach a footbridge over the river. Cross it and follow the trail another 500m to the main road of the Urubamba Valley about 5km from Salinas. Turn right to reach Urubamba in about 6km, or pick up a *colectivo* on the road.

A touch of luxury in the Sacred Valley

If you're hiking or biking around the Sacred Valley and feel that you deserve a real treat, try to eat at the **Huayoccari Hacienda Restaurante**, in the Urubamba valley 64km from Cusco (tel: 622224 or 226241; email: hsilabrador@latinmail.com). This 65ha hacienda was growing corn until 1997 when it was converted into an up-market restaurant. The place is steeped in history, having been in the same family for 350 years. The name means 'Hanging Man' after a 17th-century chief who met his end here. The house and garden are simply stunning. Roses bloom against a backdrop of mountains, with incongruous cacti to remind you that you're in Peru. The food is equally exquisite.

The hacienda lies about 2km from the main road and does not serve lunches every day, so it is essential to book first.

THE VALLEY OF LARES

Trekking in this area takes you into the remote and rarely visited Lares Valley with the spectacular backdrop of the Urubamba Mountains. The Urubamba range lies to the east of the Sacred Valley. It stretches for 30km, and has several snow-capped peaks, the best known of which is Veronica (5,750m), the most prominent snowpeak that can be seen from the Machu Picchu train. The Urubamba range in its entirety is seen at its best from the road between Cusco and Urubamba. This is one of my all time favourite views. The Lares Valley lies to the east of the Urubamba range and is easily accessible from Cusco by taking a local bus to Calca and then on to Huaran, in the Sacred Valley. The area offers moderately strenuous trekking, through small mountain villages, crossing passes of over 4,000m with spectacular views of the surrounding snow-capped peaks of Pitusiray, Sawasiray and Chicon. The trek, described here, gives you the rare opportunity to see how the Quechua-speaking Indians of the high mountain villages live by farming potatoes and *oca*, and herding llamas and alpacas on the inhospitable flanks of the towering peaks.

The Lares Valley is particularly well known for its very high-quality, brightly coloured weavings and characteristic upturned hats, many of the popular tourist markets being supplied from here. There are several variations on this trek which you can do according to how much time you have available. Even in the dry season be prepared for bad weather and take a map and compass for

GREENFORCE
Tania McCrea Steele

Greenforce, a British-based organisation, runs an Amazonian environmental project in the Madre de Dios Region of Southeastern Peru. The work takes place in the Tambopata Candamo Reserved Zone up-river from the jungle town of Puerto Maldonado. The lodge is accessible only by boat and the journey to and from Maldonado can take anywhere between three to eight hours, depending on the tides and the boat being used.

Permanent scientists co-ordinate and oversee the volunteers that come for ten-week periods to partake in the biodiversity surveys of the flora and fauna in one of the most biologically rich areas of the world. Staff carrying out the research have degrees, in biological sciences or related areas, as well as relevant field experience and first-aid training. Some of those working for Greenforce are ex-volunteers who underwent an extended period in the field as trainees (contact the office or website for more details of this particular programme). The projects include monitoring the birds, mammals and trees, and new surveys are presently being established. Volunteer work can comprise a trip up into the canopy to take a sample of leaves for identification, walking transects to scout for large mammals, catching birds in mist nets, recording their data and re-releasing them, identifying bird species by their morning chorus or observing the behaviour of giant otters in a nearby oxbow lake.

The information gathered is then passed on to INRENA (Instituto Nacional de Recursos Naturales). INRENA has funding from various organisations, including the WWF. Though INRENA is a part of the Ministry of Agriculture for Peru it functions independently. The Greenforce research data is kept on record and used to aid in the management of protected areas. Other interested environmental groups may also have access to the information. INRENA is itself faced with the difficult quandary of balancing environmental issues with the well-being of the indigenous people who rely on their traditional activities in what have become protected regions.

your own safety. Although in this area there are always people not far away, they often don't speak Spanish. If you want to take mules or porters and a guide you will probably have to organise it through one of the agencies in Cusco.

Huaran to Lares and Paucarpata

To start your trek get a local bus from the bus station in Cusco in Avenida Huascar to Calca, a distance of approximately 80km. From the square in Calca take a bus going towards Urubamba and get off after 10 minutes in the small village of Huaran. While in Calca check for frequency of transport from Lares and Paucarpata to Calca for the return journey. There is currently one daily bus leaving around noon. You can also stock up at the market with fruit,

Other organisations are also sent research data from the Greenforce project. Copies of the bird songs are sent to the British Museum's sound library. Digital images of leaf, fruit and nut samples are passed onto the Edinburgh Botanical Gardens, where a database of Amazonian plants is being established. Greenforce is also working alongside INRENA to improve one of its visitor centres and thus provide more information for tourists and locals alike.

Two Peruvian volunteers, supported by Greenforce, from the nearby university work alongside those from abroad, giving all involved the opportunity to practise their Spanish, as well as providing invaluable knowledge of the surroundings, both culturally and biologically.

The majority of Greenforce volunteers are from Britain, in their late teens to mid twenties, biology students, or taking time out from work. Normally an expedition consists of around 19 people, including staff, who come from different backgrounds, and volunteers. You don't need specific skills, as training will be provided in the field. The research work is funded by the volunteer's donation; each individual is asked to contribute.

Living conditions at Bahuaja lodge are basic, with volunteers responsible for cooking and cleaning. Greenforce staff and volunteers occupy the accommodation, tourists have the option of visiting other lodges along the river. All the buildings are long houses with the kitchen and *comedor* positioned near the sleeping quarters. Trips to one of the toilets after dark can be especially interesting as a two-toed sloth has often been spotted in one of the cubicles. Washing in the river and wallowing in the mud-baths are two ways to relax and enjoy your free time.

I personally had enormous fun while learning a great deal about the Amazonian wildlife, scientific-monitoring techniques, tropical conditions and teamwork. I would recommend Greenforce to anyone looking for a challenging and rewarding expedition. The friends I made and the lessons I learned will remain with me for ever.

You can contact Greenforce by email (greenforce@btinternet.com) or via its website (www.greenforce.org).

vegetables and basic supplies. Calca has a couple of *hostales*, and there are many places to stay in the nearby towns of Pisac and Urubamba.

Route description Set out from Huaran (2,840m), climbing gently out of the Vilcanota valley (directly northwards) on a well-marked trail up the Quebrada Cancha Cancha to the small village of the same name, situated a long way above you at 3,800m. The trail follows the course of a mineral-rich red river flowing off the mountains up ahead, and it'll take 3–4 hours to reach the scattered houses of Cancha Cancha. By now agricultural land has given way to dramatic mountain scenery. The villagers are tough Quechua-speaking Indians who herd llamas and alpacas, and grow hardy, high-altitude crops such

Distance	Huaran to Paucarpata approximately 60km
Altitude	Between 2,838m and 4,400m
Rating	Moderate
Timing	To Lares 3–4 days, to Paucarpata 5–6 days
Start of trail	Huaran (also possible to trek from Urubamba to Lares or Huaran to Urubamba)
End of trail	Lares (3–4 hours by bus/truck to Calca, not every day, usually 4 days a week) or Paucarpata (2–3 hours by bus to Calca, not every day).
Maps	IGN sheet *Urubamba* (27-r), 1:100 000 (buy this in Lima)

as potatoes and *quinoa* (*armanath*) on the steep valley sides. They live as they have for centuries; expertly weaving their own bright-coloured clothing from the spun, silky hair of the camelids, celebrating ancient pagan festivals, and living in thatched stone houses. Guinea pigs running loose around their houses are an important source of protein. There is good camping near the school in the village, up the side valley to the left (west) of the village, or at one of the many beauty spots on the way up the trail. Continue walking for 20 minutes up the flat valley bottom beyond the village (northeast). If you look up ahead you will see the trail on the right slope of the valley. Heading north again, the path now begins to climb very steeply towards the first pass, Pachacutec (4,458m). Looking down to the left, as you climb, you see the flat *pampa* where the villagers of upper Cancha Cancha have their houses and stone corrals. The pass is a strenuous 2–3-hour climb from the village. As you look back from the pass, surrounded by the weirdly contorted forms of wind-eroded rocks, the Sacred Valley is visible a long way below and even Chinchero can be made out in the distance. Pachacutec Lake and the peaks of Pitusiray loom out of the swirling clouds. Proceed along the ridge following the trail, now going northwest for an hour, 3km, until the path drops steeply down to the left into a dramatic cliff-lined corrie. There are superb camping sites on the shores of the glacier lakes found in the corrie, and this is an ideal spot for observing Andean geese, caracaras and coots. From the lip of the corrie descend into the next valley, following a series of nine cascading waterfalls to the village of Quisuarani (3,700m), 1 hour from the corrie. Camping is possible in the village.

Don't drop down to the bottom of the village, but leave Quisuarani heading directly west, steeply up to the left behind the school. If you were to continue down the valley ahead you would end up in Lares, but miss a beautiful part of the trek. There is a steep 2–3 hour climb ahead, on a good path, to reach the second pass, known as Kochuyckaza (4,200m), but marked as Abra Huillquijasa on the map. Your walk takes

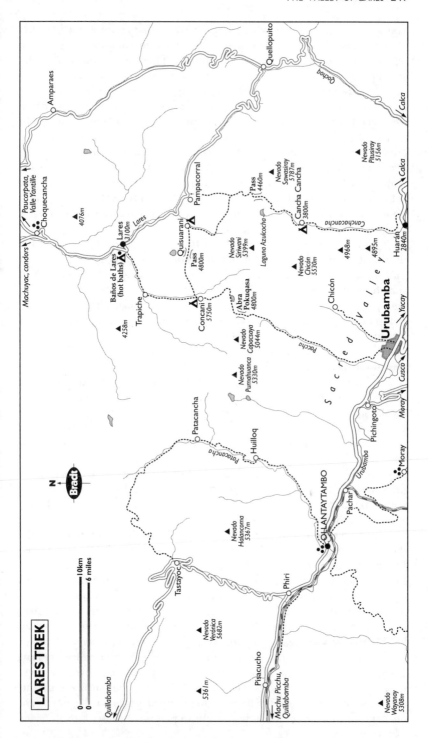

you across grazing areas where large herds of llama are tended by shy children. Watch out for their protective and sometimes very aggressive dogs; keep a few stones handy just in case. There is a good trail all the way up, but if you happen to lose the trail look out for a large lake near the head of the valley, approximately 1½ hours from the village. It is easy to pick up the trail again at the far end of the lake, from where you begin the steep final ascent zigzagging up to the steep rocky slope to the right of the sharp peak ahead. From the pass, there is a stunning view of emerald-green glacial lakes. Andean geese, gulls and caracara fly overhead. Drop down to pass the lakes on the right (north) side, cross, from right to left, the waterfall flowing from the corrie and follow the valley down to the village of Concani (3,750m) in the valley bottom (1½ hours from the pass, 1 hour from the lakes). You can camp at the lakes or in the valley bottom.

From here it is a 3-hour walk down the valley to Lares (3,100m) to the north. It is possible to head south from Concani, over the pass of Pumahuancajasa (4,900m) and straight down the valley to Urubamba. You should allow 2 days for this option, from Concani. If you set off walking at first light you may be accompanied by local farmers traditionally dresssed in bright red ponchos going to work their fields, singing and playing musical instruments as they go: an unusual sight!

For Lares a clear path follows the right slope of the valley down (northwards) alongside the white, frothy River Concani until 30 minutes before reaching the village of Lares where weary limbs can be soaked in thermal springs (take a swimsuit). Keep a look-out to the left below the path for the springs soon after the trail turns to the right (northeast) at Trapiche, after walking 2½ hours. You'll see five open-air pools with some small-built changing rooms. Lares itself is a grey and uninteresting semi-tropical town with little to offer, other than a welcome beer and a chance to restock supplies. There is a hostel (El Paraiso) to stay at on the square if you can find someone to open it for you but there isn't much to hang around for if you don't have to. You may of course have to wait for transport out: approximately 4 hours to Calca.

If, however, you decide to continue trekking for a few more days, take the road to the north from the bottom of the town towards Choquecancha, 3–4 hours from Lares. Follow the road down from Lares for 2 hours through rich vegetation, before turning right after crossing the river and heading steeply upwards on the road to Choquecancha (3,200m). A 14-niched Inca wall lines the square of this small ancient village, and a glance up the hillside reveals further neglected archaeological remains. You may be able to camp in the school grounds if you ask the resident teachers, or find a nice spot by the river before climbing to the village. From Choquecancha head out of the top-left corner of the village over the ridge to the northeast and towards Paucarpata. It is a 2½ hour steamy climb to the ridge top, where views of the snow-capped peaks to the north are outstanding. There are some beautiful camping spots here, but no water very near. However, this is the best spot in the Cusco area I've found for observing Andean condors, which nest in nearby cliffs. From the top of the ridge descend to the northeast for 1 hour to reach the small village of Paucarpata, where you will find a shop and perhaps a passing vehicle. It's 2½ spectacular hours from here to Calca along the road; again check in Calca before setting off for frequency of transport. It is possible to continue walking from here to Paucartambo, in 4–5 days, but there is no map for that route so you need plenty of time to allow for getting lost. It is also possible to take a route to Ollanytaytambo through Yervabuenayoc, Cochayoc, Kelkanka and Patacancha, allowing 4–5 days from Paucarpata, using the same map.

OLLANTAYTAMBO AND REGION
For Inca admirers, Ollantaytambo is one of the most thrilling places in Peru, and far too often rushed through by tour groups. The town still retains its Inca layout; many of the houses show signs (such as wall niches) of their Inca origins, and most of its inhabitants preserve their traditional lifestyle.

Ollantaytambo deserves a stay of a few days, offering as it does a wide choice of accommodation, spectacular Inca ruins, and local walks.

Getting there and away
Trains The trains from Cusco to Machu Picchu stop in Ollantaytambo (see page 223).

Buses These leave Cusco every 20 minutes for Ollantaytambo via Chinchero or Pisac.

Tour buses A good option is to sign up for a tour of the Sacred Valley, leaving the tour in Ollantaytambo. This ensures you get a tour of all the Inca sites (recommended).

Sleeping and eating
La Miranda One of the cheapest hostels at US$4 per person. Basic but adequate if you are on a budget.
La Chosa Just off the Plaza. US$5 per person. Not always open. Basic but adequate.
Urpi Wasi Next to the station. US$7 per person. Nice garden and restaurant.
Hostal Las Orquideas . On the road to the railway station; tel: 084 204032. US$10 per person with breakfast; dinner also available. Nice, clean, comfortable rooms; garden. Recommended.
El Albergue At the railway station. An atmospheric, popular place which is very handy for trains. Some visitors love it, others find it rather spartan, with shared bathrooms opening on to a chilly courtyard. It is run by American painter Wendy Weeks, whose late husband Robert Randall contributed his knowledge of local practices to this book (see page 22).
Pakaritampu On the road leading to the railway station. Tel/fax: 20 4020; email: pakaritampujps@terra.com.pe. US$50–80 per room. The most comfortable hotel in Ollantaytambo.

TAMBOPATA: A RAINFOREST EXPERIENCE
John Forrest

The Tambopata Reserved Zone (TRZ) was designated in 1977: 5,500 hectares of rainforest on the banks of the Tambopata river, three hours upriver from the frontier town of Puerto Maldonado. Over the ensuing years biologists from around the world, staying at the adjacent Explorers Inn jungle lodge, established that the TRZ contained an incredible diversity of flora and fauna, and could lay claim to several world records. Over 580 bird species, 1,200 or so butterflies, 91 mammals, 127 amphibians/reptiles, 135 species of ant in the canopy alone and more than 600 leaf beetles amongst others were recorded, as well as 165 species of tree in just one hectare.

Lobbying by Conservation International, the Asociación por la Conservación de la Selva Sur (ACSS) and the UK-based Tambopata Reserve Society (TReeS) and others, led to the creation in 1990 of the Tambopata-Candamo Reserved Zone (TCRZ) (1.54 million hectares). In 1996 the Bahuaja-Sonene National Park (BSNP) (325,000 hectares) was designated and in 2000 the National Park was extended to cover 1,091m hectares with associated buffer zones in which only a variety of sustainable activities are permitted. In addition to the luxuriant sub-tropical moist forest, swamp forest and bamboo thickets of the lower Tambopata drainage basin, the BSNP now also encompasses tropical savannah and cloud-forest ecosystems, through an increased altitudinal range (2403,500m).

There are now several lodges along the Tambopata river, including Explorers Inn (Peruvian Safaris, PO Box 10088, Lima 1; tel: 1 447 8888; fax: 1 241 8427; email: safaris@amauta.rcp.net.pe); Tambopata Jungle Lodge (Peruvian Andean Treks, PO Box 454, Cusco; tel: 84 225701; fax: 84 238911); Posadas Amazonas (Rainforest Expeditions, Galeon 120, Lima 41; tel: 1 4218183; fax: 1 4218347; email: rforest@perunature.com); Wasai Lodge (c/o Hotel Wasai, Plaza Grau 1, P.Maldonado; tel: 84 572290; fax: 84 572825; email: lima@wasai.com or maldonado@wasai.com). Perched on raised ground above the river, they can be reached by air from Cusco in less than an hour followed by two to four hours in a canoe. Extensive trail systems run into the surrounding forest and allow the visitor to enter a

There are a couple of restaurants: the **Alcazar** on Calle del Medio and the **Fortaleza** on the plaza. **Café Kapuly** and **La Ñusta** are reasonable cafés. Try the market for excellent fresh fruit juices.

Places of interest

The tourist focus of Ollantaytambo is the magnificent Inca fort and temple above the town. Get there as early as possible in the morning or late in the evening to avoid tour groups, and buy a locally available guide book or hire a beautiful and fascinating world, where patience and a quiet step are essential if wildlife is to be observed. The standard of the facilities at the lodges is good, with most guiding undertaken in English.

On the upper Tambopata, Posadas Amazonas operate the more basic Colpa Lodge. It is located close to one of the largest known Colpas (macaw salt-licks). On most days this offers a fantastic display of colour and a cacophony of sound as the parrots assemble to nibble at the mud forming the river cliffs from which they derive important minerals. Other lodges offer camping trips to the Colpa.

There's the chance to do some volunteer work at the Picaflor Research Centre (Dr Laurel Hanna, Jr Piura 1345, Puerto Maldonado, Madre de Dios; tel/fax: 00 51 84 572589; email: picaflor_rc@yahoo.com). This dedicated research facility has a few vacancies at special rates for travellers wishing to spend a few weeks in the rainforest in return for assisting with the maintenance of trails, etc.

The communities of Baltimore, on the Tambopata river, and Sandoval (Familia Mejia), on the Madre de Dios river, have recently established Casas de Hospedaje. These mainly consist of a few rooms attached to the family home of one of the community members with whom meals are taken and trips arranged. They are considerably cheaper than staying in one of the lodges but are only Spanish speaking and may not always have transport to their casa. A community member often meets flights at the airport.

TReeS was founded in 1986 to promote the conservation of the Tambopata area on a sustainable basis in the long term. The society supports Peruvian biologists to enable them to undertake field research and applied investigations; works with the local native people to empower them to retain their traditional activities, especially with respect to health care; supports the responses of local representative organisations to explorations within the region by multi-national oil companies; and provides advice to those visiting the area from abroad. Resident Naturalist Programmes offer a few places annually to biology graduates, enabling them to undertake research while guiding tourists to the lodges. Further details from TReeS, c/o J Forrest, PO Box 33153, London NW3 4DR, UK; web: www.geocities.com/treesweb.

guide to show you round. The Inca stonework here is as good as you can see anywhere, and there are numerous things of interest, from the ancient adobe that faces some of the secular buildings which was strengthened, according to some guides, with guinea pig hair, to the *pedros cansadas* ('tired stones') that were cut but then abandoned en route from the quarry on the opposite side of the Urubamba. The **Baño de Ñusta** (Princess's bath) should also be seen.

The CATCCO **Museum** at the old Parador, one block from the Plaza and overlooking the river, is recommended. Set up by the Cusichaca Trust, this exhibition is a must for anyone wishing to understand more about the way of life of the inhabitants, past and present, of the Sacred Valley of the Incas. The museum depends on its entry fees and donations. Open 10.00–13.00, 14.00–16.00, Tuesday to Saturday.

Cusichaca Trust

The Cusichaca Trust (see page 112) was active for 20 years in this region (1977 to 1997) and, as part of its work restoring Inca agricultural devices for the benefit of their descendents, rehabilitated the Pumamarca Canal up the Patacancha Valley. It provides constant irrigation for some 160 hectares of agricultural terracing and is a prime source of sustenance and income for many families. A visit here is a stimulating day-hike amid beautiful scenery and an excellent warm-up for the Inca Trail. Equally interesting is the restored fort of Pumamarca en route to the canal.

Local hikes: Ollantaytambo to Pumamarca

Distance	6km each way
Altitude	From 2,800m up to 3,400m
Rating	Easy walking
Timing	4–6 hours return
Start of trail	Ollantaytambo

Leave Ollantaytambo on the road that heads northwards out of the village alongside the Patacancha River. Follow this for about half an hour until the last houses in the village of Munaypata. Here cut up a steep path on to the hillside above. Follow the trail as it heads eastwards, contouring along the side of the Patacancha Valley. Most of the time now you will be walking through cultivated farmland, fields of maize, potatoes and beans, grown on well-preserved Inca terraces. After 90 minutes or so of walking you will see the stone buildings of Pumamarca above you on the hillside. It takes about two hours of walking from Ollantaytambo to reach the site. The site is well preserved and a joy to look around. Its exact function remains something of a mystery, like so many Inca sites. It is thought that Pumamarca was an Inca fortress, strategically located to control access to the Sacred Valley from Antisuyo, one of the four quarters of the empire. The high surrounding walls would support this theory, but then why locate what appear to be food stores outside the main site? You can follow the canal that runs from the site on up the hillside for even better views of the surrounding area.

The Cordilleras Vilcabamba and Vilcanota

10

Now you are acclimatised, you are ready to tackle some of the longer walks that are the goal of most of the hikers who come to Cusco. The Cordilleras Vilcabamba and Vilcanota offer some of the best hiking on the continent; not only snow-covered mountains, but subtropical valleys and outstanding Inca ruins, along with the traditional way of life unchanged for so many centuries.

Below is a list of hikes covered in this chapter:

The Vilcabamba Region
The Inca Trail
- From Kilometre 88
- Other starting points
- Chilca to Huayllabamba

Salkantay hikes
- Mollepata to Soray
- Soray to Huayllabamba
- Soray to Santa Teresa
- Soray to La Hidroeléctrica

Vilcabamba hikes
- Cachora to Huancacalle, via Choquequirao
- Huancacalle to Espíritu Pampa

The Vilcanota Region
Ausangate hikes
- The Ausangate Circuit
- Pitumarca to Laguna Sibinacocha
- Pitumarca to Tinqui, via Chillca
- Raqchi to Pitumarca or Tinqui via Chillca

THE VILCABAMBA REGION
The Vilcabamba range, approximately 85km long, is a really spectacular part of the Andes, located northwest of Cusco, between the Apurímac and Urubamba Rivers. Many people just visit Cusco and Machu Picchu and go no further, but

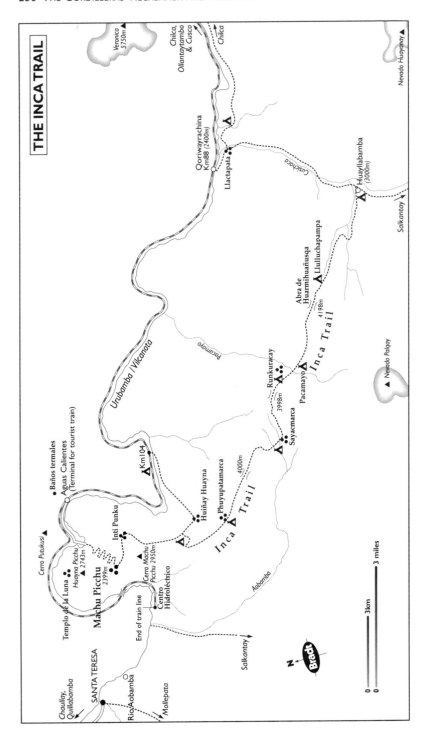

THE INCA TRAIL

there are lots of routes for trekking to suit all tastes within just a few hours of Cusco amongst the Vilcabamba mountains. If you can't face the rules and regulations (and the hoards of people) on the Inca Trail it's even possible to trek to Machu Picchu avoiding the trail altogether if you go from Mollepata to Soray via Salkantay and Santa Teresa.

Several giant snow-covered peaks rise out of the Vilcabamba massif, often clearly visible from the Lima to Cusco flight (sit on the left side of the plane). Salkantay (6,271m/20,575ft) is the highest peak in the area, towering above all the others. This mountain was highly revered by the Incas and is still very important to the people living in the Cusco area. Its name in Quechua means wild mountain. The other big snow-covered mountain you'll see is Pumasillo (6,075m), west of Machu Picchu and the highest peak in the mini Sacsarayoc range, seen in glorious close-up on the Choquequirao trek.

Typical of the region are the verdant cloudforest of the rugged eastern side of the Vilcabamba mountains and the deep gorges of the Apurímac and Urubamba. These gorges have been gouged out of granite by centuries of glacier-melt water torrents forcing their way north and eastwards on the way to the rainforest. The area is rich in Inca history: for nearly 50 years this remote region served as a hideout for its resistance movement as it tried to regain control from the Spanish invaders in the 16th century. The Incas left behind many ceremonial platforms, gatehouses (*tambos*) and a network of beautifully constructed pathways linking its strongholds, the well-known Machu Picchu, and lesser-known but equally important sites such as Choquequirao and Espíritu Pampa.

It's well worth taking a couple of weeks to explore this relatively unknown mountain area and its pre-Hispanic archaeological treasures. You are unlikely to meet many other trekkers, and you can have that unique experience of being amongst the glaciers of the high peaks one day and on the edge of the Amazon basin just a few days later.

THE INCA TRAIL

This is deservedly the most famous footpath in South America. It has everything: gorgeous mountain scenery, cloudforest and lush subtropical vegetation with numerous species of flowers, a stunning destination (Machu Picchu) and, above all, the Inca remains that give the trail its name. There are Inca paving stones, Inca stairways, an Inca tunnel, and of course the ruins: Runkuracay, Sayacmarca, Phuyupatamarca, Huiñay Huayna (Wiñay Wayna) and Machu Picchu itself.

Getting organised

During 2000 and 2001 the Peruvian government proposed numerous changes to the way the Inca Trail was to be administered in an attempt to protect it from further damage by overuse and misuse. The main impact for backpackers has been the stopping of individuals from trekking the Inca Trail on their own, and the prevention of backpackers from using the cheap local train service. This means that you have to hire a licensed, qualified local guide or trek with one of the many registered agencies in Cusco, and you have no choice but to travel on the tourist train (see page 223 for train details).

If you want to employ the services of a local guide try to arrange this in advance and expect to pay US$60 a day. Each guide is allowed to accompany up to nine trekkers, so this is a good way to go if you can get a group of people together, want to remain as independent as possible and are happy to carry your own kit. Be warned though that it is not easy to find a guide willing to walk with independent trekkers, as they have to carry their own belongings and rely on you for their meals. If you do hire your own guide you are not allowed to hire other staff to go along, such as cooks and porters. Think carefully about this, as hiring porters to carry your bags can certainly make the trek more fun, especially if you are not as fit as you could be. Many people do opt for porters so they can fully enjoy the hiking. If you trek independently it is worth buying your train tickets for the return journey before you start the trek as they can be scarce at Aguas Calientes.

The number of trekkers to walk the trail is now limited to a daily maximum of 500, so it can happen that you arrive in Cusco and find the Inca Trail in effect sold out. It is worth making a reservation in advance. The company will need your name, age, nationality and passport number when you make the booking and a signed photocopy of your passport on your arrival in Cusco.

The companies that operate along the trail have to have permits and pay a hefty fee for the privilege. There are around 30 operators in Cusco licensed to operate group treks along the Inca Trail (see page 229 for specific recommendations). Be very selective about choosing a tour company or guide. Discuss and write down all details beforehand. There have been problems with cheap and consequently poor-quality tours not fulfilling their promises, supplying poor camping equipment and food, leaving rubbish behind and not paying the porters the minimum wage. Be wary of choosing the cheapest, and if you are not happy with the organisation take time to report it to iperú (tourist protection) or one of the conservation groups in Cusco (see next page).

For an organised trip you should expect to pay at least US$245 each. The price depends on: how informed and comfortable you want to be; the quality of the equipment, food and guide; which train service is used to get you back to Cusco; the size of the group; the number of porters; and the experience of the guide. Make a list of the services you'd like on the trail before choosing a tour company. The service should include: hotel pick-up and drop-off; private bus to trek start; licensed guide; Inca Trail and Machu Picchu entrance fee; train back to Cusco; two-person tent with mats to sleep on; porters to carry camping equipment; cook, all meals while on trek (three breakfasts, lunches and dinners), and boiled water for drinking. Expect to pay extra for: the bus from Machu Picchu down to the train station (US$5) or walk; any meals in Aguas Calientes; tips; hot springs entrance; and porters to carry your personal gear (around $50 for 4 days, maximum weight 20kg per porter).

The entrance fee for the trail and Machu Picchu has increased to US$50 for tourists (US$25 for students with an ISIC) and US$10 for trekking staff. Check with your company to make sure this is included.

What to bring

Because so many people with no previous hiking experience do this trail it is worth emphasising the importance of careful preparations. If you decide to cook for yourself remember that tinned food is heavy and you will be tempted to leave the cans behind: bring packaged, dehydrated foods such as dried soup, thin noodles (which cook quickly), cheese, some fruit, and chocolate and raisins for energy. Rice takes a long time to cook so uses up your valuable fuel supplies. Oatmeal (*avena*) cooks quickly, and is filling and energy-producing. You will be drinking purified water so bring something to hide the taste of iodine. Lemons are good value for weight.

Be prepared for warm days and freezing nights. An alpaca sweater is light and warm so ideal for the Inca Trail. Thermals will help keep you warm at night and weigh very little. A woollen Cusco hat will make a big difference on the cold nights as will gloves or mittens. A scarf (muffler) takes up almost no room and keeps your neck and chest cosy.

Be prepared for rain: carry high-quality waterproofs.

Don't forget a good supply of plastic bags for carrying out your rubbish, toilet roll and matches (so you can burn it), and 'Wet-Ones' or equivalent for washing when water is scarce.

Bring insect repellent against the very persistent biting flies in the lower areas and at Machu Picchu.

Safety

It is not dangerous to hike the Inca Trail. Given that tens of thousands of hikers now do the trail each year, those who fall victim to robbers are statistically few. Check the current recommendations on safety when making your preparations in Cusco, and always follow standard safety precautions such as never leaving anything outside your tent at night.

Another, perhaps more important, safety consideration is the slippery state of some of the Inca stairways in the rainy season. During these months (December to April) the trail can be very muddy, and the passes covered in clouds and/or snow. Be careful.

Conservation

The Inca Trail has been abused by hikers for over 25 years. Litter is the main problem, but this is largely aesthetic. Pollution of water supplies by human faeces is more serious, and worst of all is the destruction of Inca stonework by lighting fires against the ancient walls. Damage done here is irreversible.

Most readers of this book will be only too aware of the need and importance of leaving no trace of their passing. They should also try to encourage the local people – sometimes the worst culprits because their needs and values are different – to protect their heritage. Small organisations have always been the most effective in taking care of the Inca Trail. The first clean-up was done by the then South American Explorers Club along with the Peruvian Andean Club in 1980. It took years to get permission to remove the rubbish. The team collected 400kg of tin cans along with a mini-mountain of other trash. Other organisations, such as the Earth Preservation Fund, continued the job. They picked up 700kg of rubbish.

As the trail becomes increasingly popular, local bodies are starting to take responsibility for conserving it. The INC (see below) at one time built pits for the disposal of rubbish at campsites. The problem was – and this happens in national parks throughout the world – visitors then just threw all their trash there and carried nothing out, so the pits were often disgusting and overflowing. Now, with the recent regulations, all rubbish has to be carried out. Do make sure you carry out all your own rubbish. The organisations below are involved in conservation and need your help and encouragement:

Instituto Nacional de la Cultura (INC) Calle San Bernardo, Cusco. They collect the entrance fees to the Inca Trail and Machu Picchu. In theory this money is used to conserve the area.
Instituto Regional del Inca next door to the Hospital Seguro on Av de la Cultura, Cusco
National Parks Department Av Sol, between blocks 5 and 6, Cusco
Ministry of Tourism Av de la Cultura 73, 3rd floor, Cusco; tel: 084 223701

Starting points
All routes end in Machu Picchu (it is forbidden to do the trail in reverse) but there are various starting points. The most popular route starts at Kilometre 88 (inaccessible by road, but the train stops here). Organised groups usually start in Chilca (Kilometre 82) because they can drive there with all the equipment and meet the porters there.

From Kilometre 88
If you have joined a group through an agency in Cusco, you will probably start the trail at Kilometre 82 as this is as far as it is possible to go by bus along the Vilcanota valley. If travelling by train from Cusco you can get off the train further down the valley at Kilometre 88.

Distance	49.5km
Altitude	Between 2,400m and 4,198m
Rating	Moderate
Timing	3 days
In reverse	Not permitted
Entrance fee	It costs US$50 per person to hike the Inca Trail. The price includes the entrance to the ruins of Machu Picchu, so save your ticket until the end.

Getting to the trailhead Most tour groups will travel by bus to the start of the trail. If you go for the option of just hiring an official guide you will need to get yourself to the trailhead. Take the train (see page 223) from Cusco or Ollantaytambo. It's a 3-hour journey from Cusco to Kilometre 88 (88km along the railway from Cusco to Machu Picchu), which is immediately after the first tunnel, about 22km beyond Ollantaytambo. You can't miss it: your guide will know the stop and you will spot a number of hikers with backpacks making for the train door. Keep an eye out of the right-hand window for the kilometre markers along the track.

Route description At Kilometre 88 (2,400m) you walk down to the entrance, where your tickets are checked. Sign in, cross the bridge and make a left turn following the trail gently uphill through a eucalyptus grove to Llactapata and the first major ruins on the route. Vast retaining walls have converted the steeply sloping hillside into agricultural terraces: an amazing sight. There is a campsite here, and it is a possible stop for the first night. It is not permitted to camp in the ruins themselves.

Just below Llactapata the Río Cusichaca, a tributary of the Urubamba, takes a spectacular plunge into the ground and runs through a subterranean channel for some way. The trail climbs steeply out of the ruins over a low pass, and the hike up the valley begins. After about an hour you'll reach a bridge, putting you on the other side of the valley, and will continue on to the village of Huayllabamba (3,000m). You will reach it in a further half hour. By this time it is likely to be very hot and you will welcome the cold drinks at the village, which makes its living out of Inca Trail hikers.

At Huayllabamba the trail turns right (northwest) up the Llullucha valley. After slogging and sweating upwards for about 1½ hours you will drop down to a grassy clearing, popularly known as The Forks. There is a designated campsite here. The path then enters woods – first scrub, then very beautiful cloudforest where the trees are hung with moss. These fairy-tale woods will help keep your mind off the fact that you are still going steeply uphill with no sign of respite. Eventually, however, the trees become more stunted and you emerge into a meadow, Llulluchapampa. There are proper toilets with running water and sinks here. Higher up in the meadows there are some pit latrines as well. From The Forks to the meadow is about 2 hours. This is the last campsite before the pass, aptly named (if you are a female hiker) Abra de Huarmihuañusqa, 'Dead Woman's Pass' (4,198m), which you can see ahead of you.

It will take you about 1½ hours to climb to the top of the pass. This is the highest point on the trail, so take heart – if you survive this, you'll survive the other passes. Take time to look around you. You should be able to pick out the circular ruins of Runkuracay ahead, just below the next pass. The descent is steep but not difficult. Just follow the trail on the left side of the valley to the valley floor and the next designated campsite at Pacamayo (3,600m). Nearby are some huts and toilets with sinks and running water built by the INC. From the valley floor it will take you about an hour to reach Runkuracay, a ruin not, perhaps, very impressive in itself, but occupying a commanding position overlooking the valley, and at the end of a series of rock-hewn steps that at last give you a feeling that you are on the trail of the Incas. There is another campsite here. You can also camp further up above Runkuracay near a small lake to the left of the trail.

From Runkuracay the path is clear over the second pass (Abra de Runkuracay, 4,000m) and, excitingly, much of the time you are on Inca steps. The descent down the steps is steep, so take care. Just before the trail turns right, you'll see the sign for Sayacmarca. These ruins lie about an hour from the top of the pass and the name, which means 'the Inaccessible or Secret City', is apt. You approach Sayacmarca up a superbly designed stone staircase. This is a diversion (the main trail continues its gradual descent to the right) but don't let fatigue persuade you to miss it.

Like so many Inca ruins, no one really knows the purpose of Sayacmarca, but these are the visible facts: it was built on a precipice commanding a spacious view; there are no agricultural terraces so the complex could not have supported many inhabitants; ritual baths and an aqueduct run round the outside of the main wall; there are curious stone rings set in the wall by trapezoid openings. For me the mystery adds to the beauty, and it is beauty all the way from here – if you are fortunate with the weather.

The trail continues down to the valley floor. From here it becomes a glorious Inca Road, being on a raised causeway over marshy ground that then rises up through cloudforest. Stone paving on raised stone foundations, steps and a gentle gradient make for easy walking, and even if it is raining (and it often is) you will marvel at the Inca workmanship. Before the climb to the third pass there is a campsite with toilets. During the ascent you climb through two Inca tunnels, and if it is a clear day you will have the added bonus of a view of Salkantay over to your left. The pass (3,700m) is used as a campsite, but it gets crowded and water is some way below. Just below the pass, about 2 hours from Sayacmarca, are the impressive ruins of Phuyupatamarca. Access is down a steep flight of stairs. Clear water runs through the channels cut into the rock that feed five baths, leading one from the other down the hill. Backpackers are advised to camp near Phuyupatamarca for the final night. Beyond here the only camping place is the crowded and unscenic area near the hostel at Huiñay Huayna (Wiñay Wayna); in the peak season you are likely to find it full of groups.

Leave early in the morning with a full canteen of water. An Inca staircase leads from the west side of the ruins (the far end from the baths) and disappears into the jungle, leading you down a thousand steps. Literally. You'll think that your knees will never feel the same again.

The end comes in the form of the hostel which marks the beginning of the trail to the ruins of Huiñay Huayna (Wiñay Wayna). This is the last camping spot before Machu Picchu and it is almost always full to bursting. Floor space is usually available in the hostel as well as dormitory accommodation, which must be booked in advance. There is a small restaurant. Beer! This is also the last place to fill up with water before Machu Picchu itself.

Huiñay Huayna lies just below the hostel round to the right as you are descending, and is the most extensive of the ruins so far. It has some beautiful stonework (though spoilt by clumsy restoration), a fantastic location, and an air of mystery often lacking in the crowded Machu Picchu ruins.

The trail from the hostel to Machu Picchu (1½ hours away) is clearly marked. Most people try to leave Huiñay Huayna by 05.30 so they can get to Machu Picchu before sunrise. The sky starts getting light by 06.00 and the first rays of the sun reach Machu Picchu around 07.00. The trail contours a mountainside and disappears into cloudforest full of begonias, bromeliads and tree ferns, before coming to a steep flight of stairs leading up to the first Inca gate. The path continues to the main gate, Intipunku – 'the Gateway of the Sun' – and suddenly the whole of Machu Picchu is spread out before you. A magical moment.

After drinking in the scene, you can stroll down to the hotel, radiating smugness amongst the groups of tourists who arrived by train, and have a slap-up meal in the Machu Picchu Sanctuary Lodge hotel. You might even take a look at the ruins! There is a place for storing your luggage near the entrance (a small fee is charged).

Try to arrive at Machu Picchu several hours before closing time. Your ticket will be stamped on arrival so leave yourself enough time to look around. You will be charged US$20 for re-admission if you return the next day.

Most organised groups will take the train back to Cusco the same day they arrive at the site, or stay at Aguas Calientes. Few backpackers stay in this hotel (it is very expensive, US$275 plus tax for a double, and usually fully booked) but for the incomparable experience of sleeping near the ruins (and I speak as one of the lucky ones who slept *in* the ruins during my first visit in 1969) the less impecunious might see if there has been a cancellation. Otherwise you can camp down by the river or, if you feel like a bed, take the bus or walk down to the railtrack town of Aguas Calientes.

Walks in the vicinity of Machu Picchu

After exploring the site of Machu Picchu, if you still have the energy there are three walks well worth doing before heading down to Aguas Calientes.

Machu Picchu mountain just south of the site, and overlooking it, is a 500m climb, up a well-made Inca pathway. There are some Inca constructions on the top that were probably for religious ceremonies, given the prominent position of the mountain. They look as though they have been damaged by treasure seekers. Allow 2 hours each way through lush forest, keeping a look-out for interesting birds, flowers and snakes sunbathing on the path. The path up Machu Picchu mountain starts from the terraces where the Inca Trail comes in to Machu Picchu at the top of the site.

Huayna Picchu mountain is a steep 1-hour climb (200m in height difference), much of which is up Inca stairs. Try to get there early, before the hordes, as it's a popular walk.

Less popular and an equally beautiful walk is to the **Temple of the Moon**. There is some high-quality Inca stonework inside a cave, which was obviously a sacred place. This is on the west side of Huayna Picchu mountain, 400m below the summit. For this and the previous walk head for the path leading out of the north end of Machu Picchu.

Putucusi, the verdant rocky lump on the east side of the river, oppposite Machu Picchu, is a challenging climb. Take a guide with you if possible. Most of the ascent is up rickety wooden ladders, with short sections of path in between. This scramble should only be attempted by serious climbers. The views from the top, of Machu Picchu and beyond to Salkantay, are pretty spectacular, but be warned: it's a hot, sweaty, slippery struggle to get there.

Aguas Calientes

Aguas Calientes is the ever-sprawling, ramshackle railway town that is the gateway to Machu Picchu. It is right on the banks of the Urubamba river, several hundred metres below Machu Picchu. The town is the last stop for the trains from Cusco and buses shuttle people from here up the hairpin road to the entrance to the Machu Picchu site, approximately 4 km from the town. It's the sort of place you'll either love or hate, with plenty of character and quite unlike any other town in Peru. It is named after the hot springs at the top of the town (15 minutes' walk), which are certainly worth a visit if you've just trekked the Inca Trail. If you have arrived by train you may not appreciate the hot baths, which seem to be in a constant state of refurbishment, and are not particularly clean. Basic changing facilities and showers are available, but there's nowhere to leave your valuables.

The town exists solely for tourists and hence has plenty of hostels, hotels, restaurants, small shops and an avenue of handicraft stalls. It is worth spending a night here at the end of the Inca Trail in order to spend a bit more time at Machu Picchu, and fully enjoy the site and the cloud forest around it. Guides to Machu Picchu are available from the agencies along the railway track. Information on Aguas Calientes is available at www.machupicchu.com.

Getting there and away

Buses to Machu Picchu leave from next to the railway at the end of the only road in town. They depart regularly throughout the day from 06.30, with a rush on departures when the tourist trains arrive. The last bus leaves Machu Picchu at 17.00. Tickets cost US$5 each way, and are purchased at the little ticket office next to the railway before getting on the bus.

If you walk down from the ruins allow an hour, and take the short cuts sign-posted off the road. The modern train station for all tourist trains to Cusco is a five-minute walk from the main rail track. For train times, see page 223.

There is also a daily helicopter back from Machu Picchu to Cusco; see Helicusco on page 230 for details.

Sleeping and eating

There are literally dozens of small restaurants all along the side of the railway and lining the pedestrian street that climbs through the town to the hot pools. It is not usually necessary to book accommodation, as there is such a plentiful supply to suit all budgets.

Las Rocas At the top of the hill; tel: 11049. US$10 per person, with bath and breakfast.

Gringo Bill's Tel: 211046; email: gringobill@yahoo.com. From US$10 per person. A rambling place, with a variety of rooms of all shapes and sizes.
La Cabana Tel: 211048. Halfway up the hill. US$15--20. Clean and friendly.
Machu Picchu Hostal By the railway; tel: 211065. US$20--30 with bath and breakfast. Central, clean and comfortable.
Machu Picchu Pueblo Tel: 211032; email: reservas@inkaterra.com.pe; web: www.inkaterra.com.pe. For that very special treat, it is well worth staying at this elegant and luxurious hotel. Bungalows in the forest, with a superb orchid garden, botanic garden, and several trails. Excellent for bird watching. From US$200 for a double room.

Other starting points
From Kilometre 104 to Machu Picchu via Huiñay Huayna
A mini Inca Trail has been opened from Kilometre 104 (on the railway line) up to Huiñay Huayna and then on to Intipunku. It takes about 3 hours to Huiñay Huayna, where you can camp or stay in the hostel if there's room (or if you have booked). From Huiñay Huayna to Machu Picchu is an hour and a half. It's a lovely hike for those who can't face the whole Inca Trail and you will get to walk on original Inca paving and up those narrow Inca stairways, as well as passing a waterfall and masses of orchids on your way to Huiñay Huayna. The trail fee is US$25. Take plenty of water as it can be a hot and dusty climb for the first two hours. Be aware of the time as the gate at Huiñay Huayna officially closes at 14.00, so if you arrive later you will be forced to stay overnight, and won't reach Machu Picchu that day. You need the catch the first train in the morning to do it all in one day.

An organised tour through an agency in Cusco costs US$120–150 per person, including transfers, train tickets, entrance fees, guide, overnight camp at Huiñay Huayna and some meals.

Ollantaytambo or Chilca to Llactapata
These two towns are on the Urubamba River, providing a gentle day's walk before the strenuous part, and removing the hassle of the train journey. From Ollantaytambo to Chilca (not really a village, just a few houses) is a 3–4 hour hike – about 7km. Unless you are a strong walker, you will need two days to reach Llactapata from Ollantaytambo – 8 hours is a fast time for this stretch; from Chilca it is a one-day hike.

Route description Cross the road bridge in Ollantaytambo and follow the dirt road along the south side of the river to the Chilca bridge, about 7km away (you may catch a ride on this stretch). You will pass some fine Inca terraces and ruins before reaching a very arid region of dry tropical vegetation. After Chilca the trail passes the interesting remains of a Spanish *estancia*. Note the ruined church and the beautiful courtyard; both buildings are still used, but no attempt has been made to restore them to their former elegance.

From Chilca it will take 3 or 4 hours to reach Llactapata. The trail is always easy to follow, and more or less level until the last section where it climbs to the rim of a spectacular canyon full of tropical vegetation. The descent and ascent up the other side are very steep. You can camp in the gorge and Llactapata is less than an hour away.

Chilca to Huayllabamba

This trail also starts at Chilca but is a dramatic, not easy, option. It adds another two or three days to the Inca Trail and includes a steep pass and the lovely *nevados* (snowpeaks) Huayanay and Salkantay Este, sister to the region's highest mountain, Salkantay, to the west.

Distance	30km
Altitude	Between 2,800m and 4,600m
Rating	Moderate/tough
Timing	2–3 days
In reverse	Inadvisable since you would have to pay the Inca Trail fee.

Route description From Chilca, head due south up the valley opposite the bridge across the Urubamba River, and follow the trail, which keeps close to the *quebrada*, west and northwest. After about 5 hours you reach the small village of Ancascocha. Turn right here (southwest) and head up the valley to your right. There are waterfalls here and some good camping spots. The trail continues towards a pass, skirting left of a small lake and reaching the top at 4,600m, some 2–3 hours of strenuous climbing from Ancascocha. The two snowpeaks on your right are Salkantay Este and Huayanay.

The trail now drops down towards the village of Quesca, 2–3 hours away, going to the right of the broad *pampa*, and down to Quebrada Cusichaca and some Inca remains (probably a *tambo*). Follow the left slope of the valley to Quesca. From the village to Huayllabamba is 3 hours. En route is the Inca fortress of Paucarcancha, an almost unknown semi-circular ruin in an inspiring position at the junction of two rivers, about 2 hours from Quesca. From here to Huayllabamba is about an hour. Cross the Cusichaca river and follow its left bank downstream.

Paucarcancha is the focal point of several alternatives. If you continue to Huayllabamba you have the choice of doing the Inca Trail or hiking to Kilometre 88 and taking the train to Machu Picchu or Cusco, or you can head south up the Cusichaca and do the Salkantay hike (see below) in reverse.

SALKANTAY HIKES

The *cordillera*'s highest mountain, Salkantay (6,271m), provides an awesome backdrop for these hikes. You then have a choice of keeping high or dropping down to the subtropical regions. The area is seldom crowded – this is Peru at its most perfect.

All three treks share the same route from Mollepata to Soray – a beautiful

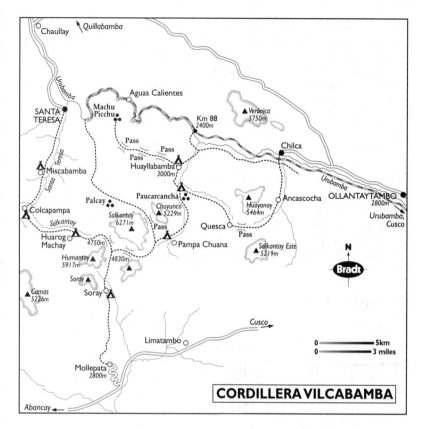

Map labels:
Chaullay — Quillabamba — Aguas Calientes — Machu Picchu — SANTA TERESA — Km 88 2400m — Verónica 5750m — Chilca — Pass — Pass — Pass — Huayllabamba 3000m — Urubamba — Miscabamba — Santa Teresa — Paucarcancha — Ancascocha — OLLANTAYTAMBO 2800m — Palcay — Chuyunco 5229m — Huayanay 5464m — Colcapampa — Salkantay — Salkantay 6271m — Quesca — Urubamba, Cusco — Huarog Machay — 4750m — Pass — Pass — Humantay 5917m — 4830m — Pampa Chuana — Salkantay Este 5219m — N — Soray — Camas 5226m — Soray — Bradt — Cusco — Limatambo — 0 —— 5km — 0 —— 3 miles — Mollepata 2800m — Abancay — **CORDILLERA VILCABAMBA**

walk with the added bonus of the chance to visit the lovely Inca site of Tarahuasi before arriving at Mollepata.

Mollepata is at a subtropical 2,803m. It overlooks a citrus growing area where flocks of parakeets screech overhead. The gradual ascent towards Salkantay is made up a valley full of flowering shrubs buzzing with hummingbirds, across streams and past isolated grass-thatched houses, while ahead of you the snow-covered flanks of Salkantay and Humantay gleam in the afternoon sun. At the head of the valley, in the tiny settlement of Soray, you have the choice of three treks: the subtropical delights and thermal baths of the trail to Santa Teresa, the icy, breathless, but stunningly beautiful Salkantay trek to Huayllabamba, or the middle route, combining elements of both: Inca ruins, ice and snow, and subtropical forests.

Limatambo and Tarahuasi

Unless you're in a great hurry I strongly recommend you spend the first night in Limatambo, about 10km before the Mollepata turnoff. It is a pleasant, low-lying little town with basic accommodation or camping possibilities. Nearby, at Tarahuasi, is an Inca temple with one of the finest examples anywhere of Inca polygonal masonry in a long retaining wall. On the upper level are 28 tall niches, thought by John Hemming to have been for liveried attendants or for mummies. The stonework, in rosette patterns, is orange-coloured through its covering of lichen. This amazing place sees few tourists.

Tarahuasi was on one of the main Inca roads (*chinchaysuyo*) leading to Cusco. It was probably a control gate at the site of a battle between the Spanish and Incas. Hernando de Soto and his soldiers were resting here on their way to Cusco when they were attacked by 4,000 Inca warriors; four Spaniards were killed and many injured.

About 15km beyond Limatambo the rivers Apurímac and Colorado meet, at a place called Airahua. Just down the river you can visit the hot springs at Cónoc. There are also some good routes to explore on foot round this area. You can walk the Chichaysuyo Inca trail, which goes towards Cónoc (2–3 hours), or take a path going upwards and northwards towards Rumirumi and Minaspata, from where you have a great view over the Apurímac canyon. The Incas had a hanging bridge over the Apurímac at Maucachaca, just where the Quebrada Honda reaches the Apurímac. This immense bridge was 45m long, and amazed the early chroniclers.

Mollepata to Soray

Distance	About 16km
Altitude	Between 2,800m and about 3,500m
Timing	1 day
Maps	Sheet *Machu Picchu* (27-q) and *Urubamba* (27-r)

Getting to the trailhead Get transport from Cusco to Mollepata by bus or truck, leaving from Avenida Arcopata early in the morning. The 05.00 bus is recommended if you want to reach Soray that day. The ride of 76km takes 3–5 hours.

***Arrieros* and pack animals** Horses and mules are available in Mollepata. Some hikers hire pack animals to take their luggage to Soray only: a sensible idea because this gives a good start on that long, uphill first day. It is also possible to hire pack animals in Soray.

Route description Mollepata has improved from the days, a century ago, when George Squier described it as a 'place unsurpassed in evil repute by any in Peru'. There is an attractive green plaza, some pretty houses, and even basic accommodation. There is a dirt road some of the way from Mollepata to Soray now, but the short cut via the footpath is much more scenic and you don't even cross the road.

The path heads steeply uphill just outside Mollepata, in the direction of the mountains. Ask locals if you're not sure, but it's a pretty obvious trail, going out of the plaza in the northwest corner, then right at the T-junction.

Continue up the left side of the valley (northwest), following a cement irrigation ditch. Follow the trail along this canal until the top of a pass (3¹/₂ hours from Mollepata). Then, instead of continuing beside the canal, head steeply up to the right. These trails will eventually take you to over a pass and into the next valley, Río Blanca. Look out for a cross on the hill where the last possible campsites are (Marcocassa). Below the cross, a difficult-to-follow trail bears round to the right, keeping on high ground, heading northeast through shrubs and bushes. There are many paths through the bushes, all leading to the same main trail, about 45 minutes from the cross. You should be on the west side of the Río Blanca valley.

Once you join the main trail the way is clear (and uphill) and you will shortly come to a stream. The trail continues round a corner and a splendid view of Humantay (5,917m) comes into sight. The path climbs up the long Humantay valley, following the water canal, to Soray, which is reached in about 3–4 hours of easy and beautiful hiking (7–8 hours total from Mollepata). The view of Salkantay appears just before Soray. Campsites are found just above the village, across the river, or – even better – an hour higher up.

Soray to Huayllabamba

This is the spectacular option, but also the toughest, passing high around the flank of Salkantay and visiting some interesting Inca remains. You may then link up with the Inca Trail to complete an Inca-saturated trek.

Distance	About 40km
Altitude	Between 2,800m and 4,880m
Rating	Difficult
Timing	2–3 days
In reverse	Yes, if you start from Chilca (see *Chilca to Huayllabamba hike*, page 266).

Route description An hour beyond Soray is the giant V of a moraine spreading down from Salkantay. The trail, not very clear, runs northeast up the right side of the moraine, crossing some streams which run from it. After some steep climbing, the terrain levels out and the trail turns sharply to the right and uphill, near a big boulder, and continues along the right-hand bank of a small stream for about an hour (the stream may be dry). Before reaching a flat, boggy meadow, you'll see a low cliff (about 5m) hung with icicles formed by the dripping water. Cross the stream below the cliff and climb straight up to the meadow. The trail seems to disappear in this boggy stretch, but you can pick it up where the meadow starts to dry out towards the centre and follow the path a little to the left. It's worth making a detour to the glacier. You can see the layers of ice representing annual precipitation, rather like the annual rings on a tree-stump. Notice, too, the quality of the ice: the old, compact ice is blue and almost clear, while new ice is frosty-looking with trapped air.

Above the plateau the path zigzags up the reddish coloured scree slope, becoming more conspicuous as it nears the top of the pass of Incachillasca, which lies at the top of the scree in the saddle of two minor ridges. This is an impressive 4,880m (over 16,000ft) and it will take you 5–6 hours to climb here from Soray. The view makes it all worthwhile. The path descending on the other side is quite clear as it traverses the right-hand (east) side of the mountain. There are some good camping places (about 1½ hours from the pass) at the point where the river and trail make a sharp left turn down the valley.

The trail continues down the right bank of the stream to some stone corrals, about 3 hours from the pass, then crosses the *quebrada* and follows it down the upper Cusichaca valley. Keep to the left-hand bank of the river as it turns northeast, picks up speed, and descends through a small gorge. About an hour past the moraine, just past a *campesino* settlement (Pampachuana) on the right-hand bank, the river is canalised for draining the *pampa*. Shortly after the end of the canal, cross to the right bank via a footbridge and follow a good path along the right-hand side of the river down the narrow, steep valley to the Quesea river junction and settlement some 1–1½ blister-making hours away.

The Inca fortress Paucarcancha stands here. From the foot of the fortress you'll see the trail leading to Chilca, one day's hike away. To reach Huayllabamba, cross the river and follow the left-hand bank on down the Río Cusichaca, about 20 minutes beyond the crossing. From Huayllabamba you can join the Inca Trail for the 3-day hike to Machu Picchu, or hike out to Chilca in 4–5 hours, or to Kilometre 88 in 2 hours. However, in the lower Cusichaca valley you can enjoy looking at the complex of Inca sites studied by the Cusichaca Trust from 1977 to 1988. Don't miss the view from the tableland of Huillca Raccay en route to Chilca. Here you are also surrounded by pre-Inca sites on the ridges. Below Kilometre 88 a visit to the Inca sites of Machu and Quente, on the left-hand side of the Urubamba valley, would take half a day.

Soray to Santa Teresa

This lovely and varied hike is the 'soft option' from Soray since the pass is lower (though still a tough 4,750m (15,580ft) and then it is mostly downhill through forested valleys, above deep ravines, past (or in) a wonderful thermal spring, until you end up in the citrus groves of Santa Teresa. This small subtropical village used to be linked by rail to Machu Picchu, but both the village and the railway were completely destroyed by a landslide in 1998. Santa Teresa today is an unattractive collection of temporary constructions, mostly wooden houses with tin roofs. The remains of the old town are interesting to visit – 'impressive houses split like a cake, steel railways twisted like hair'. From here you can walk to the train station at the hydroelectric plant up the valley (4 hours' walk to the station, 1 hour more to Aguas Calientes) or take a bus or truck out towards Quillabamba. Check locally for transport details.

Distance	About 50km
Altitude	Between 1,500m and 4,750m
Rating	Moderate to difficult
Timing	3–4 days
In reverse	Possible – but you'd better like walking uphill!
Getting to	Check bus and truck details for getting from Santa
Machu Picchu	Teresa to Quillabamba, or train details to Aguas Calientes, before you leave Cusco.

Route description Go up the left side of the moraine at the head of the valley, crossing to the left bank of a stream to pick up a path leading up the side of the mountain. It goes steeply uphill for half an hour, then comes to a series of zigzags (Siete Culebras is the local name of this stretch). At the top of the seventh switchback the terrain levels out under Salkantay's lateral moraine, and drops gently down to the small Laguna Soirococha. The pass you see above is, alas, a false one; the main pass is a little further on, but the view of Salkantay looming above you more than compensates for the effort. The real pass at 4,750m is reached after 3–4 hours from the moraine, and is marked by a pile of stones, *apacheta*, which grows daily as each traveller adds his pebble to thank the *apus* for a safe trip (see box, page 326). A few cattle skulls add a macabre touch.

The trail descends to the left-hand side of the valley, becoming indistinct in swampy areas. If the weather is bad there are caves providing shelter about 20 minutes below the pass. Once the valley narrows there is only one obvious trail on the left of the river. Some 2–3 hours from the pass you'll reach a small hut and a level area which is a popular camping spot. This place is called Huayrajmachay ('Eye of the Wind').

You'll leave the beautiful pyramid-shaped peak of Humantay behind as you drop below the treeline, known as *la ceja de selva* ('eyebrow of the jungle'), and walk through groves of bamboo with many orchids and other flowers and lots of hummingbirds. Don't forget to keep looking back at the snowpeaks behind you, framed by bamboo fronds. After about 2 hours the trail crosses an old landslide and in another 2 hours you'll drop steeply down to the bridge across the Río Chalhuay. This is a beautiful camping area, but there's an even better one an hour further on. Twenty minutes beyond the tiny settlement of Colpapampa are the hot springs: turn right at the trail junction by the river. Just before the bridge a single stream of hot water is piped into a semi-natural pool on the right-hand side of the trail. Look out for the parakeets that abound in this area.

You are now at the confluence of two rivers, the Totota and the Santa Teresa, and you'll be following the latter all the way down to the town of the same name. The best campsite is the other side of the turf bridge, and the best mineral deposits from the thermal springs are a short way below the campsite, following the river bank (scramble over the rocks).

After the bridge the trail stays close to the river (ignore a fork to your left) and then, surprisingly (because you were expecting 'downhill all the way'), climbs up to contour round the mountainside through bamboo groves. Soon you will come to a stream which disrupts the trail. Go up this for about 8m to pick up the trail again on the other side. Carry on uphill to a spectacular waterfall. This cascade drops some 300m and the trail crosses it midway! A perfect shower, and the water/air temperature is now warm enough for you to welcome a bath. Following the trail up and down, you come to a second waterfall, with swimming in the pool above. This is an incredibly beautiful stretch, with begonias, purple and orange orchids and strawberries lining the path.

Some 5 hours after the hot springs you'll come to the hamlet of Miscabamba. Basic provisions and drinks are available here. Camping in Miscabamba is not recommended, however, because of problems with theft, so it is better to camp well outside the village. From Miscabamba to the small village of Paltachayoc and the start of the dirt road will take 2–3 hours. There are good campsites near the bridge. From the bridge it's another hot 2–3 hours through citrus, banana and coffee plantations to Santa Teresa. This once attractive small town is slowly being rebuilt after the devastating landslide of 1998. There is little in the way of supplies. You can take the train to Machu Picchu (45 minutes) from the station at the hydro-electric plant about 4 hours' walk up the valley, or take a truck or bus to the Cusco–Quillabamba road. Check the transport situation in Cusco before you leave.

VILCABAMBA HIKES
Cachora to Huancacalle via Choquequirao
This is a spectacular trek of approximately 100km, with over 5,000m of ascent and slightly less descent. You cross the entire Vilcabamba range in about 8 days of trekking. You pass through an immense range of vegetation types and temperatures, with a variety of panoramic views to match: from the ice-capped peaks of the high Andes, their sharp ridges, deep gorges and raging rivers to the lush flora and prolific wildlife of the subtropical rainforest. There is not much water around for the first few days, so be sure to have the capacity to carry at least 2 litres each. You need to take your passport also as there are police checks at Puquiura.

Distance	100km
Altitude	Between 2,400m and 4,600m
Rating	Moderate
Timing	8 days
In reverse	Possible
Maps	*Machu Picchu* (27-q)

Getting to the trailhead Take the Abancay bus from the bus station in Cusco. It leaves early, usually at 06.30, so it's a good idea to buy your ticket the day before. The bus stops at Curahuasi for breakfast for around 40 minutes. This is an area of aniseed production, on the edge of the Apurímac gorge. Four hours (145km) after leaving Cusco get off the bus at the road junction (3,695m) for Cachora near the Inca site of Sayhuite, 45km before Abancay. (Some of the buses to Lima also go this way and take just 2 hours to do the same journey).

Don't miss the huge carved boulder of Sayhuite (4,000m) and its surrounding site of baths, plaza and carved rocks. The monolith of Sayhuite has over 200 figures carved into it; they are animals that were important in the beliefs of the Incas such as the jaguar, lizard, monkey and snake as well as anthropomorphic forms and various plants. To get to the site from the main road walk left down an obvious dirt track for 5–10 minutes. Pay a small entry fee of US$2. Allow at least an hour to visit the site. You can buy snacks such as deep-fried pork (*chicharron de chancho*) and maize from the houses by the roadside.

Head back up to the road junction, cross the road and follow the dirt track up to the top of the ridge. From here you will see the village of Cachora far below. Well beyond it is the dramatic Apurímac gorge. It takes 1–2 hours of fast downhill walking to reach the village. You can follow the road, taking short cuts where possible, or try to get a ride if there happens to be any passing transport. There are buses from Abancay to Cachora in the mornings, the last one leaving Abancay at 11.00. Cachora (2,875m) is a small town of around 3,000 people, with stunning views across to the snow-capped peaks of the Vilcabamba range on the far side of the Apurímac. The mountain of Ampay towers above. In Cachora basic services are available. You can rent donkeys for treks and there are several shops, bars and a hostel (**Hospedaje Judith Catherine** tel: 084 320202; US$2 per bed). You can find mules and guides in Cachora too. Seferina and Celestino Peña, have been recommended, and seem to be the best known, but there are plenty of others. Expect to pay US$10 a day for an *arriero* and US$5 a day per animal. You need to pay for the *arriero* and animal to come back, and also provide them with food and sometimes even a tent.

Route description COPESCO has recently done a lot of work on the path that you follow to get to Choquequirao. There are signposts and generally it is in excellent condition. From the plaza in Cachora take the road that leaves town heading downwards from the bottom-left corner. There is a signpost after about 20 minutes indicating a left turn and from there the path continues to wind its way leftwards along the side of the valley. There is little or no water on the route until you reach an old farm house at Chiquisaca (17km from Cachora), just 3km before you reach the mighty Apurímac river (20km from Cachora), so you need to carry several litres with you.

After a 2–3-hour walk (10km) from Cachora you reach the edge of a ridge and a picnic/camping spot known as Capilliyoc (2,800m). You can just make out where Choquequirao (3,050m) lies, in the distance, slightly above you on the far side of the river. There are a couple of thatch-covered huts on the ridge, which makes for a scenic though somewhat exposed camping spot with just enough space for two or three tents. From here a further 10km (2–3 hours), this time all descent, takes you down to the new bridge across the Apurímac (1,550m). There is water at Chiquisaca (1,930m), 2 hours from Capilliyoc, and fruit if you are lucky from the trees at the abandoned farm there. The flies bite nastily from here on down though, so insect repellent comes in handy. Looking across the river you can see only too clearly the steep climb that awaits you.

You can camp by the river if you can stand the biting flies here.

Head slowly up the steep zigzags from the river to bring you, after a hot and sweaty 1½–2 hours, to the sugarcane camp of Santa Rosa (2,200m, 22km from Cachora). Here you will find plenty of fresh water right down by the houses where they turn sugarcane into alcohol. If there is anybody about they might show you the primitive machinery used for brewing this strong and noxious spirit. A further steep climb (1½–2 hours) takes you to the grassy field at Maraupata (2,850m, 25km from Cachora now). Views of Choquequirao gradually appear ahead, and it's just 90 minutes of relatively flat walking to get there. This last part of the walk is through typical cloudforest, replete with orchids, bromeliads and lichens. There is ample camping space on the extended terraces that you reach at the beginning of the site. There is water here also and a drop toilet has been built.

The site is gradually being restored under the guidance of Peruvian archaeologist Percy Paz, who is usually to be found on site with a team of workers. He is often willing to show people around the 30% of the site which has been cleared and explain something about the many different sectors of Choquequirao, including the main square, long terraces, ceremonial platform, palaces, houses and water canal. Before work began the whole site was almost completely engulfed by the thick vegetation which grows so prolifically at these altitudes.

It is believed that Choqueuirao was constructed during the reign of the ninth Inca lord Pachacútec, dedicated to the sun, the water and the *apus*. Some of the temples have trapezoidal doors and windows typical of the palaces and temples of other Inca sites. The location is dramatic, views over the Apurímac gorge are spectacular and in the distance are the snow-capped peaks of Ampay, Panta and Quishuar. Condors are often seen soaring overhead and the men that work on clearing the site claim many sitings of the spectacled bear (*oso de anteojos*).

Head out of the site on the path signposted from the water-pipe down the bottom, where you first arrived. Alternatively, from the highest cleared point of the site a rather overgrown path leads straight upwards for 200m, then join the main path. Turn left and continue through rich cloudforest on an exposed section for an hour to reach a great look-out point on a sharp ridge with spectacular drops to the Apurímac gorge. Ahead is a steep grass-covered hillside, down which the path zig zags. Across the valley you can see where you will be heading; there are huts and yet another steep zigzagging climb.

Part way down the slope is another Inca site, known as Pincha Unuyoc or Pinchunío (2,470m), where there are water and extensive terraces probably used for agriculture. Keep a careful eye on the path as it is quite easy to get lost amongst the terraces. The path winds down leftward through the terraces and then heads more to the right to leave this area in the bottom-right corner of the lowest field. This is where the water source is, and some Inca buildings. The path follows the stream of water downwards and from here on takes a more obvious course. The temperature rises considerably as you continue descending to reach the River Victoria (on some maps Río Blanco) (1,990m) where you can have a welcome wash in the cold meltwaters from Corihuaynachina. Take care when crossing the river. There is no bridge and it can be quite fast flowing. There are camping spots on the far side about 200m downstream from where you emerged, if you can stand the flies, known locally and very appropriately as *pumahuacachi*, 'that which makes the puma scream'.

It is a long steep climb of over 2,000m to the pass of Abra Victoria (4,130m). It is possible to accomplish this climb in one day with an early start, but is perhaps better to take it more easily over two days. Be warned that there is no reliable water source on the way up. About 3 hours up from the bottom of the valley you reach several small houses, inhabited for only part of the year by families from Yanama who grow crops nearby. There is some water here, but it doesn't look too savoury. It is at least another 5 hours to the pass itself. The transition from hot, dry bamboo-rich scrubland through dense cloudforest and then out into typical high mountain *paramo* is remarkable. Even more surprising are the entrance and slag heaps of the Victoria mine, just an hour below the pass, apparently so high in the mountainside and so far from anywhere. This silver and lead mine was successively exploited by Incas and Spaniards alike. From the mine a beautifully constructed Inca road leads to the pass, where a superb view of the impressive snow-capped peaks of the Cordillera Vilcabamba awaits.

The bottom of the next valley is now your destination, at the small village of Yanama (3,480m). The Inca trail continues, carved expertly into the cliff side, leading you downwards along an impossible-looking, somewhat vertiginous route. There is water not far from the top of the pass. It is something of a relief to get to Yanama, a beautiful setting and one of the most cared for mountain villages I have seen in the Andes. Typical adobe houses are surrounded by small cultivated plots. There is plenty of water and the village is very clean and friendly. You can hire mules and muleteers here if you need to. The cost is approximately US$7 per animal and US$5–10 per person per day, and you will need to supply food and accommodation for the muleteer. You will also have to pay for the return journey for the team.

From Yanama there are good paths leading in several directions. There is no road access to the village so everything is brought in and taken out by mule. Go east up the valley, over the pass, and you can join the route to Santa Teresa or Mollepata. For Huancacalle follow the river downstream, westwards, crossing over a large bridge before continuing up the valley known locally as Quebrada de Quilcamachay but named on the map as Quebrada Otiyoc.

There is no shortage of water on this walk. Follow the path, keeping right at any junction, up this broad U-shaped valley. Look out for the many species of orchid growing in the forests you pass through, especially the rare and exquisite *Waqanqi*. Towering granite spires loom on the right, and spectacular mountain vistas appear as you climb. It is approximately 6–8 hours from Yanama to the pass Abra Choquetacarpo (4,600m). There are plenty of places to camp on the way up the pass. The last few kilometres of ascent are on Inca trail again, of amazing quality. Some sections are 3m wide, paved beautifully, and have weathered the test of time remarkably well. At the pass, after an extremely steep last section, there are cairns constructed as offerings to the *apus* and the spirits of the mountains that watch over walkers.

From the pass it takes around 4–5 hours to get to the road head at the village of Huancacalle. There are camping spots on the way down. Follow the Inca road, then a well-marked path until you reach a dirt road, at which go left to Huancacalle. Huancacalle boasts a couple of pensions, the best known of which is **Hostal Sixpac Manco**, run by the Cobos family (tel: 084 270298; US$5 per person, hot water and food available). There are a few shops and basic restaurants and a police checkpoint here too. Buses/trucks leave for Quillabamba at 09.00, 13.00 and 16.00, taking 5 hours and costing US$3. A taxi will cost around US$20 and take just 2–3 hours.

From Huancacalle it is well worth spending half a day visiting the remains of Rosas Patas and the Palace of Manco Inca and Ñusta Hispana. The local official responsible for all of the archaeological sites of the Espíritu Pampa area is Genaro Quispicusi. He is willing to discuss the sites with you if you can pin him down. The Cobos also have a long history of working in the area with explorers (Gene Savoy and Vincent Lee), and are a mine of local information.

Ñusta Hispana is an immense carved boulder, even bigger than Sayhuite. It is 5m high with finely carved steps and angles. All around it there are extensive terraces linked by water canals, probably used for irrigation.

Huancacalle to Espíritu Pampa

This hike is mainly for those with a serious interest in Inca history, and to get the most out of a visit to these important Inca ruins some background reading is essential (see *Further Reading*, page 400). The brief history below is just to whet your appetite.

Although Inca ruins are the goal, the opportunity to walk through sparsely populated low-altitude rainforest gives this hike an added appeal to naturalists and birdwatchers.

History

One of the last Inca rulers, Manco, installed himself in this area around 1537 while fleeing from the Spaniards; he planned to regain control over Tawantinsuyo at a better moment. The Spaniards finally conquered the area in 1572, with a large and thoroughly prepared expedition, and killed the very last Inca ruler, Túpac Amaru. Thus ended the Inca empire. Later the area was used for silver mining and the cultivation of sugar and coca, but there was little effort to settle this humid rainforest area and Vilcabamba became a memory until the 20th century when men of science began to take an interest in ancient Peru. Hiram Bingham, the 'discoverer' of Machu Picchu, found Vilcabamba in the same year: 1911. Gene Savoy organised expeditions to this area in 1964 and 1965, and Vincent Lee became very interested in the region's large concentration of Inca remains. In 1976 a Lima historian claimed to have 'discovered' Bingham's ruins at Espíritu Pampa and suddenly the place was off limits. Appearances of terrorists around 1983 made it even worse, and the area became overrun with soldiers and police. Fortunately these problems are now over and hikers are again visiting the area without problems. Projects are planned for more research on these Inca remains. It is hoped that the area will receive more protection before the Inca roads disappear under modern road construction.

Ruins near Huancacalle

Very interesting and important ruins are situated just outside Huancacalle, at the start of the Vilcabamba hike (see above):

- **Vitcos** (also called Rosaspata), a huge fortress uphill from Huancacalle (1 hour).
- **Yurac Rumi** (Ñusta Hispana), an enormous carved rock, the showpiece of an entire complex of ruins, including impressive baths, near the end of the valley (under an hour from Vitcos or Huancacalle).
- **Los Andenes**, a system of finely built terraces and rock shrines, in the valley beyond Vitcos.

Hiking to Vilcabamba (Espíritu Pampa)

Distance	About 60km
Altitude	Between 3,850m and 950m
Rating	Moderate, but the steep muddy paths can make hiking difficult.
Timing	About 8 days, including transport there.
In reverse	Possible
Maps	The entire trek falls between several sheets: Quillabamba (26-q), Machu Picchu (27-q), Pacaypata (27-p) and Chuanquiri (26-p).

The book *Sixpac Manco* (available in Cusco bookshops) is a great guide for this area.

Getting to the trailhead The only way to get to the trailhead, since the train line washed out below Machu Picchu, is to take the bus on the Cusco–Quillabamba route over the Abra de Malaga (500m) and get off at

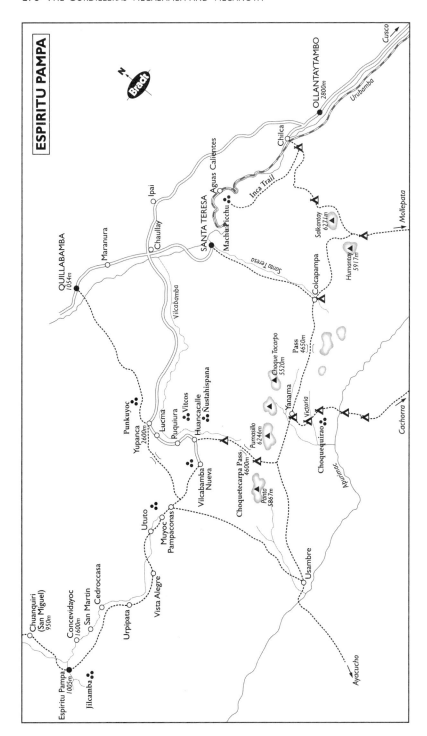

Chaullay (8 hours). Cross the bridge to the road to pick up transport to Yupanca, Puquiura and Huancacalle. If there is no transport ask at the house about accommodation or camping spots. From Chaullay the journey takes about 3–4 hours by truck or pick-up. At Puquiura there is a police checkpoint where you need to register and show your passport.

Huancacalle (2,900m) is the starting point of the hike to Vilcabamba (Espíritu Pampa). You'll need a day to get organised. It's best to hire a local guide in Huancacalle to show you the ruins, which are hard to find and overgrown. Expect to pay a guide about US$5 per day, and the same amount for a pack animal. **Sixpac Manco Hostal** has good-quality accommodation and meals in Huancacalle, and can find guides and animals for you. Narciso Huaman, who lives near Huancacalle, is recommended – ask Genaro, the top INC man in Huancacalle. There are a couple of other basic places to stay.

Route description The dirt road extending from Huancacalle to Vilcabamba Nueva has been greatly improved recently. Follow it out of the village for about 1km (10 minutes), where it forks. Stay to the right and pick up the footpath about 100m further along (5 minutes), climbing uphill, making short cuts across the switchbacks. The trail splits and forks in several places, but always rejoins itself. After about 2 hours you reach the small Spanish village of Vilcabamba Nueva. Accommodation is available at **Coleygo** (some sort of mission). The trail continues from here up the left side of the drainage channel towards the pass of Kollpakasa at 3,850m, which you'll reach after about 2 hours. Camping is possible on either side of the pass. The path descends into the valley of Concevidayoc along the south slope, over a fine Inca road, until you reach the bridge of Maucachaca over the Río Chalcha, about 1 hour from the pass. Camp just before the bridge. Take the route through the Pampaconas which forks uphill to the left. You will reach a clearing among low woods at a place called Muyoc, 1 hour later. Another hour of easy, level walking gets you from Muyoc to Ututo (3,000m), where there's a bridge to the north bank of the Río Concevidayoc.

Cross the bridge and hike down a forested ravine on sections of Inca road to Cedrochaca. There are several good campsites along the river. Recross to the south bank at Cedrochaca and traverse up a steep mountainous slope. After 1 hour you pass the hamlet of Tambo and 45 minutes later, descending, you cross the Río Zapatero, which joins the Río Concevidayoc close by.

Continue along a stretch of broad floodplain to the tributary Río Sucsuchincana with good campsites, about 1 hour. The hamlet of Vista Alegre, also with good campsites, lies about 10 minutes downstream. From Vista Alegre to the village of Concevidayoc (1,600m) the trail is quite easy to follow, once you get used to ducking under overhanging vegetation. After passing the tiny clearing of San Guillermo, a deep-forest trail brings you to Urpipata. Here the trail follows a ridge-top among tall trees to Huaynapata, a cleared hill with a primitive sugar mill atop it and sugarcane growing nearby. The trail continues to Cedroccasa, where the forest gives way to scrub slope and cultivation until you reach the village of Concevidayoc, where you can camp. Altogether this is a 7-hour walk if you don't stop along the way.

The trail continues in the direction of Espíritu Pampa about 2 hours away.

Avoid the right-hand trail fork, 20 minutes beyond Concevidayoc, which descends towards Chuanquiri. At Espíritu Pampa (1,005m) camping space is a few cramped square metres by the houses of the *campesinos*.

Visiting the ruins of Vilcabamba and Chuanquiri

The ruins are situated in the dense forest up the gentle slope beyond the settlement, between two small streams that merge below the settlement and in turn join the Concevidayoc a short distance downstream from their junction. You are recommended to hire a guide in Espíritu Pampa for about US$2, to make sure you don't miss the main parts; few ruins are visible, and unfortunately most are still overgrown. You will need a machete to cut through the vegetation to the ruins. Ask at the houses for a guide.

From Espíritu Pampa to Chuanquiri (also called San Miguel) is a hot steamy day's walking over many steep sections. Take the trail leading down to a footbridge (not for mules) which crosses the gorge of the Río Chontabamba to the north bank. Then follow the trail downstream, high above the Río Chontabamba, to its intersection with the main valley trail, about 45 minutes from Espíritu Pampa. Mules must backtrack the long way round (1½ hours) to this river junction. About 3 hours from here you will come to a cable and concrete footbridge over the Río Concevidayoc. Cross it and begin a steep, twisting ascent of 1½ hours to a grassy height. Descend for another sinuous hour to the Río San Miguel. Cross the bridge here, and climb up again to Chuanquiri (San Miguel): 950m, about half an hour. This is your final campsite.

Getting back to Cusco

From Chuanquiri (San Miguel) there are trucks (only Friday to Monday) to Kiteni from 14.00. Taking about 3 hours, this journey has been described to me as 'a 3-hour buttock-numbing, rib-cracking, back-snapping ride from hell'. If there aren't any trucks you'll have to charter a pick-up for around $40 or hike this part, following the dirt road, taking 9–10 hours. There are a couple of basic hostels and simple restaurants in Kiteni. Daily trucks do the route between Kiteni and Quillabamba, usually overnight, in about 8 hours, the last ones leaving Kiteni by 15.30. In Quillabamba you can catch a bus back to Cusco (8 hours, 08.00, 17.00 and 18.00).

THE VILCANOTA REGION

The Cordillera Vilcanota is named after the Vilcanota River lying to its west (which drains east into the Atlantic). This range is the second-largest glaciated system in Peru (after the Cordillera Blanca), with over 500km² of glacier, and with the largest single glacier in Peru, the Quelccaya ice cap. This impressive range of mountains, 80km long and 40km wide, includes the massive Nevado Ausangate (6,372m). Ausangate is the highest mountain in the department of Cusco and, like Salkantay in the Vilcabamba range, was highly revered by the Incas and continues to be sacred today. Offerings are often made by the local communities and individuals seeking good harvests, fertility, health and prosperity. Hiking opportunities here are excellent, but the toughest in the region, so you need to be fit and acclimatised. The whole area lies above the treeline and is populated with traditionally dressed Quechua-speaking *campesinos* cultivating the barren *altiplano*. This is alpaca country. Enormous herds graze in the already eroded valleys. Typical Quechua festivals are popular in this region and you might find yourself drinking the local brew of *chicha* with the villagers. Their major fiesta is *Qoyllor Rit'i* ('The Ice Festival'), around the second week of June (see box on pages 284–5) and – also in mid June – is the fiesta of *Raqchi*. The most popular hike is the circuit around Nevado Ausangate, but there are many other interesting and spectacular hikes in the area to the south and it is an ideal region for finding your own route, with plenty of paths and local people to give you directions.

Conditions

This is a remote area, so prepare carefully, particularly if exploring off the main route. Always carry enough food and a compass. Plus some stones to fend off the dogs. Camp outside the villages and ask permission when possible. Be prepared for very cold nights (well below freezing) and strong sun during the day. It can be dangerous to hike in this area during the rainy season when clouds and snow cover the passes and hide important landmarks.

Theft has been a problem near the villages on the Ausangate circuit, especially Tinqui and Upis. However, most of the time this happened when hikers made no contact with the villagers, or left things outside their tent.

The Ausangate Circuit

This 5–6 day hike has everything: herds of llamas and alpacas, traditionally dressed Indians, hot springs, turquoise lakes, glaciers, ice caves, and even *vicuñas*. Not surprisingly, it is increasingly popular with trekkers. The route takes you right round the massif of Ausangate and over three high passes before returning you to your starting point, the small village of Tinqui.

Tinqui

Tinqui is near Ocongate, southeast of Cusco. The easiest way to get there is to catch a bus to Urcos, leaving from the Coliseum in Cusco – and taking about 1 hour. From here catch a truck to Tinqui, leaving at around 11.00; the journey takes 5–6 hours. It is a beautiful but dusty and very cold ride.

This little town has two basic hostels, Hostal Ausangate and Hostal Tinqui, both great sources of information about the hikes in the area, so worth staying at for that reason alone. The guides Crispin Cayitano and Teo work out of these hostels and probably know the area as well as anyone.

There is an association of *arrieros* (about 50 members) at Tinqui, and prices are set: *arriero* about US$6 per day, and US$7 per day for his animal. Contact them in Tinqui at Hostal Tinqui, or from the South American Explorers in Cusco.

Providing you have a map and compass and know how to use them, you will not need a guide.

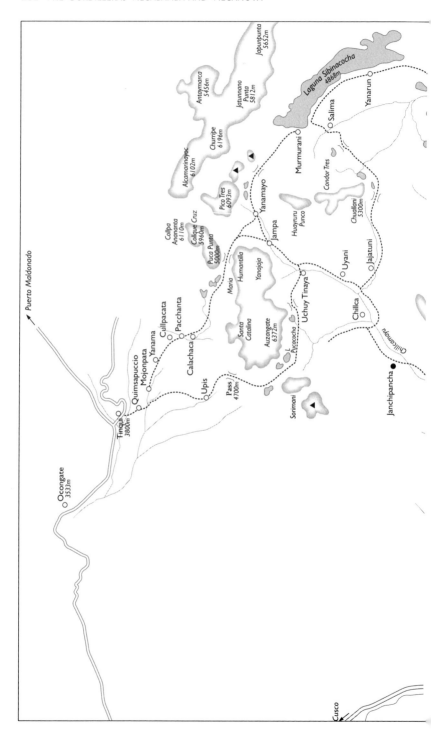

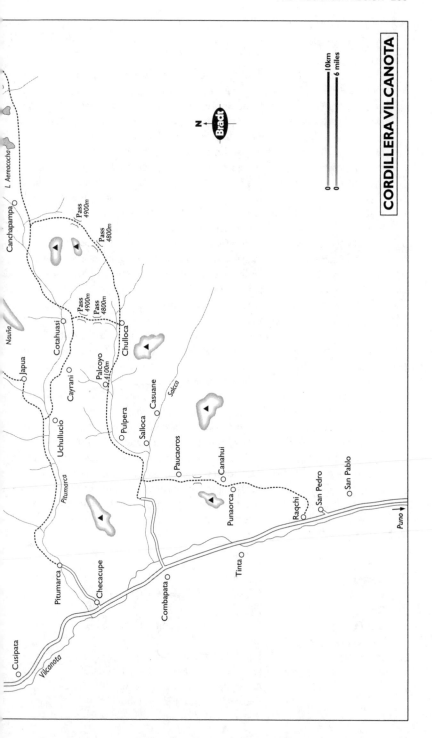

CORDILLERA VILCANOTA

QOYLLOR RIT'I
Chris Hooker

The spiritual beliefs of most Andean *campesinos* are more complex than they might at first appear. Native *campesino* communities tend to follow a syncretic religion in which the ancient worship of nature spirits is overlaid with a Christian veneer. At the pilgrimage of Qoyllor Rit'i, perhaps the most impressive Indian fiesta of all, veneration of Christ and of the sacred peak, Ausankati (Ausangate), have become mythically intertwined.

At a breathtaking 4,750m above sea level, three massive glacial tongues reach down to the desolate Sinakara valley. On a scree slope sits a stone chapel enclosing a rock outcrop on which is painted a figure of Christ crucified. This is the miraculous Señor de Qoyllor Rit'i (Lord of the Snow Star), the Cusco region's most important Indian shrine and the scene annually, between the Christian feasts of the Ascension and Corpus Christi, of an explosion of colour, noise and ritual as 25,000 pilgrims (predominantly Quechua-speaking highland Indians) converge.

The elaborate pageant of timeless devotion has its official origins in a Christian miracle of 1783. Legend tells of a mysterious pale-skinned stranger, Manuel, who befriended Mariano, a native shepherd boy, and was one day transformed into the figure of Christ crucified upon a nearby Tayanka shrub. Mariano witnessed the miracle, died suddenly and was buried beneath an adjacent crag. Churchmen from Cusco looked on as the Christ figure then disappeared, leaving behind a crucifix where the bush once stood.

Mariano's crag, later embellished with the painted Christ figure and surrounded by a chapel, today forms the focal point of devotion, while a copy of the cross (crucifix of the Lord of Tayankani) plays an important but secondary role. However, there is a lot more to Qoyllor Rit'i than a simple Christian mythohistory. Anthropologists and historians recognise that this ancient pilgrimage, like many other Andean fiestas, was hijacked by the Catholic church at a time of rising Indian unrest. The roots of Qoyllor Rit'i lie firmly planted in the ancient animistic religion of the Andean people; and more specifically, in the veneration of Ausangate, the 6,350m snowpeak in

Distance	About 80km
Altitude	Between 3,800m and 5,100m
Rating	Difficult
Timing	5 days (with pack animals); 6 days backpacking.
In reverse	Equally good
Maps	IGN *Ocongate* sheet (28-t), 1:100,000; *Ausangate Circuit* from the South American Explorers or the IGN in Lima.

whose shadow the festival unfolds. The region's highest mountain, and its foremost *apu* (mountain deity), is still seen as the primary weather creator of the Cusco area; an ambivalent god whose power can blight crops or bestow health and fertility. His devotees come to appease him, as did the Inca who regularly made offerings of gold.

The central day of the pilgrimage is Trinity Sunday, by which time most of the devotees are gathered at the Sinakara shrine having trekked the 8km from the village of Mawallani, connected by road with Cusco. A scattering of city-dwelling Peruvian pilgrims and a few foreigners attend, but it is the sea of colourfully dressed *campesinos* which dominates the scene. Village dance groups or *comparsas* come from far and wide to render homage to the *taytacha* (little father) through formalised choreography. The *ch'uncho* groups, representing jungle ancestors who long ago migrated to the highlands, wear bright, feathered head-dresses, while the *q'apaq qollas* (symbolising llama herders) wear flat embroidered hats and carry rope whips. And liberally scattered about the heaving crowd are the ubiquitous *ukukus*, or bear-men, sporting brightly coloured woollen masks. Disorderly and anarchic, they speak in bizarre falsetto tones, yet they are the guardians of order. The whip each *ukuku* carries is not merely a prop, but will be used summarily to punish any devotee found flouting the strict alcohol ban.

The dancing continues throughout the day and most of the night. In the early hours massed ranks of *ukukus* set off to ascend the glaciers, prepared for battle with the malevolant spirits of the damned thought to dwell on the icy slopes. The *ukukus* plant giant candles, retrieve a cross left there a few days earlier, and return to the valley at first light laden with blocks of ice sawn from the glacier with their whips. This, when melted, will provide a supply of holy water through the coming year.

On Monday morning, a final mass is held as dancing resumes. Throughout the day, a stream of people returns home. But a significant number remains for the overnight pilgrimage which, to the accompaniment of music, retraces the mythical steps of Mariano and Manuel on a 25km trek, interspersed with of ritual dance, via Tayankani to the town of Ocongate.

Route description Take the broad track from the school in Tinqui and cross the river via a bridge behind the school. Cross a second smaller bridge and head up to houses on the right. Continue on a wide trail to open *puna* with house-sized boulders on the left. Continue on a deteriorating trail, cross a small stream and head south-southeast across the *pampa* towards Ausangate. There is no real trail here, just cattle paths. After about 2 hours, cross a small stream by a stone footbridge and ignore the track on the right immediately beyond the bridge. Instead, look for a wide track on the left which climbs gently beyond a group of houses, then crosses an irrigation ditch and soon drops down through a green, boggy valley to Upis. It takes about 5 hours from Tinqui to Upis. There are hot springs, a fantastic view of Ausangate and a great campsite (but beware of theft).

From Upis continue up the valley towards Ausangate, crossing the swampy area as soon as possible to the right of the valley where a faint narrow footpath is found. This continues to a grassy meadow. Cross the meadow and climb to the right to some stone corrals. Here two passes are visible, to the left and right of a yellow/orange hill. Both go to the same place. The lower path is longer but easier, the higher route more spectacular. It's about 2–3 hours to the top of the pass from Upis.

From the pass descend roughly south-southwest into the valley until you reach a lilac-coloured moraine. From here you can see Laguna Vinococha, with a waterfall. Head left (southeast) under the jagged and obvious rocky spires of Nevado Sorimani to the top of the waterfall cascading out of the turquoise lake. Hike over the top of a small hillock to the right of the lake and waterfall. From here continue to the right of another small hill on the far right of the lake, and continue roughly east to the base of an obvious red-coloured mountain by Laguna Pucacocha – about 5 hours away from Upis, and a possible campsite. It's worth climbing up the small ridge to the north of the campsite for the close-up views of Ausangate and, if it's clear, far off to the left (northwest) the pyramid of Salkantay can be seen.

Ten minutes from Pucacocha you reach some corrals (Pucapata). Head right around a small rocky hill, and continue roughly east on fairly good trails below red cliffs. After about 1½ hours you'll reach the top of a small pass with the main pass to the left (east) and Laguna Ausangatecocha below. Head down fairly steeply and for quite a long way to pasture at the right end of Laguna Ausangatecocha. There are some lovely campsites here (4,631m). When you've reached this lake, cross the small stream at the right end and then head northeast on trails behind the moraine, on the east side of the lake. You'll reach this spot about 2 hours after leaving Pucapata. The long, steep climb to the highest pass (5,100m, 17,000ft) is ahead of you. There are two choices: up a gully to the east (longer, but less steep), or continue northeast up a ridge (steeper, but more direct). Head roughly northeast to the pass of Palomani about 4–5 hours from Pucapata. From the pass to the next campsite you can go cross-country, or follow the trail roughly southeast for about 1 hour through a desert-like landscape, to the camping area under Cerro Puca Punta (which means 'Red Point').

From Cerro Puca Punta, continue east to a broad green valley (Pampa Jatunpata). Cross a stream (there is a bridge) near some houses and skirt the swampy green valley to the left (northeast), climbing over the hill to the left rather than dropping to the bogs below. Head northeast up Quebrada Jampamayo, a valley full of viscachas. You will hear these little animals whistling their alarm calls as they scurry for cover among the rocks. It's best to stay left of the river. At the small community of Jampa bear left (north-northwest) around the mountain and arrive at the very small Laguna Ticllacocha (4,850m), which is not visible until you are there. There are some excellent camping places around here. It takes 4 hours from Cerro Puca Punta to the lake.

Head approximately northwest out of Laguna Ticllacocha and soon you'll come to the pass of Campa at 5,000m. It takes about an hour. This pass used to be almost completely covered with glacier and the site of a spectacular 100m-deep ice cave. Now, alas, the glacier has receded and although a line of cairns guides you up to some small ice caves they lack the drama of their predecessor.

At the pass, the northwest trail heads through the long scree slope of Quebrada Caycohuayjo and emerges above and to the left of several lakes. At the final lake, Laguna Comercocha, head past a few houses and drop down into the valley below. There's a fairly clear trail which crosses the meandering river via four bridges. Continue on a good and pleasant trail along the left bank of the river, past occasional pools and lakes, until you reach the small village of Pacchanta. There's a bridge over the river before here. Pacchanta has two hot springs and good campsites. It takes 5 hours from Laguna Ticllacocha to Pacchanta.

From Pacchanta you have to cross the river via a bridge and then follow the obvious trail northwest to Tinqui, about 3 hours away.

Pitumarca to Laguna Sibinacocha
Route information from Apus and Incas by Charles Brod
This very long, rigorous, but infinitely rewarding trek visits the largest lake in the area (18km long), and can be done as a circular hike or joining up with the Ausangate circuit. One advantage is that it is much easier to get to the starting point of Checacupe. You start lower, walking up a lovely river valley of cultivated fields then climbing high to the *puna*. There are two passes over 5,000m so this is a tough hike.

Getting to the trailhead Take a bus or *colectivo*, which leave Cusco every half hour or so for Sicuani. Get off at Checacupe, about 1½ hours from Cusco. From here you can catch a truck or pick-up, or walk, to the small village of Pitumarca.

Before leaving Checacupe try to visit the church (which is often closed but you may find the *portero* who has the key). Unremarkable from the outside, its interior is a lovely example of colonial workmanship with some marvellous paintings, a fine altar and a beautifully carved pulpit.

Distance	About 145km back to Pitumarca and 160km to Tinqui
Altitude	Between 3,440m and 5,300m
Rating	Very strenuous
Timing	7–10 days
In reverse	Equally good
Map	IGN sheet *Ocongate* (28-t), 1:100,000

Route description From Pitumarca follow the trail up the valley along the left bank of the river until you reach the small village of Uchullucllo, about 4 hours from Pitumarca. Just before the village is an area of extraordinary eroded

THE CASITA

When leading a trek in the Ausangate region I had to evacuate a hiker because of altitude sickness. On reaching Ocongate I was anxious to get back to the group so Lynn agreed to return to Cusco alone. Faustino, the *arriero*, agreed to lend me a horse so we could travel faster, but to spread the journey over two days instead of his customary one. He provided Sambo, a scrawny black pony hung about with flour sacks containing my sleeping bag, etc.

Faustino looked magnificent. Now that he was master, not servant, he'd changed into a splendid multicoloured poncho, and his bearing and the respect with which he was greeted as we trotted through the town showed that in Ocongate he was a man of considerable status. We trotted through the town, we trotted out of town, and we trotted off the road and along the track towards Pacchanta. I hadn't ridden for several years, and my bottom and knees were screaming for mercy.

I wondered where we were going to spend the night. Since it would be below freezing I hoped we'd be under cover. Yes, said Faustino, a friend of his had a *casita* in the next valley. Here we encountered the friend screaming Quechua curses at a herd of serene-looking llamas and alpacas. He and Faustino disappeared into a grass-thatched hut chattering volubly, and I decided to see if my legs still worked by climbing a nearby hill to watch the evening sun paint golden rings round the alpacas and touch the white bulk of Ausangate with pink.

It was almost dark when I returned to the *casita*. The interior was lit by one guttering candle and I ducked through the low door and groped my way to a seat by the wall – a remarkably comfortable and well-sprung seat,

rocks. The village lies on the other (south) side of the river, so cross over the bridge. Above the village there are some rather unrewarding hot springs. The trail continues across the courtyard from the school, climbing up the slope and heading towards the village of Anaiso, about 3 hours away to the east. The trail drops down to the Río Pitumarca again, before reaching the village.

From above Anaiso, continue up the right-hand side of the broad valley to where it narrows. Cross a bridge to the left side, then follow the wide path through a narrow canyon, fording the river twice. The canyon opens on to a cultivated area. The path then crosses the river once again, climbing up the valley's right-hand slope, and finally arrives at a broad marshy plain, 4 hours from Anaiso. The Río Pitumarca changes its name: it is now the Río Yanamayu ('Black River'). Hike across the marshy plain to the upper end where there is a small settlement. Don't enter the settlement but cross the river to its left side. The trail then curves to the left, heading east over a spur in the valley. Coming off a steep slope, the trail splits and runs along both sides of the river. Stay on the left side and continue up the valley, remaining near the watercourse. The small village of Canchapampa lies 2–3 hours beyond the marshy plain.

covered with a sheepskin. My host's daughter gave me a plate of tiny potatoes and I gave them some chocolate. Then I prepared myself for sleep. Father and daughter watched entranced as I laid out my requirements. I unrolled and inflated my Thermarest, stuffed a sweater into a T-shirt for a pillow, and pulled my sleeping bag from its stuff bag. In the background I could hear incredulous squeaks from the daughter punctuating the steady drone of man-of-the-world Faustino explaining what everything was for. When I actually climbed into the blue cocoon of a sleeping bag, it was too much for her. She burst into hysterical giggles and little explosions of laughter accompanied the rest of my preparations. When the show was over, she just curled up on a pile of sheepskins and went to sleep.

The girl was up again at 4.30 to start a cooking fire (inside) with llama dung, and to round up the horses. It was bitterly cold, and dark and eye-smartingly smoky in the hut, and I buried myself in my sleeping bag until it was light enough to see my surroundings. I was rather surprised at what I saw. To begin with, my comfortable seat of the previous evening turned out to be half a sheep carcass with a well-sprung rib cage. There was no furniture, and no windows, but Inca-style niches made useful shelves for more pieces of sheep, half-spun wool, burnt-out candles and a safety pin.

After a breakfast of potatoes we saddled up and set off for the final stretch. After labouring up the 5,000m pass, with Sambo equally breathless on the lead rope beside me, we stopped at a rocky knoll overlooking Ticclacocha. Rumbling glaciers and spiky snowpeaks surrounded me on all sides, with ice-cream cornices bulging over the ridges. I was well content to wait there for the group's arrival.

From here the trail continues in an easterly direction, leaving the stream and crossing over hilly terrain to Laguna Aereacocha, about 2 hours from Canchapampa. From the lake continue across the plateau before descending on to a vast plain laced with rivers. Follow a path leading over the ridge that lies to the east. Once over the ridge, the path swings north and heads to the southern end of the enormous Laguna Sibinacocha (4,868m). It's 3–4 hours from Laguna Aereacocha to Laguna Sibinacocha. Vicuñas roam this highland region. Spend a day camped at the lake, exploring its shores and the nearby hills. The lake and its surroundings provide an ideal habitat for numerous species of birds. When you are ready to leave, follow the shores of the lake to its northern end.

The mountain ridge that borders the lake's left shore dips low, providing easy access to the village of Sallma on the other side. You are now heading south back towards Pitumarca. From Sallma, cross the nearby stream and make your way to the opposite side of the valley, a short distance below the village. Here the trail climbs the slope to a marshy pasture overlooking the valley. Continue to the left of the pasture before climbing to the right of a rocky crag. The pass lies just above 5,050m, and overlooks another broad valley. Laguna Chullumpina can be seen on the far side of the valley. Descend to the left of the open area before heading for the valley below.

Cross the Río Chumayu and climb towards Laguna Chua (4,900m); there are several houses nearby. Continue past the houses to a different trail that runs along the slope above the lake. Take this trail over the spur of Nevado Chuallani (5,300m) on your right. Standing on the spur, you look down into a basin of pasture-land with a small pond (Laguna Negromutayoc), dry most of the time. Above the pasture to the west you can see the pass leading out of the region around Sibinacocha. The trail crosses the pasture below the pond, then climbs steeply up the mountainside near Nevado Chuallani. This pass also lies at 5,050m and takes 1–2 hours to reach from the small lake. The trail comes down from the pass through Quebradas Lloclla and Misquiunuj, passing the small settlement of Jajatuni, until you reach the large valley of the Río Chillcamayu, some 3 hours from the pass. You have two possibilities here: hike back to Pitumarca in 2–3 days, passing through the small community of Chillca; or join up with the Ausangate Circuit trail to Tinqui, taking 2–3 days. For the latter, cross to the right-hand side of Quebrada Chillcamayo to hike up to its northern end where it becomes the Quebrada Jampamayu, and part of the Ausangate Circuit – about 4 hours.

Pitumarca to Tinqui, via Chillca

This is a variation on the hike above combined with the Ausangate Circuit. Starting in Pitumarca rather than Tinqui gives you the advantage of easier access, and a chance to get acclimatised as you walk gently uphill along a well-used trail trodden by countless *campesinos* and their laden llamas heading for Pitumarca.

Distance	About 70km
Altitude	Between 3,440m and 5,000m
Rating	Moderate to difficult
Timing	5–6 days
In reverse	Possible, and less strenuous because you start higher.
Map	IGN sheet *Ocongate* (28-t), 1:100,000

Route description Follow the trail up the valley along the left bank of the Río Pitumarca, passing the village of Uchulluclло on the other side of the river, about 4 hours from Pitumarca. Do not cross the river but stay on the left side until you reach Quebrada Chillcamayo on your left (the third *quebrada* from Pitumarca), about 1 hour from Uchulluclло. Go up this *quebrada*, following the left bank of the Río Chillcamayo until you reach the village of Japua, situated on the other side of the river. Cross by the bridge and follow the path alongside the river, crossing it once more, to the community of Chillca at 4,200m, about 5–6 hours from the start of the *quebrada*. Chillca lies at the confluence of two rivers. Follow the right-hand branch, the Río Chillcamayo, heading northeast, to the even smaller community of Uyuni at 4,400m, about 2 hours away, and for another 4 hours up Quebrada Jampamayo to the community of Jampa at 4,600m. You are now on the Ausangate Circuit.

From Jampa you can take a side trip to Laguna Sibinacocha. Follow the river valley to your right (northeast) to the community of Yanamayu, about 1 hour from Jampa. From here you start the climb to the pass of Huayruro Punco at about 5,150m, passing Lagunas Osjollo and Ananía – about 3–4 hours. From the pass you get a spectacular view over the impressive Laguna Sibinacocha and marvel at its size. Descend along Quebrada Huampunimayo to the lake (no path) in about 2 hours. The camping by the lake is beautiful, but cold and windy. An option from here is to follow the banks of the lake south and pick up the trail to Pitumarca described earlier, or to hike back to Chillca (also described earlier) to rejoin the trail towards Tinqui.

Raqchi to Pitumarca or to Tinqui via Chillca

The southern loop was an accidental discovery during our first trip to the Cordillera Vilcanota in 1979, so I have a special affection for it. We set off on impulse from Raqchi without a map, so every pass was like approaching a new world: we had no idea what lay the other side. The most dramatic was our 'landing on Mars' when I slogged, exhausted, up the last few metres of a pass just before sunset and found a landscape unlike any I had seen in South America. It looked as though every hill was wearing a striped poncho in green, lilac, ochre and a variety of rich reds and terracotta. There was not a living soul, man or beast, as far as we could see in all directions. The exhilaration of such a sight, especially when totally unexpected, is what *real* backpacking is all about!

The extra bonus of this hike, and the one which enticed us to it in the first place, is the Inca temple of Viracocha at Raqchi. By combining the southern route with the extension to the Ausangate circuit you are giving yourself one of the most scenically varied, if strenuous, hikes in Peru. The full trek is a serious venture – about 110km, or 8–10 days of hiking – and you need to be confident of your physical abilities.

Raqchi

The village is accessible by bus or truck, about 2½ hours from Cusco, or by train to San Pedro 2km away. Even without the astonishing Inca temple this would be a remarkable village. Centuries ago a violent volcanic eruption spewed black lava all over the area, and this has been put to good use by the resourceful villagers. Numerous walls and corrals have been built from it, and hunks of the stuff still litter the surrounding hillsides. The church in Raqchi is exceptionally attractive, as is the entire village. Perhaps civic pride has something to do with it: once a year, in mid June, there is a fiesta here which is said to have some of the best costumed dancers to be seen anywhere in Peru.

The Inca temple of Viracocha

The bare facts do nothing to prepare you for the amazing spectacle that greets you as you pass through a little gate to the right of Raqchi church, nor for the legends surrounding the temple. A long single wall of magnificent Inca stonework is topped by an adobe extension bringing it to a height of 15m. The lower wall is nearly 1½m thick with typical trapezoid windows and doorways. The remains of a row of stone pillars run on each side of the wall, but only one has retained its adobe top. No other Inca building has pillars and none is as tall. The adobe wall is now protected with a little tile roof, but this is a recent addition. Beyond the temple are rows of identical buildings made from rough stone, and originally topped by adobe. These are arranged round six identical squares. In another area, towards the road, are the remains of 200 small circular constructions, arranged in lines of 12.

These are the basic facts but what on earth was it all for? We asked at the archaeological museum in Cusco, and there we struck gold in the form of George Squier's fascinating account of his travels in Peru, published in 1877. In line with all 19th-century explorers, Squier had a meticulous eye for detail and the patience to write it all down. I owe the following information to him, and to subsequent writings by Luis A Pardo in the Revista del Instituto Arqueológico del Cuzco.

The most fascinating aspect of the Temple of Viracocha is the story of how it came to be built. Some people think it was to appease the god Viracocha, after a volcanic eruption. I suppose that's the most logical explanation but I prefer the account by the notoriously inaccurate Inca (he was *mestizo*, actually) chronicler, Garcilaso de la Vega, who described the building in all its glory.

This version is that the temple was built by Inca Viracocha, the son of Yahua Huacac. The father was a mild, ineffectual man with little patience for his son's ambitions and impetuosity, so he sent the prince to the village of Chita, three leagues northeast of Cusco, in honourable exile, to supervise the royal herds pastured there.

After three years the prince returned, saying he had had a vision. During a *siesta* in the fields, a white-bearded, celestial being appeared before him saying 'I am the son of the sun, brother of Manco Capac. My name is Viracocha and I am sent by my father to advise the Inca that the provinces of Chinchasuya are in revolt, and that large armies are advancing thence to destroy the sacred capital. The Inca must prepare. I will protect him and his empire.' Inca Yahua Huacac was unmoved by this warning, however, and took no precautions against the coming invasion. When the attack took place, as predicted, he fled to Muyna.

The people, abandoned by their Inca, scattered in all directions, but the prince (who had now assumed the name of Viracocha) arrived with some shepherds of Chita, and persuaded them to return and defend Cusco. Prince Viracocha fought valiantly, though his forces were greatly outnumbered. 'The very stones rose up, armed, white-bearded men, when the weight of the battle pressed hardly on the youthful Inca.' He won, of course, and deposed his father at the request of a grateful people.

The new Inca Viracocha ordered the construction of a marvellous temple, different from any preceding it, at Cacha (de la Vega glosses over the mystery of why the temple had to be built there, rather than at Chita where the vision had appeared, or on the battlesite).

The temple was to be roofless, with an elevated second storey. It would contain a chapel with the image of the God Viracocha, as he had looked when he appeared to the prince. The floor was paved with lustrous black stones brought from afar.

De la Vega describes the temple in detail, but his descriptions don't fit with the present ruins, so it's likely that he relied on secondhand reports. However, his sorrowful statement that the Spanish destroyed this magniflcent temple in search of gold is certainly true. According to Squier, the churches of San Pedro and Tinta are built of stones from the temple walls, as is one of the bridges across the river Vilcanota.

Looking at the present ruins, you can see that the rows of pillars probably supported a slanting roof. The second floor could have been sustained on the columns, with beams running from them to holes in the centre wall.

De la Vega doesn't mention the other ruins, but it's probable that the identical houses were priests' dwellings, or perhaps barracks. The 200 small circular buildings were thought by Squier to be pilgrims' lodgings, but it's more likely they were warehouses or granaries.

There is one other Inca site here, and that is the baths to the left of the temple. You will have to leave the temple area by the gate you came in, and follow the path between stone walls. The baths have some fine water channels, and fresh running water can still be collected there. There is good camping nearby.

Distance	About 50km/110km
Altitude	Between 3,440m and 4,900m/5,000m
Rating	Moderate to difficult
Timing	4–9 days
In reverse	Possible for both routes
Maps	IGN sheets *Sicuani* (29-t), and *Ocongate* (28-t), 1:100,000.

Warning Do not attempt this route without an IGN map and plenty of time. The route is not always clear and there will be few people around to tell you the way.

Route description The trail starts northeast of the Inca temple, goes past the Inca baths and climbs steeply uphill to the main trail, which snakes through the lava. Turn right and walk between stone walls until you reach an open area, then continue in the same direction to the foot of a stone-free hill. Turn left here and follow paths up the valley, above some houses sheltered by large trees. Go north up the valley on the right-hand side of the gorge, on a good trail which crosses the stream near the top and climbs over the pass. The path becomes fainter here, but you can follow it into the valley as it zigzags down a

TAQUILE ISLAND
Kathy Jarvis

Taquile Island lies 4 hours by boat out from Puno in Lake Titicaca, to the east of Peninsula Capachina and to the south of the Island Amantani (also accessible) and is a wonderful place to visit if you have at least two days available. It doesn't offer great potential for trekking, being only 4km long by 2km wide, but does have fascinating pre-Inca archaeological remains, golden sandy bays, total peace and quiet, and an intact culture far removed from our own. It has become a bit of a tourist spot in recent years, with several boats making the long trip out and back in a day. However, by staying overnight and keeping away from the main square at midday, instead exploring the many trails leading away from the centre, you will be able to experience a unique island life unchanged in centuries.

Taquile was highly prized by the Incas and when it became part of their empire the local Aymara-speaking Indians had to adopt the Quechua language. Likewise the Inca deity *Inti* (the sun) became their highest god, and *Viracocha* was worshipped as the creator. Under the Incas the island was divided into two *ayllus* or sections, Uray Ayllu and Hanaq Ayllu, each of which was further sub-divided into three *suyos*. Today these divisions continue and the *suyos* are ruled over by six families who carefully control crop rotation and grazing on the steep terraced fields. A limited variety of crops is grown in each *suyo*: oca, potatoes, broad beans, maize and wheat, and a few scraggly sheep and cattle are grazed. Not much will grow here because of the altitude and harsh climatic conditions, but the diet is supplemented with eggs, deliciously fresh lake fish and rice. During the coldest months from June to August the potatoes are repeatedly frozen outside overnight, trampled in the morning to squeeze out the water and then made into *chuño*, the freeze-dried potato.

scree shoulder towards the village of Paucaoros. There is good camping in the area or you can descend to the Río Salca through a eucalyptus plantation on the right-hand side of the stream. It takes about 5–6 hours from Raqchi to the river.

Turn left at the Río Salca and follow it along a good track for about 2km until you see a village on the opposite bank. A kilometre further down you'll find a cable across the river with a small wooden platform dangling below it – and that's how you cross! Once on the other side walk back up the valley to the village of Salloca – 1–2 hours. From here, if you want to terminate the walk, you can hike out to the village of Combapata.

To continue the circuit to Pitumarca, when you reach the first houses of Salloca look for a well-marked path heading up the valley. It is exceptionally beautiful, crossing and recrossing the tumbling river over well-made bridges. There are flowers and flowering shrubs everywhere and plenty of hummingbirds. You'll reach some idyllic campsites about an hour after leaving the Salca valley.

Folk dances, music and the islanders' traditional clothing have all survived the passage of time and many pre-Columbian festivities are still celebrated. I have never seen anything quite like the festival of Santiago (July 25), patron saint of Taquile. This is a week-long extravaganza, fuelled by sugarcane alcohol, in which the islanders dress in extremely elaborate and colourful costumes, complete with veils and head-dresses, to compete, one *suyo* against the other, in dance and music. Offerings are still made to the deities, and it is fascinating to see the traditional customs associated with coca leaves and *chicha*, a fermented corn beer which is poured on to the ground in the name of Pachamama before a drink is taken. Coca leaves are read to reveal the future, placed on different parts of the body for healing purposes, chewed to ward off pain and hunger, and play an important role in all ceremonies and fiestas.

Taquile is probably best known for the high quality of its elaborate and sophisticated weavings. Both men and women weave from a young age, the women specialising in *chumpis* (wrap-round belts) made on ground looms, and the men in the black woollen trousers and waistcoats cut from cloth woven on treadle looms. From about six years of age boys are taught the complex designs used to knit *chullos* (hats) and *chuspis* (coca-carrying bags). The islanders spin, knit and weave whenever there is a free moment in the day or a quiet spell in the agricultural calendar.

You can stay overnight on Taquile for US$5, and will be allocated a family to stay with when you arrive. There are several basic restaurants around the square which serve simple but plentiful local food, and a couple of small shops sell the most basic provisions and drinks, including water. At the island shops on the square you can buy woven or knitted items unique to Taquile. Take a Taquile boat from the docks in Puno (US$6 return), leaving Puno at 08.00 and returning at 14.30.

The first community you come to is Pulpera, after about 3 hours. From here the path curves round to the right, up Quebrada Palcoyo, and after 2 hours of steady climbing you reach the compact small village of Palcoyo at 4,100m. Continue up the valley on a well-used path, probably together with a herd of llamas and/or alpacas, to the small community of Chulloca, about 3 hours from Palcoyo. Just before the village a path climbs up the valley to your left. Follow it to some corrals, and continue climbing steeply to the pass at 4,800m – about 2 hours. The landscape takes on a lunar quality and even the alpacas look extra-terrestrial. At the top you may feel, as I did, that you've landed on Mars.

Don't kid yourselves that it's now downhill all the way: you have a 4,900m pass before you can descend to the Río Pitumarca. Dave Carmany, who attempted this hike in 1997, writes: 'At the top of the pass ... instead of looking at a descent to Cotahuasi and then a valley to the west, we were looking at a 700m descent to a valley and then a climb to another high pass.

We turned round and went back the way we came. After all we had a plane to catch.'

Two paths lead down the valley from the pass. One runs to the right (southwest) down the side of the mountain ridge into the valley; the other continues northeast. Take the latter and follow it to a village on the valley floor. The trail traverses a rather nasty scree slope so you may prefer to drop down to the village before this stretch. Continue up the valley past the houses, following any handy alpaca tracks you may find. There's no trail. The pass at 4,900m is on the right-hand side of the valley head. It's a hard slog and will take a discouraging 2 hours from the village. But an incredible view will greet you when you finally reach the top: Ausangate and the whole Vilcanota range stretches along the horizon. If you are finishing your trek at Pitumarca your climbing is over: it is downhill virtually all the way. Just descend to the Río Pitumarca, make a left turn (west) and follow the river until its junction with Quebrada Chillcamayu – about 2 hours – then continue to Pitumarca.

To continue your trek north to Tinqui, from the river junction (Pitumarca and Chillcamayu) continue west on the south side of the rivers until you reach the Uchullucllo bridge, where you cross. From here follow the directions for the *Pitumarca to Tinqui* hike.

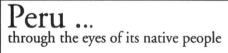

The Arequipa Area

The valley around Arequipa, 1,000km southeast of Lima and 320km from the Chilean border, is a sunny, fertile pocket tucked between the coastal desert and the high Andes. It has a lot to interest the hiker: snow-capped volcanoes, remote Quechua villages, the Colca Canyon, archaeological sites and the dazzling white colonial city of Arequipa. Given the dry climate of the area, trekking is possible all year round.

AREQUIPA

Peru's second-largest city lies at 2,380m and enjoys an almost idyllic climate: sunny and mostly dry, with a mild rainy season between December and April. Often called 'the White City' after the volcanic *sillar* from which its older buildings are built, it is overlooked by the sometimes snow-capped, perfectly shaped, volcano El Misti (5,822m).

Arequipeños have never been able to agree on how their city got its name. Does it come from the Aymara 'Ariquipa', meaning 'the place behind the peak'? Or did it originate with the Inca Mayta Kapac who was so gripped by the beauty of this valley that he ordered his retinue to stop, calling out '*Ari quipay*' ('Yes, stay')?

Although an important settlement since pre-Inca times, Arequipa was refounded by the Spanish in 1545 and this gives *Arequipeños* an excuse to celebrate on and around August 15 every year. Unfortunately the valley is prone to earthquakes and volcanic eruptions. The city was totally destroyed in 1600, and in 1991/92 the volcano Sabancaya erupted again, covering a huge area in volcanic lava and almost engulfing the village of Maca. Then in 2001, Arequipa had the misfortune of being near the epicentre of a large earthquake which did a fair amount of damage to many of its buildings. Luckily several of Arequipa's 17th- and 18th-century buildings, including the Santa Catalina monastery, have escaped destruction and are now tourist attractions.

Getting there and away
To and from Lima
By air 70 minutes. All the domestic airlines serve this route. There are at least four flights daily.

By road (via Nazca) 10 hours. Several bus companies operate on this route; Ormeño and Cruz del Sur's first-class service are recommended. Most companies operate from the *terminal terrestre* a little way out of town (there are two terminals next to each other). Be warned that the bus station area has a bad reputation for theft so it's best to use taxis to get there and away, and watch your luggage like a hawk.

To and from Cusco
By air 40 minutes. Many travellers take this flight as an alternative to the Arequipa to Cusco train, especially in the rainy season when the trains are often cancelled. There are daily flights (see Lima listings for details of airlines).

By train Via Juliaca/Puno, see below for details.

By road 12 hours (longer, and sometimes not possible, in the rainy season). Buses and trucks daily. The road is in much better condition than it used to be, and some sections are now even surfaced.

To and from Juliaca, Puno and Bolivia
By air Half an hour. Daily flights.

By train 9 hours. Night train to Puno, Sunday (21.00), day trains Saturday (08.00) and Wednesday (07.00). US$30.

By road 9 hours, depending on the weather and state of the road. Buses and *colectivos* daily. Most continue to Puno in a further half hour. Daily transport from Puno to La Paz, 8 hours.

To and from Tacna and the Chilean border
By air Half an hour. Two flights daily.

By road 5 hours. Several buses and *colectivos* daily.

Sleeping and eating
There is no shortage of places to stay in Arequipa. Just a few of the many are listed here.

Oro Blanco San Juan de Dios 117; tel: 054 206770. Double room with bath US$40. Friendly, clean and comfortable.
Miamaka San Juan de Dios 402; tel: 054 201496. Double with bath US$28. Clean and pretty.
Colonial House Inn Calle Puente Grau 114; tel: 054 223533. Double with bath US$12. A fun and friendly old colonial house.
Los Balcones Calle Moral 217, near the Plaza de Armas; tel: 054 201291. Double with bath US$30. An old house, very clean.

The popular Cusco vegetarian restaurant **Govinda** also has a branch here, on Jerusalén 505. There are many good places in the vicinity too. Excellent stuffed potatoes (*papa rellena*) and peppers (*rocotto relleno*) are for sale outside the market.

Useful addresses

Clínica Arequipa Esquina Puente Grau y Av Bolognesi; tel: 054 253416. Medical emergencies.

Centro Odontologico San Lazaro Av Juan de la Torre 201, San Lazaro; tel: 054 225904

Casa de Guías Pasaje Desaguadero 126, San Lazaro (see below)

Tourist information office Portal de la Municipalidad 104, Plaza de Armas, opposite the cathedral. Helpful and friendly and they have a good city map.

Tourist police Calle Jerusalén 315; tel: 054 239888. May be able to help if you have problems or complaints.

Touring y Automóvil Club del Perú Av Goyeneche 313; tel: 054 215631/215640

Campamento Base (Adventure Shop) Jerusalén 401-B; tel/fax: 054 206217. Rents and sells camping equipment and IGN maps.

Museo Santuarios de Altura de la Universidad Católica de Santa María Santa Catalina 210; tel: 054 252554/200345/00345; email: jchavez@ucsm.edu.pe; web: www.ucsm.edu.pe-sanctuary. Mon–Sat 09.00–17.30. US$2. Auditorium, audiovisuals, translators, guides in English, French and German, souvenir shop. A fascinating museum containing the ice-maiden Juanita, and many other treasures.

Tour operators

As in Cusco and Huaraz, beware of using cheap, non-professional agencies. There are many agencies along Calle Jerusalén and around the Plaza de Armas that offer trips to the Colca Canyon and Toro Muerto. But be warned: some are unreliable – make sure you understand exactly what you are paying for. It's definitely better not to pay in advance as your tour may be cancelled (possibly at the last minute) if not enough people turn up. For treks or climbs ensure your guides are experienced and qualified (check their *carnet*, and ask at the Asociacion de Guías if in doubt) and make sure you get a contract, detailing the services you have paid for. From June to September you should be able to find organised group treks and climbs to Misti, Chachani and Colca (see listings).

Following the devastating earthquake in the Arequipa area in June 2001 many walking routes, particularly in Colca Canon, were closed for several months. However, as most of the paths are in constant use by local people they were repaired quickly and are now usable again. Do be aware of the constant danger of falling stones and landslides, particularly after heavy rains.

Carlos Zarate Aventuras EIRL Calle Santa Catalina 204, Office 3; tel: 054 202461; tel/fax: 054 263107; email czarate@rh.com.pe; web: www.rh.com.pe/zarate. Information on trekking, maps and photos. Carlos Zarate is the recognised expert on the region, and a UIAGM-qualified guide. Offers equipment to rent and buy. Organises treks and climbs for individuals or groups, with professional guides. Treks in Colca, Misti and Chachani, from US$60 per person.

GA Travel Expert Calle Santa Catalina 312, Office 3; tel: 054 247722; fax: 054 272845. A reputable travel agent that sells airline tickets and good-quality Colca tours.

Vita Tours Jerusalén 302; tel: 054 224526. A reputable agency offering 2-day Colca tours, and adventure trips in Colca.

Campamento Base Jerusalén 401-B. An agency that also rents equipment, sells maps etc.

La Liga de Andinismo y Club de Andinismo de Arequipa (Instituto Peruano de Deporte, Coliseo Arequipa) occasionally arranges rock climbing and hiking trips for club members. Worth contacting if you are going to be in the area for some time.

La Asociacion de Guías de Montaña Pasaje Desaguadero 126, San Lazaro; tel: 054 204182; email: casaguias@correo.rh.com.pe. Information office open Mon–Fri 09.30–18.00. Can provide you not only with a guide but also with information and equipment to rent. Regular group treks and climbs from June to September. Guides US$30–50 per day, *arrieros* US$10, donkeys US$5, 4WD US$80 per day (for a driver, 100km, 6 hours). There's also a search-and-rescue team based here.

Club Deportivo Turismo de Aventura Calle La Merced 125, Of 139. Tel: 054 234818. For walking, trekking, and rafting.

CLIMBING THE VOLCANOES

The dominant geographical feature of the area is the volcanoes, so these are the focus for most hikers. This is a very dry area and little natural water is available: it must all be carried with you. You climb more for a sense of achievement than for the ever-changing views.

Practical information

Climate

Although enviably sunny for much of the year, the Arequipa area can be subject to heavy downpours between December and April, making trails muddy and dangerous.

Conditions/what to take

Make sure you carry enough warm clothing and good camping equipment for those freezing nights! For much of the time you'll be hiking above 4,000m, so take time to acclimatise. Wear a hat and protect yourself from the sun. Take plenty of water – several litres per person.

Maps

The topographical maps of this area from the IGN are especially useful, as few others are available. You can get these in Lima and locally at Jerusalén 401-B.

Guides and pack animals

You don't normally need a guide to hike in this area. Most trails are obvious, and there's usually someone to ask in case of doubt. On the volcanoes, however, routes can be confusing and weather conditions can change quickly and dangerously. For these a guide is recommended, or at least someone who's done it before. Choose your guide with care; many are unreliable. Ask at the Club de Andinismo and they will be able to put you in touch with one (see *Tour operators* above). A trekking guide will charge US$30 per day; a climbing guide $40–50.

You can arrange for *burros* or mules if necessary, at one of the villages near the starting points of the hikes. *Burros* cost about US$8 per day; *arrieros* US$10.

Equipment

Very basic gear can be rented at some travel agencies, at the Club de Andinismo, Casa de Guías, and from Campamento Base, Jerusalén 401-B.

Food and supplies

Buy your main supplies in Arequipa, where there are several good supermarkets and a market (the best central one is El Super on the Plaza de Armas). Govinda has muesli and good bread.

Volcán El Misti (5,822m)

This volcano, which provides Arequipa with its splendid backdrop, is a popular climb, best done late in the season when there's less snow. Although not a difficult ascent, El Misti shouldn't be taken lightly. The weather can change without notice from extreme heat to snow, making it easy to get lost, cold and dispirited – a perfect recipe for disaster. If no-one in your party has done the climb before, you should consider taking a guide. Allow at least 2 days for the trip.You need to carry a lot of water (there's none along the way other than at the reservoir of Aguada Blanca), together with cold-weather clothing and camping equipment. The ascent doesn't, however, involve any technical climbing.

Distance	25km
Altitude	Between 2,950 and 5,822m
Rating	Moderate
Timing	2–3 days
Maps	IGN sheet *Characato* (33-t), 1:100,000

Getting to the trailhead Buses for Chasqui used to take you to the trailhead. However, they now go along a new road to the north of Chachani. To get to the trailhead you need to take a 4WD vehicle. Ask to be let off at Aguadas Blancas, a hydro-electric station, where the Chivay and El Fraile roads meet.

Route description Follow the El Fraile road to the far side of the first dam. (You may have some difficulty getting through the hydro-electric station's security system.) Then continue for 5½ hours to Monte Blanco, a flat area with corrals where you should camp. From Monte Blanco a zigzag path will take you in 4 hours (rather more if there's a lot of snow) to the summit, which is marked by a 10m iron cross. Trekking poles are invaluable, as the path often crosses bad scree. On fine days the view is magnificent. From here you can continue to the edge of the inner crater where fumeroles can occasionally be seen.

Volcán Ubinas (5,672m)

Robin Eckhardt recommends this climb for 'its lonely position and the salt lake with flamingoes which you pass on the way to it'.

Altitude	Between about 4,000m and 5,672m
Rating	Moderate
Timing	2 days

Getting to the trailhead The starting point for this walk is Laguna Salinas Borax, 150km from Arequipa on the road to Puno. To get there from Arequipa, take a *colectivo* at 06.00 to the village of Ubinas from Sepúlveda 200. This street is reached by the yellow-white bus '5 de Agosto', and it's best to book a seat the day before. The *colectivo* should take you all the way to Ubinas. Going via Salinas Borax, you reach the junction of the Puno-Ubinas road in about 4 hours, and after continuing towards Ubinas for another 1½ hours you come to the foot of the volcano.

Route description From Laguna Salinas Borax it can be seen that the volcano has three peaks. The southern one to the right is the highest; for this you must ascend by the southwest route. There are many things to see from this peak: jets of steam, fumeroles and a turquoise crater lake 270m below. (If you go down to the lake, leave plenty of time to climb back or you'll be returning to Arequipa in darkness.)

Getting back This can be a problem unless you've booked a *colectivo* in advance. 'If not, it is impossible to get a seat. The second possibility is a huge truck which travels by night and passes the volcano between 17.00 and 19.00. Extremely cold, and the drive lasts 6–7 hours.' (R Eckhardt)

Volcán Chachani (6,076m)

An impressive volcano about 20km north of Arequipa, this high and cold climb should be tackled only by experienced mountaineers with full snow- and ice-climbing equipment. Do not climb alone. Take plenty of water.

Altitude	Between 4,700 and 6,076m
Rating	Difficult
Timing	2–3 days
Maps	IGN sheets *Arequipa* (33-s), and *Characato* (33-t), 1:100,000

Getting to the trailhead You can climb from either the north or south side. The buses to Cusco and Colca can take you to the north side of the volcano. They will drop you at a starting point at 3,200m. To get to the starting point on the south side you need to go by 4WD, to 4,900m. You can hire a 4WD in Arequipa for around $100 return.

Route description (south side) Walk 8km to the end of the jeep track, gaining 430m, and continue for another 1½ hours to a campsite in the shelter

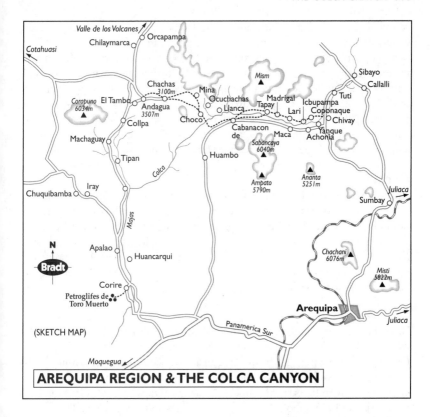

Valle de los Volcanes
Orcapampa
Chilaymarca
Cotahuasi
Chachas
Mina
Mism
Sibayo
3100m
Callalli
Corapuno
6034m
El Tambo
Andagua
Ocuchachas
Madrigal
Tuti
Icbupampa
3507m
Llanca
Tapay
Lari
Coponaque
Collpa
Choco
Chivay
Machaguay
Cabanacon
de
Maca
Yanque
Achonia
Tipan
Sabancaya
6040m
Huambo
Colca
Ananta
5251m
Iray
Juliaca
Chuquibamba
Ampato
5790m
Sumbay
Majes
N
Apalao
Chachani
6076m
Huancarqui
Bradt
Misti
5822m
Corire
Petroglifes de
Toro Muerto
Arequipa
(SKETCH MAP)
Juliaca
Panamerica Sur
Moquegua

AREQUIPA REGION & THE COLCA CANYON

of some stone corrals, just below a saddle. After camping here (camping higher will expose you to fierce winds), turn left and drop 200m before starting the final ascent. The summit will be reached 10–12 hours after leaving the corrals.

THE COLCA CANYON

A hundred kilometres long, this incredible gorge is said to reach a maximum depth of 3,400m – twice that of the Grand Canyon. It was formed through a fault in the earth's crust being eroded during thousands of years by the largest river of the Peruvian coast, the river Colca. Although a mere 160km north of Arequipa, its full extent was recognised only as recently as 1954; the first major explorations took place in 1978 and the first descent by raft and canoe in 1981. The Colca is a wild and dangerous river – not for the faint-hearted!

On both sides of the canyon you'll find picturesque villages whose inhabitants will help you with directions. Cave paintings suggest that people have lived here since the first humans arrived in the Andes.

The characteristic terraces of the Colca valley rival those of the Incas. They were carved out of the land 1,400 years ago by the Collaguas, who were Aymaras from Tiahuanaco, and the Cabanas, who were of Quechua origin, both pre-Incan peoples with an advanced level of agricultural development. The terraces are still widely used. Many local people still wear distinctive and colourful traditional costumes, and the valley boasts an extraordinary genetic variety of potatoes, corn, quinoa, maca, oca, and isaño.

Most people go to Colca Canyon to see the condors. Unfortunately some of the local restaurant owners have decided that capturing these majestic birds and putting them on display for tourists is an added attraction to their customers. Don't take pictures of these captured birds, and do complain to the businesses concerned; this is surely not something we want to promote. Also be careful where you put your rubbish, as many of the bins on the edge of the canyon are emptied over the edge. It's best to take your rubbish away with you.

Chivay

This small town is the centre for conventional tours exploring the Colca Canyon. It can be reached in a pretty rough, but memorable, journey of 4–5 hours by bus from Arequipa. If you stay the night here you can take early-morning transport on down the valley, passing the villages of Yanque, Achona, Maca and Pinchollo, to Cruz del Cóndor, a famous observation point for views of the canyon and its majestic condors. Cabanaconde is a better place to base yourself for treks into the canyon.

Getting there

Buses between Arequipa, Chivay and Cabanaconde leave throughout the day, taking 8–10 hours to Cabanaconde and costing US$5. To the Cañon de Cotahuasi departures go from Arequipa early afternoon, returning early morning. To Valle de los Volcanes departures go from Arequipa early afternoon, returning early afternoon. An alternative route to Cabanaconde is via El Alto and Huambo, Mondays, Wednesdays and Fridays at 05.00.

Sleeping and eating

Posada del Inca A modern, clean 4-storey hotel with a restaurant.
Casa Blanca Its estaurant does a lunchtime buffet; good value.
Hostal Anita Plaza de Armas 607; tel: 054 521114. US$6/10.

Tour operators

Colca Adventures Plaza de Armas 301, Chivay; tel: 054 531137. A new agency that runs rafting in the Colca Canyon, bike tours, trekking etc.

Hot springs

Some excellent hot springs are located at the Colca river at Calera, 3km from Chivay. There are four pools with changing facilities.

Cabanaconde

La Posada del Conde Highly recommended. Clean and comfortable, with hot water, private bathrooms and an excellent cook.
Valle del Fuego Tel: 054 280367. US$3. Also recommended.

In the canyon itself there are two dedicated camping areas, which also have rustic rooms. **Paraiso** is recommended as being better than **Oasis**. Both are in the bottom of the canyon by the river. Paraiso is clean and peaceful, with a swimming pool. US$3 per person for a shared room, US$2 for camping. Camping at Cruz del Condor is not allowed.

HIKING IN THE COLCA CANYON

Clive Walker reports on a promising-looking hike which goes from the pools at Calera, along the river to a fairly large canyon (one hour from the pools) and continues to Canacota village (3 hours' walk).

Cabanaconde to Andagua

This is justifiably one of the most popular of the Colca Canyon hikes. It takes you to the bottom of the canyon, up the other side, over a 5,000m pass and down to the village of Chachas, before going on to finish at Andagua, gateway to the 'Valley of the Volcanoes'. This is a very strenuous trek because of the altitude gain and loss: 3,200m or nearly 10,500ft! And do watch out for stone-fall in the canyon. Be sure to carry plenty of water (3–4 litres per person).

Altitude	Between 1,800m and 5,000m
Rating	Moderate to strenuous
Timing	6 days
Maps	IGN sheets *Chivay* (32-s), *Huambo* (32-r) and *Orcopampa* (31-r) 1:100,000. Also a small picture book, *Arequipa and the Colca Canyon*, can be bought in Arequipa for US$10. It includes a map of the canyon.
Conditions	Water is scarce; carry as much as you can at all times. Protect yourself from the burning sun.

Getting to the trailhead Cabanaconde – the best base for canyon excursions – can be reached in 9–10 hours by bus from Arequipa: a rough, dusty trip but with good views. Several buses leave daily from the bus station. En route you'll pass Chivay, a worthwhile stop, from where you can hike in half an hour to swim in the very pleasant hot pools at La Calera, or cross the canyon to the village of Sibayo on the one and only bridge built for vehicles. This 35km journey takes an hour by pick-up. From Sibayo you can continue to Cusco or to Andagua (also spelled Andahua).An alternative route to Cabanaconde goes round the other side of Sabancaya via El Alto and Huambo – a 12-hour journey, longer in the rainy season.

Route description Cabanaconde is a sleepy village at 3,287m, where the road ends on the edge of the canyon. You'll find its friendly inhabitants dressed in beautiful hand-embroidered clothing. There are several hostels on the plaza (see listings). Several restaurants offer meals, and there's a minuscule market.

THE ICE-MAIDEN 'JUANITA'

In 1995 Johan Reinhard, anthropologist and Senior Research Fellow of the Mountain Institute, and Miguel Zarate, his Peruvian climbing partner, climbed the volcano of Ampato (6,310m) on a scientific expedition to search for Inca remains. Since the nearby volcano of Sabancaya had erupted in 1990, spewing hot black ash over Ampato, there had been a melting of a considerable amount of snow from the top of this mountain.

They made an amazing discovery: a small, frozen body, tightly wrapped in textiles sitting in the foetal position surrounded by scattered pieces of pottery, llama bones, corn kernels, cloth pieces and a spondylus shell figurine.

The team photographed the site, collected the various treasures, wrapped up the mummy to keep her frozen and tied her to Reinhard's backpack. They set off on their long return journey to Arequipa, where the body was put in a freezer at the Catholic University. Fortunately, the precautionary wrapping of the body had protected it from damage.

This was the first intact female mummy to be found anywhere in the Andes, and she was in remarkably good condition, with skin and even her nails complete. The objects found alongside her had also survived well over the centuries. The fact that the body had been frozen as opposed to freeze-dried or desiccated meant that biological tests could be run on internal organs, which gave scientists an insight into the body's health and nutrition. Work later carried out on the 'ice-maiden' showed her to have been a healthy young girl, between 12 and 14 years old. It's probable she was sacrificed to the mountain gods by Inca priests.

Reinhard later returned to Mount Ampato on a National Geographic Society expedition. They discovered more ritual platforms, the body of an eight to ten year old girl, and the less well preserved skeleton of a third person.

All objects are on display in the Museo Santuarios de Altura in Arequipa, and you can read more about this discovery in *National Geographic*, June 1996, January 1997 and November 1999.

The hill 10 minutes' walk to the west of the village is an excellent place for viewing the canyon's much-publicised condors. There are conflicting views on the best time for viewing condors, but most locals say between 06.00 and 09.00 and also around 18.00.

A word of warning: landslides and rockfalls are quite frequent in the canyon. Other than the obvious danger of rocks falling on your head, these can also obscure paths, and make for very loose, sometimes treacherously slippery, ground underfoot. Ask locals, whenever possible, about conditions of paths and any recent route changes.

Leaving Cabanaconde for the canyon is rather confusing, as there are many paths. Ask locals for the way to Choco and they'll point you in the right direction (northwest). A road has been built down this way, but apart from a short stretch you don't need to follow it; take the footpath instead.

After passing the hill just behind the village, the well-used stone path drops gradually into the canyon, keeping to the right, until it crosses a dry river at the bottom of a *pampa*. From here climb the hill to your left, passing a small house, and keeping left until you see the road. Now make a sharp right turn on a faint short cut to meet the road about 2 hours from Cabanaconde.

The road winds its way into the canyon. Follow it for half an hour until you see a gap in the stone wall and a well-marked trail climbing the hill to your left. This is your path to Choco. It drops gradually westward, with spectacular views of the canyon, to a footbridge over the Río Colca 5–6 hours from Cabanaconde. The first water of the day is found in a stream just before here. This bridge, Puente Colgado de Choco, lies at a mere 1,800m and until recently was one of Peru's last remaining Inca *manguey* fibre bridges. It became dangerous and has now been reconstructed, but the remains of the fibre bridge have been put on top of the new one. On the other side you'll find some small camping places between the rocks.

From Puente Colgado the path climbs steeply up the other side to the village of Choco (2,473m), taking about 3–4 hours. It gets hot in this valley so it's important to make an early start from the bridge.

Choco is one of those increasingly rare Andean villages – beautiful, friendly and so far unspoiled! Resting in the plaza, you'll soon attract an audience, and if you ask around one of the *señoras* may be willing to prepare you a meal. Water is available in Choco.

From Choco a long and steep climb begins. Ask locals for directions here, as there is more than one possible route. There is a stone path that starts on the left-hand side of the plaza (facing the mountains) and follows the river (northwest) for about an hour, then goes up the mountain to the right, heading for an elusive 5,000m pass. The first stream is 4–5 hours from Choco.

Alternative route *There is also a path up the right side of the valley out of Choco, that initially follows the left side of the valley but then crosses the river several times. This path goes to the village of Miñas, where there are some possible camping spots, but if they show signs of cultivation be sure to ask permission first. Try the football pitch. From the village ask locals for the path to Chachas. From Miñas to the pass is around 4 hours. Follow the river on its left bank, climbing switchbacks tending left (southwest), then following a ridge to the pass. From the pass descend for 20 minutes to meet the valley up which the other route comes. Cross the river and follow the path on the left bank, gradually climbing. Carry on up the valley, passing waterfalls on the left, to a pass (5,000m), 3 hours. Go over the pass on loose gravel, taking care, and begin the descent. There's a good camping spot after 1½ hours in a flat pampa with corrals and water available. From here follow the path to the right (north) over a small hill, across a further pampa, and then dropping steeply to cross a river. Head for the settlement of Umapalla way below you. From the village ask for the path to Chachas, 5–6 hours from camp.*

Continue climbing towards the pass, banishing feelings of despair (it seems to get no nearer) and filling your water bottles wherever possible as the valley is dry higher up. There are good campsites before the pass, but it will be freezing cold and there is no water. From Choco to the pass will take 10–13 hours.

As it approaches the summit the path becomes very faint, but always picks up again. At last you reach a moraine, and a final steep climb will bring you to the top of the pass. Incredible views! From here it's all downhill to the village of Chachas: a steep descent at first, but then easing off into meadows. Stay on the left side of the valley. About 2 hours from the pass you'll be able to take a well-deserved (cold) shower! From this point to Chachas will take another 3 hours.

Overlooking a huge lake and surrounded by rich farming land, Chachas (3,100m) is another beauty of the Andes. As in Choco, its people aren't used to strangers and you may find yourself the centre of attention, but the stares are friendly. The village has no shops, but if you ask around you may be able to get a meal and even accommodation. It might be better, however, to camp across the river. Ask the villagers where.

Daily trucks and buses make the journey from Chachas to Andagua (2 hours), but really the walk is too good to be missed (6 hours so don't forget to fill your water bottles). Begin by climbing to the pass on your right, almost at the end of the mountain range, taking a footpath which short cuts the road. The summit is about an hour from the village, giving breathtaking views of the 'Valley of the Volcanoes' on the other side.

Follow the road from the pass down to the river, taking short cuts when they appear, then, leaving the lake on your right, take the footpath up the hill directly opposite for the final climb to Andagua. From the pass to Andagua is 4–5 hours.

Andagua is a small mountain village at 3,587m where the road from Chachas joins the Arequipa–Orcapampa road. Basic food and meals can be found in the plaza, and there is also a basic hostel. Or camp outside the village. The villagers here are very friendly, well acquainted with gringos, and happy to chat.

Buses leave for Arequipa daily at 18.00, and trucks almost daily. The 12-hour trip passes two of the most dominant of the western Andean peaks, the beautiful snowy peak of Coropuna (6,425m), the biggest volcano in Peru, and Solimana (6,323m). Both are considered sacred peaks. You could stop at Corire in the valley of Majes (accommodation at **Hotel Willy's** and also **Hostal Manuelito**) and visit the interesting Toro Muerto ('Dead Bull') petroglyphs. Mosquito repellent is needed here!

Detour via Hacienda Tauca
If you want to spend an extra night in this area, take the path to the right from the highest pass (between Choco and Chachas), and follow the ridge down into the next valley. There are great views and it's a nice hike, but make sure you have enough water as it will be hot in the valley. The path drops down to the river where you'll find some houses which are known as

Hacienda Tauca. Ask the way to the bridge (up the hill behind the *hacienda*). Just before the bridge, a short way to your right, are some good camping spots by a waterfall and pool. From the pass to the bridge will take about 7 hours. From the bridge a well-marked path climbs upwards, steeply at first, through rich farmland to Andagua.

Pinchollo to Cabanaconde
Linda Guinness and Renaye Upton
This hike offers spectacular Inca stonework, fine village churches, ancient terracing, more condors and, near the Choquetico viewpoint, tombs and crude paintings high on sandstone cliffs.

Note Hikers doing this route will need the spirit of adventure since these directions are for guidance only. An IGN map of the area would be useful.

Rating	Moderate
Timing	2 days
Conditions	Hot sun and little water
Map	IGN sheet *Chivay* (32-s)

Getting to the trailhead Pinchollo is a small, cold village on the Chivay–Cabanaconde road. You can walk along the road from Chivay in a long day, passing the villages of Yanque and Achoma with their Collagua carvings and huge churches, or you can take the bus. In Pinchollo very basic accommodation and simple meals are available.

Route description From the church in Pinchollo, take the lower of two stone-walled paths through maize fields, and follow it for 20 minutes to a wooden bridge over a stream. Climb up the other side to an edge, and follow this for 10 minutes to join a road at a point where a water-pipe crosses. Look here for a path to the right, and follow this past some houses, veering left downhill to a small lake. Go to the right of this and climb to join some animal tracks, which lead through giant cactus gardens parallel to the road.

Between here and the viewpoint called El Cruz del Condor, reached in 1½ hours from Pinchollo, there are plenty of places to camp, but no water. The Cruz del Condor is easy to see. It's where the buses from Chivay stop to let passengers see the canyon. From the road beyond, animal tracks lead off in the direction of Cabanaconde, which is reached in 2–3 hours (longer if you follow the road).

Cabanaconde to San Juan on to Oasis and back to Cabanaconde
Leave Cabanaconde, taking the path which leads past the Restaurante Colca, and once outside the village bear left at each fork until, after 10–15 minutes, you come to the canyon edge. Ask the locals for the path to the *puente colgado*

Rating	Moderate
Timing	2 days
Conditions	Hot sun and little water
Map	IGN sheet *Chivay* (32-s)

de Sangalle. The 2–3-hour descent is hard on the knees, but at the bottom you will find the lovely Sangalle tropical gardens where you may camp (see listings). You can bathe here in the refreshingly tepid springs.

You can return to Cabanaconde by the same route, a climb of 3–4 hours. Alternatively, it is possible to cross the river on the *puente colgado* de Sangalle and climb up to Tapay on the other side in 2 hours. From Tapay there's a walk to the small village of San Juan de Chucco and from there the following day you can return to Cabanaconde via the *puente colgado* de Chucco on another path. Ask the locals for details.

Part Three

Bolivia

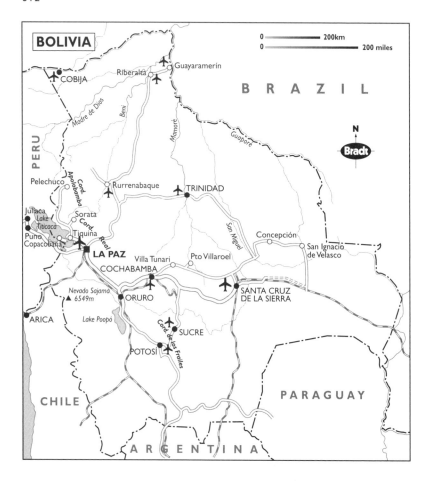

General Information

Bolivia gets its name from the great Venezuelan liberator of so much of South America, Simón Bolívar, but it was probably discovered by Europeans even before Pizarro set foot in Peru. Around 1524 a Portuguese explorer called Aleixo García journeyed west from Brazil and encountered the Inca in Tarabuco – close to modern-day Sucre. Loaded with the silver still found in the region today, he returned east to report his findings but was murdered by his guides on the return journey.

THE COUNTRY
Physical and social geography
Bolivia is dominated by the Andes, which break from a broadly single range to the north of Lake Titicaca in Peru. The Western Cordillera of the Andes forms a natural border with Chile. To its east lies the high, barren Altiplano bounded by the Eastern Cordillera before the Andes drop down to the Amazon basin to their northeast. The Cordillera Real, which provides the best hiking and climbing in Bolivia, is part of the Eastern Cordillera.

Rising moist air from the Amazon rainforest is trapped as it heads towards the Andes, so the eastern slopes are thickly forested and the rainfall is high. Northeast of La Paz this eastern region is known as the Yungas, divided into Nor and Sud Yungas. Being warm and wet, the Yungas produces large amounts of coffee, cocoa and all sorts of fruit. This is also the main area for legal coca production.

The people of present-day Bolivia are nearly three-quarters Indian, and 70% of the population lives on the unproductive Altiplano, which comprises 10% of the country. The largest body of water in the Altiplano is Lake Titicaca which, for this landlocked country of people clinging to their ancient beliefs, has a spiritual significance far greater than its economic importance.

Climate
Bolivia shares Peru's highland climate, with a dry, sunny season from April to the end of October and a rainy season from November to April. On the Altiplano during the dry winter season it is bitterly cold (around or below freezing) at night and in the early morning and evening, and cool on cloudy days, although these are rare at this time of year. Daytime temperatures range from about 10°C to 18°C.

The Yungas shares the same dry/wet months but varies from quite wet to very wet depending on whether it is the 'dry' or the rainy season.

BOLIVIA'S CHANGING CLIMATE
Jim Conrad

Western Bolivia's Altiplano region once was covered by a huge lake extending from north of Titicaca to southwestern Bolivia: Titicaca, Poopó and other of the region's high-elevation lakes, marshes and salt-plains are remnants of that vanishing lake. In fact the whole region seems to be drying up, possibly as a reaction to man's influence. In 1993 a resident of the deep valleys in the Bolivian Yungas told me this: 'Forty years ago, before they began clearing even the steep slopes for coca and other crops, this valley stayed so moist and misty that you never saw the sun until 09.30. Now as soon as the sun rises above the peaks its rays are bright and hot. Moreover, new plants are invading the valley, especially weeds. Some of the prettiest wild flowers we used to wait for at certain times of the year don't even flower any more, or maybe they flower, but at the wrong times. Everything is all messed up nowadays...'.

A brief history
Pre-conquest
Unlike Peru, where various civilisations rose and fell before the advent of the Incas, in Bolivia one culture dominated: Tiahuanaco or Tiwanaku, by Lake Titicaca. Their beginnings are dated around 1000BC and their achievements in stone masonry and grandiose religious structures rival those of the Incas. However, they were not conquered by the Incas but collapsed through some natural disaster around AD900. Archaeologists believe that Lake Titicaca was once much larger than its present size and that whatever forces caused its diminishing spelled the end of Tiwanaku, which is now some way from the lake.

For some 300 years the people of Tiwanaku shared aspects of their culture such as road-building, land terracing and irrigation with the Huari of central Peru, with whom they probably had commercial links. Unlike the Huari, the descendants of the Tiwanakans, the Aymara, resisted the Incas who never really achieved domination over these fiercely independent people.

Post-conquest
Bolivia was conquered by the Spanish in 1538, its vast resources of silver making it a very valuable possession. It became part of the Viceroyalty of Peru, but there were revolts as early as 1661. By 1824 a series of uprisings had prepared the way for independence. Bolívar's general, Sucre, invaded Bolivia after winning the Battle of Ayacucho in Peru, and the Spaniards were defeated in the Battle of Tumusla in 1825. Later that year Simon Bolívar named the country after himself.

Bolivia has become progressively smaller since independence, losing a series of territorial wars. The most painful loss was that of its Pacific coast to Chile in the War of the Pacific from 1879 to 1883. Both Brazil and Argentina followed suit by annexing Bolivian territory, and the greatest loss in terms of size came when Paraguay seized a vast chunk of Chaco in the first half of the 20th century. Bolivia's aggressive neighbours usually built a railway in compensation, which explains why this country has one of the most extensive railway networks in South America.

When not under attack from outside its borders Bolivia suffered internal strife and a succession of military governments which at one time gave it the dubious distinction of having had more political coups than years of independence. The last *de facto* military government left power in 1982, but throughout that decade economic chaos undermined the country, with inflation at one point standing at around 20,000% per annum. Not surprisingly, strikes were part of everyday life.

The 1990s have seen the arrival, at long last, of both political and economic stability, with democratic elections leading to a peaceful hand-over of power and considerable continuity of policy. Inflation is now down to a very respectable 10% or so. The elections of 1997 returned Hugo Banzer, a former military dictator from the bad old days of the 1970s, to the presidency. In the summer of 2001 ill-health forced Banzer to stand down – he died from cancer in May 2002 – and vice president Jorge Quiroga, just 41, assumed the presidency. Elections in June 2002 will see a new candidate assume the presidency on August 6 – Independence Day.

GETTING THERE
Tour operators
A UK-based and an American tour operator specialising in Bolivia are listed below. There are several others based in La Paz whose details appear on page 335. In an often demanding country joining a group or requesting a tailor-made tour is a sensible option for those with little time or special interests.

Magic of Bolivia 182 Westbourne Grove, London W11 2RH; tel: 020 7221 7310; fax: 020 7727 8756; email: magicofbolivia@bigfoot.com; web: www.bolivia.co.uk. Escorted tours of Bolivia are arranged by this company, with whom you can hook up in Bolivia or travel out from the UK.

Explore Bolivia 2510 North 47th St, Suite 207, Boulder, CO 80301; toll free in the US: 877 708 8810; tel: 303 545 5728; fax: 303 545 6239; email: xplorbol@ix.netcom.com; web: www.explorebolivia.com. Covering all sorts of active pursuits from travel by foot and kayak, to fishing and birdwatching. Among the tours they advertise are sea-kayaking on Lake Titicaca and hiking Inca trails over the Andes, finishing the descent by kayaking a whitewater river.

Red tape
At present all EU nationalities, US citizens, Canadians, Australians and New Zealanders can enter Bolivia on a Tourist Visa, which is available at the airport or land frontiers. Most will receive a 90-day card, but it is possible that you will be issued with a 30-day visa unless you request otherwise. If your 30- or 90-

day permit needs extending you have two options. Cross the border for 48 hours and receive a new visa on your return, or visit the Immigration Office in La Paz and arrange an extension.

It is always wise to get the very latest travel information on visas before travel. If you have access to the web look at www.embassyofbolivia.co.uk for information covering all nationalities.

Arrival and departure

When arriving in Bolivia overland or at the airport it is as well to heed Jon Derksen's advice: 'To avoid hassle – and I've seen many people hassled by officials – avoid wearing clothes that have "I might be the kind of person to buy or sell drugs" written all over them, for example dirty jeans, well-worn alpaca ponchos, T-shirts with holes, sneakers beyond their prime. And unfortunately long, unkempt hair is sometimes a sure way to prompt the "fickle finger", a rather uncomfortable sort of body search. Being rude is also a fine way to complicate your entrance into or out of the country. Although this may sound prudish, it is best to present yourself respectably.'

At land frontiers there's no insistence on a return ticket although in theory this is required, along with 'sufficient funds' for your stay.

When you leave Bolivia, even if only for a day, don't forget to ask for an exit stamp.

If leaving by air you'll be asked to pay a departure tax of US$25 for stays of less than 90 days, and US$50 if your visit was longer. For onward travel you can get a visa for neighbouring South American countries from consulates in most large Bolivian cities and in many smaller towns near the frontiers.

CURRENCY

During the 1980s Bolivia's economic problems were legendary. Inflation percentages were measured in thousands, people went around with neat newspaper parcels of banknotes, and beggars didn't even bother to pick up low-value notes. Today the economy is stable and inflation is down to an acceptable level, but at considerable cost: Bolivia's wage levels are the lowest in South America.

The currency is the *boliviano*. Occasionally you'll hear these being referred to as *pesos*. The rate of exchange is now relatively stable at Bs7.04 (April 2002) to the US dollar.

COMMUNICATIONS
Internet

Bolivia is no different to much of the rest of the world and enjoys a good presence on the internet. Likewise, internet access is fairly good in tourist areas. Prices vary incredibly from as little as Bs4 an hour in La Paz and Santa Cruz up to the ridiculous price of Bs24 in more out-of-the-way places. Having a web-based mail account (Yahoo, Hotmail, etc) is the easiest way to stay in touch. As far as net traffic, the busiest – and therefore slowest – time of day is between 17.00 and 19.00.

Telephones

The Bolivian telephone system has undergone a near revolution in recent years. Modern telephones using chip phonecards are replacing the magnetic-strip *tarjetas telefonicas* system. Phones are found in many hotels, bars and on the street. *Tarjetas* range in value from Bs10 to Bs50 and can usually be bought from someone in the vicinity of the telephone. Local calls are Bs6 per hour, to the USA Bs 6.50 per minute, to Australia Bs11 per minute and to Europe Bs13.50 per minute. You can make international calls from these telephones but be sure to buy the higher-value cards. (Bs50 provides just over three minutes to Europe.) Mobile telephones are popular in Bolivia and are often used as a contact number. Calls to mobiles eat up money quickly so make sure you have a number of cards if you're calling a mobile.

If you need to make several calls it can be easier to head for the Entel office where there are many telephones, a fax and internet service. As in Peru, reverse-charge (collect) calls can be made but they are more expensive. If your friends call you, Bolivia's country code is 591.

Mail

The mail system is efficient – although postal charges are surprisingly high (letters and postcards up to 20g to the US, Europe and Australia are 5, 6 and 7 *bolivianos* respectively). Each town and city has its *centro de correos* (usually situated near the main plaza) with a few secondary post offices starting to appear in larger cities. In the main post offices you will find a large bin where you post your letter according to the continent to which you are sending it.

As in Peru, if you wish to receive letters they should be sent to the *Lista de Correo* or c/o American Express. It will take about two weeks for your letter to arrive in Bolivia from North America or Europe. When writing to businesses, always use their *casilla* (PO Box) number.

Newspaper

The English-language *Bolivian Times* is published on Fridays and often has articles on hiking as well as other subjects of interest to travellers. Its offices can be contacted on tel/fax: 244 1348; email: info@boliviantimes.com; web: www.boliviantimes.com

Business hours

Traditionally business hours are 08.30–12.30 and 14.30–18.00, Monday to Friday. Government offices now work *hora continua*, which means they work straight through lunch from 08.30 to 16.30. While the office may be open all day, don't expect full services for a couple of hours around lunch. Bank hours are generally 09.00–18.00 weekdays, and increasingly Saturday morning 09.00–13.00.

Holidays

The ones that are likely to catch you out are Alacitas (the end of January), Labour Day (May 1), Independence Day (August 5 to 7) and La Paz Day

THE COCAINE TRADE
Claire Hargreaves

Cocaine took off in the West in the 1970s; seen as glamorous, harmless and socially acceptable, it was the rich man's drug. Then in the 1980s came crack, which is far more harmful. In the United States, where most cocaine and crack were consumed, drugs became a political issue and the government launched a 'War on Drugs'. Bolivia and Peru, which produce virtually all the raw coca leaves used to make cocaine, became, together with Colombia, the main targets of the 'war'. Their governments came under strong US pressure to eradicate coca fields and put the drug barons out of business.

In Peru, coca is grown mainly in the northern Amazonas Department. In Bolivia it is produced illegally in the Chapare, between Cochabamba and Santa Cruz, and legally in the Yungas. In 1990 an estimated 51,000 hectares in the Chapare were planted with coca.

When President Banzer came to power he promised zero tolerance on coca growing and promised the international community that coca production in the Chapare would be eradicated. True to his word, despite a difficult few years marred by extensive protests from the *cocaleros*, coca production in the Chapare is believed to be almost non-existent as the presidential term of office comes to a close.

The first stages of processing are carried out in primitive 'pits' or *pozas* in the jungle. The leaves are mashed with chemicals by barefooted men

(October 20). These days are marked by military parades and virtually all shops and businesses close. In villages, fiestas are frequent and fabulous (see page 29). The tourist office in La Paz (see *Useful addresses* on page 335) will confirm the date and place of the best fiestas.

MISCELLANEOUS
Laundry

As in Peru there are *lavanderías* where you can take your washing, but most hotels will do it for you and the cheaper the hotel, the cheaper the laundry charges. Make sure you know what the cost will be, however, before emptying the contents of your bag on the reception counter.

Handicrafts

Good-quality tourist items are not particularly cheap, but on the whole the quality is better than in Peru and there is more variety and ingenuity. Although you can find goods for sale dotted throughout the country, the best one-stop shop is Calle Sagárnaga in La Paz, behind and above the church of San Francisco on the main road through La Paz.

Machine-knitted alpaca sweaters are a good buy, and there are some 'designer label' sweaters that are almost the same price as you'd pay at home but gorgeous! Bolivia's traditional weavings – ponchos and *mantas* – are second known as 'stompers'. The last of the three stages of processing is carried out in sophisticated laboratories in northeastern Bolivia, in the Beni. You are unlikely to see one, as they are well hidden (and if you do, make yourself scarce as quickly as possible).

In Santa Cruz you can see the luxurious houses inhabited by many of Bolivia's drug barons, and the businesses like discos and car dealerships which grew on recycling drug cash.

Even today, if you are travelling in the drug-producing areas, you should be very careful. Remember that if you have a white skin, drug dealers will assume you work for the CIA or the DEA (US Drug Enforcement Administration) and will not want you around. On the occasions that Westerners have run into trouble it has almost always been because they were in the wrong place at the wrong time.

Many of the *campesinos* who grow coca for cocaine would prefer to grow a legal crop, but find that coca is the only product that pays. Attempts to grow alternative crops such as coffee, tea, cocoa and citrus fruits have failed because of the difficulties of penetrating the Western markets. You can help by buying products like Cafédirect which cut out the middle person and give a better return to the producer.

Clare Hargreaves is author of Snowfields: The War on Cocaine in the Andes; *see Further Reading, page 401.*

to none. The most beautiful are undoubtedly those made in the Potosí and Sucre areas. Designs on the ponchos and *mantas* woven here incorporate all sorts of mythical animals, and are unique. There is usually a good selection in La Paz, especially from street vendors up Calle Sagárnaga, although, inevitably, prices are higher than for those bought direct from the makers.

Leather goods are excellent and inexpensive; gold and silver jewellery is good value and often beautiful; and the tin cutlery and other tableware sold on Calle Sagárnaga is attractive and cheap, although it tarnishes easily.

Guitar players will probably fall for a *charango*, a small twelve-stringed instrument with an armadillo shell as a sound box. If you buy one, be sure to get an instruction book as well or even a beginner's lesson from a local musician.

You can buy just about anything at low cost in the *Mercado Negro*, black market, in the Calle Max Paredes area.

Hot baths

La Paz and other Altiplano towns are freezing at night, and a hotel without hot water is a real misery. If circumstances or economy force you to sleep cold, go to the public baths (*baños públicos*), which exist in most towns. They are usually very good value with lots of hot water.

For a real treat in La Paz, spend an afternoon in the sauna at the Plaza Hotel, and follow it up with a massage. Bliss!

Security

Jon Derksen writes: 'My wife and I feel very safe in Bolivia. We have never met such friendly and generous people as in the Bolivian countryside. But many have deep-rooted traditions and suspicions. Simple foresight and respect will help you to avoid most undesirable situations. For example, always ask before taking a picture – many native people truly do believe that a camera steals their souls. While visiting the town of Tarabuco, I tried to photograph a lady in the market. She called out to me, "If you take my picture I'll throw this bag of food at you!" My brother Craig, who was with me, called back jokingly, "If you do, we'll eat it!" At that moment a local passer-by, who had overheard the exchange, whipped out a knife and held it to my throat. "Take the picture and I'll cut you!" he said. Now, this may sound frightening, but the man was right; I'd overstepped my bounds. Luckily for me he put the knife away and smiled victoriously.

'Don't assume that if country people are dancing and having fun they want you to be part of it. On the other hand, if you are cornered or approached by festive, drunk or perhaps belligerent individuals, don't panic and try not to look afraid. Use whatever Spanish you have to offer to buy a round of beers, or share a few coca leaves with them. I've won more than a few friends in the *campo* this way. Every so often you might run into a truly dangerous situation.

'As in any other country, racism is alive and well in Bolivia, and whatever you do or say, the colour of your skin may sometimes serve as an unspoken provocation. Try to read the situation as best you can.

'Use your common sense. People in remote areas are understandably wary or curious about you. If wary don't approach them too openly. In many parts of Bolivia backpackers are still a novelty. If the people are curious, invite them over, but be prepared to talk for a couple of hours about everything under the sun.'

When the inevitable question comes up of how much everything you own cost you, it may be prudent to say it was a gift rather than revealing its price tag.

PROTECTED AREAS OF BOLIVIA

The national parks and reserves in Bolivia were created for the protection, preservation and survival of Bolivia's diverse wildlife. Only the native population may live within the national parks and reserves, although some non-native populations have been given consent to open up reserve lands in the jungle lowlands. In theory, the rainforest and cloudforest reserves were established to ensure that rare species of plants and animals would not be destroyed by human encroachment. However, in practice the decimation of forest lands and uncontrolled hunting have led to the tragic and rapid decline of rare natural habitat.

Since the late 1980s and early 1990s certain groups, both local and international, have been struggling to conserve endangered areas. Fundación Amigos de la Naturaleza (FAN) in Bolivia and Conservation International and Nature Conservancy in the USA are just three organisations that have helped establish new protected areas. Some organisations have attempted debt-for-nature exchanges where part of Bolivia's external debt is cancelled in return for greater local commitment to financing conservation projects.

In 1992 the United Nations organised ECO-92, a massive meeting held in Brazil to discuss the more serious global environmental issues, especially the fate of the Amazon Basin. Since then, Bolivians seem to be more cognisant of the threat to their precious resources, but finding ways to put thoughts into action has proved difficult, given the lack of direct government involvement and funding as well as the conflicting interests of loggers, agro-industries and peasants eager to exploit new lands.

Is there an answer to these problems? Groups blamed for the irresponsible development of resources must be shown viable alternatives. Long-term sustainable development programmes must be effectively publicised so that those in positions of power feel the need for change and, at the same time, realise that such schemes can procure a profit. Stephen Schmidheiny, Swiss billionaire and chairman of UNOTEC, who has funded several sustainable development projects in Bolivia, states the following in his executive summary of *Changing Course: A Global Business Perspective on Development and the Environment*:

> Clean and equitable economic growth, which is integral to sustainable development, requires more efficient use of resources ... such growth ... requires open and competitive markets. It also requires a break with conventional wisdom that sidelines environmental and human concerns.

For example, by logging selectively, timber prices may rise, but there would not be the complete devastation caused by clear-cut logging. 'Extractive reserves' are an alternative. These try to use the forest as a renewable resource, harvesting such things as brazil nuts and rubber, thus avoiding deforestation. In the Pando, Bolivia's northernmost province, it is illegal to cut down a brazil-nut or rubber tree; as a result, huge tracts of land have, to a large extent, been spared.

As ever, the course of development and protection of land is an ongoing process. Many of the protected areas of Bolivia are poorly understood and research is still very limited in most cases.

National parks and protected areas of Bolivia

These are listed according to their number on the map on page 324. A useful map that can be bought in La Paz is *A Travel Map of Bolivia Highlighting the National Park System* (2nd edition). It is available by mail from Liam O'Brian, 28 Turner Terrace, Newtonville, MA 02160, USA and from good bookshops.

Information is provided overleaf of many of the protected areas in the central highlands.

Parque Nacional Madidi (1995) This park includes Bolivian's western frontier with Peru from Puerto Heath in the Amazon Basin south, joining to Ulla Ulla National Park. From the Peruvian border the 1.9-million-ha park stretches

PROTECTED AREAS IN THE CENTRAL HIGHLANDS

Name	Department	Date est'd
National parks		
1 Parque Nacional Amboró (637,000ha)	Santa Cruz	1973
2 Parque Nacional Carrasco (620,000ha)	Cochabamba	1988
3 Parque Regional El Pirai (250,000ha)	Santa Cruz	1984
4 Parque Regional Lomas Arena (13,200ha)	Santa Cruz	1989
5 Parque Nacional Llica (97,500ha)	Potosí	1990
6 Parque Nacional Madidi (1,894,750ha)	La Paz	1995
7* Parque Nacional Mallasa	La Pax	1955
8 Parque Nacional Noel Kempff Mercado (914,000ha)	Santa Cruz	1979
9 Parque Nacional Sajama (149,940ha)	Oruro	1939
10 Parque Nacional Santa Cruz La Vieja (17,080ha)	Santa Cruz	1987
11 Parque Nacional Sehuencas	Cochabamba	1989
12 Parque Nacional Torotoro (16,570ha)	Potosí	1989
13 Parque Nacional Tunari (approx 60,000ha)	Cochabamba	1962
14 Parque Nacional Tuni Condoriri (30,000ha)	La Paz	1942
15 Parque Nacional de Ulla-Ulla (240,000ha)	La Paz	1972
16 Parque Regional Yacuma (130,000ha)	Beni	1987
17 Parque Nacional y Area de Manejo Integrado Cotapata (40,000ha)	La Paz	1993
18 Parque Nacional y Area de Manejo Integrado Kaa-Iya del Gran Chaco (3,441,115ha)	Santa Cruz	1995
19 Parque Nacional y Territorio Indígena Isibore-Sécure (approx 1,200,000ha)	Beni	1965
National reserves		
20 Reserva Nacional Amazónica Manuripi-Heath (1,800,000ha)	Pando	1973
21 Reserva Nacional Cordillera de Sama (108,500ha)	Tarija	1991
22 Reserva Nacional Eduardo Avaroa (440,00ha including 10km² surrounding Laguna Colorado)	Potosí	1973
23* Reserva Nacional Incacasani-Altamachi		
24* Reserva Nacional Lagunas Angostura y Alalay		
25 Reserva Nacional Noel Kempff Mercado (21,900ha)	Santa Cruz	1988
26 Reserva Nacional de Vida Silvestre Ríos Blancos y Negro (1,400,000ha)	Santa Cruz	1990
27 Reserva Nacional Tariquia (246,870ha)	Tarija	1989
28* Reserva Nacional Yura	Potosí	1974
29 Reserva de la Biósfera Estación Biológica del Beni (135,000ha)	La Paz	1982
30 Reserva de la Biósfera Territorio Indigena Pilón-Lajas (400,000ha)	Beni	1992

Name	Department	Date est'd
31 Reserva Fiscal (Forestal) Bella Vista (approx 90,000ha)	La Paz	1964
32 Reserva Forestal de Inmovilización Covendo (approx 294,195ha)	La Paz	1984
33 Reserva Forestal de Inmovilización Iténez (approx 1,500,000ha)	Beni	1986
34 Reserva Forestal de Inmovilización Río Boopi (approx 128,100ha)	La Paz	1979
35 Reserva Forestal de Inmovilización Río Grande Mascicuri (242,000ha)	Santa Cruz	1979

Wildlife reserves

36 Reserva de Vida Silvestre Cerro Tapilla (Pelcoya)	Oruro	1940
37 Reserva de Vida Silvestre El Dorado (170,000ha)	La Paz	1988
38 Reserva de Vida Silvestre Est. Elsner San Rafael (20,000ha)	Beni	1978
39 Reserva de Vida Silvestre Mirikiri y Flavio Machicado Viscarra (37.25ha)	La Paz	1946
40 Reserva de Vida Silvestre Huancaraoma (11,000ha)	Oruro	1975
41 Refugio de Vida Silvestre Est Elsner Espíritu (73,000ha)	Beni	1978
42 Santuario de Vida Silvestre Cavernas El Repechon (1,500ha)	Cochabamba	1986

Forest reserves

43 Bosque Permanente de Producción Bajo Paragua (3,382,200ha)	Santa Cruz	1988
44 Bosque Permanente de Producción Chimanes (1,164,220ha)	Beni	1978
45 Bosque Permanente de Producción El Chore (approx 900,000ha)	Beni	1966
46 Bosque Permanente de Producción Guarayos (1,500,000ha)	Beni	1969
47 Bosque Permanente de Producción Quimera del Aten (20,000ha)	La Paz	1977
48* Bosque Permanente de Protección Sajta-Ichilo	Cochabamba/ Santa Cruz	–
49 Area de Protección de Cuencas Eva Eva – Mosetenes (approx 225,000ha)	Beni	1987

*The national parks department is unable to supply statistics on these reserves.

eastward to encompass the River Tuichi basin that flows out from Rurrenabaque. Ranging in altitude from 6,000m above sea level down to just 250m, this park is one of the main areas of biodiversity in the world and the subject of a classic *National Geographic* article in March 2000. Contact: Eco Bolivia Foundation, La Paz; tel/fax: 02 231 5974; email: ecobolivia@mail.megalink.com; web: www.ecobolivia.org.

Parque Nacional Ulla Ulla (1972) This reserve is located in the remote Apolobamba mountain range near Bolivia's western border with Peru. The 240,000ha park spans three major zones: glacial highlands, tundra (altiplano) and subtropical Yungas. The tundra portion of the park not only harbours Bolivia's largest concentration of vicuñas, but its numerous shallow lakes also provide safe haven for waterfowl like the Andean goose and Chilean flamingo. For more details see page 394.

Bosque Permanente de Producción Quimera del Aten (1977) Protected forest reserve to the north of Lake Titicaca on the upper Amazon slopes.

Parque Nacional Tuni Condoriri (1942) includes a chain of mountains approximately 60km east of La Paz. The area is best known for the snow-

PACHAMAMA IN BOLIVIA

In Bolivia, people of all classes make the traditional *Pago a Pachamama* or sacrifice to Mother Earth to ensure good luck (or rather to prevent bad luck) when building a new house. A Bolivian friend described an elaborate ceremony which she attended to inaugurate a glass factory. One llama was sacrificed for the sales department and one for the plant itself. First a pit was dug, oriented east to west, and prepared with coca leaves, herbs and incense. Bottles of beer and sweet wine were placed at each corner of the pit, which was then blessed by the priest. A *brujo* (sorcerer) was called in to 'read' the coca leaves to see what colour the sacrificial llama should be.

The beast arrived, washed and groomed and wearing a silk coat decorated with gold and silver 'coins' and paper money. It was made to drink three bottles of beer and one of *aguardiente* (apparently it offered no resistance throughout the ceremony), then to kneel first towards the sun and then towards Illimani before its throat was cut. Even then it did not struggle; it did not even blink.

The blood was sprinkled around the perimeter of the factory and in the pit, which then became the llama's grave.

On a less lavish scale, but still symbolising an offering to Mother Earth, is the *mesa con sullo*. This is what the dried llama foetuses and strange herbs and objects that are sold at the 'witches' market' near Calle Sagárnaga in La Paz are for. If Pachamama can't have a live llama, she'll settle for a dried foetus, rubbed with fat to simulate the real thing. This must be laid on a bed of wool (white for purity), along with sweets in the shapes of different animals and devils, nuts and seeds, and gold and silver trinkets. All this is by way of returning to Mother Earth what has been taken from her. The foetus may be dressed in a coat, like a real sacrificial llama, and little bottles of sweets may take the place of the beer in the full sacrifice. The whole thing may be topped with a piece of cat's skin to represent the untameable, which still succumbs to the power of Pachamama.

When complete, the objects will be blessed, then parcelled up and buried, to the accompaniment of incantations and sprinkles of alcohol, either under the foundations of a new house, or in the countryside in view of the major snowpeaks and their *achachilas* (mountain spirits).

APACHETA

On every high pass of the Andes you'll see an *apacheta* (a piles of stones). These are built gradually through the custom of each traveller carrying a stone from the valley to place at the highest point as an offering to the *Apus* (gods of the *nevados* or snowpeaks). This has been going on since pre-Hispanic times.

When the pass is a major one, connecting two important valleys or villages, or overlooked by a mighty snowpeak and its *Apu*, the pile may be enormous and is sometimes topped by a cross. The ritual thanks the *Apu* for leading the traveller safely up to the pass; when the stone is deposited the *Apu* will give you protection for the rest of your journey.

capped peak, Chacaltaya, and the subtropical Zongo Valley. Andean condors, foxes and highland deer frequent the area. Contact: Señor Alfredo Martinez Delgado at the Club Andino Boliviano (tel: 225 0658) or Hugo Berrios at Hotel Continental (tel: 245 6717).

Parque Nacional y Area de Manejo Integrado Cotapata (1993) protects areas of the Yungas and the high Andes, preventing forestry, fishing and hunting – except for traditional Aymara communities living in the area.

Parque Nacional Mallasa (1955) This includes lands bordering the river beds just below La Paz, and covers the eco-region of dry inter-Andean valleys characterised by bizarre, eroded sedimentary deposits, locally known as 'Valleys of the Moon'. Viscachas (rodents related to the chinchilla) are commonly seen.

Reserva de Vida Silvestre Mirikiri y Flavio Machicado Viscarra (1946) is an area south of Lake Titicaca known for its gently rolling hills and extensive meadows. Guanacos may be seen here.

Parque Nacional Sajama (1939) Touching the Chilean border the park protects the area around Sajama Volcano – Bolivia's highest peak at 6,549m. This is a good area for spotting condors, llamas and other highland wildlife. Access is now considerably better since the construction of a new road to Arica, Chile.

Reserva de Vida Silvestre Huancaroma (1975) Privately owned land 200km south of La Paz along the Desaguadero River. Although used as grazing for livestock, it protects a large area of dry *puna*.

Reserva de Vida Silvestre Cerro Tapilla (Pelcoya) (1940) This is one of the oldest reserves in the country, originally set aside for breeding chinchillas (*Chinchilla brevicaudata*), which may now be extinct in the area, if not in all of Bolivia.

Ecotourism

Ecotourism by responsible visitors who respect the rules and pay the required fee will help conserve threatened habitats in Bolivia, so do inform yourselves about the protected areas and make a point of visiting them. If you wish to help further, any of the organisations below would be pleased to hear from you

GIVING SOMETHING BACK

Additional information from Phil Deutschle, resident of La Paz
Web: www.FarJourney.com.
By supporting the following charities, rather than giving to beggars, you are doing your bit for the Bolivians whose country has given you so much enjoyment.

Hogar Mixto is a children's home in Sopocachi, working with runaway, orphaned, abused and abandoned children in La Paz. Home to about 50 boys and girls aged between six and 12, the running of the home is greatly assisted by donations of time and money. The volunteer programme includes creative activities, games, gardening and reading. There is a minimum eight-week commitment unless it's the flying visit of an impromptu juggling or theatre performance. Extra finances not only help the day-to-day running of the home, but also help to employ a family therapist. Hogar Mixto hopes to begin working with deaf and disabled children so there will shortly be a need for these skills as well. For information contact Diane Bellomy at cnsorata@ceibo.entelnet.bo or the volunteer co-ordinator at adh_volunteers@yahoo.com. Or telephone the director, Marina de Ascarrunz, on 243 1071.

WSCS is the Women's Society for Christian Service, which donates money to a number of organisations that desperately need financial assistance. They give to orphanages, drug and alcohol rehabilitation projects, elderly residences, and to individuals in need of help. Contact Gaila Chambi at gchambi@acslp.org.

Habitat for Humanity helps finance and construct housing for low-income families. Volunteers donate both funds and labour. This is a very successful endeavour in Bolivia. Contact Mirna Aliaga, PO Box 9573, La Paz; fax: 591 2284 5878; email: habitaea@ceibo.entelnet.bo.

CAZUR is a small group of volunteers that provides catechism and a snack on Saturday afternoons to children from the Zona Sur who sell candy or shine shoes or are otherwise employed during part of the day. These youngsters have parents and a place to live but have very little stimulation in their lives. CAZUR works with ages four through 16 and also with a group of mothers. They go on outings, have parties, try to get their teeth checked, etc. Contact the president of CAZUR, Augusta Ocampo, in La Paz on 279 1071.

FAM is Fondo de Ayuda al Menor, which works with sick children who need urgent treatment. They pay for operations, medication, tests, etc. In the three years they have been working they have been able to help around 20 kids. This group has a great need of funds to assist children in truly desperate situations. Contact: FAM Board Members, Erika Asbun (tel: 277 0768) or Mercedes Calvo (tel: 271 2591; email: mcalvo@acslp.org).

Social Exchange is a website that has recently been established by concerned La Paz residents who wish to facilitate communications between service organisations and individuals who wish to donate time, resources, or money. Eventually most aid organisations will be listed with full contact information. See the site at www.social-exchange.net.

Pre-Kindergarten and Kindergarten for children from low-income families, where they receive education, food, sanitary facilities, and parental guidance. Donations are always needed and appreciated. The centre is located at Felipe Pizarro Street 2247,Miraflores, La Paz; tel: 591 2 222 1268 or email: fundadler@yahoo.com.

Animales SOS Bolivia is really the only animal rights organisation in Bolivia. It is recognised by the Humane Society of the US (HSUS) and by the Humane Society International (HSI) as well as by the WSPA. As a volunteer organisation, it has been working for over five years in La Paz and has expanded in the last few years to most of the major Bolivian cities. They work with stray animals that are injured, sick, have been hit by cars, are ready to give birth in the street or animals that have been abused. They also confiscate wild animals from owners and rehabilitate them before sending them to a refuge in the Chapare. (It is illegal in Bolivia to own wild animals such as parrots and monkeys.) They currently have a small shelter that operates in a private house where there are animals available for adoption, but the ultimate goal is to build a permanent, modern shelter which requires a large sum of money. There is a need for monetary donations and volunteers with veterinary experience. Additional information can be found at www.animalessos.org. Contact Animales SOS, tel: 591 2 248 3333 or email: bolivia@animalessos.org.

Inti Wara Yassi gives volunteers the opportunity to work with wild animals that were injured or abused as pets, with the aim of returning them to the wild. The project is at Parque Machia, near Villa Tunari. Volunteers are asked to give a minimum of two weeks of their time.

La Paz

13

The city huddles in a bowl-like valley with the Altiplano forming the rim. Whether you arrive by air or by bus, you won't forget your first sight of the city lying below you surrounded by the high peaks of the Cordillera Real. It's the highest seat of government in the world (the legal capital is actually Sucre) at a cool 3,632m. Altitude sickness hits most people flying here, and you'll soon find out if you're a *soroche* sufferer – a problem compounded by this being one of the hilliest cities in the world. Except for the Prado, the main street down the centre of the valley, everything of interest seems to be at the top of a steep hill. At least it's difficult to get lost in La Paz, which is like a giant funnel: walk downhill from anywhere and you'll arrive at the Prado.

The Prado, whose official name is Avenida 16 de Julio, is broad and lined with modern shops and offices, but the old city, up on the hill around the government palace, is full of character. The endless streets of Indian markets in the districts above and behind the church of San Francisco are fascinating. Here you can buy a llama foetus to bury under the foundations of your new house for luck, or more mundane things like an aluminium saucepan and food for your next hike.

There is a handful of museums (open daily) a few blocks north of Plaza Murillo down Calle Jaén, one of the best preserved colonial streets in the city. There is also a new and interesting Coca Museum showing the history of coca through the years, just off Calle Sagárnaga on Calle Linares, open 10.00 to 18.00.

When you are tired of sightseeing, relax by sitting on the steps of the San Francisco church and do some people-watching.

To see the modern and lively side of La Paz, jump on an 'Ñ' bus and head down to the Zona Sur and the districts of Calacoto and San Miguel, home to several contemporary art galleries and a bustling nightlife.

GETTING THERE
Transport between Peru and Bolivia
Several bus companies provide transport between Copacabana on the Bolivian border and Puno on the northwestern shores of Lake Titicaca in Peru. There

is also a direct daily bus service between Cusco and La Paz with Transporte Internacional (Bs120 for the 13-hour journey).

AeroPerú and Lloyd Aero Boliviano (LAB) fly several times a week between Cusco, Lima and La Paz. LAB, for example, flies to Cusco three times a week, approximately US$100 one-way. It also does daily flights to Lima, US$185 one-way.

Transturín runs comfortable buses between La Paz and Puno with links to Cusco and a rather chic (and pricey) daily catamaran boat service across Lake Titicaca.

At the airport

El Alto is the highest commercial airport in the world and surely the most beautiful. You step out into bright sunshine, your heart fluttering through lack of oxygen, and see the entire Cordillera Real ranged in front of your admiring eyes. It could not be a better welcome for mountain lovers! The good impression is maintained in the airport itself, which is calm and efficient and even provides trolleys for your luggage – free of charge! There is an exchange bureau, ATM machines, a small restaurant and a telephone office in the main departures area.

It is only a short drive into La Paz and since most international flights arrive in the early morning you will probably prefer to take a taxi for around US$8, which allows you to stop and take photos of the spectacular setting of the city. Alternatively, minibuses leave the airport for the city every ten minutes or so. They wait just outside the arrivals building until full and drop you in the centre of town along the Prado for US$0.60.

Buses

International buses and those to southern Bolivian cities arrive and leave from the *terminal terrestre* at Plaza Antofogosta. Most others leave from the cemetery area, easily reached by taking a bus or a taxi.

City transport

The most convenient way for tourists to get around is by taxi. Radio taxis are efficient and their numbers are posted everywhere. Short trips cost from Bs5 (about US$0.60) to Bs10 and longer trips Bs10 to Bs15. Taxis can be a useful way of getting to trailheads but you will have to negotiate the price. Radio taxis may be reluctant to travel down really bad roads, but keep trying! In La Paz *trufis* follow set routes and are recognised by the green pennants flying from their bonnets (hoods). Journeys cost Bs3. Minibuses run along the major routes; they are crowded but cheap, costing Bs2.30. The cheapest way around town is on the city buses, which crawl through the streets charging Bs1.40 for the journey.

SLEEPING AND EATING
Accommodation

Libertador Obispo Cárdenas 1421; Casilla 8412; tel: 02 220 2424/0599; fax: 02 220 0584; email: libertad@ceibo.entelnet.bo. The best value mid- to upper-range hotel.

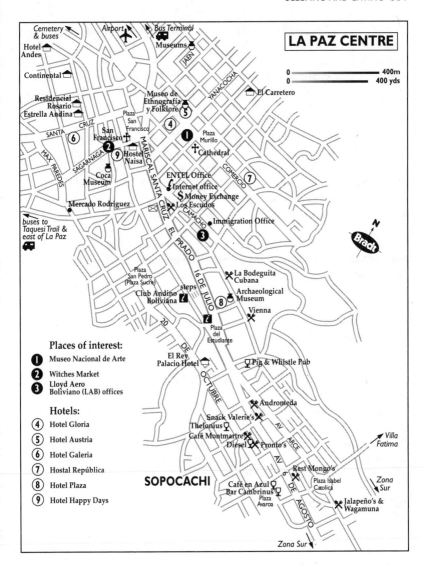

LA PAZ CENTRE

Places of interest:

❶ Museo Nacional de Arte

❷ Witches Market

❸ Lloyd Aero Boliviano (LAB) offices

Hotels:

④ Hotel Gloria

⑤ Hotel Austria

⑥ Hotel Galeria

⑦ Hostal República

⑧ Hotel Plaza

⑨ Hotel Happy Days

Hotel Gloria Calle Potosí 909; tel: 02 237 0010; fax: 02 239 1489; email: gloriatr@ceibo.entelnet.bo; web: www.gloria-tours-bolivia.com. Smart multi-storey hotel with a wide range of services including a pleasant top-floor restaurant. Double US$60.

Residencial Rosario Calle Illampu 704; tel: 02 245 1658; fax: 02 245 1991; email: reservas@hotelrosario.com; web: www.hotelrosario.com. Has 32 clean rooms, and good services including a restaurant. US$37 for a double room, including breakfast – popular with travellers and groups but getting pricey.

Hotel Galería Horizontes Andes 4th floor, Calle Santa Cruz 583; tel: 02 246 1015; fax: 02 246 1253; email: hgaleria@horizontandino.com.bo; web:

www.horizontandino.com.bo. Has 30 rooms with private bathrooms and TV. A comfortable option with a good view from the restaurant, internet service and helpful staff. US$35 double.

Hostal Estrella Andina Av Illampu 716 esq Aroma; Casilla 1546; tel: 02 245 6401; fax: 02 245 1401; email: estrellaandina@latinmail.com. Has 32 clean and comfortable rooms, many decorated with murals of Andean life. US$32 double, US$20 single, including breakfast.

Hotel Continental Calle Illampu 626; Casilla 479; tel: 02 245 1176; fax: 02 245 1176; email: bolclimb@mail.megalink.com. Its 40 rooms are OK, but could do with a lick of paint. This is the main contact for the *refugio* near Huayna Potosí.

Hostal Naira Calle Sagárnaga 161; tel: 02 235 5645; fax: 02 232 7262. A beautiful hotel right on the main tourist thoroughfare. Double US$32.

Hostal La Republica Calle Comercio 1455 esq Bueno; tel: 02 220 2742; fax: 02 220 2782; email: marynela@ceibo.entelnet.bo. A pleasant courtyard in a former presidential home, close to the centre but away from the busy parts of town. Small café and travel agency. Doubles from US$24 with bathroom, US$16 without.

Hotel Andes Av Manco Kapac 364; Casilla 2233; tel: 02 245 5327; email: hotandes@caoba.entelnet.bo. A mixed bag of 60 rooms, some sleeping up to four, good value at US$10 with a private bath, US$8 with a shared bath. Price per person includes breakfast.

Hotel Happy Days Sagárnaga 229; Casilla 13586; tel: 02 231 4759; fax: 02 235 5079; email: happydays@zuper.net. Two dozen spotless rooms. The better beds are in rooms with shared bath, but rooms with private bath are still excellent value at US$8 per person. Very clean, run by the incredibly friendly Leonor Arocha – justifiably the budget traveller's first choice.

Hotel Italia Av Manco Kapac 303; tel: 02 245 6710. Has 33 rather tatty rooms but is good value at US$4 for a single and US$6 for a double.

El Carretero Calle Catacora 1056, between Yanacocha y Junín; tel: 02 228 5271. The laid-back hangout for travellers on the gringo trail. One report said you either love the place or you don't. Hot showers, kitchen available. US$3 per person.

Restaurants and nightlife

The Prado is dotted with endless cheap restaurants. Particular recommendations along or close to the Prado include the following:

The Bolivian way of life includes mid-morning snacking on *salteñas*. Readily available on the street, the best in the city are from **Snack Valerie** at Av 6 de Agosto 2187, a few blocks on from Plaza Estudiante.

Hotel Gloria provides a variety of eating options. The vegetarian restaurant on the ground floor is popular with those seeking a vitamin-filled vegetarian meal at lunchtime. There is also an excellent coffee shop on the ground floor and upstairs a restaurant provides good food à la carte and an excellent view across the city. Main dishes start at US$3.

Restaurant UTAMA, Hotel Plaza Av 16 de Julio 1789 (Prado); tel: 02 237 8311. The restaurant on the top floor provides a mix of European and Bolivian dishes, is reasonably priced (US$15) and has stunning views. A perfect way to end a trip!

One road north of the Hotel Plaza is **La Bodeguita Cubana** on Federico Zuezo 1653, serving Cuban dishes while the music and cocktails keep flowing. A few blocks down is **Restaurant Vienna** at Federico Zuazo 1905. Serving European cuisine, this is a long-time favourite, popular with expatriates. A bit pricey but worth getting the credit card out for.

Andromeda Av Arce and Aspiazu, a few blocks south of the university. Serves good food in a comfortable setting – very popular for *almuerzo* (US$3).

Pronto serves good pasta and pizza in a quiet little restaurant on Pasaje Jáuregui, Sopocachi. **Jalapeno** (Mexican) and **Wagamama** (Japanese) on Avenida Arce at the corner of Pasaje Pinilla are a couple of restaurants showing the increasing diversity of the *paceño* palette.

Also popular are the *peñas* with traditional dishes and dances. Try **Los Escudos**, in the basement of the building opposite the post office on Av Mariscal Santa Cruz; tel: 02 231 2133, or **Peña Huari** on Calle Sagárnaga 339; tel: 02 231 6225.

For a treat go to one of the Kuchen Stube tea-rooms, either in Edificio Guadelquivir on Calle Rosendo Gutiérrez (a few blocks up from the Sheraton Hotel) or in Edificio Mariscal Ballicán at Calle Mercado 1328 (the same building as the tourist office – see *Useful addresses*, page 336). How better to prepare for a hike than by gorging yourself on German cakes?

In the district of Calacoto in Zona Sur on the main road is the popular British pub **The Britannia** on the corner of Calle 16 and Av Ballivian. Next door is the **Abracadabra Restaurant**, which will happily send a pizza or hamburger over to the Britannia. A short walk towards the heart of San Miguel leads to an area that buzzes with life. **La Terraza** is the place to be seen for a drink. If you're looking for one special meal try **Maphrao On** on Calle Claudio Aliaga 1182; tel: 02 279 3070, for excellent Thai cuisine.

A little further down the valley in La Florida try the outdoor **Las Cholas** on Calle 7. The specialities are cheap local and imported beer, pickled onions and Chola sandwiches. The latter are snacks prepared by *cholitas* (local girls) and consist of a bun filled with pork, tomato, onion and *escaveche* (pickled this and that) – a direct contravention to every guideline on safe eating.

If you're looking for a drink in the evening **Mongo's** on Hermano's Manchega is a popular choice, especially on Friday and Saturday nights. A wide selection of bars is found close to Plaza Avaroa. Try **Café en Azul** for clear-headed drink and chat, **Cambrinus** for a quiet sit-down drink or **Diesel Nacional** for post-industrial mayhem, and you've got a good overview of where the nightlife in this once-quiet city is heading. The more sober headed might want to listen to some excellent and thriving local jazz at **Thelonius** on 20 de Octubre between Fernando Guachalla and Rosendo Gutierrez.

MAPS, EQUIPMENT AND GUIDES
Hiking maps
Bolivia used to produce some of the best topographical maps in South America but, sadly, most of the popular ones are now out of print. There are two Instituto Geográfico Militar (IGM) sales offices. The most accessible is in

Edificio Murillo. It is easy enough to find the front entrance, but map purchasers must go to the back of the building: go up Calle Oruro by the main post office and you will see the blue-and-white Edifico Murillo to the right. Turn left, *away* from the building, and after about 50m make a sharp right on to Calle Rodriguez, which runs uphill at an acute angle, then take the first road (unpaved) to the right. This is Pasaje Juan XXIII. Edificio Murillo and the back entrance to the IGM will be visible once you turn the corner. Open Monday to Friday 09.00–12.00 and 15.00–19.00. The second and larger office is across town at the Estado Mayor, easiest to reach by taxi going to Avenida Saavedra Final 2303; tel/fax: 02 222 9786. Open Monday to Friday, 08.30–16.30. Maps cost Bs42. Take your passport. The IGM has a website at www.igmbolivia.com

Imprenta Don Bosco publishes contour maps by Walter Guzmán Córdova which are fairly accurate although they repeat many of the errors of the IGM maps in terms of trails and the extent of glaciers. The Choro–Takesi–Yunga Cruz map is one of the better ones, showing altitude, vegetation, lakes, mines, water supplies, towns, roads, trails and camping sites. Another privately published map is the *New Map of the Cordillera Real* by Liam O'Brien which provides a useful overview of the *cordillera*. All these maps are normally available at Los Amigos del Libro (several branches in town on the Av 16 de Julio at Edificio Alameda, tel: 02 235 8164) and other good bookshops in La Paz. You can obtain them internationally at good bookshops, and South American Explorers. Contact Liam O'Brien direct if you prefer at O'Brien Cartographics, 3806 Lynn Regis Ct, Fairfax, VA, 22031, USA; email: bahrain@boo.net. The cost is US$10 plus postage.

Buying and renting equipment

Renting equipment is getting easier in La Paz to the extent that you don't have to have all your own gear if you fancy going on a trek. Two-person tents start around US$5 per day, sleeping bags US$3 and cooking stoves US$1.50. You will be required to leave a deposit for rented items.

Camping Caza y Pesca Local 9, ground floor of Handal Centre at the corner of Av Mariscal Santa Cruz and Calle Socabaya; tel/fax: 02 237 9207. Sells Bolivia's widest range of outdoor equipment, and is a good source of gas canisters for Camping Gaz Bleuet stoves.

Condoriri Galeria Sagárnaga, Calle Sagárnaga 343, Local 8; tel: 02 231 9369; fax: 02 241 9735. Offers new and second-hand trekking/climbing equipment; also has hiring and repair services.

Sarañani Calle Sagárnaga and Murillo 189, second floor of the Doryan Shopping Centre, Local 25; tel/fax: 02 237 9806; email: saranani@latinwide.com. Has a wide range of equipment for hire, with bespoke services available – say what you need and they'll give a price.

Andean Summits Local 27 of the Doryan Centre (two doors from Sarañani, see above); tel: 02 231 7497; email: andean_summits@hotmail.com. Specialises in climbing equipment for hire and sale. Can also organise English- and French-speaking guides.

Colibrí Calle Sagárnaga 309; tel: 02 237 1936; fax: 02 235 5043; email: acolibri@ceibo.entelnet.bo; web: www.colibri-adventures.com. Mainly involved with mountaineering but can rent equipment such as camping stoves; also has jeeps which you can hire (with driver) to take you to the trailheads.
Bolivian Journeys Calle Sagárnaga 363, 1st floor; tel: 02 235 7848; email: boljour@ceibo.entelnet.bo; web: www.bolivianjourneys.org. New and second-hand equipment, maps, camping gaz and white gaz available for rent or to buy. Good general information available.

Mountain guides
There are several good guides living in La Paz and a system of recognised guides is being slowly introduced. The best way to contact them is through Alfredo Martínez Delgado of the Club Andino Boliviano (see below). Sr Martínez is one of the most experienced mountaineers in the country. The Club will also recommend drivers if you want to get to any particularly difficult areas.

Erik Nijland recommends the brothers Bernado and Eduardo Guarachi who run a trekking office in La Paz: Andes Expediciones, Plaza Alonso de Mendoza, Edificio Santa Anita, third floor, Local 314; tel: 02 232 0901.

Tour operators
America Tours SRL Av 16 de Julio (El Prado) 1490, Edificio Avenida, Ground Floor No 9 (at the back), across from Monje Campero Cinema; tel: 02 237 4204; fax: 02 231 0023; email: jmiranda@ceibo.entelnet.bo; web: www.america-ecotours.com Good on logistics if you want to get off the beaten track.
Andean Summits Calle Armaza 710, Plaza Adela Zamudio, Sopocachi; Casilla 6976; tel: 02 242 2106; email: info@andeansummits.com; web: www.andeansummits.com. Co-owners José Camarlinghi and Javier Thellaeche offer adventure tours in Bolivia and neighbouring countries. They are experienced mountain guides and I can personally recommend José as one of the best trekking guides in La Paz.
Traveline Expeditions Av Mariscal Santa Cruz 1392, Edificio Camara Nacional De Comercio, Of 6 and 7, basement; Casilla 110, La Paz; tel: 02 233 6599; fax: 02 237 2934; email: info@travelinexpeditions.com; web: www.travelinexpeditions.com. Offers a broad range of travel services and drivers for getting off the beaten track.
Bolivian Journeys (see above) offers climbing, trekking and mountain-bike guided tours.
Paititi Av 6 de Agosto esquina Aspiazu; tel: 02 244 0061; fax: 02 244 0999; email: paititi@ceibo.entelnet.bo; web: www.paitititravel.com. Organises climbing and trekking trips.
TAWA Calle Sagárnaga 161; tel: 02 233 4290; fax: 02 239 1175; email: info@tawa.fr; web: www.tawa.fr. A French-run tour operator with an extensive programme of treks, jeep expeditions and rainforest excursions.
Turismo Balsa Ltda Capitan Ravelo 2104; PO Box 5889, La Paz; tel: 00 591 2 244 0817/244 0620; fax: (00 591) 2 244 0310; email: jjv@turismobalsa.com. Contact Jean-Jacques Valloton. Day hikes in the Cordillera Real, Isla del Sol, and Amboro National Park.

USEFUL ADDRESSES

Ministry of Immigration Av Camacho 1433, opposite Banco Santa Cruz. Open Monday to Friday, 08.30–16.30.

Club Andino Boliviano Calle México 1638; Casilla 1346, La Paz; tel/fax: 02 231 2875 and tel: 02 232 4682; Monday to Friday 09.30–12.30, 15.00–19.00. Has a small library with maps and a meeting place for members. Also some maps for sale and equipment for rent. Pretty casual – opening hours not guaranteed, but a good source of information if you can get there when they are open!

Club de Excursionismo, Andinismo y Camping (Contact via Luis Zapata, tel: 02 279 5596) Meets Wednesdays, 19.30–21.00, Calle Riobamba 502 – call in advance. Members may be able to offer information on hiking, climbing, skiing, mountain biking and even kayaking. Has some equipment to rent.

Vice Ministerio de Turismo 16th floor, Edificio Palacio de Comunicaciones (the post office – a great little plaza overlooking the busy street to sit, hide and people-watch), Av Mariscal Santa Cruz; Casilla 1868; tel: 02 235 8213; fax: 02 237 4630; email: t-mercadeo@mcei.gov.bo; web: www.seebolivia.com. Open Monday to Friday 08.30–12.00 and 14.30–18.30. Offers general tourist and travel information.

Tourist Information on Plaza Estudiante, open Monday to Friday, 08.30–16.30.

Transturín Alfredo Ascarrunz Street 2518, Sopocachi, Casilla 5311; tel: 02 242 2222; fax: 02 241 1922, email: sales@turismo-bolivia.com; web: www.turismo-bolivia.com.

Camera repair Rolando Calla is highly proficient and speaks perfect English. Calle Victor Eduardo 2173 (Parque Triangular); tel: 222 3701; email: rcc@ceibo.entelnet.bo He can also be contacted at Foto Color Capric, Av Mariscal Santa Cruz 1299 esq Colón; tel: 02 237 0134.

EXCURSIONS AND DAY HIKES FROM LA PAZ
Tiwanaku (Tiahuanaco)

Don't miss Tiwanaku, Bolivia's main ruin site. Travellers coming from Peru will note that the people of Tiwanaku were as expert at carving stone as the Incas – some people believe the Inca inherited the skill from the Tiwanakans – and added interest is provided by the enigmatic carved figures and the wonderful Sun Gate. An excellent small visitors' centre gives, with the help of models, a detailed and understandable account of this culture.

On the way to Tiwanaku you pass through the small town of **Laja**, which was the original La Paz, founded in 1548 by Alonzo de Mendoza. The town is dominated by its church, across a large plaza with bizarre-looking giant cacti interrupting the view. The church is usually locked (it is said to have a solid-silver altar) but there are some interesting stone carvings on the outside pillars, including a monkey. The walls, as with all Catholic churches, are decorated with the 14 stations of the cross. The paintings are radical, contemporary and reflect the torments that may have faced a late-20th-century Christ in Latin America. The works go unsigned.

Getting to Tiwanaku on public transport is an easy ride on regular minibuses, departing from the cemetery district and costing about US$1. Alternatively, consider taking a tour with one of the agencies down Calle Sagárnaga for about US$15.

Urmiri

The thermal baths and hotel to the south of La Paz provide an excellent base for day hikes and the chance for a little pampering after a few longer hikes – massage, shiatsu and reflexology are available. In 2002 one of the simple rooms cost about US$18 per person for a two-day, one-night package including food. Day trips are available for US$8, with charges for additional services, leaving at 08.00 and returning at 16.00, giving you about 5½ hours at the hot baths. The hotel is owned by the Hotel Gloria in La Paz – see page 331. Reservations are recommended at weekends.

A day hike near La Paz

This hike will lead you through wonderful countryside with superb views both of the city and of all the major mountains around La Paz. The first part is steep but it becomes easier later. It is a good hike to get accustomed to the altitude if you have plans to do one of the longer ones in the region.

Getting to the trailhead Take a microbus 'Ñ' to its terminus at Ovejuyo. Then take any minibus going to Chasquipampa, from where the walk begins down the road past the police checkpoint.

Route description Immediately after passing the Chasquipampa checkpoint, take a path on your right that descends to a riverbank and then goes steeply upwards in the direction of Collana. On the way up you'll twice cross a road (this is the one on which you'll return later). After 1½ hours you'll find yourself at a minor pass, from where there are good views back to La Paz. At this point avoid the temptation to follow the rolling footpath ahead of you. Instead take the road immediately beneath the pass; this way you'll be able to enjoy the wonderful views of Illimani and the flat-topped Mururata.

Keep to this road (occasionally used by trucks loaded with *campesinos*), ignoring two side-tracks on your left and passing a hill with a radio antenna on your right. After 45 minutes take a track to the right. This is used by vehicles, but probably not more than about one a week, so your hike is unlikely to be spoiled by traffic. The track descends and after half an hour you'll come to a small village called Lloto at 3,900m – the lowest point on the hike. The track turns into a footpath here. As you enter the village, look out for a trail going up slightly to your right; this will take you back to the pass. There are side-tracks, but the main trail is always clear. You will have lovely views of the city of La Paz and Huayna Potosí, and away to your left the valley of the Río Abajo, which drains the city, with Muela del Diablo ('Devil's Tooth') standing as a watchtower over it.

After about an hour on this track you'll come to the pass crossed previously, from where you can retrace your steps to Chasquipampa. The whole walk will take between 4 and 5 hours. It could also be done by mountain bike if you keep to the road.

Alternative route *Take the same bus at the start and simply head across the valley and make towards the Muela del Diablo. If you can't find your way across the network of trails* *simply ask – everyone you meet will know the way. The round trip takes about 4 hours if you don't linger too long at the tooth.*

Chacaltaya

Mount Chacaltaya, located only 1½ hours' drive from La Paz, is an ideal day hike for those wishing to acclimatise for higher hikes, like Huayna Potosí glacier or Illimani. The summit at 5,600m (18,300ft) is a suitable climb for people of varying experience.

Like most glaciers in the Andes, this one is receding rapidly. According to recent studies, the ice pack at Chacaltaya is galloping backwards at a rate of 6m a year. In ten years alone, environmental change has lopped at least 60m off the length and 10m off the width of this glacier. See it while you can.

Practical information

Although this climb is relatively easy, you should remember that you are well above 5,000m, and *soroche*, or altitude sickness, is a real hazard. Do not attempt this hike if you have recently arrived from lower altitudes. The key at this altitude is to take rests even if you don't feel you need them. Deep, controlled breathing also helps.

The lodge (see below) is a good place to see how you fare at higher altitudes during the night. Snacks and hot drinks are available, but if you want something more nourishing you should bring it with you from La Paz.

Beware of the weather, especially between March and June when the heaviest snows fall. Bring waterproof clothing that will keep you warm in sub-zero temperatures.

Getting there Rides can be arranged through most tour operators in La Paz. The Club Andino Boliviano has a clubhouse at the first (false) summit, and provides a bus service to the slope on Saturdays and Sundays, leaving 08.00, costing US$10. Tel/fax: 02 231 2875. Between January and May you can even ski on the world's highest ski slope, US$10 for equipment, US$7 for use of ski lift.

If approaching on foot, you should make your way for 1.5km on a surfaced road in the direction of Lake Titicaca, then turn right at the Bolivian Air-force base (recognised by a long, drab, grey wall with castle-like lookout towers). A wide road, paved at first, later a dirt road (to Milluni and Zongo), will lead you directly towards Chacaltaya. After 14km of easy slogging over open tundra, bear right at the sign indicating the ski resort. The road will take you up the foot of the mountain, past several glacial lakes on the right, then zigzags wildly up until a large white research building appears on the left. Just above this are the old and new lodges of the Club Andino Boliviano; the entrance fee is Bs10.

Route description The approach to the summit is by the ridge just behind the new lodge. On a clear day a spectacular view of Huayna Potosí will unfold at your left. On your right is the glacier and ski-slope, a bit anorexic by North American or European standards, but nevertheless a thrill for anyone willing to go to the trouble of donning skis, although at the time of writing the long-awaited rope tow has yet to be installed. It is only 20 minutes to the first summit at 5,400m where the rubble of an old observatory offers some shelter from the wind. The summit proper is reached by another 200m push up the slope. The Chacaltaya summits offer a panorama of the southern Cordillera Real, the Altiplano as far as Sajama, Lake Titicaca and La Paz. An alternative descent is down the west face to the Milluni road, visible below.

It is interesting to explore the glacial lakes and abandoned mines just below the foot of the glacier. I was surprised to discover a large lizard living among some ruins.

340

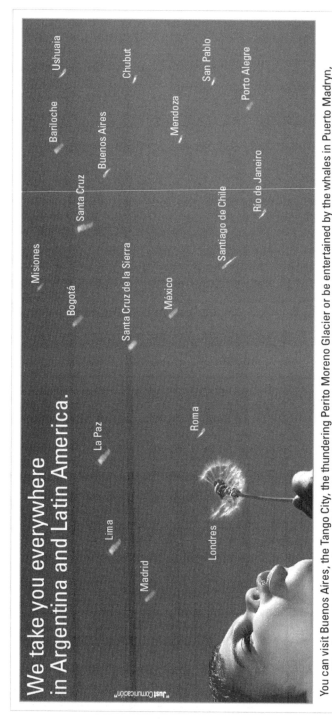

We take you everywhere in Argentina and Latin America.

"Just Comunicación"

Lima
Madrid
La Paz
Londres
Roma
Bogotá
Misiones
Santa Cruz de la Sierra
México
Santiago de Chile
Santa Cruz
Buenos Aires
Bariloche
Ushuaia
Chubut
Mendoza
Río de Janeiro
San Pablo
Porto Alegre

You can visit Buenos Aires, the Tango City, the thundering Perito Moreno Glacier or be entertained by the whales in Puerto Madryn, one of the few protected marine habitats in the world and enjoy many more things which only Argentina can offer you. Travel on Aerolíneas Argentinas and experience our country in a different way.

Consult your Travel Agent or contact us on tel: 020 7494 1001, fax: 020 7494 1002, e-mail: **aerolineas_arg@compuserve.com http://www.aerolineas.com.ar**

AEROLINEAS ARGENTINAS

Lake Titicaca

Few travellers will intentionally omit a visit to Lake Titicaca (Titikaka). It is not hard to understand why this huge lake became the focus for religion and an entire civilization; today's visitors feel exultation at their first sight of this great sapphire-blue body of water contrasting with the dried yellow grasslands which surround it, and the white peaks of the Cordillera Real against a clear blue sky.

With luck, you'll experience a phenomenal sunset as the vast surface of the lake reflects the light of the setting sun acting like a huge planetary mirror.

Most people find the Bolivian side of the lake more appealing than the Peruvian, perhaps because Copacabana is so much nicer a town than Puno.

GETTING THERE

The journey from La Paz to the lake is full of interest. You climb out of the bowl of La Paz to the dusty, bleak Altiplano where the traditional way of life is maintained. Indians herd their sheep and llamas or till the dry soil, and (assuming it's the dry season) the sun shines from a relentlessly blue sky.

Buses make the 3-hour journey between La Paz and Copacabana several times a day starting at 06.30, with the last one leaving at 16.00, Bs14 – although sometimes cheaper Copacabana–La Paz. Two bus offices are located opposite the city cemetery. A radio taxi will take you there as will any bus marked 'cemeterio'.

The first lakeside village is Huarina. As you drive west along the lake shore towards Huatajata you'll see the upmarket **Hotel Titikaka**, near Puerto Perez. This is pretty good value considering it has a heated swimming pool and a sauna, and wonderful views over the lake from the dining room. Bookings for this hotel can be made in La Paz by phone (02 244 0620/0817) or email (hrv@turismobalsa.com). A little further down the road in Huatajata is a comfortable hotel owned by Crillon Tours.

The trip to Copacabana crosses the narrow Strait of Tiquina by ferry, with a rather entertaining journey for the bus at least, and then comes a spectacular drive along an arm of the peninsula and over the headland on a surfaced, twisting road to arrive high above Copacabana with stunning views of the lake and the town. If you're really keen, you can walk west heading out of Tiquina on the southern side of the straits and walk along the coast to Copacabana.

COPACABANA

Copacabana has been a sacred place from earliest times. First the Tiwanaku culture had its sacred sites near here, then the Incas, and now Bolivia's patron saint, the Dark Lady of the Lake, is housed in the church of Moorish design. Her chapel (in the main church) is well worth a visit because of the devotions of the people, but even more rewarding is the Capilla de Velas, to the left-hand side of the church, where people burn candles in support of their prayers. They used to press home their requests to the virgin by writing or drawing on the walls with melted candle wax; much to my regret this practice has now been forbidden. A few years ago there was hardly a bare space left on the walls: houses and trucks were by far the most sought-after gift when I was there, with one worshipper spelling out 'Volvo' to make sure the virgin didn't make a mistake (after all, what do women know about such things?).

Copacabana's inhabitants and non-gringo visitors seem to spend most of their waking and praying hours thinking about trucks. There are drawings of trucks in the chapel and models of trucks that you can carry past the Stations of the Cross hoping they will be changed by divine intervention into something larger and more practical, and, when the miracle has come to pass, there is a ceremony to bless the new truck. On Sundays and holy days there is a *challa*, or blessing, of cars outside the church. A priest officiates, and large quantities of alcohol and smaller quantities of holy water are sloshed or sprinkled over the engine and other vital parts. The vehicles are wonderfully decorated with flowers for the occasion.

Sleeping and eating

In recent years there has been a dramatic increase in the number of people passing through Copacabana and, consequently, large numbers of hotels are opening up. While budget is probably the main guide, using services provided by locals is a good way of making sure the link between travellers and the community is positive.

Hotel Rosario del Lago Tel: 862 2141; fax: 862 2141; email: lrosario@ceibo.entelnet.bo. Probably the best hotel in town, with 28 rooms right on the shore of the lake. Doubles at US$48, a little lower in the low season.

La Cúpula Tel/fax; 862 2029; web: www.hotelcupula.com. A wonderful hotel with top-notch service, minutes' walk from the centre but in its own quiet atmosphere. Offers 17 comfortable rooms, an excellent vegetarian restaurant, use of the kitchen and lounge, and a good bookswap. US$18–24 for a double with private bath.

Hostal Colonial del Lago Tel: 862 2270; web: www.titicacabolivia.com. A popular choice close to the shore with 28 rooms, many having lake views, and a big garden out back. US$4.50 per person.

Emperador A long-time favourite with budget travellers. Small, clean, basic and locally owned. Why popular? Breakfast in bed for Bs7 on those freezing-cold altiplano mornings. Has 18 rooms, US$1.50 per person.

Eating options in Copacabana are numerous and there is absolutely no need to eat in the same place twice. If you're looking to get away from the

crowds, there are a couple of spots on the main square which often get
overlooked.

Communications and banking

An Alf@net internet service has opened round the back of the Hostal Colonial
del Lago (Bs20 per hour) and there is another on the main square next to the
post office. The Entel telephone office is on the eastern side of the church on
the road up to the Emperador.

A branch of Banco Union will generally change travellers' cheques.

Excursions

On the hill behind town are the **Stations of the Cross**; pilgrims climb up
here not only with model trucks, but with model houses or animals, to pray
for a little materialism. It's easy to mock, but when you climb with them and
witness the seriousness and yearning behind the prayers for possessions that
we would take for granted, it is no laughing matter.

Annual pilgrimages to the church from La Paz take place in the week
leading up to Easter. The main Copacabana fiesta takes place August 5–8.

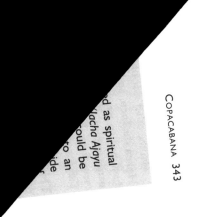

from the lake, is the path leading to the
·nuinely Inca, which is more likely to
han to have been the gallows that the
be aligned to the winter solstice. The
expect a beautiful red sunset – the

?ATA

ına Peninsula and is the nearest land
walk there, along an old Inca road
nstruction of an occasionally-used

....ɔ w ure road out of town and along the lake joining a sporadic procession
of foot travellers and their animals. One and a half hours after Copacabana the
main track goes up a hill but a lower path to the left crosses a meadow with a
stream (bridged by logs), near a house and a shrine, to climb steeply up an
obviously Inca road (stone paved) to rejoin the road again. A tiring but
scenically rewarding short cut. Yampupata is about 2½ hours after the log
bridge. You can camp in Yampupata or probably find lodging in the small
village.

Boats to the Island of the Sun

Although Yampupata is the nearest land to the Island of the Sun, you are likely
to be quoted double the normal rate (about US$8) for a specially hired boat to
take you there.

From Copacabana, where all the tourist boats leave, there are a number
of options. Boats leave at 08.15 and 13.30, going to the south of the island
and stopping at the Inca Stairway for Bs20 return. The morning departure
also goes to the north of the island, calling at Challapampa and including a
20-minute stop at the Island of the Moon on the return leg, for Bs30. If you
are staying on the island you are not allowed to buy a return ticket. The
afternoon service is perfect for hikers since it drops you at Pilkokaina, in the
south of the island, allowing you to walk gently north to spend the night in
or near Challapampa and catch the return boat at about 16.00 the next day
– check for changes to the schedule. Tickets can be bought from agencies in
Copacabana.

THE ISLAND OF THE SUN (ISLA DEL SOL)

According to legend, the Island of the Sun is the birthplace of the sun and
moon. These celestial bodies took human form as the first Inca, Manco Capac,
and his sister-wife Mama Occllo. The cultural significance of the island made
it an important pilgrimage destination and the shrines of a past civilisation
have left several ruins worth exploring.

With a network of trails covering the island and the ready availability of
fresh water, the island is ideal for camping and walking. It is also an excellent
way to acclimatise for higher treks. The three towns on the island are Yumani,

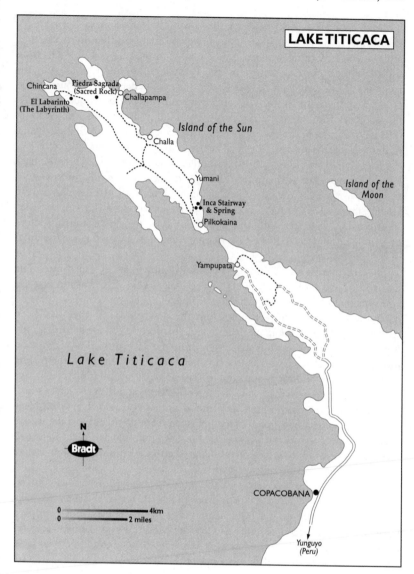

Challa and Challapampa. All have basic hostel accommodation if needed. In Yumani try the long-standing **Inti Wayra** or the new **Posada Isla del Sol** (tel: 7193 4427)

Arriving on the island from Yampupata, or direct from Copacabana, you are dropped at the 300-step Inca Stairway (Escalera del Inca) with the Inca Fountain (Fuente del Inca) running alongside. If camping, you may as well fill your water bottles to avoid having to climb down the next morning. From the top of the stairs, following the path upwards will take you to the small settlement of Yumani with several hostels.

From Yumani a short walk to the southeast leads you to the ruins of Pilkokaina, easily seen when arriving on the island by boat (but not signposted, so easily missed); campers could head directly for the ruins of Pilkokaina from the top of the stairs. Also known as The Temple of the Virgins of the Sun, the ruins are Tiwanaku in style with early Inca influences. The stonework is crude, but there are some well-preserved and interesting adobe doorways moulded in the step-pattern that is typical Tiwanaku and also seen in Ollantaytambo in Peru. Illampu, a *nevado sagrado* to the Incas, is framed by one of the trapezoid windows. You may be asked to pay a small entrance fee.

From Pilkokaina the path continues in a northwesterly direction back towards Yumani, along the spine of the island, taking you to the northwestern tip of the island towards Challapampa. The walk from Yumani to Challapampa takes around 3 hours and provides stunning views of the lake, Peru to the southwest and the Cordillera Real to the northeast. Before descending to the town, it is worth visiting ruins close by on the northern part of the island.

The path leads to Chincana, popularly known as El Labarinto (The Labyrinth), and La Piedra Sagrada (The Sacred Rock). El Labarinto is a site with a name that needs no explanation. Originally pilgrims to the island would enter the complex of tiny rooms from the downslope. As they had been requested to be truthful at an earlier 'gate', this second test ensured that only honest pilgrims successfully emerged from the labyrinth. Travellers then move on to La Piedra Sagrada (in the direction of Challapampa), the resting home of the sun and the moon, and the last point on the pilgrimage.

Challapampa is a small town to the east of Piedra Sagrada. A few small stores provide refreshments and basic accommodation is available. The town has a museum housing a range of artefacts collected from the island and the waters nearby. Underwater archaeology carried out by archaeologist Johan Reinhard recovered many stone boxes containing gold effigies from the shallow waters off the northwestern tip of the island.

From Challapampa a path follows the shoreline, taking you back to Yumani. Rising along the cliff edge, the path drops to pass through the town of Challa before rising again to join the main island path. Tourist boats stop at Challapampa on the way to the Island of the Moon. If you want to camp on the island it is possible to negotiate a lift, but you will need to take all your food with you as stores have only basic supplies.

The Cordillera Real

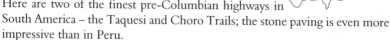

The 150km of Bolivia's Cordillera Real stretch from the Sorata Valley to Río La Paz (Río Choqueyapu), providing a splendid backdrop for the world's highest capital city. There are six peaks over 6,000m, and many more above the 5,000m mark. This mountain range is perfect for backpacking, offering days of hiking above the treeline with snow-capped mountains appearing round almost every bend, and steep descents to the tropical vegetation of the Yungas. Here are two of the finest pre-Columbian highways in South America – the Taquesi and Choro Trails; the stone paving is even more impressive than in Peru.

All the trails described in this section start within a day's journey of La Paz, and a couple are only a few hours away. The trails are listed in order on the Cordillera heading west to east. There is no problem acclimatising for the hikes: a few days' sightseeing in La Paz will take care of that. Most of the trails can be done in reverse if you prefer going uphill to downhill (and it is a serious option for those getting fit and acclimatised for a mountaineering expedition).

CONDORIRI CIRCUIT

The Condoriri group of mountains is well known to climbers as offering some of the best scenery in Bolivia and plenty of peaks to climb, varying from very easy to extremely difficult.

For hikers and backpackers there is a lovely natural lake where you can stay to enjoy the scenery, and a return route which takes you to the Zongo area and provides possible links with other treks.

Getting there The base camp for Condoriri, 5,648m, is easily reached. Take any transport in the direction of Lake Titicaca and get off at the first village, some 10–15km beyond the *tranca* (toll-gate). You will see a dirt road leading off to the right.

Route description Follow the dirt road to the top rim of a broad river gorge. Ask the villagers for Tuni-Condoriri, the name of the lake at the foot of Condoriri mountain. You may get a lift but otherwise it is a dull, 21km walk along a jeep track towards Tuni, a small village where the road ends at a gate, just below the lake (reservoir). There are splendid views of Huayna Potosí from here. Climb the dyke towards the house or follow the road after the fence and you will see an emerald-green lake. Keeping the lake to your right, walk along its shores until you come to a high-water drainage system. Leave the lake at this point and follow the road until you come to a canal that feeds into the lake. The road follows this canal upwards, giving you beautiful views of Condoriri, named as such because it resembles a condor with outstretched wings.

One hour after the fence you will reach the end of the canal and of the road. Climb slightly uphill, following the left bank of the river, to a path some 100m above the stream. Condoriri will be ahead of you. The first lake you come to is small, with a tiny island in the middle of it. Continue to the big lake, Laguna Condoriri, which is about 1½ hours from the water project. This is an ideal base for exploring the area.

One of the 'easy' peaks is El Diente (5,200m) but this still needs proper equipment (crampons and rope) and glacier experience. The mountain lies at the far end of the valley, to the right of Condoriri.

Alternative routes back *Looking towards the mountain group, and the peak known as Ilusión, you will see a huge, rocky mountain, the Aguja Negra (Black Needle). Climb the hill to the right of this peak, crossing beneath the glacier at the foot of Aguja Negra, to climb to the top of the pass. From here you can see the reservoir you passed on your way up and can join the jeep track back to the main road.*

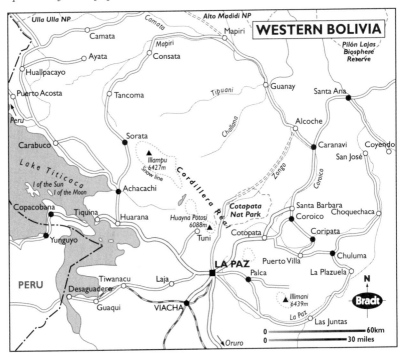

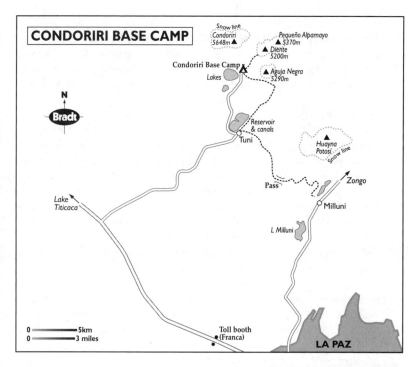

A more scenic and adventurous route back is to take the old mining road from the village of Tuni and follow it for 24km to Milluni, between Huayna Potosí and Chacaltaya. The road is rarely used these days and offers spectacular views of Huayna Potosí and other peaks. There is a pass half way, but it is not a strenuous climb. At the main road turn left for Huayna Potosí (or its refugio) or right if you want to head back to La Paz. By taking this route you are well placed to do a variety of treks or climbs in the Zongo area.

THE ZONGO VALLEY

The Zongo Valley provides an alternative, yet not necessarily easy, route to the North and South Yungas. As with all journeys through these valleys east of the Andes, you experience rapid and surprising changes in climate and vegetation. Just below the pass you might see small herds of llamas grazing on esparto grass and glaciers spilling over high cliff edges; then slightly lower down you will notice a few shrubs and trees covered with moss, which will give way to forest and, eventually, subtropical broad-leaved plants and hardwood trees. It's hard to find a more dramatic change in scenery in such a short distance.

Another bonus of this easy walk is the well-set-up boy-scout camp, which is available for use by backpackers (with a reservation).

Practical information If transportation can be found to La Cumbre anyone in shape can walk down to the scout camp in a long day – it's

MOUNTAIN CLIMBING FOR NON-MOUNTAINEERS

Bolivia has several peaks over 5,000m which can safely be climbed with no mountaineering experience. However, current conditions should always be checked before you set off and you should be accompanied by a reliable guide.

Huayna Potosí (6,094m)

This is one of the few peaks in South America over 6,000m which can be climbed by fit people with no technical mountaineering experience. The owner of the Refugio Huayna Potosí, Dr Hugo Berrios (contact the Hotel Continental in La Paz – see page 332), offers all-inclusive packages, with guides, porters, all equipment and food, and transport from La Paz to the *refugio*, for about US$160 per person. You can also contact specialist tour operators in La Paz (see page 335). The trip is done in three days, building in some training on how to use an ice axe and crampons.

Even experienced, properly equipped mountaineers are advised to take a guide and not to rely on the brief directions below.

On reaching the dam from Milluni, cross it and follow an aqueduct to a small reservoir from where the route goes up the spine of a moraine, eventually joining a rocky ridge. Pick your way up this ridge to the snow plateau called Campamento Argentino at 5,500m, where you should make your base camp. This should take one day. High winds are sometimes a problem here. Next morning an early start is essential. The route goes up the glacier towards the back wall of the basin ahead, then heads up towards the ridge on the right. Keep well to the right here to avoid crevasses. On reaching the ridge, follow it round to the left. The final part is steep.

It takes about 4 hours to reach the summit from Campamento Argentino and 2 hours to return. Dehydration is a real danger at this altitude; you should carry more than a litre of water per person for the ascent from Campamento Argentino.

downhill all the way, if your knees like that sort of thing. If you wish to continue on down to Bella Vista, you should tag on another 3–4 days from the last hydro station.

This area generally receives a lot of precipitation, so pack to stay dry. After the last station there are no villages, so be prepared with extra food. Water is available in abundance all the way down the valley.

Getting to the trailhead The approach to the valley is the same as going to Zongo Lake and the beginning of the trailhead to the Cumbre, except you continue along the well-reinforced and maintained road zigzagging dizzily down (you drop over 1,500m in a few kilometres) through a valley of waterfalls, rivers and hydro-electric stations.

Route description Simply follow the road, keeping right at any branches (I believe there are two) and continue steadily down past the hydro-electric

Japu Japuni (5,088m)

We wanted to climb a 5,000m peak, and found that this was possible starting from the 4,880m pass on the first day of the Zongo-to-La Cumbre hike. Follow the rocky ridge north of the col, keeping slightly to the right, and about a third of the way up you'll find a large cairn. The summit (reached in about 1 hour from the pass) affords an incredible view of the Cordillera beyond Huayna Potosí. The ascent doesn't require any special equipment or climbing skills, but we wouldn't recommend it in bad weather as there are cliffs below the ridge.

Huiata (5,092m)

We started from Achura, taking the steep path going north up the valley side past Waca Kunca and following the Zongo route in reverse up the wide, gentle Illampu valley. There are several excellent camping sites along the river as far as the 4,100m contour below Jishka Telata; we made our 'base camp' here.

The next day we left the main trail, continuing southwestwards up the Illampu, first on its north side, then crossing on a small footbridge before passing some big boulders and eventually climbing up the left-hand of two tributaries to a flat area southeast of Huiata at about 4,600m. From here we headed straight for the steep buttress of the lower, eastern part of the mountain. The path went to the right of this, giving a splendid view of the topaz-green waters of Laguna Chaco Kkota with the Telata glacier behind.

Keeping our elevation above the lake, we headed due west up the valley beyond, heading to the left (south) of the peak ahead, climbing a steep snowfield to a ridge, then gaining the summit from the rear (west) side.

Huiata gives excellent views of Huayna Potosí, the Telata massif, the Huarinilla valley towards the Yungas, and much more. It is easily climbed by 'ordinary' trekkers with no special equipment.

stations including Zongo, Botijlaca and Cuticucho. After the Santa Rosa station you will pass by an outdoor cement football court on your right; then, further down, a small school on your left. Just below these, to the right of the road, is a large open area of grass with a small building (bathrooms) and a thatched gazebo. This is the scout camp, established several years ago for the sole purpose of camping. Unfortunately the camp has fallen into disrepair, but even if the showers are no longer available, there are plenty of spots at the camp to pitch a tent, and a revitalising river rushes past just metres away. Here you might try your luck at trout fishing.

The Zongo, like each of the Yungas valleys, is a micro-ecosystem and you have a good chance of sighting plant- or bird-life that can only be found in these valleys.

Perhaps one of the most interesting activities in the area is to explore the numerous maintenance trails that lead both east and west into the mountains from the River Zongo at the base of the valley. One of these trails begins after crossing a narrow iron bridge just opposite the scout camp and leads you up along a steep, forested hillside, then across a large steel pipe and up the spine from where you can catch glimpses of the jungle valleys far below. Be careful: when it is rainy the pipes are very slippery. If you don't mind heights and are sure-footed, it's a thrill to follow the aqueduct that runs from Planta Harca along the side of a cliff to a village beside the Río Yohuilaque. Higher up in the valley there are canals cutting through the rock in long tunnels that are worth a look.

After the last hydro station (Planta Huaji) a rough trail leads farther down the valley until it meets with the Río Coroico. This portion of the hike might take 2–3 days, depending on the weather. I'm told a machete is indispensable here. Once you arrive at the Río Coroico, follow the path going left for several kilometres until you come to the village of Bella Vista. Here you can cross over to the town of Alcoche where transportation back to La Paz, or deeper into the lowlands, can be found.

ZONGO TO LA CUMBRE OR COROICO

This is a high-altitude walk, partly along a good trail and partly cross-country, taking you parallel to the glaciers of Huayna Potosí (6,088m), past a series of lakes, and connecting with the La Cumbre–Coroico trail. Being so close to the peaks, you may feel an urge to climb one of them. I've included three possibilities in the box on pages 350–1.

This was one of those happy hikes discovered accidentally when we were leafing through the topographical maps at the IGM while waiting for our order. The *Milluni* sheet caught our eye, covered in evocative blue contour lines, and we soon picked out a possible trail. As it turned out, this could only be followed part of the way, but the subsequent cross-country scramble was both exciting and beautiful. There are plenty of other options for well-prepared and adventurous backpackers.

Altitude	Between 4,880m and 3,900m
Rating	Difficult, with cross-country stretches
Timing	3 to 5 days
Maps	IGM sheet *Milluni* (5945 II). 1:50,000

Conditions/what to take The first two nights will be bitterly cold. Bring hat, gloves, and all the warm clothes you've got. You'll also need tough boots and a compass for the cross-country section. There is no habitation before Achura, and precious little to buy there, so stock up well with provisions.

Accommodation The **Refugio Huayna Potosí**, situated to the east of Laguna Zongo, opened early in 1995 to provide mountain climbers and trekkers with a warm place to stay. There is hot water and a log fire, US$10 per person. To book contact the Hotel Continental – see page 332. A cook can be provided if requested in advance.

Getting to the trailhead If there's a group of you, a taxi is the easiest option. Alternatively, the Hotel Continental, La Paz, can arrange transport to the *refugio* during the peak season with a daily service at 10.00, US$10. Outside these months transport is US$60 for up to six people. A cheaper alternative is to catch the bus to Zongo which leaves at 06.00 every morning from Plaza Ballivián in El Alto.

Route description Follow the Zongo road north as it continues down the valley in a series of zigzags. After 2km, just after the second hairpin bend, your trail leads off to the right and across a small stream. The path is faint at times, disappearing altogether across open pasture, but you should have little difficulty following it along the contours of the mountain, above and parallel to the valley road. The views of Huayna Potosí are splendid, and soon the snowy peak of Telata comes into view.

After 1½ hours you'll pass a small lake, and 3 or 4 hours after leaving the road the path swings round a lower peak called Chekapa and heads towards an unnamed pass at 4,880m. Beyond the pass is a well-watered valley with a series of dammed lakes, part of another hydro-electric scheme. There's good camping all along this valley.

From the dam at the first lake, continue east to the second lake, taking a path along the south shore and uphill towards Laguna Telata, whose dam is just visible. There are marvellous views of the dramatic snow-covered peak called Ilampu on the IGM map, but better known as Tiquimani to avoid confusion with Illampu in another part of the Cordillera. The last possible camping places for several hours are near this lake, either below the dam or at the far shore. This is where the cross-country stretch begins. (For a poor-weather alternative, see below.)

Walk across the dam and make your way over rocks and cliffs, guided by cairns, above the northern shore of the lake. This involves scrambling but no technical climbing. At the eastern end of the lake, start up the scree slope towards the lowest point on the shoulder above you to your left (northeast). This climb, again guided by cairns, isn't difficult and will take about an hour.

From the top you'll see three lakes and a shoulder to your right. From this shoulder you should make your way down towards the southeast and over a wall, then pick up a very faint path to the right of a stonefall. Continue steeply downhill to a swampy area studded with Andean gentians. Go down to the valley bottom and the river. As you veer east beneath the crags of Jishka Telata you'll pass a large cave beneath some monstrous fallen boulders – an excellent shelter if the weather is bad. Continue to follow the river on its left bank until the trail at last asserts itself and you can follow it easily to a *hacienda*, Sanja Pampa, and the bridge beyond.

After crossing the river you'll pass through a scatter of houses and up a steep but good path skirting round the end of a ridge called Waca Kunca. As it levels out, the trail passes several ponds, crosses a stream, then heads south, descending steeply before turning southwest to the village of Achura (Chucura). There's a bridge across the river and it is a short climb to reach the main trail just above the village.

Here you must make the decision either to go up to La Cumbre, about 6 hours away, or to continue down to Coroico which will take you 2 more days.

Poor-weather alternative *This is rather longer than my recommended route, with a bit more climbing, but may be preferable in bad conditions as it stays slightly lower.*

After coming down from the first pass, follow the path which goes round the western shore of the first lake to the dam, and then descends very steeply to the lower lake, which the IGM map describes as Laguna Kkota Khuchu. Should you lose the path, look for the bridge over the aqueduct before the steep part.

A well-used trail follows the northern shore of the lower lake before cutting down to join the river below the dam. Once beside this river, follow it for 10 minutes, and where it starts to turn northeast strike out due east across the hillside below steep slabs until you gain the next valley.

A faint path will be found running south up the near side of this valley. Ascending steeply, it soon passes to the right (west) of a lake, and – more obvious now – climbs to a second lake where there are camping possibilities, surrounded by steep slopes. Continuing south, it climbs another 150m to cross a pass at about 4,700m, before descending to the west of Jishka Telata where you rejoin the route described above.

LA CUMBRE TO COROICO

This is another of those hikes which evoke a pleasing feeling of nostalgia. It was my first in Bolivia, and our information in 1973 was vague. An American told us that a drunken member of the Costa Rican National Orchestra had told him that if he went to a big 'Jesus cross' near La Paz and followed its outstretched left hand, he would find an Inca trail that led into the jungle. The tourist-office staff were amused – and bemused – at the idea of anyone wanting to walk into the Yungas, and had never heard of an Inca trail – or any trail, come to that. However, they did know where there was a statue of Jesus. We had a wonderful and serendipitous hike, and beyond Achura (where I slept in a thatched building, under a poncho on a pile of potatoes because my sleeping bag had been stolen) we came across an 'Inca' road so amazing in its engineering that by the time we'd reached Coroico we'd decided to write a book and share this find with others.

The hike, now well known, takes you from a snow-covered 4,850m pass down to subtropical river valleys full of parakeets, blue *morpho* butterflies, flowers and wild strawberries, and ends in hot citrus groves at just over 1,500m. The first part is easy, thanks to pre-Inca roadbuilders, but towards the end it may be overgrown and difficult to follow. Tall backpackers may find that their pack keeps getting entangled in the vegetation. More seriously, be warned that the short cuts which have been forged between the switchbacks tend to be impossibly slippery and are best avoided.

You'll see plenty of llamas grazing on the first day, and will probably encounter them being used as pack animals on the trail. Stand aside and let them pass.

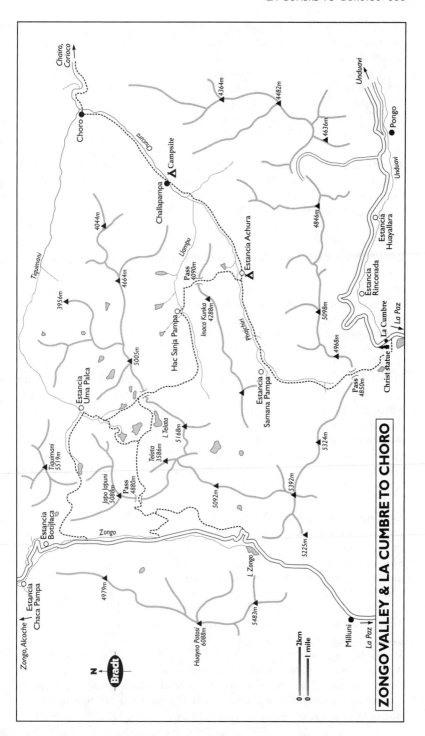

ZONGO VALLEY & LA CUMBRE TO CHORO

Distance	About 70km
Altitude	Between 4,850m and 1,300m
Rating	Moderate
Timing	4 days
Maps	IGM sheets *Milluni* (5945 II) and *Unduavi* (6045 III)

Conditions/what to take Prepare for one cold night and several warm ones. 'Avoid the rainy season (November to May) unless you like water. You'll be thoroughly soaked every hour of the day and night. Prepare as if for a white-water expedition,' warns one reader. Another adds: 'It's essential to have thin pants (trousers) for the last day, as it will be hot, the trail may be overgrown and there'll be prickly plants and biting insects.' At La Cumbre, on the other hand (whatever the season), you may encounter freezing rain, snow, hail and wind. To avoid a miserable start to your walk, dress appropriately before leaving La Paz.

You can camp at several spots along the trail and there is now basic lodging available in Challapampa and Achura.

Stock up with provisions in La Paz; although you can buy *refrescos* and beer at several points along the trail the first shops with any real supplies will not be found until Chairo. (Fresh bread can be bought in the street in Villa Fátima just before departure.) One couple suggests taking some extra food to share with the *campesinos*. 'They were some of the most welcoming, gracious hosts we've met in South America; and for the favour of being invited in out of the rain it's nice to split a pot of soup with them, or a *mate de coca*. Bread is much asked for. Most live outside the economic system and their stomachs matter more to them than their pockets.' Another essential is insect repellent. Also a machete might be useful if the trail is overgrown. But only bring one if you know how to use it; accidentally cutting off your leg on this trail would be inconvenient.

Getting to the trailhead Buses leave La Paz for the Yungas from 07.00 onwards from Avenida de las Américas 344, Villa Fátima. The short journey (about an hour) can also easily be done by one of the trucks which leave from a little higher up Avenida de las Américas throughout the day. It's best to make as early a start as possible, since mist tends to start billowing over the pass soon after midday, obscuring the view.

A special feature of this road is the dogs which stand like sentinels along it. I first noticed them in 1974, and have seen them (or their descendants) on every subsequent visit. I used to think they were just hanging around for scraps thrown from the trucks, but a Bolivian friend has since told me that they are the Guardians of the Cordillera Real. Locals placate the *achachilas* (mountain spirits) by feeding the dogs. Certainly when you see these patient figures, motionless but watchful in the swirling snow, it's easy to believe in the power of mountain spirits.

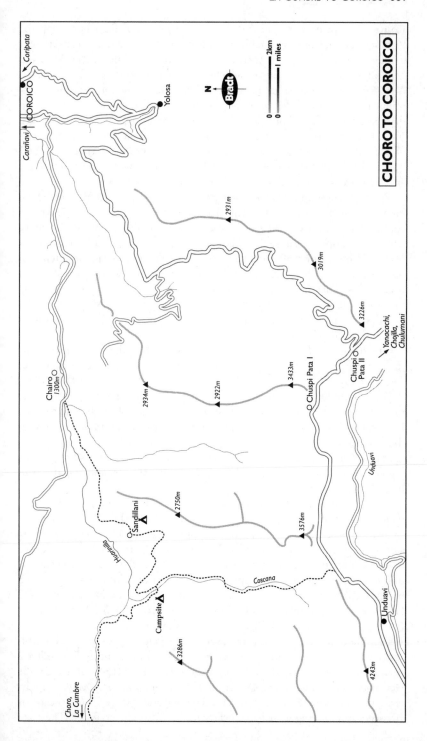

Route description La Cumbre ('The Summit') is not a village, but simply the highest point (4,725m) on the bleak mountain road before it begins its descent to the Yungas. A statue of Christ the Redeemer faces north, his left hand helpfully pointing out the trail, which heads west towards some small lakes. After recent snow you should have no difficulty following the foot- and hoof-prints. If in doubt take the most obvious vehicle track, past one largish lake and then between two small ones, before veering north up a scree slope to the pass. In clear weather you can see the stone cairn at the top of the pass. Yellow splashes of paint also indicate the way. The climb to this point (4,850m) takes about 1 hour. When you reach the *apacheta*, you'll be rewarded with a spectacular view and the knowledge that it's downhill most of the rest of the way.

The trail is now very clear, dropping steeply down a *quebrada* (ravine), which broadens out after joining the main river (Río Phajchiri) allowing the path to continue more gently to the small village of Achura (also known as Chucura). There are campsites below the village and basic lodging is available, which is reached about 4 hours after the pass. The villagers certainly take an interest in backpackers; I've had reports of hostility and robbery but also of great friendliness. This may be something to do with the way hikers are beginning to distort the local economy. Readers have told of being asked for sweets, watches and money. Rather than camp near the village it is better to push on for about another hour.

One thing you *shouldn't* expect at Achura is much in the way of provisions for sale. Steve Newman warns: 'It took us 1½ hours to buy 2lbs of potatoes and three eggs!'

Beyond Achura the 'Inca' road really comes into its own, with some marvellous paving and low steps often arranged in a fan shape around a curve. It's just over an hour down to Challapampa – the last real camping option for the first day.

Starting on what is a long second day, Choro is some 2 hours beyond this point. After about 4km of paved track you reach the treeline and the path becomes narrower.

At Choro, where several houses have been abandoned, there is a river over which a variety of bridges have served their time. In 1990 Dr Nizam Mamode wrote: 'A *campesino* pointed to a rather improbable strand of wire stretching across a cascade of white foam. I laughed, perhaps a little nervously, at the idea of my 12½ stones plus loaded rucksack crossing in this manner, but a few minutes later found myself wrapped in a piece of old cloth, hanging from a pulley and dragging myself over with white knuckles, to the amusement of the family watching from the bank.' Now this arrangement has been replaced (perhaps disappointingly) by a sturdy wooden bridge.

From here on you should carry water, as the supply is erratic. The trail is also harder to follow and may be overgrown. The next campsite is another 2 hours away at San Francisco – about one hour before the Río Coscapa. On the way you'll encounter ravines, each one containing a useful water supply, usually in the form of an icy torrent. The biggest of these, Río Coscapa, is crossed by an exciting suspension bridge set in a magnificent gorge. There are several possible campsites but most are some distance from water so you will need to be well prepared.

About 5 hours from Choro, near a place called Bella Vista, lives the Japanese man Tamiji Hanamura who has become quite famous among backpackers. He made his home here many years ago, and you'll have no difficulty recognising the rose-covered house, La Casa Sandillani. Tamiji has collected postcards from all over the world. The only fee he asks of campers is that you sign his visitors' book, but a postcard would no doubt be appreciated as well. Most people camp at Tamiji's.

The final 2-hour stretch to Chairo (1,300m) is steep and badly eroded towards the end, but you'll find the villagers very friendly, and the two stores offer bread, canned goods and beer. There are occasional trucks to Yolosa and Coroico; otherwise it's a dusty 4 or 5 hours' walk through coffee, citrus and banana plantations.

By the time you read this the new road from Coroico may well have reached Chairo. Nevertheless, a path will probably continue to take the most direct route through the citrus groves, allowing you to complete the journey to your well-earned rest in Coroico on foot. There will be plenty of people around to ask the way.

Some sturdy hikers opt to do the trail in reverse, slogging up 3,200m to La Cumbre. Jürgen Stock warns that the first section between Estancia Sandillani and Río Coscapa is particularly tricky because there are many local trails running down to the Río Huarinilla and up into the surrounding hills. You may want to take a guide for the first day.

Coroico and getting back If you are in a hurry you can skip Coroico altogether, and take a truck from the new road back to La Paz. That would be a pity, however, since Coroico is a very pretty subtropical town (1,525m), with several hotels and nothing much to do except relax after your exertions.

Flota Yungueña buses leave for La Paz at 07.00 most days, from the street to the right of the church. However, they are often booked up several days in advance.

Trucks also make the journey; or you can take a small truck from just below the square to Yolosa, and then change to the (more frequent) trucks coming up from Caranavi.

The 96km road to La Paz meets the one from Chojlla at Unduavi. Until then it's little more than a track, winding under waterfalls (have your rain gear ready if you are travelling by truck!) and alongside vertical cliffs. Its impact on impressionable travellers is heightened by the many roadside crosses commemorating those who have gone over the edge.

THE LLAMA TRAIL TO COROICO

Jonathon Exley

This is an alternative to the La Cumbre to Coroico (via Choro) trail just described. For the first half of the trek it follows llama trails across an alpine plateau and through a valley to a pass at 5,000m, then down to meet the Choro trail via an overgrown and disused pre-Columbian road and past some ruins.

This trail strays away from popular routes and should only be attempted by groups with experience in navigation and route-finding. To this end I have given a map reference (map number followed by a six-digit figure; the first three digits are the east grid reference and the last three are the north grid reference).

Conditions/what to take The first couple of nights are spent at altitudes of 4,800m and 4,400m: you need a very warm sleeping bag. A compass is useful and on Day 5 a machete would be handy. Buy it in La Paz on Calle Isaac Tamayo for about Bs15; spend a further Bs6 having it sharpened (look for one of the men who sharpen knives on the street).

Getting to the trailhead The trail starts above the hill from the village of Tapacaya (6044 III: 095713) just off the road to Ventilla.

Catch the Ventilla/Bolsa Negra bus from La Paz as though heading for the Taquesi trail (see page 364), but ask the driver to let you off at Tapacaya. Since in his mind all gringos want to go to Ventilla he'll probably think you're confused and take you there anyway. So keep track of where you are on the map and yell when you want to get off.

Altitude	Between 5,020m and 1,525m
Rating	Difficult, with some bush-whacking and a very high pass.
Timing	6 to 7 days but can be broken at Unduavi for La Paz.
Maps	IGM 1:50,000 series: *Palca* (6044 III), *Chojlla* (6044 IV) and *Unduavi* (6045 III)

Route description

Day 1 The turn-off to Tapacaya is marked with a concrete sign on the left of the road. Walk along this road for a short way, keeping right, until you can see the village down the hill. Depending on whether the bus broke down en route or if it left on time, you may not get to any water until tomorrow so it is wise to fill up from the village stream.

The trail goes up the ridge to your left as you look down towards the village. The ridge is easy to follow and there are large cairns until Cerro Achachicala where the trail moves north across Putu Pampa and the cairns head west. Continue across Sucul Pampa, keeping to the ridge on the east side, towards the lake at 6044 IV: 092780.

Groups of llamas graze on this plateau, and at 4,800m there are good views of Illimani and La Paz. It is also very cold at night – be sure to pitch camp and eat dinner before the sun touches the horizon. Expect ice on your sleeping bag in the morning.

Try to pitch your tent with the opening towards La Paz for a wonderful view of the city lights at night.

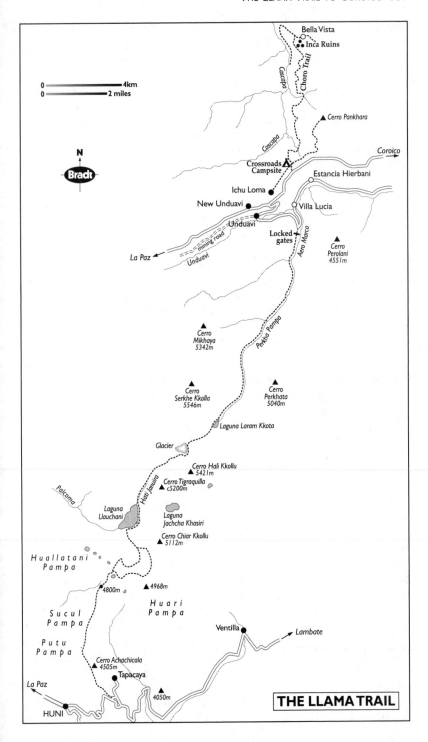

THE LLAMA TRAIL

Day 2 Expect a late start – there is absolutely no point getting up until the sun has hit your tent and started to defrost everything. The llama trail continues northeast to the valley of the Río Palcoma where it drops 500m down a near vertical scree slope to the valley floor. You would have to be mad to go down this scree slope yourself; even the locals consider it dangerous. Instead it is much safer to move east to the head of the valley and sidle down from there. There appears to be a faint track from the saddle just above the lake where you camped going northeast and around the watershed, crossing over into the valley head just south of Cerro Chiar Kkollu (at 6044 IV: 113790).

Day 3 Continue north up the Río Hati Jahuira, past the remains of an old village, to the pass at 5,020m. This pass is topped with a permanent snow cap, but there is an indistinct path around it on the right, from about 4,800m. I built cairns, but they may not still be there.

From this pass you enter a beautiful valley with tall and steep walls, waterfalls cascading down the sides and the occasional condor gliding up in the stratosphere. A path leads down the scree on the left from the pass. The path disappears and shortly you come to a flat grassy area that is too wet for camping. Scramble downriver to Laguna Laram Kkota where there is dry ground. It is best not to camp any lower than here as the rest of the valley appears to be used as a llama farm and your presence may not be too welcome.

Day 4 The first part of the day involves a bit of scrambling down rocks until the valley flattens out to llama pastures on which the walking is very easy. A track soon makes itself evident, eventually turning into a stone paved road, possibly pre-Columbian. There is a mine, Mina Rosario, high in the hills on the eastern side, and supposedly the trail was the access road.

The valley becomes more and more beautiful, with some ideal picnic and sunbathing spots. However, try not to call attention to yourselves from the farm owners.

The track follows the river down the valley past farm buildings, the weather warming up as you approach the Yungas. The trail passes a large farmhouse-looking building on the opposite side of the river, where a hysterical dog resides, and then connects with a shingle road to the valley mouth, near which there is a small bunch of buildings with a touristic look to them and a sign over the (locked) gate reading Complejo Turistico Incahuasi. This organisation produces alpaca sweaters from the animals which graze in the area. The owner, Billy Borth, does not mind backpackers passing through his land and is happy to demonstrate the process of shearing the alpacas. Phone 235 8515 or 236 6641 if you have a particular interest in this.

From the gate you can try walking or hitching down the road to Villa Santa Lucia near the joining of the Ríos Acero Marca and Unduavi (6045 III: 187969). This is easily identified by the tall chimney built by the Spanish for a smelter. The villa used to be an Inca staging house that was converted by the Spanish into a smelter for silver from nearby mines, such as Mina Rosario. It has been partially damaged by the Río Unduavi cutting into one side and is now owned by an engineer in La Paz who arranges for groups of paying tourists to stay there from time to time.

If the villa is not being used the caretaker may let you camp in the patio if you line his pockets with silver – about Bs5 per person should do. This is a nice place to stay and rest for a day. If the caretaker won't take you, or if you can't be bothered, hitch a ride up the road to Unduavi, a grubby police checkpoint and fast-food stop on the road to Coroico where you can stock up on food and petrol for your stove. Expect to pay higher prices than in La Paz. All traffic stops here so it is a good place to hitch from. If you want to head back to La Paz there are regular minibuses passing.

Catch a ride for about 2.5km along the road to Coroico to the trail going up the hill at 6045 III: 185967. The trail is quite visible going diagonally up the hill when you are on the opposite side of the valley from the stream coming down from Cerro Perolani. Follow the track up, hopping across a fence or two, to the saddle. The track will have turned into a pre-Columbian road by this time and at the saddle there is a crossroads with pre-Columbian roads going west, northeast, south and southwest.

The southwest path goes toward Unduavi but gets lost in tangled scrub just south of Ichu Loma. The south path, which leads down to the Unduavi–Coroico road, probably continued down to Villa Santa Lucia at one time but I haven't been able to find it.

The northeast path continues along the ridge tops, past a couple more sinkholes, down to Cerro Pankhara where I stopped following it. The Japanese man at Sandillani walked this road in the 1960s and said that it leads to Coroico, probably connecting with the trail marked on the map at 6045 III: 234040. The west road goes down to Bella Vista on the Choro Trail, but not how it is marked on the IGM map. This is a good place to camp, although it's damp. Water can be obtained from the large sinkhole just downhill toward the Unduavi road. There are a couple of stepping-stones on the opposite side from the path to get past the weeds at the edge. This wee lake is a definite biological hazard – treat the water!

Day 5 This day will be quite hard, so start early. Take the west road down the ridge towards Río Coscapa. This was once the main route to Coroico but now is used only occasionally by the local farmers who clear a path for themselves every time. If someone has recently used the path it will be moderately easy to follow; if not, it will be difficult. A machete would be useful here.

About a third of the way down the ridge, the road levels off and deviates from the trail marked on the IGM map, following the eastern side of the valley. The bush quickly becomes dense, and at times quite hard to move through as the path follows a gentle gradient with a couple of broken bridges. Keep your water bottles topped up as the last section of the road is dry.

To keep you company there are large yellow-and-black-striped flies that buzz around you, giving a nasty bite when they land. Curiously they get more excited the more infuriated you become. Insect repellent does not work; the only thing to do is to sit down and cool off.

The road eventually wraps around a sharp ridge at about 6045 III: 185052, where the locals usually bash down the ridge to the Choro Trail. However, if you persevere along the road through some particularly tangled bush, you will arrive at a clearing with some Inca ruins. Presumably a staging house. Continuing along the road is made near impossible by tangled spiky plants, but the road comes out in a vegetable patch in Bella Vista near a *tienda* that bakes bread. You are still some distance from Sandillani, so is best to ask the people at the *tienda* if you can camp there. Alternatively you can share the disused hut in the Inca ruins with the bats that now live there.

Day 6 You are now on the Choro Trail. Easy walking to Coroico.

THE TAQUESI (TAKESI) TRAIL

This is often called an Inca road, but was in fact almost certainly constructed before the Incas conquered the region. Whichever culture was responsible, we can admire the perfection of the work and its underlying engineering principles. The paved section covers half the trail, about 20km, and you'll see all the classic features of pre-Columbian road construction: stone paving, steps, drainage canals and retaining walls.

The walk takes only two days, but the variety of scenery is astonishing, so you might want to go a little slower and take three. From swirling snow on the 4,650m pass, you drop down to the treeline and through incredibly lush vegetation to the humid rainforest below the Chojlla mine. Above the trees the colours are soft and muted: green-ochre hills, grey stones, brown llamas. In the Yungas it's steamy-hot and bright with butterflies, flowers, green leaves and sparkling blue rivers.

The two main villages along the upper part of the trail, Choquekota and Taquesi, pursue a way of life unchanged for centuries: men herding llamas, making rope or harvesting crops; women trampling *chuños* and preparing the next meal. Below the treeline, however, *mestizos* mix traditional customs with new innovations. Women still sit weaving outside their homes, but synthetic yarn is in vogue and bright cotton dresses replace the Indian homespun.

At its beginning and end the walk is served by two spectacular and contrasting bus journeys. To reach the trailhead you drive through a lunar landscape of eroded 'badlands' offering a display of brown, red, orange and yellow tones, unrelieved by any green. But the return trip from the Yungas is perhaps the most beautiful road of its kind in South America. It is cut into the mountainside and runs parallel to a river for much of the way. Luxuriant vegetation hangs from cliffs jutting over the road as it winds up to the bleak Altiplano.

Fundacion Pueblo Casilla 9564, La Paz; tel/fax: 02 241 3662. This organisation is working in the Yanacachi/Sud Yungas region with rural development particularly in relation to tourism. It is working with the villagers along the Taquesi Trail to help the local people benefit from trekkers who pass that way. Basic tourist services have been set up in Kakapi and are planned for the village of Taquesi.

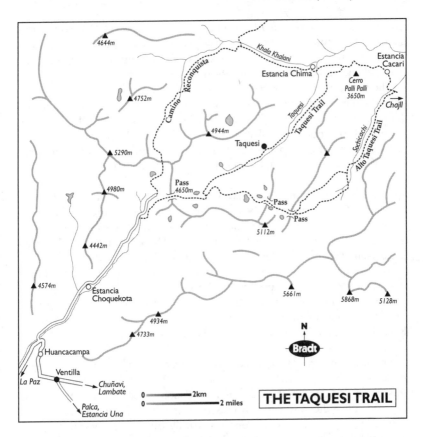

Distance	About 40km
Altitude	Between 4,650m and 2,100m
Rating	Easy to moderate, but there is an altitude gain of 1,200m at the start and an altitude loss (over 2 days) of 2,550m.
Timing	2 to 3 days
Special requirements	A tent is not essential – lodging is available in Taquesi and Kakapi – but you would be safer to carry one.
Map	IGM sheet *Chojlla*, scale 1:50,000. But the trail is very clear.

Getting to the trailhead The access town is Ventilla. Make an early start; climbing up to the pass in the midday heat is debilitating and in the early afternoon clouds often start rolling in, blotting out the views. The cheapest way of getting there is by bus from Calle General Luis Lara at the junction with Calle Venancio

Burgoa, near Plaza Libano in Alto San Pedro. The bus leaves at 09.00 costing Bs5 for the 2-hour journey. All things considered, you won't set out until midday travelling by bus so consider Plan B, a taxi. If there's a group of you the Bs150 fare is a good option, getting you starting the trek as early as you can get up.

The same bus also provides access to Tapacaya just before Ventilla, Palca nearby and the road to Estancia Una for trekking around and climbing Illimani. The bus continues east travelling north of Illimani to Tres Rios (Bolsa Negra, 4 hours, Bs9), Chuñavi, Lambate (6 hours, Bs 13)) and Pariguaya.

You can also hitch. Take the Ñ bus to the end of the line at Ovejuyo and from there walk up the hill, trying your luck when the opportunity arises.

Route description From Ventilla continue through the village and take a left fork at the Camino Precolombiano El Takesi sign towards the San Francisco mine. The track climbs steadily, passing through Choquekota after 1½ hours. The village store has basic supplies and *refrescos*. The village received electricity in 2000 and is just waking up to an altogether different lifestyle.

Keep going up the track, which is the access road for the mine at the top of the valley, staying on the path past a derelict church and a graveyard full of cigar-shaped adobe burial mounds. The snowy flank of Mururata gradually comes into view on the right, with llamas providing a picturesque foreground. Keep to the left of the widening valley, ignoring the right turn to the hut in the middle of the broad alluvial plateau.

About 2 hours from Choquekota, after a river crossing, the main track goes to the mine and a concrete signpost marks the 'Inca' trail (rather indistinct at this point) branching off to the right and soon zigzags steeply upwards to arrive at one of the most perfectly preserved stretches of stone paving in South America. This amazing road (one can hardly call it a trail) winds up the mountainside, easing the traveller's passing with a series of low steps. However, on my last trip it was 6 inches deep in snow in early October. The top of the pass (4,650m) is reached in about 1½–2 hours, and if the weather is clear you'll have a fine view of the snowy peaks of the Cordillera Real and the Yungas far below. The first good (but bitterly cold) camping place is just below the pass by a small lake. The descent from the pass to Taquesi takes about 3 hours. The path, if anything, is even more perfect; and the hillsides are dotted with grazing alpacas and livestock. There is camping by another lake shortly before Taquesi, and lodging in the village in a basic *refugio* (Bs5).

Taquesi is very attractive in its isolation and life goes on pretty much unchanged since the villagers' ancestors built the road. You can continue down as far as a small wooden bridge which is the last campsite before the river and trail part company. There is a small clean but basic bathroom beside the river – keep it that way. Shortly after the village the moist Yungas air asserts itself; boulders are covered in bright green moss and bushes and shrubs provide welcome relief from the stark mountain scene. The trail rides the contours of the valley rising high above the Río Taquesi, hugging the cliff edge. This is a dry section and you should carry water. About 30 minutes below Taquesi the trail and the river start to make a long curve round Cerro

Palli Palli. It will be a good 2½ hours before you'll see the ruins of a chapel and pass several houses surrounded by cultivated flowers. This is Kakapi; you can buy food and drink here, water is available and a solar-powered *refugio* has just been completed. Continuing straight ahead the trail drops steeply down to Río Quimsa Chata, which is crossed by a footbridge. Beyond the river is a steady climb up and over a shoulder before descending again to cross the Río Taquesi at 2,100m. There's some lovely swimming in river pools here if you can stand the cold water. Half a kilometre further on, by the beginning of an aqueduct, is a good campsite.

Chojlla – the town which you could see from up on the shoulder – is reached 2 hours after crossing the river. To reach Chojlla scramble up the steep footpath to the left, 100m after crossing the tributary below the town. A huge hydro-electric project was completed at the end of 2001 – engineers working on the project were certain that the vegetation cleared for construction would cover the pipelines within a year. Bypassing this uninspiring village – the choice of the vast majority – you can continue straight on to follow the meandering dirt road for about 5km to Yanacachi.

Staying in Yanacachi If you are ready for a rest, Yanacachi is a nice place to relax in for a few days. There are several places to stay, from 'basic but good' to 'very basic'. The map below shows their location. None has a sign, and few have names. The best is the hotel/restaurant on the opposite side of the road from the school. Apart from the basic *alojamientos* in the village there is **Refugio Don Miguel** outside the town on the road leading to the Yungas. This has a small swimming pool.

The benefit of the hydro-electric project in the valley is the presence of an archaeologist who has discovered new sections of Inca trail which were previously covered in vegetation.

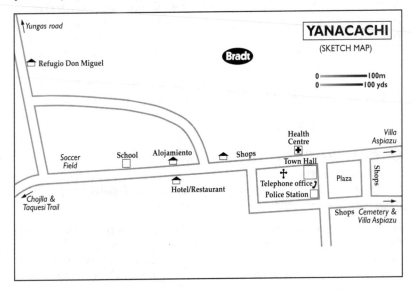

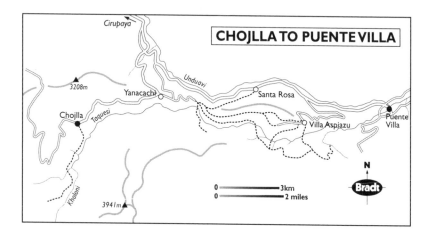

On to Puente Villa If you are in the swing of things and want to keep walking, take one of the trails east from Yanacachi and hike 10km or so to Villa Aspiazu and Puente Villa, where the beautifully situated **Hotel Tamampaya** will tend to your every need. The route is confusing since there are many *estancias* and small communities in the area so a profusion of tracks. When you leave Yanacachi simply follow the ridge, crossing the road several times, until you arrive at a football pitch with a view of the Río Unduavi on your left and the Río Taquesi on your right. Turn southeast and follow the often overgrown track which runs parallel to (but above) the Río Taquesi until you reach the old road to Villa Aspiazu which takes you to the road that runs from La Paz to Chulumani. An old road runs from Puente Villa to Coroico via Coripata. There is no regular public transport so it could be a long (but interesting) walk.

Getting back If you are leaving direct from Chojlla there is transport at around 05.30 and 13.00, passing through Yanacachi at 06.00 and 14.00. If you want to get on your way, walk the extra 4km to the Yungas road and wait for a passing bus or hitch a ride. Open trucks are a splendid way of enjoying the scenery but bear in mind that this part of Bolivia has high rainfall and that there may be snow over the pass of La Cumbre. Be prepared. It takes about 6 hours to get to La Paz, 4 hours by minibus, and a stop will be probably made at Unduavi where you can fill up on fried fish and other roadside goodies.

CHOQUEKOTA TO TRES RÍOS

This circuit involves 2 days' tough hiking, some of it cross-country, including a 4,850m pass. Be prepared! It finishes on the road to Tres Ríos and so could be combined with the Illimani to Chulumani hike.

Route description From the ruined chapel at Choquekota head northeast up the hillside towards a house. From here continue traversing the hill, which is called Cerro Altipani, until you meet a river valley coming down from the southeast. Go up this valley, aiming for the obvious col (4,700m). The country

Altitude	Between 3,900m and 4,850m
Rating	Tough
Timing	2 days
Maps	(Essential). IGM *Palca* (6044-III) and *Chojlla* (6044-IV), 1:50,000

is quite broken here, and you may find it easier to cross the ridge to the south of the col where the steep slope from the summit levels out.

Go down into the next valley, where there is camping, and follow this up into the basin below Mururata. Three streams come down to meet at the valley head. Take the first on the right, which comes from the southeast, and follow this up quite steeply to a pass at 4,850m, with Mururata on your left.

On the other side a narrow valley leads down to the southeast, and soon you'll pick up a path on the right-hand (south) side of the stream, leading to a *pampa* with abandoned houses. Improving all the time, the path keeps high above the river as it swings south. Follow it past some houses above the wet pastures of Totoral Pampa, eventually meeting the road from Ventilla to Tres Ríos at a hairpin. The trailhead for the Illimani to Chulumani (or Lambate) hike is only a couple of kilometres to your left.

ILLIMANI TO CHULUMANI

This is a rugged but wonderfully varied trek of from two to seven days (it can be ended or begun at various places), which takes you round the western flank of one of Bolivia's highest mountains, the multi-peaked Illimani (6,439m), then, like all the other Cordillera Real hikes, down into the tropical Yungas. And like the other trails, it provides contrasts of glaciers and citrus groves, goose-pimples and sweat, passing through some very remote areas where you are unlikely to meet anyone, only condors.

Getting to the trailhead The trek begins at Tres Ríos, near the mining town of Bolsa Negra, about 37km (but 3–4 hours' drive!) beyond Ventilla. See page 366 for advice on transport. If you go by truck dress warmly: there is a 4,700m pass before Tres Ríos. There is a good place to camp near the river, below the town and just below the bridge; take water from the standpipe in the village square, not from the polluted river.

Route description

Tres Ríos to Totoral (2 days) From Tres Ríos look for a track that climbs the hill by the bridge above the campsite, to the right of the river. A road also goes up the valley but it is easier to keep to the path, with the river to your left, towards the head of the valley and Illimani. This will take 2 hours. You'll see the abandoned mining camp of Bolsa Blanca across the valley. Then it's a steep climb, still on the right, up to a level *pampa* full of grazing horses and llamas, with lovely views of Illimani. Whatever time of day you arrive, camp at the end of the valley by some abandoned buildings (where there's some shelter from the cold wind). It's beautiful, freezing, and the last good campsite for several hours.

Looking up to the pass from your campsite your heart will sink. There is no obvious route up and the top seems vertically above you. In fact there is a trail: climb up behind the buildings to the right of the scree, to pick up the path which zigzags to the top of the pass, 4,850m, and a very tough 1-hour climb. Catch your breath before turning sharp right and follow a clear path along a rocky ledge towards a cleft in the rock. Beyond the cleft, head left towards the valley, making your way down the steep slope, over grass and boulders, or sliding down a dusty trail. A difficult descent. At the head of the valley make your way over to the right-hand side of the river and follow an improving path down that valley (always keep the river to your left) to the village of Totoral and the road to La Paz or Lambate. This is a long, tough descent from 4,700m to 3,400m, and is very steep towards the end.

Totoral is a friendly, cheerful village, seemingly involved in a continuous game of football. Beer is sold at one of the shops, and you can camp by the river. From Bolsa Blanca to here is about 7 hours. You can return to La Paz (there should be an early morning truck) or continue to Lambate (another day) or to Chulumani in 5 days.

Distance	About 100km
Altitude	Between 4,850m and 1,800m; altitude gains and losses of over 2,000m.
Rating	Moderate to difficult
Timing	2, 5 or 7 days, depending on your route and where you finish
Special requirements	Pack for some very hot days and bitterly cold nights. Biting insects (not mosquitoes) can be a problem below the treeline. There's a small selection of provisions in Lambate and Chuñavi. Pack animals and arrieros can be hired (with luck) in Tres Ríos and Lambate.
Map	IGM sheet *Palca* (6044 III), 1:50,000, shows the first part. 6044 II and 6044 I probably show the rest of the trail but are hard to obtain.

Totoral to Khala Ciudad via Chuñavi (2 days) Jürgen Stock from Germany recommends the following 'short cut' to Khala Ciudad. Fit hikers could do it in a day; tired trekkers will take two and save themselves the tough climb over to Lambate and the punishing descent to Chungu Mayu on the standard route. This route does, however, deprive you of the glorious campsite by the lake of Khala Ciudad unless you decide to make a loop and head back to Lambate along the standard route. Not a bad option.

From Totoral follow the road some 6km to the community of Chuñavi. Or take the bus/truck from La Paz to this small village where you can sleep in the school on payment of a fee. Basic meals are available. Fill up with water here; once on the trail it is difficult to find.

Shortly before the end of the village turn left on a track which heads east and then northeast, following the ridge of Cerro Aro Pampa. From the trail you can enjoy good views of Nevado Mururata. When the path divides, choose the one that takes you on the left-hand side (north) of the ridge. After 1–2 hours there are possible campsites on the ridge or at the source of two rivers (Río Tilacachi and Río Locotoni) though these are often swampy. The next campsites are about 4 hours away.

Continue climbing northeast and east, with the Khala Ciudad range on your right, to the upper valleys of two rivers where there are possible campsites. Your altitude is now just under 4,000m.

The trail now takes you up and down towards a pass and the junction with the 'main' path from Chunga Mayu.

Totoral to Khala Ciudad via Lambate (3 days) Make an early morning start to reach Lambate for lunch (cold beer!) with super mountain views en route. Cross the river by the bridge and follow the road for 20m. Just beyond the second bend in the road a steep track leads up to the right. It runs parallel to the road for a while, then forks right over a grassy hill from where you get good views of Illimani. Also, look in the opposite direction. See that far mountain range silhouetted like the Manhattan skyline? That's Khala Ciudad, 'rock city', and your destination in a couple of days' time.

After about 3 hours you descend, following steep gullies lined with foxgloves, to Lambate. As you approach the village take the left-hand path to the plaza. Lambate is an attractive town, full of character – and characters – and beautifully situated on a promontory. If you need pack animals to take you to the next pass, ask for Don Rosario. He lives in Lambate and generally works for the trekking company TAWA, but if he's available there is no better *arriero*.

Your next destination is the Chunga Mayu valley, way below you. From Lambate continue along the road, crossing a ford, and after about 1 hour you'll reach a new road leading off to your left. Before that, keep an eye out for the clear trail running up the valley the other side of the river to a village. You'll be toiling up this tomorrow.

Follow the new road until you are just above a small house with a path leading towards it. Take this path, going to the right of the house. The trail is clear, contouring the mountain through increasingly verdant vegetation (you start to see bromeliads and orchids and also parakeets), but don't be misled into following animal tracks. Keep an eye out for footprints. Five minutes before reaching the river you come to the remains of an old *hacienda*. Only some walls and two splendid conifers remain. Descend to the bridge and a welcome bath in the river (there are some reasonably private pools on the left). By this time your knees will be killing you – you have just descended 1,400m.

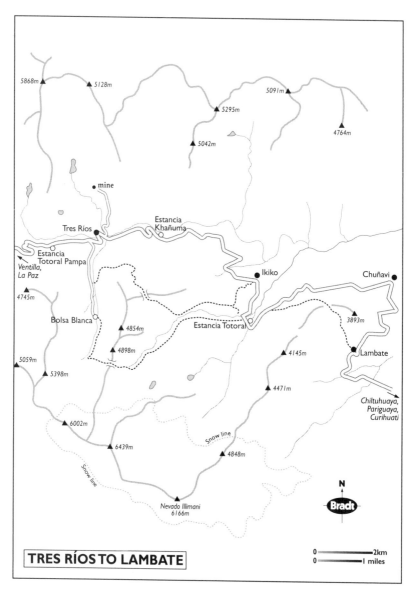

TRES RÍOS TO LAMBATE

Finding a camping place is not easy. Groups camp at a deserted fruit farm 5 minutes along the trail (turn right after the bridge). Try to find someone to ask permission. Sometimes families in the next village, Ranchería (also known as Quilcoma), will give hikers a place for their tent.

Now comes the toughest part of the trek. The Chunga Mayu is at a tropical 2,300m; the next pass is 4,300m! Even taking 2 days over the ascent this is hard work. The first part is very hot and there is no water for about 2½ hours so be sure to fill your water bottle at the river.

To reach Ranchería follow the path parallel to the river (ignore trails climbing up to your left) to the first building. Then turn left and climb steeply through the village to some eucalyptus trees and three conifers that you can see on the skyline. Continue climbing – hot and steep – for 2 hours until you come to a ridge and the beginning of the cloudforest.

Suddenly your efforts will seem worthwhile. The temperature drops, tree ferns and bromeliads adorn the trailside, and brightly coloured birds start to show themselves. Take your time to enjoy it. When you reach the campsite in about 4 hours from Ranchería you are amply rewarded. The river, which has been inaccessible as you sweated up the ridge to the left of its gorge, flows through meadows into pools and waterfalls, while at the head of the valley is the rock amphitheatre below Khala Ciudad. It's a magical place. Not as magical, however, as Khala Ciudad itself, which is my favourite mountain spot in Bolivia.

To reach it cast around for the path, which you pick up by climbing high above the campsite on the left. You will know when you're on the right trail – it's pretty clear, although sometimes confused by cow paths. It goes to the left of the sugarloaf that dominates the valley and then zigzags up the right side of the next shallow valley, reaching the top through a 'V' in the cliff wall. The focus of Khala Ciudad is the lake, or rather two lakes, which reflect the rock buttresses surrounding them; they seem as high as Illimani, once again visible across the valley.

If you are with a local *arriero* he will find an excuse not to camp by the lake. Several generations ago, so the story goes, the lake was dominated by an evil creature or spirit. The pilgrims heading for the Sanctuary of Irupana were not molested, but individuals and small groups disappeared. This was the only route to the Yungas and finally the locals became so desperate they asked the priest to perform an exorcism ceremony. The priest put a cordon of incense around the lake, whereupon a huge, three-headed serpent emerged from the water, broke through the cordon, and slithered away. The giant serpentine tracks can still be seen in the rock. The serpent still lives in the lake, they say, but these days it is subdued and causes no harm. The locals light fires around the lake to remind it to stay that way.

Khala Ciudad to Chulumani (2 days) Traverse high on the rock to the right of the serpent's lake, and start the climb (1¹/₂–2 hours) to the final pass at 4,200m where you can add your stone to the large *apacheta*. The view here is magnificent: behind you is the Cordillera Real and ahead lie the steamy forests of the Amazon basin, stretching uninterrupted as far as the eye can see. It is not exactly downhill all the way, since the path skirts the mountains and climbs other small passes, but it is excitingly evident that you are now on an Inca (or pre-Inca) trail. From the pass the path goes to the left, contouring the mountain, and over a low pass to continue its contouring on the left side of the ridge.

Don't worry if you lose a bit of height but be careful not to descend too much. If you lose the path keep close to the crest of the ridge and you will

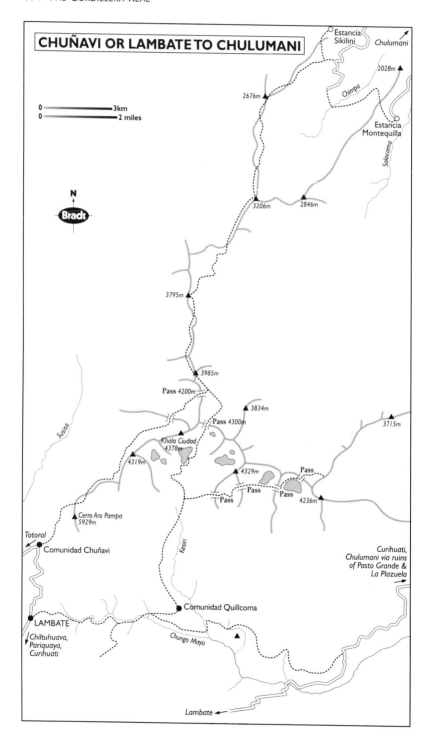

CHUÑAVI OR LAMBATE TO CHULUMANI

Estancia Sikilini

Chulumani

2028m

Chimpa

2676m

Estancia Montequilla

Solacama

N

Bradt

0 _____ 3km
0 _____ 2 miles

3206m

2846m

3795m

3985m

Pass 4200m

3834m

3715m

Pass 4300m

Khala Ciudad 4378m

4319m

4329m

Pass

Susisa

Pass

Pass

Pass

4236m

Pass

Cerro Aro Pampa 5929m

Kesiri

Curihuati, Chulumani via ruins of Pasto Grande & La Plazuela

Totoral

Comunidad Chuñavi

Comunidad Quillcoma

LAMBATE

Chiltuhuava, Pariquaya, Curihuati

Chungo Mayu

Lambate

pick it up when it joins the very clear trail (from the left) from Chuñavi, about an hour from the pass. This is the best 'Inca' section, with stone paving and steps. Three of the four times that I have done this trek I have seen condors; once four huge birds circled above us for some minutes, so close you could clearly see the white neck ruff. If you want to shorten your trek you can reach Chuñavi in a day.

From this point (the trail junction) to the next pass is about 4 hours. You should not lose your way (providing you take the upper path if faced with a choice) and with the walking easy and mainly level you can thoroughly enjoy the feeling of isolation and space. Everywhere you look are hills and forests – no sign of humans except in the far, far distance.

The final low pass faces you with a choice. Two trails lead through two notches in the mountain wall. Take the upper, left one. From there it is about 2 hours to the next – and last – campsite. You plunge dramatically into cloudforest, then out again. The campsite is at the second river crossing at about 3,300m. Beyond here there are very few camping possibilities.

The next day is a very tough one, so make an early start and keep the Band-Aids handy. You are going to descend about 1,500m (nearly 5,000ft). After the campsite the trail narrows, sometimes running along a stream-bed and past stands of bamboo – typical vegetation of this altitude. Once the trail starts descending it becomes very narrow, passing between steep banks and often through tunnels of vegetation, with great views when there's a gap in the trees giving you the startling realization that you are skirting the edge of a 300m precipice. There's not much water, so fill up when you get the chance. About 3 hours after the campsite you'll emerge into a grassy clearing with a dome-shaped hill ahead. This is where everyone gets lost.

The correct trail leaves the clearing at the far end, heading towards the dome-shaped hill, and soon forks. Take the right-hand branch that runs uphill for a good 20 minutes, then through more forest (giving you your first views of Chulumani) for 1½ hours before emerging into a cleared, grassy area and views of Chulumani, which looks temptingly near. It isn't. There's a final steep descent (watch out for snakes on this section, and fierce dogs guarding the coca plantations). Cultivation in the area has interfered with the trail so be careful not to get lost.

Finally you arrive at the elegant gates of Hacienda Siquilini with its private church, its fruit-bearing citrus trees and refreshing fresh water. It will have taken 6–7 hours from the campsite to here, and your knees and toes will be screaming for mercy. I'm afraid it's another 2 hours to Chulumani because the road has to skirt an immense gorge. There is a short cut (which you should take) through an orange grove down to the 'main' road and another short cut across the gorge but I'm not sure it's worth the effort of yet another steep descent and steep climb. Better, I think, to take your time walking along the road, help yourself to oranges and tangerines, view the coca plantations where the precious crop is grown on neat terraces, and enjoy your achievement. And hope for a lift.

Chulumani lies at only 1,800m, and is the capital of the Sud Yungas. It is a very attractive town with several hotels. If you feel that you deserve some luxury, the **Prefectural** and **San Bartolomé** are the best.

Getting back There is a wide choice of buses and minibuses, mostly leaving in the morning, to take you back to La Paz (5 hours) up the dramatic 'Route of the Abysses'. Book well in advance, and remember to bring warm clothes with you: it's hard to believe as you board the bus in sultry Chulumani that 4 hours later you may be braving the snow on the break for refreshments in La Cumbre.

THE CONDOR'S NEST: ILLIMANI BASE CAMP

Many hikers who have just arrived in La Paz are tempted by the majestic sight of Illimani (6,439m), overlooking the city and shining in the evening sun. Although this is a challenging and technical climb, backpackers can enjoy an excursion to the base camp called El Nido de Condores (The Condor's Nest). This lies at 5,600m, giving you the chance to test your fitness and to check out your cold-weather gear, while watching the lights of La Paz twinkling below you as you listen to the cracking of the surrounding glaciers.

Altitude	Between 3,300m and 5,600m
Rating	Strenuous
Timing	3–4 days
Maps	*Cordillera Real de La Paz (Sur)*, 1:50,000, by Walter Guzmán Córdova (available from Los Amigos del Libro).

Getting there Follow directions for getting to the Taquesi trail (see page 365). When you reach Ventilla look for transport as far as Cohoni, and get off at Estancia Una (3,330m), a settlement on the left side of the valley shortly after a low pass about 2 hours from Palca. The driver will know where this is. There is one truck a day from Palca to Cohoni, leaving early in the morning – so you may find you have to arrange transport from La Paz.

Route description The villagers of Estancia Una will want to rent you a pack animal. This is not a bad idea: you will need your energy for the final, steep climb to the base camp. From Estancia Una to a possible camping place, will take about 4 hours. It is a pleasant walk up the valley to the tiny village of Pinaya at the foot of Illimani. Just before you reach Pinaya, turn right and cross the river. From here head straight for Illimani, slowly climbing up through meadows and flat plains until you reach a broad, flat plain at an altitude of 4,500m. Any local person will point out the way. There are plenty of suitable camping places here. If you have hired pack animals they will leave you here – after this point the path is too steep for them!

It will take 5 very strenuous hours to reach the Nido de Condores from here. Shortly after the plain you will come to an old mining road. Follow this

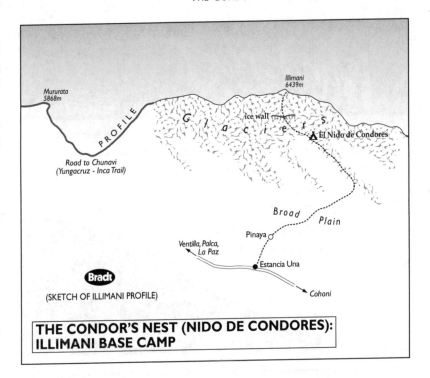

(SKETCH OF ILLIMANI PROFILE)

**THE CONDOR'S NEST (NIDO DE CONDORES):
ILLIMANI BASE CAMP**

for about 15 minutes until you cross a bridge, and shortly afterwards a path leads steeply up a scree slope towards a ridge. Follow this to the Nido de Condores.

Warning Illimani yearly claims the lives of climbers who are unprepared for the altitude, capricious weather and testing conditions. Do not climb the mountain without a local guide and full climbing gear.

Sorata, Illampu and the Tipuani Valley

This is a wonderful region for hiking or just hanging out in the almost subtropical climate. There is a growing choice of options from gentle day hikes, trips lasting a few days exploring the lagoons on the lower slopes of Illampu, through to strenuous treks of a week or longer; you can walk through snow or citrus groves or a combination of the two, and return to Sorata for relaxation. Life doesn't get much better than this!

Nestling at the foot of the Cordillera Real, Sorata has one of the finest settings in Bolivia. The second-and third-highest mountains in the country (Illampu, 6,362m and Ancohuma, 6,427m – although their heights and therefore claims to eminence are disputed) overlook the town, which lies at a mere 2,695m and has swanky palm trees in the plaza as proof of its mild climate. After a few days spent gasping and freezing in La Paz, it's a great relief to spend some time in Sorata, especially on a Sunday when the market is in full swing. Sorata's main fiesta is held between September 12 and 16 each year.

Getting there and away
The buses from La Paz to Sorata depart from Calle Manuel Bustillos, three blocks up Avenida Kollasuyo from the cemetery in La Paz. They leave every hour between 05.00 and 16.00 and the ride takes 4–5 hours (US$1.50). You don't usually need to book your seat in advance, just turn up. Be careful as the area around the bus office is well known for pickpockets and thieves.

If you are coming from Peru and Copacabana, you can avoid the long trip into La Paz by changing buses at Huarina to pick up one of the regular buses heading for Sorata.

Sleeping and eating
Two of the gringo hotels – the Residencial Sorata and the Landhaus Copacabana – are owned by expats with a passion for films, so evenings can be spent in front of the video catching up on missed movies.

Residencial Sorata On the corner of Plaza Enrique Peñaranda; tel: 813 5044; fax: 811 5218; email: resorata@ceibo.entelnet.bo. Hot water, good restaurant and nice

FROM SORATA TO THE YUNGAS BY ROAD AND RIVER
Matthew Parris

Many travellers treat Sorata as a dead-end: a pretty town to be reached by bus from La Paz, used as a base for some smashing local walks and climbs – and then left by the same bus, back to La Paz. The more adventurous, of course, may try the Gold Diggers' route down to Mapiri; the most adventurous brave the Mapiri trail.

But there is another way out of Sorata, as beautiful as it is plain-sailing even for the more timid. Try going down to the Yungas via Consata and Santa Rosa – then Mapiri, Guanay (by canoe-bus) and back up to La Paz by bus or onward toward Brazil. A motorable track leads down the mountains from Sorata to Consata, and Louis Demers at the Residencial Sorata can help find transport – though, walked over two days, the journey would be lovely on foot.

I went by Toyota, reaching Consata, a tropical village in the foothills of the Andes, after lunch. We pulled ripe oranges off trees where we lodged – a tiny but friendly *hostal*, Don Betus, run by an immensely attentive elderly couple, the hospitable Rosa and her friendly husband. The *hostal* is on the left before you enter the village. Should we lock our valuables? No. There was a thief here once but they shot him.

Santa Rosa is 30 miles on down the river. The dawn brought no transport so we started to walk. It did not matter that nothing came. Our morning stroll along a jungle track through hills, alongside rivers, overflown by

gardens. A popular choice in a handy spot, managed by Canadian Louis Demers. US$3–6 per person.

Hotel Landhaus Copacabana Av 9 de Abril; Casilla 3452; tel: 813 5042; fax: 813 5042; email: kramer@caoba.entelnet.bo; web: www.khainata.com/sorata. German-owned (Eduardo) and home to the offices of the Club Sorata – a good source of hiking information. A bit out of town. Bs18 per person.

Gran Hotel Ex-Prefectural Sorata On Av Samuel Tejerina (the main road to town about 10 minutes' walk from the centre although the bus will drop you off if you ask); Casilla 11023; tel: 813 7378 (La Paz 02 277 2846). Quite a luxurious hotel with 28 rooms (with or without bathroom). Also has a restaurant, living room with fire and swimming pool. Prices from US$11 for just the room, US$18 full board (when there is space).

Hotel Panchita Plaza Enrique Peñaranda, next to the church; tel: 813 5038 or 831 3700. US$4.50 per person. Clean, bright and friendly with hot water in shared bathrooms. A good choice.

Hotel Paraiso next to Residencial Sorata; tel: 813 5043.

Also try **Hostal Mirador**, one block west of the plaza, if all these are full. Ten clean rooms with shared bath and spectacular views down the valley. US$4.50 per person in rather dark rooms.

Altai Oasis is a fair trek out of town down on the valley floor – follow the signs. It's a great spot with a number of options, including camping (US$1.50), rooms with shattering green parrots, attended by butterflies the size of handkerchiefs, observed by bird-spiders from giant webs and ignored by armies of leafcutter ants on the march, and surrounded by flowering trees and waterfalls ... was like paradise.

Lunch was at Incachaka after 15 miles; rice and fried egg (they never have less in Bolivia, and rarely more), and we marched on into the afternoon sun. Suddenly there was a swimming pool – a big, roadside, concrete pool fed by cool clear water from a nearby stream – so we stripped off and swam. Then onward, the forest trees growing more huge as we descended into the heat. Next, a bend in the track, a giant mahogany, and a liana rope hanging from 50 feet above. We all swung and shrieked like kids.

Then on. All at once a swarm of black hornets attacked from the trees. We fought them off. Our losses amounted to five stings: six hornets bit the dust.

Another corner: and a river to cross. A wide, deep and turbulent river. Boots off, we waded over with sticks. The track began to climb. We began to tire. After climbing a thousand feet, we were strung out single over a mile, all exhausted.

Lights! A bar! Music! We had reached a mining settlement called (confusingly) Consata Limitada. From here it was only a few miles through gullies by Land Rover to Santa Rosa and the Hotel Ruth – the noisiest hotel in the world. But that's another story.

shared bath (US$2–4.50), and fully equipped, self-catering cabins (US$4–5.50) – all prices per person. Also has a good restaurant.

For food the first stop is normally **Altai** on the main square, owned by the friendly Pete Good who, on top of running a fine restaurant, is an excellent source of local information. This has a good menu with vegetarian and meaty dishes side by side, and is wonderfully relaxing after several days of roughing it. The **Spider Bar** is worth a visit if you still have energy in the evening. This is an expat-run gringo hangout at the lower end of the village. Follow Muñecar down past Calle El Mirador.

Cafe Illampu is a long way out of town on the road to the San Pedro caves so makes a great stop on your way back to town. It offers excellent freshly baked cakes, coffee and hammocks for relaxing. **Italia** is the best of a clutch of pizzerias on the corner of the plaza. There are several local restaurants serving traditional Bolivian meals on the road heading downhill from the plaza – try **El Ceibo** for starters.

Handicrafts

Artesania Sorata not only gets you a colourful sweater, but helps to employ between 150 and 200 low-income families and supports the continuation of traditional handicraft techniques. It allows artisans to earn a living working in their homes, while still caring for their families or crops and animals. To learn more check their website at www.peopline.org/partners/bo/so/.

HIKING IN THE REGION

In former years trekkers came to Sorata to do the Gold Diggers' Trail (Camino del Oro). It used to be a wonderful hike, much of it on a pre-Inca trail, but is now partly destroyed by the activities of the eponymous miners. José Camarlingh, co-owner of Andean Summits in La Paz, writes: 'We have not been there for many years because it was already very decayed. There was a lot of rubbish and pollution from the gold miners and all the fauna had run away. The forest had been destroyed by high-pressure water machines and although it is interesting to see what humans can do to nature it is a miserable scene.' The first half of the trail is still intact, but even this is under threat by another mining company.

In recent years the three-lakes trek has become the main attraction. A 3- or 4-day trek up the lower slopes of Illampu to camp on the shores of Laguna Chillata, from where it's a day trip climbing higher to Laguna Glacial, set against snow-covered slopes well above the snow-line. Several other new day treks are also available.

José suggests a longer alternative such as the Illampu circuit, described here by Kathy Jarvis, or the trans-Cordillera trail down to Condoriri, or the trail from Sorata to Curva in Apolobamba. The truly ambitious could even attempt the trans-Cordillera trek, first trekked by Yossi Brain and now offering a challenging walk heading for the *refugio* at Huayna Potosí (10–12 days) or lasting up to three weeks and travelling as far as Cohoni for the truly adventurous. Contact the guides association in Sorata or tour operators in La Paz for details.

There is also the Mapiri Trail. Matthew Parris, travel writer and *Times* columnist, wrote graphically about his trek up the Mapiri Trail in 1997. He describes an easier hike in the box on pages 380–1. None of these hikes should be attempted without a guide. And if you're determined to do the Camino del Oro you will be able to get directions in Sorata. The trail is reasonably clear. For the Mapiri trail, the guide Eduardo Chura has been recommended.

Guides and *arrieros*

There is a guides co-operative association in Sorata; the Oficina de Guías (tel: 813 5044; fax: 813 5218), located on Plaza Peñaranda facing Residencial Sorata. In 2002 the association was charging US$12 per day (guide's food and supplementary equipment are not included). As yet this organisation lacks the sophistication of its counterparts in Peru. Your guide will know the way but will probably only speak Spanish and may be poorly equipped. Check that he has proper equipment for spending nights out in the chilly mountains.

Safety

It is unfortunate but true that there have been several problems for trekkers in the hills above Sorata. General responses suggest that the problems –

which include armed hold-ups but as yet nothing more than robbery – emanate around the Laguna San Francisco region, which is passed on the last days of the Illampu Circuit trek. Even if the problem is geographically contained, the advice to people wanting to trek the region above Sorata is to go with a guide until full confidence has been restored. Unfortunately, the rumours which circulate this town are unlikely to make that a reality for some time to come.

SHORT HIKES IN THE SORATA AREA
San Pedro Cave
This is a large cave with a lake inside. You can explore it with the aid of the electric lights, for a fee, or by torchlight for a smaller fee. The legends surrounding the cave are interesting: the *conquistadores* are said to have buried a large treasure somewhere deep inside the cave and some say the cave was deliberately flooded to conceal the treasure. In addition to the cave and its lake, there is a large population of bats.

Probably the lake inside the cave is natural, but *El Dorado* is still in the minds of the local people. Divers have been discouraged from exploring the cave to its limits by a fatal accident (attributed to an Inca curse).

San Pedro is a small village some 3 hours' walk from Sorata along a path down the valley (or rather along a ledge halfway up the valley side). When you see San Pedro's church, climb uphill to reach the village and continue to its far side. The cave is 20m above the jeep track – which, incidentally, gives you an alternative route back to Sorata in about 2 hours.

Continuing down the valley You can continue hiking down this beautiful valley to the towns of Quiabaya and Tacacoma. There may be transport, but most likely you will be walking so be sure to bring sufficient food. The way is easy (following the road), but for the truly adventurous, with a map, there are all sorts of possibilities in this area.

THE ILLAMPU CIRCUIT
Kathy Jarvis
This is a spectacular, tough trek of 7 days, starting out from subtropical Sorata at 2,695m and passing high around the flanks of Illampu and Ancohuma, before returning to the starting point. There are four passes on the trek, the fourth and highest, Abra de La Calzada, taking you up to a breathtaking, heart-pounding 5,045m. Other highlights are the remote highland villages, herds of grazing llamas, awe-inspiring mountain scenery, stunning views over shimmering Lake Titicaca to Peru on the far shores, and the chance of seeing viscachas, Andean geese and soaring condors overhead. See *Safety* above.

Conditions/what to take The trek is best done in the dry season between April and October, but be prepared for cold and wet at any time.

You can buy basic provisions in Sorata at the many shops lining the square, so it isn't necessary to bring food supplies with you from La Paz. However, you will need to rent equipment in La Paz if you haven't brought your own.

If you are going to trek with a local guide you won't need your own stove. Buy your maps in La Paz too, as there is nowhere in Sorata that sells them.

Guides and pack animals While doing this trek with an excellent guide named Eusebio, his mule Pancho and his son Elias, a trainee-guide, we encountered two trekkers without guides who had got seriously lost. This is because of the frequent difficulty in choosing the right trail from among a myriad of tracks, or choosing the right direction when there is no sign of any track! With a good map and compass you can of course go it alone, but if you decide to hire a guide and mule the Oficina de Guías will help you. Assuming you are a couple, the cost of a guide and mule for the 7-day trek will be around US$100 (excluding food).

Distance	About 90 km
Altitude	Between 2,695 and 5,045m
Rating	Difficult
Timing	6–7 days
Maps	Club Andino Aleman *Cordillera Real Nord* (*Illampu*) or IGM *Sorata* (5846)

Route description Set off from Sorata heading past Residencia Sorata up Calle Sucre. Turn right at the top and then left up Calle Illampu, leaving Sorata on a wide path heading southeast. After approximately 30 minutes take a steep path left (east) off the main track heading up above the valley of the River Lakathiya towards Quilambaya (1¹/₂ hours' walk). At Quilambaya head left and on up through the cactus avenue. There is a water tap just off the path to the left where you can fill up your bottles (use iodine). Continue climbing steeply for 15 minutes before the path levels out and you contour round to the left to cross a bridge over the River Lakathiya. Go straight on after the bridge, zigzagging steeply up to reach the village of Lakathiya in 45 minutes. There is a shop here with basic provisions. Walking through the village keep an eye out to the left for the point where two branches of the river meet. You want to follow the left bank of the left branch, crossing the river on a small stone bridge and heading on up the track for an hour until the valley widens out and there are good camping spots. From Sorata it takes 4–5 hours of steady climbing to reach this camping place, about 2km beyond Lakathiya at 4,000m.

From where the valley widens and the stream you are following swings round to the left (north), 90 minutes' steep walking takes you to the Abra Illampu (4,741m). As you climb past grazing llamas, there are breathtaking views of the glacier covered Illampu peak up ahead, and plunging deep, green valleys behind. From the pass follow the track heading down the grassy valley of Quebrada Illampu to the northeast until you reach the valley of the River Chuchu Jahuira and the dirt road from Sorata to Ancohuma and Cocoyo. Follow the road to the right for 3km, about 45 minutes, and then head right

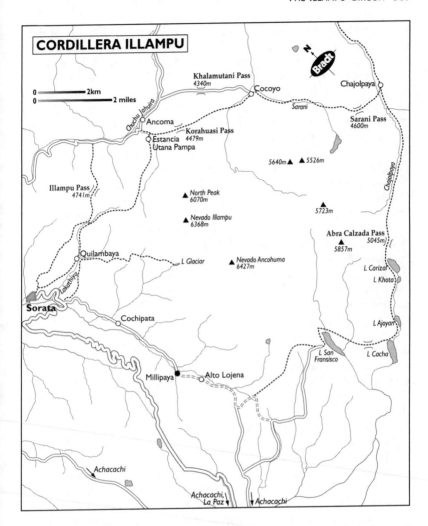

(south) at the small hamlet of Estancia Utana Pampa, just before the road bridge. Cross the River Ancohuma Jahuira on a stone bridge and continue heading up the valley. After 10 minutes take the steep path going off to the left (southeast) up and into the hanging valley below Abra Korahuasi (4,479m). This is the second pass, which is reached after 2 hours' ascent from the valley floor. There are good campsites after leaving Ancohuma in the main valley and at the base of the hanging valley. Once over the pass follow the track down, through luxuriant vegetation, dropping 1,000m to the flat-bottomed, green valley with the small village of Cocoyo ahead. You may be able to buy fresh trout from local children tending llama herds and fishing in the many streams meandering through the valley. Stay on the left side of the rivers along the edge of the valley until you reach Cocoyo where you cross the river over a bridge (2 hours from the pass). There is a small shop on the right of the bridge, where very basic supplies can sometimes be purchased. Turn left after crossing the river and head first right up past the school and then along the bank of the thundering waters of the River Sarani. Keep the river on the left and do not cross again, but remain on the right bank ascending the Sarani valley. Cocoyo is a village of llama herders and miners, which we had the good fortune to come upon at carnival, at the end of February. This meant being bombarded with water bombs then followed by crowds of giggling, inquisitive children and inebriated, curious adults. Trekkers are often asked to donate a few *bolivianos* to the school as they pass through the village. There are plenty of campsites on the banks of the river 30 minutes from Cocoyo.

From Cocoyo, 3½ hours of gentle climbing brings you to Paso Sarani (4,600m). The path from Cocoyo initially follows the right side of the river, crossing a huge boulder to the left bank after 2 hours and then rising steeply to the left as you reach a few thatched stone houses on the valley floor. Water cascades all around into the flat boggy *pampa* land at the head of the valley, which you leave to your right as you ascend. Just over an hour before the pass and 20 minutes above the stone houses there is a wonderful camping spot next to two abandoned buildings, with dramatic views over the valley below. Look out for condors overhead and viscachas on the boulders on the way up the pass.

Cross the pass and descend steeply towards Chajolpaya. After 15 minutes' descent from the top of the pass, cross a stream to the right and follow the good trail down to the village (1 hour from the top). There are several houses in Chajolpaya, but little sign of life other than llamas and sheep in this remote inaccessible place. Aymara is the only language spoken here and the nearest shops are two days' walk away in the town of Achacachi far beyond Abra Calzada. After passing through the village turn immediately right up the valley skirting the boggy ground bordering the River Chajolpaya. From here it is 5 hours' steady climbing to the highest pass on the trek, Abra Calzada (5,045m). There are abundant camping spots on the way up the pass and even at the top, rubbing shoulders with the glaciers, if the altitude doesn't bother you. The trail here is obvious and there is plenty of water on the way up. The climb, although long, is steady and the reward worthwhile as you reach the top and have spectacular views out to the southwest over Lake Titicaca, and all around of ice-capped rugged peaks. The pass itself is broad and almost barren, with a few hardy plants struggling for survival amid ice-scraped boulders and melt-water lakes.

The initial descent from the pass is steep and tricky for mules, as you make your way through large boulders on a trail heading southwest towards the deep blue-green lakes of Carizal and Khota. After 30 minutes the track levels out and passes close to the lakes, crossing a scree slope of deep red-coloured rock. From Laguna Khota (1 hour from the pass) finding the way becomes more difficult as the path goes off to the southwest and you want to head northwest towards Laguna San Francisco. It is a 1½-hour slog across the grassy *pampa* of the Quebrada de Kote. You should stay on the right (north) side of the river after Laguna Khota and then on reaching the far end (south) of Laguna Ajoyan head cross country up and over the boulder-strewn ridge lying to the west above you (a 1-hour climb). The views of Lake Titicaca to the west and the high peaks of the Cordillera to the east from the top of the ridge are astonishing and the light over the altiplano is unsurpassably beautiful. To the northwest lies Laguna San Francisco, your destination. Head for the right (north) end of the lake about 1.5 hours from the top of the ridge. There are several places to camp before reaching the lake, or at the north end of the lake, where there are a few stone houses and possibly grazing Andean geese. It is best not to camp within sight of any houses as you may attract the unwanted attention of local farmers, who are not always friendly and may demand money from you. Finding a way across the numerous silted streams flowing into the Laguna San Francisco isn't easy, unless you have the assistance of local children who may come running. If there is no-one around and you don't want to get wet feet, head north up the valley until you see a suitable place to cross. From Laguna San Francisco head steeply west up the track towards a disused road you see above you. Cross the disused road on the track and continue heading up to the top of the ridge (1½ hours from the lake). Again, finding the way becomes a bit tricky as the path heads down to the left (southwest) and you want to go straight ahead (northwest). From the top of the ridge where there is a rocky cairn (4,867m), continue northwest down into the next valley and up the other side (30 minutes), over the ridge and down into the next valley too (20 minutes), always heading northwest. In the second valley turn west and follow the valley down until you reach a track crossing your path (40 minutes). It's all down hill from here back to Sorata. Cross over the track and continue westwards across the *pampa* and the head of the valley of Quebrada Tiquitini to rejoin the same track 50 minutes later. Follow this track down until it joins a dirt road leading to the village of Alto Lojena after 30 minutes. This relatively new road (not marked on the maps) sees very little traffic, but you could catch a truck down to the La Paz to Sorata road from here. Alternatively walk down the road through Millipaya (45 minutes from Lojena), cross the river in the middle of the village and continue down the right bank of the river all the way to Sorata (4 hours from Millipaya). There are good camping spots at the old mine on the left of the road, 1 hour from Millipaya before the village of Cochipata. As you descend to Sorata the landscape changes totally from high mountain *puna* to cultivated fields of maize, potatoes and beans, human habitation becoming much more apparent as you pass through many small villages of adobe houses. You still catch glimpses of the glaciated massifs of Ancohuma and Illampu up to the right with melt-water cascading down erosion-formed gullies towards the valley bottom. Vegetation becomes prolific, the temperature rises and birds sing all around as you return to subtropical Sorata and a welcome rest.

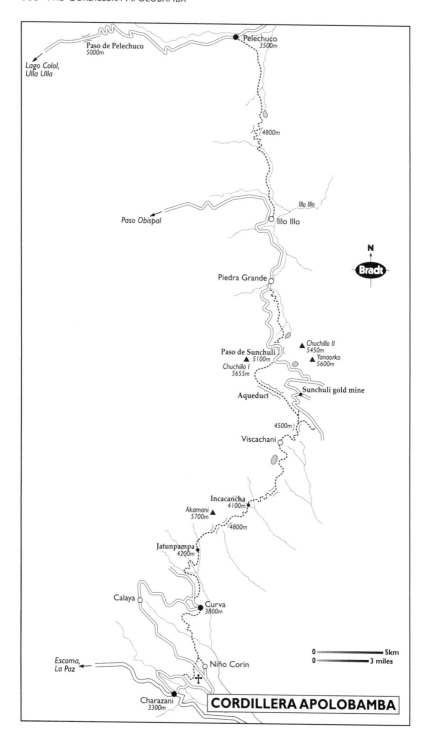

Paso de Pelechuco
5000m

Pelechuco
3500m

Lago Colol,
Ulla Ulla

(4800m

Illo Illo

Paso Obispal

Illo Illo

N

Bradt

Piedra Grande

Chuchillo II
5450m

Paso de Sunchuli
5100m

Yanaorko
5600m

Chuchillo I
5655m

Sunchuli gold mine

Aqueduct

(4500m

Viscachani

Incacancha
4100m

Akamani
5700m

(4800m

Jatunpampa
4200m

Calaya

Curva
3800m

Escoma,
La Paz

Niño Corín

0 ———— 5km
0 ———— 3 miles

Charazani
3300m

CORDILLERA APOLOBAMBA

The Cordillera Apolobamba

Less known and less accessible than the Cordillera Real, the Apolobamba lies to the north and west of that range, rising abruptly from the Altiplano and straddling the Peruvian frontier directly north of the tip of Lake Titicaca.

This is the place for truly adventurous hikers with lots of time. The beauty of the mountain scenery equals or even exceeds that of the Cordillera Real, and the glimpses of Indian life and wildlife (there is a vicuña reserve in the foothills) are even more interesting than to the south.

The Apolobamba owes its network of good trails to the Spanish lust for gold. This has been a gold-mining area since the conquest, and ruined mines can be visited in remote valleys.

One of the biggest problems confronting the Apolobamba explorer is the lack of maps. The one opposite is drawn from a variety of sources and is as close as we can get. I am indebted to Peter Hutchison and John Pilkington for correcting and updating it.

GETTING THERE

For those without their own transport, just getting to the Cordillera Apolobamba is challenging enough.

Via Pelechuco From the decrepit and smelly Calle Reyes Cardona, four blocks up Avenida Kollasuyo from the cemetery in La Paz, an equally decrepit bus of the Héctor Pastén company leaves on Wednesdays at 11.00 and reaches Pelechuco 20 excruciating hours later. Tickets for this journey (US$6) are sold on the bus, which is parked at the point of departure from 11.00 the previous day. It goes via Escoma, close to Lake Titicaca, then north to Ulla Ulla (see page 394) before turning east past Lago Cololo and over the 5,000m Paso de Pelechuco. Passengers may have to walk a kilometre or two at the summit if the road is bad. The bus makes the return journey from Pelechuco on Saturdays at 14.00.

There are also irregular truck departures, either from Calle Reyes Cardona as above or from Mercado Tejar, opposite the cemetery's main entrance. Pete Lawrence and Rachel Scott warn that the journey can be very cold – be prepared! 'Our truck took 19 hours, including a stop of 2–3 hours at night in the middle of nowhere. There are settlements of sorts – mostly mudbrick shacks, seemingly deserted. Occasionally a figure emerges, or else someone jumps down from the truck and disappears through a silent doorway...'

Via Charazani Buses of the Trans Altiplano company (tel: 02 238 0859) leave from Calle Reyes Cardona in La Paz (see above) daily at 06.30. The trip costs US$4 and takes 8 hours. The bus continues for another 2 hours to the village of Curva, US$4.50. Return journeys to La Paz leave from the plaza in Charazani daily at 20.00, leaving Curva a couple of hours earlier.

As with Pelechuco, there are also occasional trucks from Calle Reyes Cardona or Mercado Tejar in La Paz (though very few continue to Curva).

So, if travelling by public transport you're probably better off going to Pelechuco and having a regular bus service to catch out of Charazani. If you want to organise a jeep to collect you in Pelechuco, starting in Charazani is good option.

PELECHUCO TO CHARAZANI

I did this magnificent trek with TAWA (see *Tour operators* on page 335), who solved the logistics of getting there and of carrying a pack over a 5,100m pass. It was a 6-day trek (including one rest day), and so spectacular and interesting that I wouldn't hesitate to recommend it to backpackers who are willing to face the transport difficulties or to groups looking for an exceptional organised trek. The clear trail runs along the eastern side of the Cordillera from Pelechuco, a village founded in 1560, which is at the crossroads of Amazon and Andean trade.

Apart from the breathtaking scenery, this trek was special because of the contact it allowed us with the Calahuaya Indians who are the traditional healers of the area. Highly respected throughout South America (they journey as far as Patagonia and Panama), they are expert in the use of herbal medicine and the art of making diagnoses by 'reading' a llama's entrails or scattered coca leaves. The Calahuayas were our *arrieros* and I am perfectly willing to believe that their acts of propitiation to the *achachilas* (mountain spirits) helped to make this the least problematic trek I have made in Bolivia. Bottles of the local *aguardiente*, Caiman, were opened at regular intervals, and the alcohol was sprinkled around the wheels of the truck as we approached the trailhead, and on the hoofs of donkeys on the trail, amid muttered incantations. So accustomed did we become to the ritual that we felt uneasy without it when later we headed for a high pass in a truck. One of the group commented 'Shouldn't we Caiman the wheels?'

There is basic accommodation in Pelechuco if you have time to kill – which is pretty normal in reality.

Distance	About 70km
Altitude	Between 5,100m and 3,500m
Rating	Difficult
Timing	5–6 days

CLIMBING IN THE CORDILLERA APOLOBAMBA
Paul Hudson

The attractions of the Cordillera Apolobamba for a climbing expedition were its feeling of remoteness, mostly good weather, Alpine-like peaks and high base camps.

The area has been visited by British climbers on various occasions and 47 of the 101 identified peaks had been conquered by British climbers. We climbed 13 peaks in the southern part of the range, 10 of which were first British ascents. Our first camp was at Paso Osipal, from where we climbed Sunchuli (5,306m), Cololo (5,916m) and Iscacuchu (5,650m). From the next camp, near the village of Sunchuli, we ascended Chuchillo 1 (5,655m), Corohuari (5,668m), Yanaorco (5,600m) Cavayani (5,700m) and Chuchillo 2 (5,450m) together with a number of unnamed summits. The best excursion was a two-day trip which started high up the valley west of Sunchuli, and saw us climbing on to the ridge via one of its side valleys. The trip west along its spine was excellent despite its difficulties and saw us bivvying east of Cavayani itself.

Our equipment included snow stakes which were invaluable both as abseil anchors and running belays, the 3ft ones being better than the shorter ones. The glaciers we encountered were straight forward and the difficult and dangerous sections could easily be avoided. We employed only a few ice screws so there is no need to take too many; the rock gear remained unused mainly due to the poor rock. Our 9mm Cairngorm ropes were employed on a ratio of one to two people. We bivvied out on two occasions without sleeping bags, our duvets and Phoenix bivvy bags being adequate, although for real comfort extra layers and a Karrimat would have been good.

It is necessary to bring mountain food from home; this is essential if you are planning to stay up high on a multi-day route. We took multi-fuel stoves and bought paraffin from a garage in La Paz.

Maps are a problem, and a sketch map was drawn of the entire area by Paul Hudson. This, and a more detailed account of the ascents, is available by writing to P Hudson, 88 Ash Rd, Leeds, LS6 3HD (SAE please).

If you want to climb in the area, contact the tour operators listed on page 335.

Guides and pack-animals The best guide for the area is Alcides Imaño Pérez. The Royal Dutch Alpine Club used his services in 1996 and endorse the recommendation given by other readers: 'He was the most helpful and careful guide we had, and made the contact with the inhabitants of the cordillera much easier. He knows many other good routes as well ... He is desperately seeking a good tent.' Sr Imaño Pérez lives in Pelechuco but can sometimes be contacted through the Club Andino in La Paz.

If you will be spending some time in the Apolobamba consider following the example of some Dutch climbers: 'Pelechuco has a nice little school which we visited. It is in need of materials such as pencils, pens, exercise books, posters and so on. After we paid a visit to the school the contact with the people became very friendly and warm.'

Conditions/what to bring Days will be cold and nights very cold, and you may encounter rain and snow even in the dry season. Around Pelechuco and Charazani, however, it will be warm enough for T-shirts and shorts. Don't forget your sunglasses against the glare of the snow. Although provisions (including bread) may be available in Pelechuco, don't bank on it; stock up in La Paz.

Route description
Updated by John Pilkington and Peter Hutchison

Pelechuco is quiet and pretty, with a strong Spanish flavour. There are cobbled streets, colonial-style courtyards and a general air of decay. The church clock and the splendid wrought-iron fountain in the plaza were donated by Karl Francke, a 19th-century immigrant who made a fortune mining the area's gold. In the same plaza is Hotel Llajtaymanta – the name is Quechua for Pelechuco – run by friendly Reynaldo Vasquez and his wife María (US$2 per night and good meals for $1). A few small shops sell basic provisions; and if you see a basket covered with a white cloth outside someone's front door it means they have fresh bread for sale.

To begin the walk, climb the steps by the church and turn left at the top. After crossing a small stream make a right turn and follow this path out of town towards the first pass. Where the path forks, take the higher right-hand branch. After about 2½ hours a small house will come into view. Bear right here and continue for 1¼ hours to an excellent campsite. The path is clear and well used, and another 1¼ hours will bring you to the top of the pass at 4,800m. A steep half-hour descent follows to the Río Illo Illo and good camping.

Follow the river downstream past more good campsites, ignoring the path which, after half an hour, ascends to a couple of hamlets on the right. After a further half hour, cross a side stream on a stone bridge and climb gently up the valley side to the village of Illo Illo, where shops sell basic provisions.

From Illo Illo a jeep track leads over the next pass towards the mining settlement of Sunchuli. You can join it above the village, but the most direct route leaves the plaza by the church and descends to a stream before climbing steeply to join the jeep track in half an hour. Follow this track for a further hour to the village of Piedra Grande, then continue for another half hour, and after fording a stream turn left up a steep path to join an old, possibly pre-Hispanic, route. A further 2 hours of climbing, with ever-improving views of Chuchillo II (5,450m), will bring you to a pleasant camping area. The

Sunchuli Pass is now in view straight ahead, with the road leading diagonally down from it to the right.

The path heads straight for the pass, crossing a marsh before zigzagging steeply up to the road. From the summit (reached 1½ hours after leaving the camping area) follow the road down to the Sunchuli Gold Mine, once abandoned but reopened in 1992 and now clearly prospering. The rough-and-ready village nearby has shops selling basic supplies.

From the mine take the well-used jeep track which zigzags up the right-hand valley side. After perhaps half an hour it levels out, and at this point look for a minor track leading uphill and to the right. This doubles back above the mine before crossing the ridge via a 4,900m pass with stunning views of the Cordillera Real to the south. You may see condors here. (Note that you can reach this point without descending to the mine by striking out southwest after the Sunchuli Pass, contouring round the valley above a prominent aqueduct.)

From the pass the track descends steeply to Viscachani, a mining village that has seen better days, which you'll reach 2–2½ hours after leaving the Sunchuli Pass. You can camp beyond the village. There is a deserted gold mine here which may be fun to explore.

From Viscachani your route heads up the right-hand side of the valley beneath the village and drops down into a neighbouring valley where you'll find a small lake. A short climb takes you into a third valley, with a village away to the left. Go down to the right towards a gap between two crags, and about an hour from Viscachani you'll come to a magnificent viewpoint from where the next and final pass can be seen. An hour-long hair-raising descent (or breathtaking ascent if you coming from Charazani) brings you to a river at a place called Incacancha. This is an enchanting spot with a stone bridge, a waterfall nearby and a wonderful campsite from where you can contemplate the mountains all around.

The next climb takes at least 2 hours and is bedevilled by false summits. Akamani (5,700m) is in view to the right. From the true summit it's downhill – well, almost! – for the rest of the walk (watch out for more condors). First descend to the right, traversing round the head of the valley to a gap. Pass through this and drop straight down the next valley to another good campsite, an hour from the top, at a place called Jatunpampa. If it's late in the day you should consider stopping here, because the countryside ahead is intensively farmed and campsites are harder to find. Otherwise continue descending through stone enclosures, cross the main river and climb diagonally to the left onto a spur. Descend again to ford a second river (an hour from Jatunpampa) and follow the path up the valley side to meet a disused irrigation channel. Follow this for 15 minutes before turning off to the right, from where a further hour of gradual ascent will bring you to a jeep track. When you come to a junction carry straight on, and Curva will almost immediately come into view on top of a small hill.

With no accommodation (yet) and limited food supplies, Curva will offer little encouragement to stay. Luckily, an excellent ancient path leads down from its main square, giving magnificent views of the terracing opposite, and after descending for an hour and climbing for a second hour you'll find yourself at a fork. The route to Charazani goes vertically up from here. When, after half an hour, you reach a church, look back for a final view of the Akamani massif and forward for your first sight of Charazani. From here the direct route drops down steeply to a road, which you follow for a short distance before turning left towards a cross and descending to the river. The more obvious path descends gently to the road, which you can then follow round the valley to Charazani. Either way, the town is reached about 1¼ hours after leaving the church.

Getting back Buses to La Paz leave from the plaza in Charazani daily at 20.00, leaving Curva a couple of hours previously. The journey takes 10 hours from Curva. Occasionally, trucks leave Charazani early in the morning, taking 12–16 hours. Alternatively, you could walk to the junction with the Pelechuco road – a long day, but with plenty of good campsites and water en route in case you should decide to linger.

Pete Lawrence and Rachel Scott report that a vehicle track leads west from Calaya (the village in the valley below Curva), over a pass and then down to join the Ulla Ulla road. They had no trouble following this in the opposite direction, and found lakes and potential campsites en route. This could be yet another way out of the area if transport can't be found. Again, allow at least a day, and preferably two.

ULLA ULLA NATIONAL PARK

Some people ask for remoteness, others ask for nature in its undefiled state; Ulla Ulla National Park offers both. Located deep within the Apolobamba Mountains and approximately 100km north of Lake Titicaca, the park is not only a wonder to see but a true challenge to get to.

The park has a roughly defined area of just over 200,000ha, and was first established as a vicuña reserve in 1972. At that time, the vicuña count in the area had dropped to a mere 72 animals due to unrestrained poaching. In 1977, UNESCO managed to raise the park's status to Biosphere Reserve in the hope of protecting not only the native vicuña population, but the entire ecosystem. That same year, the Instituto Nacional de Fomento Lanero (INFOL) was created and put in charge of conducting vicuña research and safeguarding the reserve. Now Ulla Ulla boasts a swelling population of 2,500 vicuñas and healthy numbers of black ibises, Chilean flamingos, Andean geese and viscachas.

The village of Ulla Ulla itself is located in the middle of a sprawling *bofedal*, or ancient lake bed, which extends the length of the Apolobamba range. Most residents are alpaca farmers who share local water and other resources with adjacent villages.

There is much to see and do in the park if you have your own transport and don't mind the rough ride. Otherwise you'll get fleeting glances from a bus or truck. The wild vicuña herds can be observed at close range and followed cross-country. During the day, the vicuñas graze with the alpacas, but towards evening, when their domesticated brothers and sisters head home to their stone-wall corrals, the vicuñas wander to more isolated pastures. It is especially beautiful to see these graceful cameloids grazing along the plains at dawn against a backdrop of snow-clad peaks.

In the Apolobamba foothills there are a number of lakes to visit including Katantira and Kanahuma, where you encounter flamingos, ducks, Andean geese, black ibises and other waterfowl. Slightly further north, just east of the road to Pelechuco, are the Putina hot springs, where you can wallow in steaming, sulphur-rich waters while watching isolated rainstorms sweep in over the broad plains.

Practical information Travelling by car from La Paz follow the road to Lake Titicaca, then bear right at Huarina and follow the dirt highway to Achacachi and Escoma. In Escoma, the road turns north, traverses several passes, and then just after the turn-off to Charazani (stay left) descends into the Apolobamba valley. The total drive takes 8–12 hours. To reach Ulla Ulla by public transport see page 389.

Although Ulla Ulla offers no hotel accommodation, lodging may be found with local families. There are also plenty of campsites on the outskirts of the village. In fact, almost anywhere outside the village is a campsite. Supplies in the local store are limited but sufficient. Be sure to bring warm clothing as temperatures often drop below zero at night.

For further information contact INFOL (tel: 02 234 9048) at Calle Bueno 444, Casilla 732, La Paz.

HIKING THE ROAD TO APOLO

One of the most thrilling, or perhaps terrifying, things about being in Bolivia is road travel. Some of the most spectacular drives might include the roads to Coroico, Sorata, the Zongo Valley or Illimani, or along the Carretera Cochabamba. A relatively new road has recently penetrated deep into the department of La Paz that rivals all of these: the road to Apolo. Apolo is a small jungle town lying at the edge of the Amazon basin, several hundred kilometres north of Lake Titicaca.

Roads in the area were first built to access a number of mines (some of which date back to pre-Columbian times) just past the town of Charazani. Visitors without their own vehicle can derive just as much enjoyment from hiking this road, and exploring some of the side-trails, as can the car driver or mountain biker.

Distance	About 90km
Altitude	Between about 3,800m and 1,500m
Rating	Moderate
Timing	7–10 days

Conditions/what to take The only towns between Charazani and Apolo are Camata, about halfway between the two points, and Correo, about three-quarters of the way. In an emergency there are several military/mining construction camps where help may be sought. But remember, this place is remote, so prepare for the worst as well as the best. If you plan to hike down from the pass, make sure to bring clothing that will guard against freezing temperatures and precipitation. We had snow in November, when it's supposed to start warming up in that area. Bring extra water purification tablets, a well-stocked first-aid kit, sturdy boots, a tent, and surplus food.

Route description From Charazani the dirt track winds down through a land of grassy mountains and running waters. Every bend offers breathtaking views of what were once heavily terraced hillsides (pre-Columbian), now often covered with thick forest. Waterfalls tumble down from the Andean heights to feed the many rivers that flow through the steep valleys.

At an altitude of 3,000m the valleys take on a distinctly tropical atmosphere. Butterflies, disturbed from puddles on the road, flit about in colourful clouds, small flocks of parakeets screech noisily overhead and orchids and other flowers adorn the roadside.

Lower down still, the road meanders along the foot of towering cliffs, streaked with white and yellow from hot springs, while massive boulders, that years ago tumbled from above, sit in their final resting place at the base of the valley.

Small green areas invite you to camp beside rushing streams and rivers, and for the more adventurous there are mines to explore, trails to hike and ruins to discover. About 2 hours (driving) below Charazani a hot spring pours across the road. Bathing here by moonlight is an experience beyond words, and if you are lucky, you'll see *guácharos*, a nocturnal bird, doing aerial acrobatics in small squadrons in the night sky.

Appendix 1

LANGUAGE
Spanish
Below is a basic vocabulary to help hikers with only a smattering of Spanish to communicate with campesinos. For general travel purposes a good phrase book is indespensible.

On the trail
Observing the courtesies of greetings is an essential part of hiking in the Andes. If you observe the local people they will always exchange a few words with a stranger on the trail, however brief the encounter.

Buenas días	Good morning
Buenas tardes	Good afternoon
Como está?	How are you?
Vaya bien	Go well
Adios	Good bye

Most frequently asked questions (theirs):

De donde es (son)?	Where are you (sing. or plur.) from?
De donde viene?	Where are you coming from?

Most frequent unwelcome question:

Dame, regálame	Give me

Most frequent questions (yours):

How much is it?	*Cuanto vale?*
Is it permitted to...?	*Se puede?*
What is this place called?	*Como se llama este lugar?*
Where does this trail go?	*A donde va este camino?*
May we camp here?	*Podemos acampar aquí?*

Most frequent answers:

Muy cerquita	Very near
Lejos	Far
No puede perdirse	You can't get lost
Izquierdo/derecho	Left/right

Backpackers' vocabulary

equipaje	baggage
mochila	backpack
pueblito; poblado	settlement or small village
carpa	tent
río	river
puente	bridge
derrumbe; huayco	landslide
carro (Peru); mobilidad (Bolivia)	truck or bus
trámite	red tape; transaction
tienda	shop

Quechua and Aymara

English	Quechua	Aymara
Hello	*Maynalla*	*Kamisaki*
Where is...?	*Maypi...?*	*Kaukasa...*
Yes	*Ari*	*Jisa*
No	*Mana*	*Janiwar*
good	*walej-pacha*	*walikuskiu*
bad	*mana-walej janiwa*	*walikiti*
food	*mikuna*	*manka*
water	*yaku*	*uma*
house	*huasi*	*uta*
river	*mayu*	*jawira*
bridge	*chaka*	*vhaka*
lake	*cocha*	*vota*
footpath	*chakinan*	*tupu*
help	*yanapaway*	*yanaptita*

Phrasebook

Quechua phrasebook, Ronald Wright, published by Lonely Planet.

Appendix 2

FURTHER READING

I once asked an impressively fit woman how she had prepared for the trek. 'I did a lot of reading,' she responded.

Background reading and a companion guidebook will help you get the most out of your trip. Here are a few suggestions, with subjective comments on those I particularly liked, but I would welcome further recommendations.

Readers wanting a complete bibliography of Peru and Bolivia should get hold of a copy of the World Bibliographic Series published by Clio Press (UK) and ABC-Clio (USA): *Peru* by John Ridley, with 705 entries, and *Bolivia* by Gertrude M Yeager, with 816 entries.

The Hispanic and Luso-Brazilian Council at Canning House, 2 Belgrave Square, London SWIX 8PJ provides Londoners with an excellent library of books pertaining to South America.

Novels

Vargas Llosa, Mario, *Aunt Julia and the Scriptwriter*, Avon (1982). A funny, imaginative novel which gives a good insight into life in Lima. Ideal for a long bus or train journey.

Wilder, Thornton, *The Bridge of San Luís Rey* (1927). The classic novel of South America. The collapse of an Inca bridge throws five people to their deaths. Who were they and why were they there? If you haven't yet read it, now's the time. You will never forget it.

Travel narratives

Murphy, Dervla, *Eight Feet in the Andes*, John Murray (1983). An entertaining and insightful account of the author's trek from Cajamarca to Cusco, accompanied by her ten-year-old daughter.

Parris, Matthew, *Inca Cola*, Weidenfeld and Nicolson (1990)/Phoenix (1993). One of the best modern travelogues about Peru and Bolivia. Much of the narrative covers a hiking trip to the Cordillera Huayhuash. Witty, evocative and accurate.

Simpson, Joe, *Touching the Void*, Jonathan Cape (1988). An award-winning description of a climbing accident in the Cordillera Huayhuash. An extraordinarily vivid and moving book.

Thomson, Hugh, *The White Rock*, Weidenfeld and Nicolson (2001). Very readable account of Thomson's modern-day travels into the Inca Heartland, with plenty of information on previous explorers.

History

Savoy, Gene, *Vilcabamba Last City of the Incas*, Robert Hale (1971). Fascinating account of the author's explorations in Peru, mostly in the 1960s.

Lee, Vincent R, *Sixpac Manco: Travels Among the Incas*, self published (1985). Useful guide for the Vilcabamba area, with maps and diagrams of some of the more remote sites.

Burger, Richard, *Chavín and the Origin of the Andean Civilization*, Thames and Hudson (1993). The definitive book on a fascinating subject.

Hemming, John, *Conquest of the Incas*, Macmillan (1970). The outstanding book on the Incas and their conquest by the Spanish. A hefty 640 pages but eminently readable and a perfect length for a 3-week trip.

Hemming, John and Ranney, Edward, *Monuments of the Incas*, University of New Mexico Press (1990). Studies of the better-known Inca sites, beautifully illustrated with black and white photographs. Highly recommended.

de la Vega, Garcilaso, *Royal Commentaries of the Incas*. Fascinating because it was originally written in 1609 by the son of a conquistador and an Inca princess.

Bingham, Hiram, *Lost City of the Incas*, New York (1972). Original tale of the rediscovery of Machu Picchu. A classic.

Muscatt, Keith, *Warriors of the Clouds*, University of New Mexico Press (1998). A vivid account of living in, and exploring, the Chachapoyas area.

Mountaineering and trekking guides

Sharman, David, *Climbs of the Cordillera Blanca*, Whizzo Climbs (1995). One of the few technical climbing guides for the Cordillera Blanca.

Mesili, Alain, *La Cordillera Real de los Andes – Bolivia*, Los Amigos de Libro, Bolivia (1984). Descriptions of all the routes up the peaks of the Cordillera Real (Spanish).

Neate, Jill, *Mountaineering in the Andes: A Sourcebook for Climbers*, Expedition Advisory Centre, Royal Geographical Society, London (1994). An extremely thorough and accurate survey of all the Andean Cordilleras. Includes mountaineering history and a comprehensive bibliography. An essential book for those planning a mountaineering expedition.

Brain, Yossi, *A Climber's Guide to Bolivia*, The Mountaineers (1996). La Paz-based Yossi Brain was the acknowledged expert on Bolivia's mountains. Includes Bolivia's four main cordilleras.

Brain, Yossi, *Trekking in Bolivia*, Cordee (1997). Very useful for those wanting to spend longer exploring Bolivian trails.

Biggar, John, *The High Andes: A Guide for Climbers*, Andes (1996). 174 route descriptions in all, including every 6,000m peak and a selection of 5,000m ones.

Biggar, Cathy and Biggar, John, *The Andes: A Trekking Guide*, Andes (2001). From Venezuala to Patagonia, the classic treks and some useful background information.

Bartle, Jim, *Trails of the Cordillras Blanca and Huayhuash of Peru*, new edition due to be published in 2002.

Health

Darvill, Fred, *Mountaineering Medicine*, Wilderness Press, USA (1992). A compact, 100-page booklet which should be carried by all North American backpackers.

Steele, Peter, *Medical Handbook for Mountaineers*, Constable, London. The best pocket guide on the subject for British readers.

Wilson-Howarth, Jane, *Healthy Travel: Bugs, Bites & Bowels*, Cadogan (1995). A super book! New edition due August 2002. Practical, sensible and entertaining, written by a doctor who has lived and travelled extensively in the developing countries.

Wilson-Howarth, Jane, *Your Child's Health Abroad*, Bradt (1998). Any hesitation about taking children trekking will be dispelled by this reassuring and inspiring book. Don't leave home without your kids; don't leave home without this book!

Miscellaneous

Hargreaves, Clare, *Snowfields: The War on Cocaine in the Andes*, Zed Books/Holmes and Meier (1992). The background to one of the most serious problems affecting Peru and Bolivia.

Strong, Simon, *Shining Path*, Harper Collins (1992). A powerful and first-hand account of the terrorist movement which vividly evokes life in Peru in the early part of this decade.

Chamalu, Luis Espinoza, *The Gates of Paradise: Secrets of Andean Shamanism*, Gateway Books (1997). A spiritual exploration into the minds and shamanistic arts of the Andean people, as told by the leading Bolivian practitioner.

Right, Ruth, *The Machu Picchu Guidebook*, Johnson Books (2001). Includes a self-guided tour of the site.

Frost, Peter, *Exploring Cusco*, Nuevas Imagenes (1999). Extremely useful, pocket-sized guidebook with all the information you need for the Cusco area.

PromPerú have produced the following guides, which are available from the tourist information offices throughout Peru. The publication date is 1999.

Beaches and Adventure Sports in Peru
Nature and Protected Areas in Peru
Trekking and Mountaineering in Peru
Watching Wildlife in Peru
Festivities, Music and Folk Art in Peru
Cusco, The Sacred City
Lima, the City of Kings

Index

*Page numbers in bold indicate main entries;
those in italics indicate maps*